The Best
AMERICAN
ESSAYS
2024

GUEST EDITORS OF THE BEST AMERICAN ESSAYS

The Best
AMERICAN
ESSAYS®
2024

Edited and with an Introduction
by WESLEY MORRIS

KIM DANA KUPPERMAN, Series Editor

MARINER BOOKS
New York   Boston

FIRST EDITION

ISSN 0888-3742
ISBN 978-0-06-335155-4

24 25 26 27 28 LBC 5 4 3 2 1

Contents

Foreword

For the Sake of Argument

> Time spent arguing is, oddly enough, almost never wasted.
> —Christopher Hitchens

WHAT IS IT about argument that is so dangerous? When thoughts blossom into ideas, argument refines them. To argue is to clarify, demonstrate, prove. For an essayist, argument drives thought on the page, urging the writer's mind to meander associatively until it makes meaning of experience. Argument asks the essay to risk collapse—where do you take thinking when faced with experiences without conclusions, which may seem impossible to mend? Often, there are no answers to the essayist's questions, though readers may think up their own. Sometimes the argument fails its assignment as a proof, and a new essay—a renewed attempt to decipher how one thinks—argues its way into beginning.

It seems to me that what is today called argument is really dispute (a word derived from *disputare*, to think contentiously). Nonfiction prose that seeks quarrel is highly polemic, and the essayistic quality of weighing and appraising (*arguing*) is not present. Contentious thinking knows that losing is almost always guaranteed when each of two sides clings to right and wrong. *Dispute*, its etymology suggests, describes a state of thinking that cannot be settled. In this binary, someone is destined to be the victor, someone the loser. Losing and loss terrify, particularly in a culture in which winning and gain define success, and losers are dismissed or shunned for their perceived failures. Especially at a time when those who win often deploy intellectual brutality to silence the kind of argument that results in bringing people closer instead of pushing them apart.

Thinking combatively is a hallmark of social polarization, a phenomenon firmly gripping democracies everywhere. In the fevered pitch of polarized dispute, censorship is never too far behind. Such an environment renders books, including anthologies such as the volume you hold in your hands, dangerous. "Books are inseparable from ideas," writes Viet Thanh Nguyen about censorship, "and this is really what is at stake: the struggle over what a child, a reader and a society are allowed to think, to know and to question."

Censorship is what happens when argument is no longer supported and tolerated, which allows those with power and privilege to silence the powerless. As I write this foreword, I am dismayed, but not surprised to learn, that book banning surged in 2023 to the highest level ever reported, with over 4,200 individual titles targeted for removal from libraries in America. This upward trend corresponds to the increase of legislation regulating the content of libraries and growing prohibitions against "woke" curricula in classrooms. What should be shocking here is that these specific types of censorship are law in regions of a country whose constitution guarantees the freedom of expression to all its citizens.

Of course, it's not shocking anymore. Writers of all genres have warned us what's coming, not only politically, but ecologically, emotionally, and spiritually. The last five years have been catastrophe-inflected: violent in every possible way, environmentally disastrous, and ill in epidemic and pandemic proportion. Compared to the number of people and other species killed, injured, traumatized, and displaced and the ceaseless assault on the Earth itself, the removal of four-thousand-plus books from library shelves might be considered trifling.

In fact, the removal of those books is one cut in the death by a thousand small cuts being meted out to democracy. Given that so many of the recent political cataclysms have unfolded when more countries than at any time call themselves democracies, just imagine the number (and severity) of calamities possible in a world dominated by totalitarian regimes. Picture America being one of those countries, ruled by an autocrat, with no regard to the history that has shaped us, and nothing but disdain for anyone who does not hold the methods of tyranny close to the heart.

We might be fooled into believing that things aren't so bad because today's publishing landscape offers a multitude of platforms for new voices. Peruse the American print and online periodical literature and you'll find a roared-to-life diversity in which everyone is "everywhere whispering essays," as Alexander Smith put it. Such publications preserve a record of our troubled times, authored by a robust number of writers with everything and nothing in common. I suspect every authoritarian would be afraid to read these publications. These new voices in print represent the marginalized claiming centrality—evidence, to dictators and tyrants at least, that democracy can overtake them.

Authoritarian regimes are characterized by the threat—particularly to their artists and intellectuals—of oblivion. This cruel unremembering drives the type of censorship called deplatforming,* which not only removes someone or their work from the commons but seeks to permanently obscure the removed artists and their work. It has a side effect of arresting the critical thinking required for argument, ultimately silencing and distancing not only the censored, but their allies, whose fear of reprisal prevents them from articulating disagreement. Such censorship is unusually disquieting when the people imposing it decry tyranny while acting, mostly unwittingly, as the agents of tyrants. These censors assert political affinities that are admirable: they are firmly against totalitarianism, massacres, hatred, the flagrant injustice of a culture bequeathed us by too many centuries of colonialism. Scarier still is when the censors are both activists and respected guardians of free speech (academics, editors and publishers, intellectuals), whose work it is to nurture, publish, and protect narratives, not obliviate them. This type of censorship is one sure path toward a democracy in ruin. Lest we forget that the real adversaries—an authoritarian

---

* This is a word I had hoped to never use. It is cold and technocratic and dehumanizes the people who are made to suffer because of it.

with a mob retinue—are lurking offstage, content they don't have to dirty *their* hands in dismembering our First Amendment.

One has only to look out a window for respite from such grim contemplations: In North America, where the essays in this book were published, winter is waning, light returning. Soon spring will swell the continent's colder reaches with green. By the time these words appear in print, autumn will gild the dimming light. This increase and decrease of light—each reality with its own beauty and enduring nature—occur side by side with the pervasive uncertainty and doom of today's global turmoil. It is the essay's nature to contemplate opposites, I think, in this case beauty and ugliness, which will never cease to coexist.

I take a break to peruse previous volumes of *The Best American Essays*—an essayist's digression is her prerogative. Imagine all thirty-eight of founding editor Robert Atwan's forewords together in one book: an anthology comprising essays from anthologies, edited by "one of America's noted anthologists," an epithet that recalls the 2011 foreword, "Confessions of an Anthologist." It is one of my favorites.

"I'm certain no one ever sets out to be an anthologist," Atwan writes. For me, that's certainly true: I never intended to be an anthologist or to inherit the responsibility of caring for such a noteworthy anthology. But that is what happened, and I see now how natural a path it was for me. I've always liked to collect diverse examples of beauty: pebbles, feathers, the evidence of lives that once were (shells, abandoned nests, skulls picked clean by birds of prey, vacated chrysalises, snakeskins), and of course, all the stories that fill books. Where did it start, this impulse? Likely in childhood, that "jewel beyond all price," as Rilke calls it, when I organized my seashell collection into clans based on shared morphologies and launched them into epic dramas and odysseys across the ocean of my bedroom floor.

My first idea for a book was to curate an anthology of people's nuclear nightmares. This was in 1980, nine months after the Three Mile Island nuclear accident, eerily preceded twelve days before it occurred by the theatrical release of *The China Syndrome*, a film about a meltdown at an American nuclear power plant. After several of these meltdown-inspired dreams, you could say that chain-reaction accidents were on my mind. I began to suspect such disasters were on the minds of others. In the unsurprising naivete of a twenty-something, I believed that gathering evidence of a collective psychic response to the existential threat of chain reactions would reveal another hazard of nuclear energy, one summoning the kind of political attention that, years later, I realized was impossible. I posted announcements in a few bookstores, asking folks to send their dreams to the address provided. A few envelopes arrived, including one from a nuclear physicist and another from a fifth-grade teacher, who had recorded some of the dreams her students were having. I was young, and completely ignorant of how a book was made (and I certainly didn't understand my anthologist yearnings).

Forty years passed before I discovered Charlotte Beradt and her remarkable *Third Reich of Dreams*,* a suite of short essays analyzing seventy-five of the three hundred dreams the author collected in Berlin from 1933 until she fled Germany in 1939. The dreams reflect distinct practices of totalitarianism—including outright censorship (and consequent punishment), limits on the freedom of expression, and denunciations by neighbors, colleagues, and friends—which were undoing, in real time, the collective psyches of Germans who had little belief in or official affiliation with the Nazi Party. As Bruno Bettelheim writes in his afterword: "Typical is the dream of the man who writes a letter of protest about existing conditions, but instead of mailing it he puts an empty piece of paper in the envelope, without a single word on it." He's describing silencing, voicelessness, invisible protest that cannot be articulated. I wonder what similarities might be found among today's collective dreams.

Many, many years after my first failed attempt at anthologizing, I would edit and publish pamphlets from symposia and panel talks on the essay, work at a quarterly of literature and art, edit an anthology of essays devoted to the second person, and publish another featuring essays on the essay. I have many ideas for other anthologies, but I'm happy to focus on exactly where I am, anthologizing the best American essays.

---

* Charlotte Beradt, *Das Dritte Reich des Traums* (Munich: Nymphenburger Verlaghandlung, 1966), translated by Adriane Gottwald as *The Third Reich of Dreams. With an Essay by Bruno Bettelheim* (Chicago: Quadrangle Books, 1968). Beradt, a German Jew, hid the transcripts of these dreams in the bindings of books in her personal library. Before fleeing Germany, she mailed her materials to friends who lived abroad.

In "Confessions of an Anthologist," Robert Atwan describes the moment certain readers have when they acquire their first library card, and feel, as he felt in front of the card catalogs and vast shelves filled with books, "the terrifying rush of unknown possibilities." Libraries being the ultimate anthology. Just after this moment in his essay, we can imagine ourselves in the reference section, where our narrator tells us the meaning of the word *anthology*. Like any essayist, I love a good etymological romp: "The word *anthology* derives from the Greek *antholegein*, which literally means to gather (*legein*) flowers (*anthos*). The anthologist in a sense gathers a literary bouquet."

A bouquet of essays: that's what we offer you, dear reader, with this volume. Think of them as flowers that sing, arranged with fierce tenderness and a keen ear to emotional rhythms by guest editor Wesley Morris.

Acknowledgments

The practice, circulation, and reputation of the essay have dramatically changed since the first volume of *The Best American Essays* was published in 1986. No longer "the second-class citizen in the republic of literature,"* the genre has firmly established itself in American letters. In this second decade of the twentieth century, more authors write essays, more periodicals feature or are devoted to them, more editors and agents buy and sell collections of them. No one knows about these transformations more intimately than Robert Atwan, whose enthusiastic love of the essay helped elevate the genre and secure it in its deserved place. A reader of exceptional breadth and depth, Atwan is one of America's most eloquent champions and erudite scholars of the essay. He diligently nurtured this series for four decades, and I am but one essayist who is thankful to him for his endless devotion. I am fortunate to have worked with him on other deeply meaningful essay-related adventures, profoundly honored when he invited me to take the helm of this series, and grateful for his sage guidance during the last fifteen months.

It has been a pure delight to collaborate with this year's guest editor, Wesley Morris, whose style as a reader is abundant with au-

---

* Robert Atwan, "Foreword," *The Best American Essays 2023*, xv.

thentic insight, sincerity, and wit, qualities that combined like a magic elixir to assemble the contents of this anthology. I feel as if Wesley and I have danced a once-in-a-lifetime dance, at a banquet whose orchestra featured the esteemed contributors to this volume. I am grateful for their music, and for their courage to not only tell their stories, but to make meaning out of them.

Nicole Angeloro at HarperCollins/Mariner has been a source of support, assistance, and humor in perfect measure; she is possessed of that rare ability to make one feel as if she has all the time in the world even when she's managing a hundred tasks simultaneously. Joshua Levine and Cheyenne Paterson jumped into editorial internships with eager enthusiasm, intelligent questions, and a desire to read excellent work, all of which makes the uncertain world of publishing deeply fulfilling. My husband, Sami, made it possible for me to read in comfort, listened as I extolled the treasures unearthed in reading the many magazines and journals that came to fill a once-empty bookcase, and provided a sounding board for this foreword. I am deeply grateful for my family and friends (both human and nonhuman), who have kept my spirits aloft, and for the many acquaintances and former colleagues who wished me well as I set off on this editorial odyssey. And, finally, I am humbled and awed by the energy and grace of the many tireless editors who celebrate and preserve literature by meeting deadlines, polishing manuscripts, thinking about design matters, and managing the business of the hundreds of periodicals published in North America. This bouquet of the best American essays, culled from your resplendent gardens, is possible only because of you.

Nomination Guidelines

This volume of *The Best American Essays* features a selection of essays published between January 2023 and January 2024. The qualifications for nomination are: (1) original publication as an unabridged, stand-alone essay in a nationally distributed North American periodical and (2) publication in English (or translated into English by the essay's author). Writers whose essays have been published in the series and former guest editors are encouraged to nominate up to five of their own eligible essays, or up to five essays by other writers. These nominations must be submitted as tear sheets before or on December 31, 2024. Periodical editors who wish essays in their publications to be considered are invited to send subscriptions or, in the case of online essays, hard copies (up to five per calendar year, with clear citations and contact information) to the following address, to be received before or on December 31, 2024:

Kim Dana Kupperman
Best American Essays
P.O. Box 569
Hartland VT 05048

Please note: Writers whose work has not been published in the series (including those listed in Notables) are invited to email bestamericanessayseditor@gmail.com to determine if a journal or magazine in which their work appears is a periodical to which the series is subscribed. If the series is not subscribed to a particular publication, authors are invited to send the copy in which their work appears to the above address. All nonfiction is reviewed, and all eligible essays are read.

For updated and detailed nomination guidelines and eligibility criteria, please visit http://bestamericanessays.substack.com.

Postscript: Some Farewells

Contemporary literature suffered many losses in 2023, several of which directly impact *The Best American Essays* anthology.

After thirty-five years, *The Gettysburg Review* was shuttered by the college that launched and funded it. In this volume of *The Best American Essays*, you will find James Whorton Jr.'s "An Upset Place," which will be, sadly, the last essay selected for this series from this magnificent literary journal. You can read Mark Drew's moving farewell "Editor's Pages" from the final issue of the *Review* in the *Best American Essays Newsletter* at https://bestamericanessays .substack.com.

After thirty-six years, *The Briar Cliff Review* ended with volume 35. Two of the essays published in its pages are included in this year's list of Notables.

The journal *Freeman's* said goodbye to readers after eight years with the issue called *Conclusions*. Several of the short essays appearing therein are included in this year's list of Notables.

Dedication

This volume of *The Best American Essays 2024* is dedicated to Sy Safransky, the founding editor of *The Sun* and a visionary publisher, who stepped down in 2023 after fifty years at the helm of the magazine. Read his farewell missive at: https://www.thesunmagazine .org/issues/576/a-letter-from-sys-desk.

KIM DANA KUPPERMAN

Introduction

LAST NOVEMBER, this series's editor, Kim Dana Kupperman, mailed me the first of two substantial bundles. Each a manila folder taco. Spread width-wise, the shell cupped a casserole of tessellated paper, some printed out, most so diligently extracted from their sources that you could trace your fingers along the soft teeth of perforation. They were essays. And in addition to being selected, their presentation also looked picked, as in pulled up from earth, like vegetables. She secured the whole thing with two extra large rubber bands, one red, one purple. Two months later, came taco number two. Same idea. Different rubber bands. In both cases, I left it to rest on my desk and, for more than a week, I'd just look up from the television or the newspaper or from typing and just . . . admire it. To and from the kitchen, I'd cruise it. That's how handsome and attentively, imaginatively assembled it was. For decades, Robert Atwan helmed this series to perfection (the man could write a foreword). This is Kim's first edition. The craft of those bundles represents the meticulous care of her stewardship. These books are in strong hands. But let's not be *too* precious about it: They were also piles of work. Work Kim had already completed. Work I had yet to do.

Labor, however, was never a meaningful factor. Reading every single stapled sheaf she'd sent, plus a handful more, was one of the high points of my life—the anticipation of the occasional days I knew could do almost nothing but read essays was childlike, the respite a literary snow day. Even the misbegotten pieces taught me something: about what the author wanted to communicate, yes; but also that imparting some piece of yourself—any part—is arduous and warrants *some* kind of commendation. Occasionally, I'll finish writing a piece I know isn't "there" but feel relief anyway. It'll either get there or I'll get it next time. But allow me to state the obvious: this shit is hard. Every sentence is a risk. And sometimes I'm not sure why we're taking it. A rebuttal often radiated from within Kim's bundles: because we *have* to. The twenty-two essays collected in this thirty-ninth edition *really* had to. As a class, they did a little of everything to me: surprise, astound, bewitch, reframe, knock me down, crack me up, push, enlighten, inspire.

I remember where I was when I read each one of them, too—on the subway, in the window of a coffee shop, on the floor, at the kitchen table, waiting waiting waiting for trains, in the cafeteria at work, at my work desk, at my desk-desk, in a recording studio, in the back seat of a car, at my kitchen table, at my sister's kitchen table, at my man's, at restaurant bars and one sushi counter, in bed, in bed, in bed. I recall my shivers and tingles and squeals and moans of "mm mm mm." Anybody I read near would've heard me say, "Jesus fucking Christ" or "Oh man" or just a bunch of vowels leaving my mouth like slot machine coins. On a downtown 4, Jenisha Watts had me straight weeping. New Yorkers do *not* know how to handle subway tears. But I didn't even bother fighting it. Her sentences are quick, declarative, and frank. The title doesn't lie: Watts's essay is a declaration. I couldn't think of a bigger gut-punch to open this book.

Some of these essays are marvels of memory, like Amy Margolis's vignetted, intensely fragrant mosaic of arriving in New York City as a ballerina during the disco era; Michael W. Clune's personal history of childhood panic attacks, which has too many killer sentences to count and features some writing about reading that borders on the architectural; Ed Pavlić's smoky, humid, dreamily disorienting reminiscence about meeting his best friend and Anita Baker's first diamond, *Rapture*; or James McAuley's "Memory's Cellar," which celebrates an almost hidden act of memorializing. Sallie Tisdale's is a marvel of argument *against* memory, the alleged truth of it. Like so many of these pieces, hers is taught, generous, critical, *self-critical.* Some, like Jennifer Senior's essay about the shameful years-long mistreatment of her aunt, are marvels of reporting, here in which one life speaks to the lives of too many. Her piece is one of many in this volume concerned with families and their histories—Courtney Miller Santo's story about a trip to a family horse ranch, Jennifer Sinor's story about her brother's near deaths, Jonathan Gleason's reckoning with his father's incarcerated brother. My heart swelled at their insight, emotional audacity, clear-eyed vision, their resolute compassion and very different gift for pacing and rhythm, their wonder. So many of us are mothers and fathers remembering what it was like to be daughters and sons. So many of us are daughters and sons recovering from our mothers and fathers. Some of the essayists here are considering the meaning of their wounds, how, in the case of Kathleen Alcott's shockingly engineered essay, they didn't know they'd even been wounded. The paragraphs unknot themselves before your eyes. That piece is called "Trapdoor," which is what the writing plunges us through.

Some of these essays, like James Whorton Jr.'s "An Upset Place," are studies in construction, their power arising from the daring of their form. Whorton's is the sort of achievement you sense is going somewhere and when you figure it out—when it's revealed itself—you still don't know how the hell he did it, what in tarnation possessed him to tell a story of this country *this* way. I got to the end and started it over to read through the eyes of revelation. I did that a bunch. Press play again. Jerald Walker, writing so deftly, so brazenly, about the time he was, he swears, a pimp? So nice I had to do it twice. Walker's a comedian here, but a sly, thrillingly ambiguous one. The piece luxuriates in the uncertainty that Tisdale is so rigorously interrogating, but Walker just *knows* this happened. Simply terrific. He's isn't the lone comedian. There's Brock Clarke on his dog and the dog's death and Rémy Ngamije on learning to box as a newlywed. They understand how comedy is a gateway for life's more difficult stuff. They also know how to enliven that difficulty with incandescent personality.

So *many* of these essays are marvels of voice. I'd never read anything by Christienne L. Hinz. Now I have, and I'll never be the same. Her essay is titled "A Rewilding," and she means it. This person has full command of her lyrical, muscular instrument. It's a mighty performance, and the best way I could think to close this collection: with a mic drop. Hers is one of two astounding essays about gardening as metaphor and gardening as gardening. Yiyun Li wrote the other. She gets so deep inside the meaning of her yard work—as an antidote to grief—that I had to laugh at how she made such heartbreaking work go down so easily. I finished it and thought: "Everybody's getting this piece for Christmas."

Some of these are marvels of earnest charm and emotional transparency, like the essay Austin Woerner composed about his mentorship with the novelist Su Wei and how a student-teacher connection deepened into lifelong friendship. Woerner manages to bring Su and his family to bright, crackling life. Some of these essays are marvelous experiments in style whose nerve and frankness disarm you. Here, none more so than Richard Prins's. A single preposition becomes a reply that becomes an after-school punishment that becomes a parental emergency that is also a writer in astounding psychological bloom. Halfway through, I knew he'd pull this off and said aloud, "bravo." I said something like that about Anne Marie Todkill's epic about her relationship to the land and what the rest of are doing to it, but she takes an activist's approach. It's full of play and rue, bemusement and fury. It's *capacious*. While I read it, one of Andrei Tarkovsky's ravaged cinematic behemoths came to mind. So did something I read in which Sigrid Nunez mentions that she's trying to keep alive Barbara Kingsolver's challenge to do more writing about nonhumans—or maybe just animals. But this has got to count.

Then there is the miracle of storytelling that Nicole Graev Lipson achieves in an essay about how the Shakespeare she's taught to so many school kids provides a framework for apprehending her own kid's gender journey. The tone is a breeze, yet the questions are among the most fraught an American can ask right now. But Lipson asks away as though there were no risk at all. Her righteous, naive certainty curdles—as she has to learn, unlearn, and relearn—into struggle, angst, anger, and ardent acceptance. I don't know how you write about that struggle as a parent any better than this great, big airing out.

I wanted to include a work of personal criticism. And Teju Cole came through. Somehow, he got last year's most desperately pursued and hardest to attain museum ticket and modeled how to consider anew what it means to truly look at what a work of art is trying to show you. If we're talking, as Cole is, about Johannes Vermeer, what has that work of art *been* trying to tell us?

I suppose I wanted to include it because I'm a critic. Is it important to tell you that? And to tell you right here, toward the end? Well, I wanted to level with you some. For years, a top editor at the *New York Times Magazine*, Jessica Lustig, would leave the same note on pieces: "More essayistic." Not a prompt that's ever seemed inherent to criticism. All an essay ought to be is a short piece of writing. That's it. But the journey from that to what Jessica wanted essentially requires a passport. My panic disguised itself as exasperation. What was being asked of me, I feared, was to Go There. Yes, to plumb the meaning of this warping of language, this movie scene that echoes across time. But also plumb some zone of the self. If you're not ready, too afraid, if you're self-protectively closed, "plumb" sounds too much like "plunder."

Anytime I have to respond to "what do you do," "I'm a critic" is what I say. And here is this critic introducing a collection of essays— the best of them, from last year. So, in explaining that I'm a critic, that I assess, analyze, inspect, rhapsodize, reconsider, enthuse, that what I write is based on and inspired by, that my imagination corresponds to the imaginations of others, what I should also be telling you is what I'm not. And *that* is an essayist. I should be telling you— warning you, really—that the tenets of my writerly identity have always prized the impersonal and pooh-poohed too probing an exploration of my self. In other words, I should be telling you that *I* should not be this series's latest guest-editor, because it would never occur to me to tell a soul I'm an essayist. Partly because I couldn't say it to myself. But sitting with scores of essays, thinking about what each of these authors had the nerve to offer of themselves, and now having selected a mere yet triumphant twenty-two to offer to you, a kinship has set in. I can see it now, I can feel it. I do what they do. I write essays.

WESLEY MORRIS

The Best
AMERICAN
ESSAYS
2024

Jenisha from Kentucky

FROM *The Atlantic*

MS. BROWN DIDN'T TELL ME where we were going. I knew we would be visiting someone important, a literary figure, because we took a gypsy cab instead of the subway. It would probably be someone I should have known, but didn't.

A brownstone in Harlem. It was immaculate—paintings of women in headscarves; a cherry-colored oriental rug; a dark, gleaming dining-room table. Ms. Brown led me toward a woman on the couch. She knew that I would recognize her, and I did, despite the plastic tube snaking from her nostrils to an oxygen tank. Maya Angelou's back was straight. Her rose-pink eyeshadow sparkled.

My mind called up random bits of information from *I Know Why the Caged Bird Sings*. Canned pineapples—she loved them. Bailey—her brother's name. What she felt when she heard someone read Dickens aloud for the first time—the voice that "slid in and curved down through and over the words." And that, like me, she had called her grandmother Momma.

"What's your name?" she asked.

"Jenisha."

"Last name?" she shot back.

"Watts."

Maya Angelou now knew my name.

The party was for the poet Eugene B. Redmond. Amiri Baraka was there. The family of James Baldwin. And Nikki Giovanni, who once wrote—just to me, it felt like—"Though you're poor it isn't poverty that / concerns you."

By then I knew how to mingle with literary types at networking events. But I always felt like my worth was tied to my job, or my education, or my family background. This night was different. I didn't have to prove myself. It was assumed that everyone here was important, because who else would possibly be invited to Maya Angelou's brownstone? In my head, I created stories about who I might be to these people. Maybe I was a young poet of great promise, or a family friend of Maya's, or even her granddaughter. Having Maya Angelou as my grandmother would have been nice. Toni Morrison, too. And James Baldwin for a granddad.

I'd done this as a child as well, imagining who I could have been if I'd had a different kind of family. Who I could have been had my mother been a professor, an artist, a writer.

But I didn't grow up in a Harlem brownstone. I didn't have a professor or an artist or a writer for a mother. And Maya Angelou wasn't my grandmother.

I was Jenisha from Kentucky, and I was raised in a crack house.

At the Charlotte Court housing project in Lexington, Kentucky, the apartment complexes were all the same, the front yards bare dirt with patches of grass. Lexington is a very white city in an extremely white state, but the West End is Black. Lots of people were poor. I had a bubblegum-pink ten-speed that I would ride to the corner store, where older girls and I would steal Lemonheads and Now and Laters. In summer my brothers and sister and I would rush to Douglass Park to catch the free lunch truck. On weekends we'd bum money at the Plaza—the West End parking lot where people dressed up to sit on the hoods of their freshly washed cars.

The neighborhood was full of boys fighting. Once, my little brother Colby needed a haircut. Our mother, Trina, had no money for the barber, so she shaved his head with a disposable razor. His tight coils covered our floor, and the next day all the kids on the school bus laughed at the nicks on his head.

On one of my birthdays—I was maybe six or seven—Trina let me have a party. No balloons or cake or gifts—just a few girls from the neighborhood going wild. We were upstairs when another mother knocked on the front door. "I told y'all you were not allowed over here," she said to her daughters.

I knew other people who used drugs, but what happened at our apartment was different. On any given day, folks would be in the bathroom or a bedroom getting high. In return, the dealers gave Trina free drugs. Our door was always opening and shutting, strangers entering and leaving. One evening my little brothers and sister and I were in our bedroom, coloring dinosaurs with green crayons. I was about seven. I was working hard to keep them busy so that Trina could enjoy her high. I don't remember Trina ever praising me for being a good big sister, but I heard her brag to a friend about how quiet we were when she left us alone. Coloring books kept us quiet, she said.

Sometimes the cops would come, four or five at a time. My siblings and I would lie in bed as they walked through our dark apartment with flashlights, their staticky walkie-talkies impossible to understand. In the morning we'd see that they'd trashed the place: flipped mattresses onto the floor, pulled out drawers. My Aunt Soso says they once found drugs hidden in the cereal boxes.

We knew why the police came. After they kicked in the door once, a man we'd never seen before handed Colby a bag of drugs to hide. And there were guns. I was standing on the stairs one night when I saw a man in a red jacket hand someone a gun that looked like a big, black Super Soaker. Trina made an "*oooh*" sound. I could tell she was nervous from the way she looked away from the gun.

One time, Trina went upstairs with a group of people to get high. I was crying. I yelled for her because I didn't want her to leave me downstairs without her. I noticed a man with hazel eyes and a mole on his face sitting in a chair, staring at me. "Do you want me to make you feel good?" he asked. My tears stopped. I knew that wasn't something a grown man should say to a child. I was in the third grade.

The police never took Trina to jail those nights, but sometimes they would handcuff her. Once, she was sitting on the couch with my sister Ebony crying in her lap. "Can I change her Pamper?" she asked. She needed them to take the handcuffs off first.

Trina was what I called her. Even when I was little, I never called her Momma.

I don't have any photos of myself as a baby. I recently asked some relatives if they had any in their own albums. No one did, but a cousin sent me a photo of Trina at her high-school prom. Her hair was up and she wore a pastel-pink gown, tight around her tiny waist. She looked innocent. It was the kind of photo that proud daughters share on Instagram. Anyone could see how beautiful she was. I had never thought that about my mother before, that she had been beautiful once.

When I picture Trina, I see her in a hospital bed.

I was in New York City in 2010, at my desk at *People* magazine, when I got the call. Trina had overdosed and hit her head, or been beaten by her boyfriend (not for the first time), or maybe both. When I arrived at the hospital in Lexington, she was almost dead. The right side of her head had been shaved and stapled closed. She couldn't open one of her eyes, but when she saw me, a smile crawled across her face.

But I'm getting ahead of myself. Let me first tell you a bit about Trina Renee Watts.

She was born on October 16, 1965, across town from where we would live as children. Her caramel skin is pimpled and she has a birthmark that resembles a bruise over her right eye. She has always enjoyed reading and writing, and English was her favorite subject in school. She ran track. They called her the next Wilma Rudolph—she was that fast.

She got accepted to Western Kentucky University, but dropped out when I was born, in January 1985. My father's name is Levi Fishback, and he met Trina at a club called Tommy Campbell's.

My sister JaShae was born a year and a half after me. Shay was high yellow, a quiet kid who rarely cried but would suck her thumb or shake her leg when she got anxious, and sniff Trina's shirts when she wasn't around.

When Shay was a baby, Trina started freebasing cocaine, and then she began using crack. When Shay was eleven months old, Trina started bleeding and bleeding, and she didn't know what was wrong. She woke up in the hospital, handcuffed to the bed, and learned that she'd given birth to another baby. She hadn't even suspected that she was pregnant. The baby was born with crack in his system and was in the neonatal ICU, covered in tubes, tiny enough to fit into her cupped hands. This was my brother Jacobbie—Colby.

Aaron was born just before Christmas in 1990, and our youngest sibling, Ebony, in 1992. All five of us have different fathers—I don't think Trina even knows who most of the dads are.

Trina would let me change Ebony's diaper like she was my

doll. During a visit to a neighbor, the woman asked Trina, "Can I have Ebony?" as if that were normal, as if Trina might just hand her child over. She didn't, not that day. But a few months later, Ebony was sent to live with a relative, and she never came home again.

Trina was never mean, never hit us or screamed. She read us *Curious George*—the only book we owned. Sometimes she lifted us up on her feet, pretending we were airplanes, making engine noises. She put up a Christmas tree, even though we had few gifts. Once, an older boy was bullying me on the bus. I had a pencil in my hand and stabbed him on the top of his head. Stunned, he touched the spot, and blood colored his fingertip. That evening, his mother knocked on our door. "Trina, look at what your daughter did to my son," she said, showing her the mark on his head. Trina said, "Well, what did *he* do to *her*?" Trina was on my side.

Sometimes she would pack us into her bed and say, "I promise y'all. I'm going to stop using drugs."

But then we would wake up and Trina would be gone. We wouldn't go to school. We would sit like soldiers on ambush and wait, alert to any sound of chatter, footsteps, or clicking keys that would mean Trina was home. If someone knocked on the door, we knew to hush and not answer it.

One day, we were home alone, and I heard knocking. I was seven or eight. I looked through the peephole. It was my dad. I opened the door and he walked in and looked around. Clothes were scattered everywhere and dirty dishes and trash littered the floor. We didn't have any food. We thought that he would take us back to his place, where he lived with his wife and stepdaughter, or at least give us something to eat. "I gotta get you out of here," he said. But he left and didn't come back.

Another day, I was wearing the same outfit I'd had on for a week, shorts and a tank top. My hair wasn't combed. Trina had brought us over to her friend's house, so the two of them could get high. The friend was balding and fat—I hadn't known that drug addicts could be fat. Inside, the smell of crack was strong—thicker than cigarette smoke, like someone who never brushed their teeth breathing directly into your nose—so I went outside to wander the neighborhood. I ran into a group of pretty, clean-dressed girls who scanned me up and down and whispered. I didn't like them. I didn't like my ugly sister Shay, or my nappy-headed brothers. They all reminded me of what those girls thought of me.

Once, when I was about eight, we were alone and hungry. Colby opened a can of cranberry sauce. One of us poured syrup on a piece of bread. If I'd had only myself to take care of, it wouldn't have been so bad, but as the oldest, I felt it was up to me to fix things. I decided to get my grandmother, Trina's mom, to help us.

My granny worked right across the street from Charlotte Court—she was a nurse for the Health Department. I crossed the two-lane road, pushed open the glass revolving door, and walked to the front desk. "Pat Dishman," I whispered to the secretary. She made me sign in. I pulled down my baseball cap and fixed my jacket. The women were dressed in blouses tucked into slacks. Some wore suits with heels. I had scratched-up legs and my teeth were so crooked that if I smiled with my mouth shut, one poked out the side.

When I stepped off the elevator, I recognized one of my grand-mother's friends, a white woman who offered me a Thin Mint and watched with concern as I gobbled it up. My granny wasn't in the office, but the friend said she'd let her know that I'd stopped by. Walking home, I wondered if her coworkers could see me through the windows. I was mad at myself for not being pretty.

"What the fuck are y'all looking at?" I asked Shay, Colby, and Aaron. I wanted Trina to stroll in so that I could cuss her out. *You stupid bitch!* I would tell her. *Crackhead! Where the fuck you been? We need food! I hate you!*

A knock on the door turned into a bang. It sounded like the police. But it was my granny, in a teal silk coat with fur around the hood. I unlocked the door, and she rushed in.

"Why did you come to my job?" she screamed. Her makeup, as always, was perfect, her lips a deep plum. "Why did you come to my job?"

"I didn't go to your job," I said, almost believing my own lie.

"Yes she did, Granny," Shay said. I wanted to smack her. I wanted to say, *You're uglier than me.*

"Don't you ever bring yo ass to my job," Granny said. She didn't ask where Trina was or how long she'd been gone, or offer to take us to McDonald's. She just left, slamming the door.

Another time, Trina disappeared for a few hours. We were wait-ing for her when the door to the closet opened and she walked out. That entire time, she'd been sitting in the closet, high. I can still see her long leg stepping out from behind the door. She moved like a nutcracker soldier, as if her body were made of wood. Her lips were pressed together, and she didn't acknowledge us at all. She just walked out of the apartment. We were too stunned to chase after her.

When I was nine, we moved into the Salvation Army. Trina said it was because the police had damaged the apartment so badly during a raid that maintenance had to come and fix it up. We certainly hadn't been evicted, she told me, because our subsidized rent was only $50.

We ate at a brown table in the Salvation Army cafeteria and shared a bathroom with homeless people who mumbled to themselves as we brushed our teeth. We slept in a room that automatically went dark each night when the clock flashed curfew.

One day, Trina and two other mothers took us all to the park. They huddled by a tree as I sat on a park bench, keeping an eye on the little kids and on Trina. Two homeless men were pointing at our moms. One was shaking his head as if he was disappointed. I could see the fire from the lighter warming the crack pipe as Trina and the other women bent down and took turns.

I was surprised that she had found other women like her, other moms who enjoyed drugs. At the time, Trina was on crutches because she had gotten in a fight and broken her foot. *Even hopping around on one foot*, I thought to myself, *she still wants to get high.*

Aaron came down with a bad fever at the Salvation Army. He was in Trina's lap, his head on her chest. Ordering an ambulance was going to be expensive, but Trina didn't hesitate—she just wanted to make sure her baby boy was okay. Right then, she seemed like a normal mother.

My aunts, Chantelle and Soso, came to the Salvation Army with a U-Haul to get me. I sat between them. The drive to Tallahassee was bumpy and long, the inside of the truck hot and sticky. But Florida, when we got there, was peaceful and sunny and had palm trees. I moved into Aunt Chantelle's apartment, where she shared one room with her baby son and I shared the other with my seven-year-old cousin, Kiki.

Aunt Chantelle had just graduated from Florida State University and was working at Target. She tried to give me a normal life. We ate dinner at a table and had Fruit Roll-Ups for snacks. I was in the fourth grade at Apalachee Elementary School, and every day my hair was done and I had proper clothes to wear. Once, when it rained, she let Kiki and me run around until we were soaked. We filled buckets up with rainwater, which she told us was good for our hair.

But many days, I would walk down to a payphone near a convenience store, where I could call my granny collect to ask about Trina and my siblings. That's how I learned that the state had taken them away. Shay was living with my granny's sister, Jamie. The boys were in foster care with a Jehovah's Witness. They were all gone.

The adults seemed to have known that this was the likely outcome—that's why I'd been sent away, to keep me out of the system. But I felt so guilty for leaving, like it wouldn't have happened if I had been there, like I was the only one who could protect them. There were two boys in the neighborhood who reminded me of my brothers; one had the same box haircut as Aaron. I'd knock on their door and ask if they could play, when all I really wanted was to watch as they wrestled on the playground.

I had a journal with a red-ribbon placeholder that I wrote in about Trina's addiction and how much I missed my siblings. One time, I left it out in plain view, where I knew my aunts would find it. That night, I sat with my ear against the wall, listening as Aunt Soso read my journal over the phone to my granny.

I was beginning to see that writing things down, naming them, could make other people feel things. I felt freer writing than I did speaking out loud. I discovered books in Florida, too. I lived in my head and went wherever the stories took me—into the world of a boy who learned that he was diabetic because he always had to pee; or a redheaded, freckled kid who wiped his runny nose with his shirt; or a rich kid who was new to school and tried to use his money to make friends. Reading was the only time when I didn't think about Trina or my siblings.

I lived in Florida for more than a year. Then the state of Kentucky gave Trina another chance. Shay, Aaron, Colby, and I all moved into our grandmother's house—the three-bedroom house on Valley Farm Drive where Trina had grown up. Trina wasn't permitted to live with us yet, but she visited on weekends. She was in rehab and working at Hardee's. One evening, she came by with another woman—her caseworker, I think—to bring me a birthday card and a Butterfinger, my favorite candy. When she was sober, Trina would do my hair. She knew how to do cornrows in elaborate designs, any style I wanted. She took her time, and her hands were gentle.

It was a different world from the projects. My granny was a master sergeant in the Army Reserve, and she was strict, but she took care of us. She worked every day, so she'd get us up early and I'd dress Aaron for day care. We'd sing the Barney song together. We had a yard to play in, and at night, we all slept in the same bed under a blanket covered in faded-pink strawberries, me in the middle with my arms around my siblings.

Granny threw us birthday parties, too. I had a party at a skating rink with a Mickey Mouse cake. She pushed me to work hard at school, though I didn't always listen, and she got a tutor for Colby, who was struggling.

My dad would make the occasional appearance. One time, he promised to take me to the zoo. The night before, I ironed my black jeans until they had a white crease from the starch. I even ironed my cotton panties. I was picturing the day to come: He would take me to the gift shop and to McDonald's. He'd let me order anything on the menu.

In the morning, I wore my favorite purple sweater and new white ribbons in my pigtails. I went outside to wait, because waiting outside would help speed his arrival. I watched the road, leaving my post only to go to the bathroom, or to answer the ringing phone. I hoped it was him, calling to assure me that he was on his way. "He's not coming, Jenisha," my granny kept saying. I waited until the sun set. He didn't even call the next day, or the day after that.

Trina got us kids back, but she began doing drugs again, too. I was always asking if I could go to my granny's, because it was calmer there. So I wasn't with my siblings on the day when Trina dropped them off with the woman who took care of Ebony. When she didn't come back to get them, the woman called social services and reported her. I stayed with my granny while Colby, Aaron, and Shay ended up back in foster care. We never lived together again.

At Christmas, I would pick out gifts, wrapping them in forest-green paper with a Black Santa pattern. But I never saw my siblings during the holidays. Once New Year's came, I'd put the gifts in the attic. Eventually I stopped buying new ones. I brought the old presents down again and again, until the wrapping paper faded and tore.

I didn't cry. I just pushed away my emotions and eased into my new life. I had my own bedroom; the telephone worked, and the cable did, too. Eventually my granny paid for me to get braces—a status symbol in my middle-school eyes. Only white kids, and Black kids from two-parent homes, had braces.

My sister Shay lived with Aunt Jamie in the projects and we went to the same school, one grade apart. She did endless chores and rarely had any new clothes. I used to make fun of her high-water pants. One weekend, when I was visiting, she took my wide-legged jeans. When I saw them on her at school, I tried to fight her. No one knew why—most of our classmates didn't even know we were sisters.

Shay probably had it worst of all my siblings. She moved out as soon as she turned eighteen and got pregnant with her first baby around then. I wasn't much of a sister to her. I wanted to close the door on that part of my life. And I wanted to make my granny proud.

Granny was always warning me that I could turn out just like "your mammy." I was desperate for her to see me as a beautiful girl, a girl who was nothing like my mother. Maybe that's why I started calling her Momma. And for a while, she let me. But one day, I walked into her room and said, "Momma," and she looked up at me over her reading glasses. "I'm not your momma," she said.

I wasn't lonely when I was reading. And in my diary, I could say whatever I wanted, name every insecurity. Words also pulled me closer to other people—like Contessa, who had hair that ran past her shoulders and got high scores on her papers, and yet was still my friend. Both of our mothers had been in jail, and we shared the letters that they had written to us from inside.

I was a collector of words. In sixth grade I learned the meaning of *dumbfounded* from a vocabulary test. I liked the fullness of the word and how it rolled off my tongue.

I felt the same about the word *perplexed*. Tom Joyner, the radio host, said "I'm perplexed" during an interview, and as soon as the word landed on my ears, I knew what he meant. I learned *epitome* from a TLC song, and *regurgitate* from a friend's letter about her abortion.

Words were the only things that seemed attainable to me. I could look them up in my grandmother's dictionary and understand their meaning—unlike math, where, if I was stuck, I'd need someone to help me. The more words I learned, the more I realized that my own language could be deepened.

My grandmother worked a lot, and when she was home, she'd stay in her room. One day she said, "I got you some pads." I thought, *Wow, she got me some writing pads.* But when she didn't make eye contact with me, I realized that she meant something else. She must have noticed the blood on my laundry. She didn't like the word *period*—she thought *cycle* was more polite.

When I was home alone, I would read her *Jet* and *Ebony* magazines, and the laminated aphorisms and poems she'd hung on the wall. My favorite was called "Don't Quit": "When things go wrong, as they sometimes will, / When the road you're trudging seems all uphill . . ."

Trina moved in with Granny and me when I was about fifteen. We fought a lot—I thought she owed me for choosing drugs over being a mother. Once, I asked her to do my hair. She said no, and suddenly I was furious. I called her a crackhead and punched her. And then I picked up a pair of scissors and cut off a chunk of her hair.

Granny called the cops on me. I was handcuffed and driven to a juvenile detention center. They made me strip in a cold room, and a white female officer inspected my body. I told someone there that I wanted to kill myself, so I had to wear a special shirt, alerting everyone that I was on suicide watch, until they let me go home a few days later.

Around that time, I read *The Color of Water,* James McBride's memoir about his white mother's life, in which he tries to understand his identity as a Black man. I wasn't a diligent student, but I knew what I liked, and I liked James McBride. He wasn't a great student either—"my high school grades were sour, my SATs low," he wrote. He stole and did drugs. And yet he made a life from words.

Everyone around me wanted to go to the University of Kentucky.

Many of my friends got in. But my ACT score was so embarrassingly low that when I saw it, I balled up the paper and hid it under the couch. I would have to do two years of community college first.

I kept this a secret. Community-college kids lived on the same campus as the University of Kentucky students, so even as my granny and Trina moved me into my dorm room, they had no idea that I hadn't gotten in.

I was placed in remedial classes, where I learned basic things that I should have been taught in grade school. One semester, I had to select a word and write a paper illustrating it. My word was *condescending*.

But eventually, I was able to transfer to the University of Kentucky. I got a UK ID with my picture on it, and a UK wallet to put it in. Sometimes I'd pull out my ID and stare at it.

My friend Carrie was an English major and a writer. She was so free with her language, and could enunciate long, peculiar words. We'd sit on her dorm-room bed and share lines that moved us. She helped me tune my ears to the music of writing.

Another friend handed me *The Fire Next Time* and said, "You need to know this man." I loved that James Baldwin wasn't handsome like Langston Hughes. I read that he was often called ugly, ridiculed for his "frog eyes," and for the gap in his grin and his African nose. I saw beauty in him, but more than that, I admired how his intellect transcended what others thought about him.

I heard about a creative-writing professor who was supposed to be incredible, a poet. One day, I was walking with a friend, and we saw a tall, bronze-skinned woman with gold-streaked locs. My friend turned to me and said, "There she is!"

Nikky Finney. We were like teenagers spotting their favorite musician. I had listened many times to a clip of Professor Finney reading her poem "The Greatest Show on Earth," about Saartjie Baartman, the Hottentot Venus. She wrote about "the spectacle / of being a Black woman," and the "pornographic hands / fascinated with difference" that dissected her.

In spring 2007, I got to take Professor Finney's class. She acted like words were living, breathing, sacred things—like writing was serious. "Take a word on a date," she would tell us. One day, I submitted a poem called "Threadless." I used the word *panacea*, and when I read it aloud, I pronounced it "panaysha." Professor Finney

stopped the class. "Never use a word you don't know how to pronounce," she said. I think she felt that I had disrespected the word.
    And yet she was curious about me, and asked me about my life
and my interests, and that made me stand up a little taller around
her. She was the one who realized how much help I still needed
with grammar and arranged for a tutor, a graduate student who
worked with me on diagramming sentences and the parts of
speech. I resented it then, but now when I look back at the emails
I was sending at that time, I cringe—they're riddled with basic
errors. And no one told me. Professor Finney was the first teacher
who told me the truth.

    As soon as classes ended, I was gone. I left Kentucky for New York
on a Greyhound bus with a few hundred dollars in my bank account
and two suitcases: one with my professional clothes—a pair of black
slacks, a pair of gray slacks, a few collared shirts, my flower-printed
sundresses—and the other stuffed with Shay's blow-up mattress. It
was August 2008, and five days earlier I had gotten a temp job at
Essence magazine—ten dollars an hour to help move stories from
an old version of the website to a new one.
    The trip took twenty hours. I tried to lay my head against the
window and sleep, but I couldn't. It was late when the bus pulled
into Manhattan. My plan had been to spend that first night in a
hotel. I found one near the Port Authority, but when I tried to go
inside, the doorman lied and said it was closed. I think he thought
I was homeless. Instantly, I regretted my travel outfit—sneakers
and jeans, my hair undone beneath a baseball cap.
    I was too scared to try another hotel. Instead I called the young
woman who had offered to host me that first month—the daughter
of one of my college mentors—and asked if I could show up right
away. The taxi to Brooklyn cost a fortune.
    I had no idea how to navigate this new world. But I was a very
good beggar. As a child, I would approach anyone who looked re-
motely willing and able and ask them for money to buy my siblings
and me a value meal at Rally's. When I was eight, success meant
that we would get burgers and fries for dinner, instead of nothing.
Later, it meant a mentorship, an interview, a job.
    I had gotten my first position at *Essence*—an internship—thanks
to Susan Taylor, the editorial director. I loved the magazine because

it was full of stories about successful Black women, and every month I'd see Susan's face, smiling in the back of the book. In Kentucky, I'd gone to a talk she was giving, offered to carry her bags, and told her all about my ambitions.

At the office, I would watch people I admired, anyone who seemed proper and smart, and try to do what they did. I could make it in New York, I told myself, if I worked hard, wore all black, and persuaded people to look after me. I asked anyone I thought could help me for advice, or a connection. Most people, like Susan, were generous and kind, but there was also the occasional humiliation.

One time I was having lunch at a French restaurant with another editor from *Essence*. I was proud because I had connected with him over our shared experience of growing up in a small town. As we were walking back to the Time & Life Building, I told him how nice it was to "conversate" with him. "Did you just say 'conversate'?" he asked, and my face burned.

I was always a fast eater, but I'd never thought to be ashamed of it until I was having lunch with a beautiful editor from a different magazine. I guess I made a mess with the breadcrumbs. Even though she was Black herself, she asked, "Why do you Black girls eat like that?"

Every Wednesday, I went to Hump Day—a happy hour for young Black professionals where everyone talked politics and seemed to have answers to all sorts of serious questions. The men wore suits and ties and the women all reminded me of Michelle Obama: ambitious, credentialed, supremely confident. Most were Jack-and-Jill groomed. They came from intact families that understood the concept of internships. They didn't drink Olde English, and they knew how to eat spaghetti correctly. They read books at the summer houses of their parents, parents who sent *them* money—not the other way around.

At Hump Day, I hid my past. They knew I was from Kentucky, which was foreign enough. They'd complain about boarding school and I'd say, *Yeah, my private school was horrible, too.* I told myself I wasn't technically lying—I *had* attended a magnet school with a dress code: khaki pants and collared shirts.

Growing up, I'd never wanted to be white, just the right kind of Black. I'd always assumed that I was proper: I didn't have children out of wedlock; I wasn't a ho; I went to college. I had never thought much about class, but I'd never met Black people like these before.

My deficiencies haunted me: my childhood, my accent, my lack of knowledge. Silly things, like the fact that I'd never seen the movies that well-off Black kids had all watched: *Coming to America*, *Harlem Nights*. I asked "Where you at?" instead of "Where are you?" I talked quietly because I was never certain I was saying the words correctly. When I said "picture," people heard "pitcher." Eventually, I trained myself to always say "photo." I even found an acting coach online who agreed to give me voice lessons to try to change my accent, and we practiced on monologues in her studio.

I told one Hump Day guy named Brandon that I was planning a trip to Paris. He asked if I spoke French and I said, "Conversational." All I could say was *Bonjour* and *Je m'appelle Jenisha*, and I definitely wasn't flying to Europe. Each month many of my credit cards went delinquent. After Sprint turned my cellphone off, my granny shipped me one that had belonged to her dead ex-husband, Big Dishman, with one instruction: Don't erase his voice from the greeting. So whenever I missed someone's call, they'd hear a man's deep voice telling them to leave a message.

At work I never met anyone with a background like mine, and I knew why; only people with money could afford to be paid so little. There were times when I couldn't pay for lunch. One day, I walked into a Chase bank to withdraw two dollars—just enough for a hot dog and chips. I probably had about five dollars in my account, but the teller wouldn't let me make the withdrawal. She handed me a five-dollar bill from her own wallet instead.

I thought constantly about my family. Colby was mixed up in drugs and getting in trouble. Aaron was married and raising two sons with his high-school sweetheart; Shay was living in a three-bedroom house with her boyfriend and four kids. I was closest then to Shay and her children, especially my oldest niece. I didn't go home much, but when I did, I'd take her to the bookstore and spend more than I could afford on *Junie B. Jones*. My family knew I was working at a glamorous job in New York City, so they assumed I had money. I was too proud to tell them otherwise.

In October 2010, I got that call about Trina in the hospital. A friend loaned me the cash for a plane ticket so I could make it to her bedside.

The note on her chart read: "Pt. has no bone flap on right side." The doctors had taken it out because her brain was swollen and bleeding from a hematoma. The intake nurse had written that the details surrounding how she'd arrived at the hospital were "sketchy at best."

"You came all the way from New York to check on me," Trina whispered. She was wearing a diaper, and I changed it for her. She said thank you. She was too weak to use her arms, so I helped feed her a sloppy cheeseburger, watery mustard soaking the bun.

Trina's longtime boyfriend, Tim, had called an ambulance because she wouldn't wake up. She had been high, and it looked as if Tim had beaten her up. He told me that wasn't true, and claimed that she had overdosed. But I had witnessed him hitting Trina many times. They're still together, and I asked him recently why he hit her so often. "She was crazy," he said. "She's still crazy."

Sitting beside her, I couldn't bat down the flashbacks. I saw Tim pull her up by her hair like a fisherman would lift a trout. I saw her jaw widening to scream.

"What year is it?" I asked her.

"1985," she said.

"Who is the president?"

"Bush."

"*What year* is this?"

"You just heard me say what year it is," she said. Her memory was draining away like spilled water.

Whenever Trina woke up, I would ask her what I should do: Should I go back to New York? And she always said yes. "Go back. You got a dream there." I asked if she had any advice for me, and she said, "Don't be smart all your life. Always be yourself no matter who's around. You live and you learn and you learn to live."

After a day or two, she started asking me for crack. She moved her mouth from side to side as if her lips were playing an invisible harmonica. Spit bubbled on her lips. She didn't even know who I was anymore. She pleaded with me: "I want a hit."

My friends in New York had no idea what was going on. My bosses just knew that my mom was sick. She's still in critical condition, I told them. I wanted them to believe she was dying of cancer or something.

She survived that injury, survived withdrawal, and then went back

____

on crack. For at least a year, she had to wear a protective helmet. I just went back to New York.

One night not long after I returned, I was covering a celebrity event for *People*. Ne-Yo was performing, and my assignment was to interview him after his set. I got the VIP treatment, skipping the crowd and sipping free cocktails. We talked about his work and his children. It was just a normal night in my new life. But on the long commute home, I started sobbing, I didn't understand what was happening. What if someone I knew saw me crying? I couldn't stop. I could barely breathe.

I'd slept in a walk-in closet, stayed with acquaintances, lived for a while with a boyfriend. I couldn't afford rent. But I needed a steady place to live, and a family friend from Kentucky finally connected me with Marie Brown.

Ms. Brown was a literary agent who championed Black writers and artists, and she had a habit of taking in young people who needed help. Her Harlem brownstone was a library. Magazines and newspapers were piled everywhere. And books and books and books. She looked at me skeptically while I pretended to have a reasonable plan for the future. At last she offered me a room for a few months, until I got on my feet. I stayed for four years.

Much of the time, I could hide my inadequacies by working hard. Not with Ms. Brown. One day in the kitchen, she told me to add two measurements, but my math was wrong. "Why don't you know anything about numbers?" she asked. She ordered me some basic math books, and gave me a card with different percentages on it for tipping.

She gave me beauty advice, too—wear sunscreen, scrub your elbows—things I'd never discussed with Trina or my granny. When I ate quickly, Ms. Brown would tell me, "Take your time, Jenisha. Don't pick up the entire piece of bread; break off a small piece and eat it. Dip the spoon in the soup and slowly bring it to your mouth."

But the main thing she had me do was read. Read until I couldn't read anymore.

She was always saying "I left that for you." Her living-room table was covered in magazines and manuscripts, but amid the pandemonium I always knew exactly which article was meant for me. When I was at work, she'd email me links to breaking news, with the subject "Did you read this?" I'd reply, "No, I didn't hear about it. I'll check it out." And she'd write back, "What type of journalist are you?"

Whenever I was being small-town or closed-minded, or acting like a victim of circumstance, she'd say, "Quit being Kentucky."

Ms. Brown wasn't my only mentor; I had a string of them—women who talked to me about writers like Sylvia Plath, taught me how to fact-check, and invited me over for holiday dinners. But one of the most influential was someone I never met: Helen Gurley Brown, the legendary editor of *Cosmopolitan*.

One day I found, on the pile left out for me, a review of a new biography of Brown called *Bad Girls Go Everywhere*. I couldn't understand at first why I needed to read about this plain-faced white woman. But I did, and then I ordered Brown's own book.

Helen Gurley Brown grew up in Arkansas. "I *never* liked the looks of the life that was programmed for me—ordinary, hillbilly, and poor," she wrote. She quoted Carson McCullers: "'I must go home periodically to renew my sense of horror.'" She called herself a "mouseburger"—the kind of woman who wasn't Marilyn Monroe beautiful but knew how to work hard and highlight her best features. She understood me: "You may not be an intellectual or a scholar, but you *are* 'street smart.' Like a little forest animal, you are quick and adaptable. You 'know' things."

One night I saw a tweet about *The Messenger*, by Charles Wright. I'd never heard of Wright, and I immediately ordered a copy. I found his *New York Times* obituary. A quote from his editor drew me in. "He was a very strange man, and after we met I thought, 'Well, this is not going to work.'" Then "he turned in the most perfect manuscript I'd ever received."

Wright may have lacked technical skill, but raw talent throbbed beneath his sentences. He wrote about walking through Rockefeller Center with a book in his hands, "sneezing and reading Lawrence Durrell, dead drunk from the explosion of his words. I suddenly looked up and encountered the long face of Steven Rockefeller. He seemed startled. Doesn't he think poor people read?"

Wright was an outsider in New York, trying to straddle two worlds. His grandmother had raised him in Missouri after his mother died of typhoid fever. He wanted to be a writer but worked as a messenger, walking through the "rainy New York streets" until his shoes were soaked through.

"I cannot connect the fragments of my life," he wrote.

Wright was sad, with pockets full of ambition. And so was I.

Around this time, I applied to Columbia Journalism School. I did it secretly, because I was sure I wouldn't get in. But I did. All of my reading had paid off. For the first time, thanks to graduate-school loans, I could afford to live comfortably.

I called home to share the news, but no one had heard of Columbia before. "Where's that?" my granny asked. I told her that Barack Obama had gone there.

Now, whenever I went out with the Hump Day crowd, people asked me for book recommendations. "You have to read *Liar's Poker*," I'd say. "You'd really love *The Brief Wondrous Life of Oscar Wao*." The truth is, I hadn't even read some of the books I recommended; I'd just heard about them while listening to Ms. Brown and her literary friends, or read the reviews that told me they were important.

In 2011, my old professor Nikky Finney was nominated for a National Book Award for Poetry, and she invited me to go to the ceremony with her. I was in the audience when she won, and gave an acceptance speech that soon went viral: "Black people were the only people in the United States ever explicitly forbidden to become literate." That, she said, "still haunts every poem I make."

She invited me again two years later, when she was a judge. I met James McBride, and I told him that his book had changed my life. When he won, for *The Good Lord Bird*, I cheered and cheered.

The next year, I graduated from Columbia. Ms. Brown was throwing me a party, and I invited a bunch of my mentors, as well as Aunt Soso, Trina, and my granny. I had helped get some money together for Trina to ride that same Greyhound bus I'd once taken. But then I changed my mind. She was getting high a lot then, and I didn't want to babysit her. So I called her back and said to forget about it, that I didn't want her to come after all. She didn't ask why.

My granny didn't come either. I had so wanted her to see my life—my studio apartment with its bookshelves of novels and biographies, the campus filled with brilliant professors. But at the last minute she made an excuse and said she couldn't come. Many people were there to support me, but not the two women who'd raised me.

My brothers and sisters and I have never talked much about our childhood. When I went to live with my granny, I became something like an only child, and each year their absence became easier to accept. Alone, I was able to rewrite my own story: I had a good life. I went to Florida every spring break and swam with my cousins. I decorated my own room. I had only myself to look after. I tried to bury the rest of it in the ground, and I was surprisingly successful. But our silence had a cost.

Last year, I started writing what I thought would be an essay about my start in journalism, but I kept getting pulled back and back. I couldn't write about myself without writing about my family.

I always knew that I had privileges my brothers and sisters didn't have. All this time I thought that Colby and Aaron had lived with a nice foster family, but I found out this year that Colby, struggling with behavioral issues, had been sent away to live in a series of group homes when he was nine or ten. How could I not have known that? "You were just off in your own little world," he told me. "We were all off in our own little worlds."

He told me about a time when he was alone downstairs in our apartment, and the cops barged in. He'd gotten a teddy bear on a school trip to some kind of medical clinic, and it had a big bandage on it. Someone was hurt during the raid. I'm not sure what happened—or how much of this is the dream logic of a traumatized child—but he said that "somebody took my Band-Aid off my teddy bear because they was bleeding that bad."

"I was so mad," he said. "I loved that teddy bear."

Listening to his memories, I felt like a wound was reopening inside me.

I talked with my aunts and my great-aunts, with my granny's cousin and childhood friend. But the one person who didn't want to talk was my granny.

"You don't want to open that can of worms," she said.

I always saw crack as the source of my family's problems. But I learned that addiction went back in our family long before the crack epidemic—as did poverty and neglect.

Irvin Smith, my granny's cousin, is the most educated member of our family—he has a doctorate in behavioral and analytical psychology and worked as a clinical consultant for the state of Kentucky. Ours, Irvin told me, was a "female-dominated family." The women were always getting in hair-pulling, skillet-raising fights—"mother-daughter fights" about the things "that all mothers and daughters argue about: the daughter's boyfriends, the grandkids." They lived in the '40s, '50s, and '60s in a part of Lexington called the Bottoms, where the juke joints were, where people went to drink and fight.

My granny was raised mostly by her grandmother, Addie Mae Fields, who worked in the Southwestern Tobacco factory and wove beautiful baskets out of tobacco leaves. My granny's mother worked in the factory, too. Both her mother and grandmother drank heavily. Granny's mother died suddenly in her sleep, in her early forties or even younger.

My granny was fourteen or fifteen when she became a mother, to a baby girl who died. Trina was born the year after. Her father's name is Walter Watts. Walter's childhood was one of real deprivation. He told me that his mother gave him up and that he lived "in the streets." He was "the neighborhood child—people in the neighborhood at different houses would buy clothes for me, and I would have to go to their house to take a bath."

He was addicted to heroin, then to crack. "Drugs do not allow you to be a parent," he told me. "They consume your whole life."

So why did he use them? "My mother didn't love me, so how could anybody else love me? That's the way I always looked at it."

When I asked people in my family why their lives had gone so off track, they all seemed to point to the same thing: this void where a mother's love was supposed to be.

"You try to close that void, but it never happens," Walter said. "At least it hasn't happened for me."

"My mother never, never wanted me," Trina said. "She never wanted me."

Trina was in the shower one day when she heard the bathroom door opening. She was fourteen and would normally have been at school, but it was a snow day. The shower curtain came back fast and there was her stepfather's towering body. She started crying and yelled out, "No, no, please, no!" He grabbed her naked body. "I was fighting and fighting and fighting," and he was "taking his hands and sticking them up in me." He pulled her from the shower and slammed her on the bed he shared with her mother.

"He raped me," she said.

I'd known for years that Trina had said she was raped by my granny's husband, Big Dishman—the man whose phone I'd inherited. But we'd never talked about it. This year I finally asked her to tell me what happened.

Eventually, she got free and "ran out of the house with no clothes on all the way up the hill" to a friend's house. "Snow was on the ground; it was cold, but I can't remember being cold. I was just trying to get away."

At some point the police were called, and Big Dishman was arrested. Trina said she was taken to the hospital, where doctors examined her. Trina told me that her mother picked her up from the hospital and then went straight to the police station to bail Big Dishman out.

The local paper reported his arrest: "Police Charge Man With Raping Juvenile," read the headline. "William R. Dishman, 42, of 1000 Valley Farm Drive, has been charged with second degree rape."

I didn't know Big Dishman well. He and my granny separated long before I moved in with her, so I don't remember seeing him much growing up, and he died in 2005. I couldn't find any court records, so I'm not sure what happened after he was released, or whether there was a trial.

But I asked Irvin what he remembered. He said that when my grandmother found out about the abuse, she kicked Big Dishman out. He said she was the one who called the police. But then she took him back in. "You gotta remember," Irvin said: "He was still the father of three of her children."

In Trina's memory, Granny was angry at *her*—as if she'd seduced Big Dishman and then lied about it. She was mad at Trina's younger sister Soso, too. One time, Soso told me, when she was in high school, Big Dishman walked into her room naked and said, "I will give you twenty dollars if you let me eat your pussy." Soso, like Trina, went on to struggle with addiction, though she's been clean for decades; my granny has a similarly strained relationship with her.

When I asked my granny about the sexual abuse, she accused

Trina and Soso of taking money from Big Dishman in return for sexual favors. She said she blamed all three of them, but Soso especially.

But she was a kid, I said.

"She knew what she was doing," Granny said.

I'd always thought of my grandmother as my protector, my savior. She was so put together and morally upright—I couldn't believe that she would have let her daughter be abused. Easier to not believe Trina, because she's a drug addict, because I've resented her for so long. It was hard for me to see that she'd been hurt, too. But I could hear it, in the way Trina said Big Dishman's name, low and quiet, as if he still might be nearby.

Not long ago, Colby overdosed on heroin. "I just took a little line of it and next thing you know, I woke up and everybody was crying."

Aaron texted me: "I gave him narcan and cpr and he came back." He also sent a video of Colby on the floor: he was sweating, his eyes half closed, and he kept moving his mouth back and forth in this way that looked deeply familiar.

This past June, I booked a trip to Kentucky. I had so many doubts about this essay. Was it a betrayal to speak so honestly about my family? Was I "pimping my trauma"? I wanted to talk with everyone in person.

My flight was early, but my son, sensing that I was leaving, woke up crying. He wrapped his arms around my neck and wouldn't let go. Whenever I tried to put him back in his crib, he screamed. My husband finally intervened, but I'd already held my son for so long that I missed my flight.

When I finally got to Lexington, Trina was drunk. I'd been telling her for weeks that I was coming to interview her for this story. But everything, as usual, was chaos. Tim, her boyfriend, had lost his phone, and a woman who lived at the Salvation Army had found it. Trina needed me to drive her over there to get it. The parking lot looked smaller than it had when we stayed there, the entrance somehow sleeker. I didn't go in.

Then Trina insisted that she had to clean her apartment before she could sit down and talk. Enough. I stormed off. When I'm in Kentucky, the old Jenisha slips out. I drove around, steaming.

Granny's old office looked the same, but the Charlotte Court projects were gone, a new single-family home standing in the lot where Trina used to hang our clothes.

Finally I went back to Trina's. She insisted that she wasn't drunk, that she'd only had a Long Island. We sat on the side of her bed. I'd always wanted to ask why she chose drugs over us. Since her brain injury, it can be hard for her to recall things. But she answered my questions as best she could.

"It wasn't like I intentionally tried to do it," she told me. She said she would tell us that she was going around the corner to a friend's house—"'I'll be right back. I'm going to get some sugar or something. . . . Don't open the door for anybody.'" But then her friend would have crack, and people would be there partying. "I would say, 'Well, I'm just going to take one.' . . . Then one turned into another one and another one and another one." She turned her head to the headboard and cried.

Later I went looking for Colby. He's still handsome—over six feet tall with a head full of hair. A decade ago he was in college, but now he doesn't have a job or a home. Back when we were little, I found a sheet of paper where he had written: "Dear Diary, I was born on May 10, and little did I know I was born a crack baby." I can still see his soft, left-handed cursive, wobbly on the page.

As we talked in my car, he described what it had felt like when he overdosed: "I didn't see no angels, no demons, no nothing."

"You think you died?" I asked.

"I was dead. I did die." His voice was so low, I worried the recorder wouldn't pick it up.

After our last interview, he wanted me to buy him a drink, but I said no. When I left him at the curb, sadness hit me like a glob of spit.

The last thing I did was go to my granny's. She lives just across the border in Indiana now, in a nice house with a four-car garage and a pond in the yard filled with goldfish. I wore a white lace dress and made sure my hair was straightened and concealer covered up my blemishes. She stared me up and down, saving her compliments for later.

She told me that she didn't want to be part of any story that included Trina or Aunt Soso. She gave me a glass of water and I patted her dog, and then it was time for my flight home. But just as I was about to leave, she said that I could call her later with my questions—we could do my "little interview."

For two months, she dodged my calls. The whole time, I was worried about the story of the rape. Could I really write about something so painful? I love my granny, but we'd never talked honestly about the past. I had to remind myself that it wasn't a secret. It had been in the newspaper.

Then a researcher who was helping me on this story found something—files from a court case involving Big Dishman. At last, I thought, I'd have the legal record of Trina's accusation. I looked at the PDF of the crooked documents, the word DISMISSED stamped across a page.

But I was confused. The incident the complaint described was from 1988. One page was particularly blurry, but I could make out the words: "Dishman, William . . . did rub his granddaughter in the vaginal area while waiting [in] the car at Northpark Shopping Center."

The papers said the child involved was only three years old. Her initials were J. W.

I was three in 1988. My initials are J. W.

I called to ask Trina if she knew about this, and she said she'd had no idea. She seemed genuinely shocked, and insisted that she would never have let that happen to one of her kids. I called my granny next, and she said she didn't know anything about it either. She had trouble forming a response; I didn't know how to respond either.

She called me back later to say that "J. W. could've been any J. W."

She didn't understand why I wanted to dig all this up. "He's dead," she said. Yes, he's dead—and she was still trying to spare him. I was done with that.

That Sunday, I stayed in bed until late in the afternoon, trying to sleep it all off—my initials; three years old; granddaughter; DISMISSED. I'd spent so much time pushing my family's history aside, and now here it was, circling back at me.

Over the following days, I learned that there were other cases: The Fayette County court had records of four more criminal complaints against a William Dishman alleging sexual abuse of a minor.

The first was from 1986, the last from 2002. The cases are sealed because they involve juveniles. I don't know who the alleged victims were—only that there were more.

I kept thinking of something Irvin said. "Secrets never stay secret, no matter what you do."

Two years ago, when I was pregnant with my son, I was angrier with Trina than I'd ever been. As I was becoming a mother myself, the weight of it hit me. I couldn't understand a mother not being there to protect her child. I still can't.

I've talked with my husband about my childhood, but he grew up in a stable household, and he can't really understand what it's like to come from a family like mine. We're both Black, but it's like we're in a mixed marriage.

Our life is comfortable, but *comfortable* feels like the wrong word. I still worry all the time about money, about losing the opportunities I've worked so hard to achieve. I still get flustered when trying to communicate my thoughts or ideas—still worry that I might never catch up. I've spent my whole life trying not to be like my mother. I've spent my whole life trying to belong, to show people that I'm not like "them," not a Black person living in poverty, not a Black person with an addiction.

My son is one and a half now. My husband and I take him to the zoo and try to read to him every night. Before he was born, he had more books than baby clothes. I don't want him to have to hustle like I did. I want to give him the words he needs to open any doors, and if I can't, I want him to know where to find those words: in books. He already likes to pull my books off the shelf. He wrinkles the pages, bites the corners, wets a bookmark with his drool—and I don't mind.

Charles Wright said he couldn't connect the fragments of his life. That's how I feel, too. How can I connect the fragments when the ground is still heaving up new ones?

Many people told me not to write this. Trina was the one who said to do it. "The truth is the light of the world," she said. "The truth will set you free."

So this is the beginning of the story of Jenisha Watts.

TEJU COLE

Reframing Vermeer

FROM *New York Times Magazine*

THE AFTERNOON I discovered Vermeer, I was passing time by browsing the books and publications piled up on the shelves at home in Lagos. I was fourteen or fifteen. Amid the relics of my parents' college studies (Nigerian plays, French histories, business-management textbooks), I found something unfamiliar: the annual report for a multinational company. I don't remember which company it was, but it must have had something to do with food or drink, because on the front cover was a painting of peasants in a rolling field and on the back was a painting of a woman pouring milk.

I remember the quietness of that afternoon and my fascination with the images on the report, which seemed to transfigure the space around me. I learned from the printed captions that the paintings were *The Harvesters*, by Pieter Bruegel the Elder, and *The Milkmaid*, by Johannes Vermeer. These names were new to me at the time, but I was already an avid student of art and knew enough to know when something moved me. The Vermeer, especially, had a plain and impressive mystery. Never had I seen a wall so well painted or a human figure so convincingly situated in pictorial space. And all of it was suffused with a light that made it seem more like life itself than like other paintings. I would not have thought to call it "Northern light" back then, but I did know that I was looking at something foreign and alluring, something set in a world radically unlike the tropical one in which I was living.

I am still moved by the quiet miracle of that boyhood afternoon. But my relationship with art has changed. I look for trouble now.

No longer is a Vermeer painting simply "foreign and alluring." It is an artifact inescapably involved in the world's messiness—the world when the painting was made and the world now. Looking at paintings this way doesn't spoil them. On the contrary, it opens them up, and what used to be mere surface becomes a portal, divulging all kinds of other things I need to know.

This spring, at the Rijksmuseum in Amsterdam, I stood again in front of *The Milkmaid*, returning thirty-three years after that day in Lagos to her humility, her solidity and the ongoingness of her domestic work. I love it—I love her—no less than I ever did. It was she who inspired Wisława Szymborska's epigrammatic poem "Vermeer," which describes, in the unending time of a painting, the quiet concentration with which the milk is poured day after day. For as long as the milkmaid continues at this task, Szymborska writes, "the World hasn't earned / the world's end."

The curators of the Rijksmuseum have brought together, in a much-praised exhibition, the largest number of paintings by Vermeer ever assembled, twenty-eight of the surviving thirty-five or so generally agreed to be by him. It is a feat of coordination by the organizers and of generosity by the lenders, a gathering unlikely to be repeated in this generation at such a scale.

But I had not been keen on seeing the exhibition, and the reasons why not began to accumulate. The entire run of tickets, some 450,000 of them, sold out within a few weeks of the opening, and even if I did manage to get one, the galleries were sure to be crowded. I was also skeptical of the bluntly narrow focus of the exhibition: a painting by Vermeer, followed by another, followed by another; most successful exhibitions need more context than this. But what was really beginning to grate on me was the breathless critical acclaim. The name Vermeer is, by now, a shorthand for artistic excellence and so much of the praise for the exhibition sounded like emotional shorthand, too. Greatness, perfection, sublimity: the appropriate vocabulary for a certain kind of cultural experience. Those who had seen the show were envied by those who hadn't. That it represented a "once in a lifetime" experience was taken as gospel. (And yet, how many of our best encounters with art have happened in a minor museum on a quiet day? What moment, fully inhabited, isn't "once in a lifetime"?) The idea that the images were wonderful had somehow gotten mixed up with the dogma that the images were nothing but wonderful. Amid all this rapturous consensus, critical dissent was hard to come by.

But some Dutch friends arranged entry for me, weakening my resolve. Then, Martine Gosselink, director of the Mauritshuis (home of *Girl with a Pearl Earring* and one of the major museum lenders to the exhibition), invited me to walk through the exhibition with her after hours. Well, refusal at that point would have been absurd. Late in the afternoon on March 13, joined by a friend, we entered the exhibition. The last wave of regular visitors was ushered out, and there we were, three lucky viewers, with twenty-eight Vermeers.

He was not prolific: He is thought to have made as few as forty-two paintings in all. It's reasonable to assume, as art historians did for a long time, that this slow rate of production was a consequence of a particularly meticulous technique. But X-rays and infrared imaging show that he made swift underpaintings and very few preparatory drawings. So what was he doing with all that extra time? For one thing, he had a day job as an art dealer, the profession he inherited from his father. For another, he was himself father to as many as fifteen children (eleven of whom outlived him). The household must have been noisy. Against the implied backdrop of that noise, the astonishing and self-possessed pictures arrive, two or three of them a year. These are pictures that seem to be doing things with light that no pictures had ever done before. The art historian Lawrence Gowing describes it as a certain heedlessness of subject, a certain faithfulness to pure appearance: "Vermeer seems almost not to care, or not even to know, what it is that he is painting. What do men call this wedge of light? A nose? A finger? What do we know of its shape? To Vermeer none of this matters, the conceptual world of names and knowledge is forgotten, nothing concerns him but what is visible, the tone, the wedge of light."

Our little group paused in front of *Woman in Blue Reading a Letter*, and it was so beautiful that my heart almost stopped. The paint keeps to a narrow range of hues: The wall is off-white with blue undertones; the large map of the regions of Holland and West Friesland is light brown with a hint of green; the two chairs on either side of the woman have glimmering brass tacks that hold their deep blue upholstery in place. One chair is larger than the other, closer to us while the other is farther away, and between them is the space in which the woman stands. She is clad in a top of blue and a skirt of dark olive. All the colors are so muted, it is as though they are remembered rather than painted. The woman, in profile, in a deep reverie, her eyes dreamily downcast, holds the letter with both hands. There are ribbons in her hair. The blue top is a beddejak, a bell-shaped house jacket. She is pregnant. Scholars doubt that she's pregnant, or they say that we can't know. But we rely on scholars to tell us what we cannot see, not what we plainly can.

What has he written to her—for surely it's a he and surely he's the father of her child? Her lips are parted. Vermeer tightens his cord of suggestion around us. The map, the early morning, the letter that has traveled through the night to be delivered: A narrative heaves underneath the silence of the scene. There's drama here, if not melodrama. We imagine someone far away whose awayness is being imagined by this other he has left behind. Perhaps the faraway one is a soldier or a sailor. The back of the chair on the left casts soft, bluish shadows on the wall. The window from which the light comes is only implied, not depicted, and the light falls on the woman's forehead and on the gently swelling marine expanse of her beddejak. All of this is done in brushwork that is precise but not fussy, a wedge of light here, a wedge of light there. Our breath as viewers is collectively held because we don't want to interrupt whatever this is. The woman is waiting for her lover to return, she is waiting for her child to be born and the painter is waiting, after working at his easel each morning, for the next morning to arrive, and the next, waiting for those favorable hours, until the work is complete. Lawrence Gowing is right that Vermeer is a painter of light. He is also, exquisitely, a painter of time.

But let us find the trouble now. All through Vermeer's oeuvre are objects like those in *Woman in Blue Reading a Letter* that remind us the world is large. This was the world that was emerging after the protracted struggle by the Netherlands for independence from Spanish rule. During the Eighty Years' War and in its immediate aftermath, the Dutch established trading posts in Asia, Africa, and in the Americas. An efflorescence of capitalism at home and overseas followed, and with it the beginnings of a colonial empire. Their own experience of subjugation did nothing to temper their desire to subjugate others. The Dutch East India Company dominated maritime routes and its shareholders raked in profits. The Dutch West India Company, meanwhile, was a significant force in the trade in enslaved people. Ordinary Dutch citizens grew wealthy from these criminal enterprises. With a renewed sense of who they were in the world, they filled their homes with rare objects and far-fetched finery. You could have luxurious things, and you could also have them depicted in paintings. The paintings were helpful reminders that you were mortal, yes, but also that you were rich.

In his perceptive book *Vermeer's Hat* (2008), the historian Timothy Brook draws out some of the global provenances of the things we see in Vermeer's paintings. He suggests, for instance, that the silver on the table in the *Woman Holding a Balance* could have had its origin in the notorious Potosí silver mine, a hellish place run on the labor of enslaved people in what was then Peru and is now Bolivia. The felt lining the hat of the soldier in *Officer and Laughing Girl* almost certainly came from beaver pelts sourced by French adventurers from the violent trade networks of seventeenth-century Canada. Brook traces a connection between this lighthearted genre scene and the bitter history of the "starvation winter of 1649–50," when European greed for pelts led to expulsions, wars and the mass deaths of Huron Indian children.

The beddejak in *Woman in Blue Reading a Letter*, Martine tells me, is painted with ultramarine, the rarest and most expensive of the blue pigments that would have been available to a seventeenth-century Dutch painter. Ultramarine was made from lapis lazuli, which was imported into Western Europe from Afghan mines; it came from beyond the sea (Latin "ultra marinus"). Possibly the use of such an expensive pigment allowed Vermeer to attach greater prestige and a higher price to his paintings. Possibly he liked its association with paintings from earlier eras in which it was used to paint the blue of the Virgin Mary's robe. The effect of ultramarine is dazzling, emotional. But who was mining the lapis lazuli in Afghanistan and under what conditions?

Any work of art is evidence of the material circumstances in which it was produced. The very best works of art are more than evidence. Inside a single frame, within a single great painting, complicity and transcendence coexist. This is what I thought as I went through *Vermeer*. The exhibition did not broach those subjects, and I did not read the catalog, which was scholarly and insightful, until later, but earlier that afternoon I had lunch with Valika Smeulders, the head of the history department at the Rijksmuseum. Smeulders cocurated *Slavery*, an epochal show held at the museum in 2021. It made use of artifacts from the Rijksmuseum's own collections and a wide range of other sources. There were paintings, prints, drawings, and documents, as well as plantation bells, foot stocks, a brass collar, a branding iron bearing a logo (probably of the Dutch West India company), and a ceremonial glass made for the raising of toasts by successful enslavers. Visitors to the Rijksmuseum, used to more vainglorious accounts of their national history, were confronted by visions of the brutality of life on plantations in Batavia, South Africa, and the Banda Islands and by the stories of a select few of the hundreds of thousands of people enslaved by the Dutch.

One painting featured in that exhibition was by Pieter de Wit, who was possibly a student of Rembrandt's. De Wit's painting depicts the director general of the Gold Coast, one Dirk Wilre, in an ornate interior in Elmina Castle, in present-day Ghana. De Wit, as a painter, is not at all in Vermeer's league, but I'm struck by the details his painting shares with Vermeer's *The Geographer*, painted in the same year, 1669: the single open window to the left, the leaded glass, the terrestrial globe, the richly patterned rug on the table. But unlike *The Geographer*, De Wit's painting has two other figures in it. One of them is a woman: Black, naked to the waist, down on one knee, clearly in a condition of servitude. If the slippers on the floor are hers, her servitude might be sexual as well. The kneeling woman offers Wilre a landscape painting showing Elmina Castle. Her body, and her land. The brutality is explicit.

The exhibition at the Rijksmuseum, which runs through June 4, is full of arresting pictures, many of them from the mid-1660s when Vermeer's career was at its peak of focus and invention. In those years he made a number of immortal pictures, several of them variations on the theme of a woman in a hushed interior, solitary, wearing a fur-trimmed beddejak. In *Woman Holding a Balance*, she is pregnant and the room is darker than usual, lit primarily by the daylight that has sneaked around the lemon-yellow curtain. The scales the woman holds up are empty—she's balancing, not weighing. On the table in front of her are coins of gold and silver as well as pearls, and behind her is a painting of the Last Judgment. In another painting, the *Woman with a Pearl Necklace* stands in profile looking left. It's the same yellow curtain, now drawn aside to admit gentle light. On the left side, in shadow, is a dark blue porcelain jar, its hard gleam contrasting with, on the right, the softness and yellowness—a yellow slightly cooler than that of the curtain—of her beddejak. *A Lady Writing* is another arrangement in yellows and blues. We don't know who she is, this long-ago woman; we don't know who any of them are and probably never will. She, too, wears the yellow jacket. (Vermeer's few props recur like a playwright's favorite actors.) She is seated at her writing table and looks at us directly with what seems to be real human understanding. It is a stunning picture, in the collection of the National Gallery in Washington. I had seen it before but never properly looked at it. This is why, finally, one goes to museums: for the chance to learn to see again, to see beauty, to see trouble. And, yes, there is the *Girl with a Pearl Earring*, a startling and *immediate* vision. In the context of its studio mates it is just another mountain peak in the range. But what a range, and what a peak.

As we were heading out of the exhibition, I dashed back and went to stand again in front of the painting that had surprised me most: *A Lady Writing*. Her gaze has a shadowy complexity to it, a soft smile; on her irises are white points. (She feels far more real to me than the *Mona Lisa* ever has.) There are white highlights, too, on the enormous pearl earrings she wears. If real, the pearls would have been harvested by pearl divers in the Gulf of Mannar, between present-day Sri Lanka and India. In her right hand is a quill pen, paused. Underneath it, a streak of white paint perfectly denotes a sheaf of white paper. The ornate writing box, of different kinds of wood and with round metal studs, is most likely from Goa under Portuguese rule. Made by whom? I found myself asking again. Under what conditions? Behind her is a painting in dark umber of a viola da gamba, a stilled music that suggests or confirms the love theme of the picture. But if her lover is absent, who has interrupted her? At whom is she smiling with such gentle familiarity?

At you. This gaze has held yours for centuries, suspending time on your behalf. There's not a single hard line of drawing anywhere in the painting, just layers of paint set beside one another, patches of color blurring into one another as though seen through an old camera lens that refuses to focus. The softness of *A Lady Writing* is so pervasive, it's as though the picture were on the verge of dissolving. Morning after morning Vermeer sits at his easel, as the world rages out there, the world where people are kneeling in subjection, where people are being branded with a hot iron. Even right outside his own door, there's the violent brother-in-law who threatens to beat up the women in the household. But the pictures are permeable to these outside troubles, are in fact continuous with them. Those amorous soldiers aren't playing dress-up. They fight, they kill. We scan Vermeer's oeuvre in vain for an image of a simple happy family, of mother, father, child in domestic peace. No, the world of the pictures is poetic and lyrical, but it is also fractured, vulnerable, isolated, and anxious. His paintings (and those by others; the implications of this argument are not limited to Vermeer) cannot be taken as mere decorations or technical achievements. They contain the knowledge of their own sorrow and can tolerate more honest context than we often allow them. To reduce them to ads for beauty, free-floating signifiers of culture and elegance, does them a disservice. On their long journey across the ages, the paintings of Vermeer bring with them both consolation and terror. And so long as this is the case, this world has not yet earned its end.

SALLIE TISDALE

Mere Belief

FROM *Harper's Magazine*

A LONG TIME AGO, I took a yearlong course of premed anatomy and physiology. Our professor, Dr. Welton, was tall and bald, wore a white lab coat, and knew a hundred of our names after the first week. I adored him and often attended his office hours, demanding to help him file or dissect.

Once, I asked him about memory. He had devoted a few weeks to the structure and function of the brain, but had barely mentioned memory. "Why are some memories more vivid than others?" I asked. We were in his office, standing in shadow by his desk. At a small lab table along one wall, a grad student prepared petri dishes. I waited for the mechanical answer—some neurochemical explanation for the floods and droughts of time, the way memory buries delight and shears off whole years. He was suddenly still, looking up to the corner where the wall met the ceiling. This man who always had an answer was silent for a long moment.

"I don't know," he finally said. It was the only time I heard him say that. "I remember being on a train, and I looked out and saw a window in a building. And it went by." He looked back at me. "It was gone. And I remember that window as if it was right here." He looked away. "I don't know why."

I am standing in a dry field on a moonless night. Men are lifting heavy boxes, mumbling, grunting, laughing quietly. My father is a broad silhouette against the sky. Then I see a spark, hear the whistle of flight and the whump of a shell exploding, its lucent flower filling the sky. This scene is so clear, and yet so dreamlike that I am not sure it is real. Many of my memories are like this: a single scene, a tableau as still and bounded as a nativity. I am climbing a dirty heap of snow. I am holding a pair of gleaming bronzed baby shoes. I hear the distant cocktail chatter of adults. When I find the edge and pull to see what comes next, the whole thing is jerked from my hand. I am left alone, climbing a heap of snow. I am left with rubble.

Memory is mostly accurate, most of the time. We agree on the general picture of what happened far more often than we don't. In this sense, what I remember of the past is basically true. But for a writer, the details are everything. What shifts are often the small details.

We are always losing more than we keep. In 1885, the German psychologist Hermann Ebbinghaus created the "curve of forgetting," a graph corresponding to a mathematical formula that measured how quickly people lose the information they learn. The loss is exponential; more than half of what we lose is gone in an hour. The curve flattens, but within a few days a person will forget about 70 percent of any information acquired, unless she makes a conscious effort to remember. Remembering requires repetition—but repetition, as we shall see, changes what we remember.

People insist that they *do* remember, of course. In a foreword to his fantastically detailed memoir, *Speak, Memory*, Vladimir Nabokov bemoaned his "amnesic defects," the "blank spots, blurry areas, domains of dimness." But in fact he was proud of his recall. When he found himself at odds with a fact-checker at *The New Yorker* regarding the color of the funnel on a French ocean liner, Nabokov chose to omit the reference rather than admit he'd gotten it wrong.

When studying memory, neuroscientists sometimes refer to "persistence" and "transience." Is memory a recording? A storehouse? A catalogue? More like vapor. There *are* mechanical explanations for the droughts and floods, but researching them is challenging, the operations strange, and the conclusions something of a disappointment. No rabbit emerges from the hat. While reading about how RNA-binding proteins affect the long-term potentiation of neurons, with a jolt I am reminded—that word, *re*-minded—that this is you and me. This is all of it. Making love. A near-mortal wound. The dried salty grit on your hands at sunset, returning to shore. The heap of snow. All of it.

I have been studying the science of memory, those mechanical explanations, for some time now. I can tell you that procedural memory (how to brush one's teeth) is different from episodic memory (I brushed my teeth this morning), which in turn is different from semantic memory (I brush my teeth to avoid cavities). I can tell you this, and a little about those binding proteins, but I can't explain memory. No one can. All these types of memory overlap and blur; little of what we know is purely one or the other. We live in a matrix of events, facts, meanings, contexts, brief jottings on a notepad. As a writer, I am generally concerned with what is called autobiographical memory, the broad tapestry of experiences that are unique to a person and—importantly—linked over time. We are not one self; our selves give way, each to the next in a ceaseless parade. But they are intricately connected. My autobiographical memory includes digging a mud puddle, taking an anatomy exam, sitting by my mother's deathbed, and, now, drawing the line that ties all these moments together into a package I call *me*. This is the foundation of the conscious self: I am who I am because this happened. We trust it implicitly. We tend to forget that there is a gulf between autobiographical memory and autobiography itself.

I write memoir sometimes, which is to say I write about the past. For a long time, I didn't question this—neither the past nor my ability to know it well enough to write about it. Every writer makes a contract with the reader. That contract may be filled with fine print and subordinate clauses, but a few points are there in bold type. The story you are reading now is an essay, which means that it is not fiction. You are trusting me to tell the truth, that is, to use facts and lived events. I promise, pinky-swear, this is true. The same promise is made by memoir and autobiography. There is no firm line separating these forms; most definitions focus on the supposedly neutral, factual approach of autobiography and the personal, more emotional nature of memoir. Yet we are supposed to believe that both forms describe what happened.

Memoir makes a peculiar promise: it offers a true story rooted in the writer's unique past, known only to the writer. I think of memoir as a revisitation and a retelling of *what happened* with a delicate and honest overlay of *how it felt* and *what I believed* and *what it means*. I write to evoke—an emotion, a state of mind, the stillness that overcomes one when the past intrudes. Often I am writing to evoke the peculiar, ineluctable sensuality of childhood, the world immense and intimate and present with the child at the center. I evoke, but I want also to invoke, to charm something dead back into life—perhaps that center of sensuality most of all.

I grant that this is an interpretive art. The point of memoir is memory, and memory can be little more than tattered prayer flags. So I am drawn to work like *Angela's Ashes*, in which Frank McCourt uses dialogue sparingly, without quotation marks, letting the kind of conversation a child overhears become part of the description, like paint on the walls. The reader is always with McCourt in his memory, knowing it is memory.

I think most other memoirists would agree with my definition, but we often end up in different places. I have always maintained a strict (and, to many writers, too rigid) standard: no composite characters, no re-creating scenes I don't honestly remember, no invented dialogue, no compressing of time or space or moving events around. I am out of fashion in the present vogue for unfiltered confessions, with my bending over backward to avoid signs of self-indulgence—a gift from my family. And I know, have known for a long time, that this avoidance is part of the story I am writing whether I intend it to be or not. Readers have sometimes taken me for a recluse of some kind. There are many kinds of recluses, of course.

I try to verify every fact I can. I read a lot. I use books, newspaper archives, photographs, maps, interviews, yearbooks, journals, letters, visits to museums and historical societies, just as I do research for an essay like this one. I also use myself: I invade, steal, rewrite, disavow, and in many other ways make use of everything I've written, considering it a good primary source. Still, I want to be willing to change my mind about what I remember, to admit that I don't remember and sometimes remember wrongly.

I try to read new memoirs, but I often set books aside, unable to suspend my disbelief. Jeannette Walls's *The Glass Castle* includes a nuanced description of the author's serious burns at the age of three: the event, the hospital stay, the aftermath. *Beautiful Country*, by Qian Julie Wang, details a scene of the author's immigration to the United States at age seven at such length and specificity as to surely be beyond the power of most adults to remember. Maxine

Hong Kingston's much-admired *The Woman Warrior* opens with a monologue by her mother that stretches more than two pages. Kingston says nothing of how she remembers this. She recounts many lengthy, and perhaps invented, conversations.

It is tempting to substitute today's psychological truth for history. Memory is wet sand. This is what I want to interrogate: the slipperiness, the uncertainty. *What is it about that window?*

I have always been bothered by memoir writers who are obviously making stuff up, but I am now also bothered by the possibility that we are all making it up, all the time. I know that I have blended and inverted events over time, perhaps invented one or two, and it startles me to discover this. I long to correct the record. But what have I missed? I started the research for this essay wondering how often my memories are false. As I write now, I wonder whether anything I remember is true.

Some of what we remember didn't happen at all, and a great deal that did is not remembered. A small child knows faces, names, new words, how to use a toy. But she won't remember her second birthday party. Children do not form retrievable autobiographical memories until around age three, a phenomenon called childhood amnesia. Such amnesia may exist because of the immature structure of the brain or because small children lack the language with which to form and express a memory. The answer is likely a combination of factors. Not until the age of around ten does a child's autobiographical memory begin to seem like that of an adult.

People argue about this. (Some write memoirs.) They *do* remember, they say, of course they do. But many of our earliest memories are based on photographs or stories. One group of researchers describes this as a "scaffold" on which we construct a past. People recall details of things they cannot know, and know things they cannot recall. This is called belief without recollection. You may know that you had an operation when you were a baby. I know that my mother had a miscarriage when I was three. I know that I took swimming lessons, but I don't remember them—I just remember being able to swim. Freud said of the confusion of memories he encountered in analysis: "It is difficult to find one's way about in this." In crucial ways we are made before age ten. So the conundrum appears: How can I possibly know who I was? I can't, and yet I do.

A single memory is roughly the result of three separate actions: encoding, the creation of a pattern; consolidation, the storing of that pattern; and retrieval, the re-creation of that pattern. Imaging can now show us a little of this activity, but it can't tell us what is happening in the mind. Our understanding of how memory works is so rough as to seem less like "imaging" than a crude drawing.

A man lifts a box, murmuring. The complexity this image represents is mind-boggling. He murmurs, a shadow in a shadow, and in a barely measurable instant, a surge of activity pulses across a few of the millions of miles of nerve connections in the brain. A complex of pathways is laid, much of it scattered in the medial temporal lobe. The hippocampus is critical, but memory isn't filed any one place in particular; it shatters into spring rain. Memory is a kind of ceaseless remodeling. The pattern won't stay without consolidation; it slides down the steep Ebbinghaus curve. Consolidation is a cascade of processes that may work by changing membrane strengths and voltage gradients in neural cells. Consolidation takes seconds or minutes, sometimes days or longer; many studies show that sleep aids consolidation. Then newly traced pathways are linked to earlier ones, and together these are organized in obscure ways that change over time as new traces are created, forming roads with many entrances and exits. And after the pattern is laid and patted into place, what remains? Potential. Capacity. Despite the microscopic shifts, memories don't exist, exactly; they are not fixed objects. They are more akin to templates or molds—it is their empty space that counts.

How do we find the pattern again? In 1932, the great psychologist Frederic Bartlett performed a series of simple, ingenious experiments. He reported the results in his book *Remembering*. The work upended the field of memory science. Bartlett was able to demonstrate retrieval as a kind of creation. "Remembering is not the re-excitation of innumerable fixed, lifeless and fragmentary traces. It is an imaginative reconstruction, or construction," he wrote. "It is thus hardly ever really exact, even in the most rudimentary cases."

Bringing a memory into awareness is the work of an elaborate machine across a vast but measurable space. The machine does this

over and over again, but never in exactly the same way twice. Each
retrieval must be unique because the machine itself is always changing, updating, breaking down, repairing. A conscious memory is
a combination of the specific pathway encoded at the time of the
event and a lot of subsequent knowledge, inferences, beliefs, and
experience. Inference but also *interference.* We get new overlays all
the time—experience in the same place or with the same people,
similar events, similar views, new knowledge. The brain sweeps this
flotsam into the pattern every time we retrieve it. Siblings recon-
struct memories from similar fragments but different experiences.
Thus our memories are rarely exactly the same. Much diverges with
time. In 1962, Daniel Offer interviewed seventy-three fourteen-year-
old boys about their lives. He asked about relationships, punish-
ments, families, dating, school. In 1996, he interviewed sixty-seven
of the surviving seventy-one men, now forty-eight years old, using
the same questions. Comparing the answers across the distance of
more than thirty years, Offer found that virtually all their memories
had altered so much that their "recollections were about the same
as would have been expected by chance."

Twenty-eight years ago, I wrote an essay called "The Basement,"
about my brother and sister and me being required to play in our
grandmother's dim and empty basement when we visited her. I
described what I saw as my older brother's bravery with our unpredictable father, and mentioned that he hated football but knew
quitting wasn't an option. I called my sister "squeamish, chubby,
pale, and black-haired—she's the one left out, the baby."

I sent my brother the essay, and he told me a few months later,
"I *liked* football. Don't know why you thought that." Years later, my
sister, angry with me about several old wrongs, complained about
my description of her. "I was *not*," she said. "*Not* like *that.*"

Yes she was, I thought. I pulled out old photos, their scalloped
white edges beginning to curl. She is crying in many of them, forever left behind when my brother and I took off. But she's not
chubby. Why did I remember it that way? I was wrong. And I was
right, for she was what I meant by that word—fragile, weak in a
world where weakness was lethal. And why did I say my brother
hated football? Because I felt the pressure he was under, the steady
squeeze of our father's demands. The psychologist David Pillemer
says that we can, "from a functional perspective," think of memory
not as a mechanism for truth but "as a belief system."

Perhaps, as many researchers think, our memories are as good as they need to be. Memoir writing aside, we function just fine with all this forgetting, because reconstruction is adaptive. And there is social merit in reminiscence; it strengthens intimacy and community. But reconstruction also allows us to imagine the future. Our false and shifting memories of the past don't matter to anyone but ourselves. The future only cares about what we learn from them.

Even though I know that memory is not a recording, not a single thing, it *feels* as though it is. I smell chlorine's damp tang and my brain flings me back into the deep end. I am in the dim locker room, wet concrete cool against my bare feet. A stretch of water flares in the light. The diving board sings its comic bounce. Autobiographical memories seem to be linked to a kind of network, so that the sound of the diving board brings the river to mind. And that links to the strange afternoon when we found a giant fish hovering under a boulder, and my brother and I tried to lasso it. I am treading slowly in ten feet of water. My brother is anchored on the beach, holding one end of the rope. I take a deep breath and turn over, swimming down to where sound thickens like porridge, the loop of rough rope in my hand. The fish hangs under the sunken boulder, one clear eye on me. I kick closer, rope at the ready. I am who I am because this happened. Because all this happened.

I think this happened.

Jules Feiffer says that writing is "mainly an attempt to out-argue one's past." We have a "self-enhancing bias"—that is, our memories gradually make us look better to ourselves. We arrange scenes in the most flattering way. The brain edits, gently but insistently shaping the wisps into coherent scenes. We may not even notice this shifting of perspective. One tends to remember a recent event from the position of the protagonist, living it again. But over time this perspective shifts to that of the observer. We watch ourselves.

One of my earliest bright memories comes from when I was six. My family was at the boardwalk amusement park in Santa Cruz. My little sister and I rode electric cars along a track, pretending to steer. Then our car stopped in the middle of the ride. I knew I was in charge of my sister and so I climbed out of the car onto the track and helped her out. I was rescuing her. I could hear distant shouts and see my mother waving from the bridge. Then a man ran out and met us, and that is the end of the memory. I see it only from above. I am standing beside my mother, watching two small girls in danger. I am yelling with the rest of the adults. And surely this memory is only a fragment, a scene built out of the many times I heard the story told.

Many memoirs are born of vibrant memories like this one. The phenomenon known as flashbulb memory usually refers to recollections of consequential events like assassinations or the attacks of 9/11, our memories of which may seem almost photo-realistic in retrospect. (Though they are sometimes wrong.) Most people also have flashbulb memories of ordinary events with no clear significance. You remember a window, and you don't know why. I vividly recall perching in a cedar tree, swaying safe and high above an uncertain world. I can recall, as though it is happening now, the back patio on a summer evening as I take my turn at the handle of a big wooden ice cream maker. The cold, salty water pools under my feet. Adults mill about, cocktails in hand, and I lean in to the joyful work in the sweet twilight. And in one breath, I am again sitting at the dinner table when my father starts yelling, pulling my little sister out of her chair, spanking her; she is hollering and my mother is crying and I am leaping up and shouting at him to stop, to leave her alone, to leave us all alone. Then the film breaks, and there is nothing else—after the ice cream, after the shouting, what?

And so we mold our pasts into a story that may bear little resemblance to the genuine mess of actual life. When I write from memory, am I writing a history or a story? Isn't it both? In the eighties, the influential psychologist Jerome Bruner popularized what came to be called narrative theory, writing of memory that "we seem to have no other way of describing 'lived time' save in the form of a narrative. . . . We *become* the autobiographical narratives by which we 'tell about' our lives." The story seems to come from the self, but in fact the self is partly constructed from the story.

My story: a girl with a stout heart. She holds her ground. She is lonely and fierce and does not believe everything she is told. A feral child, at home with lizards and trees. An odd girl anchored to a suffocating and unpredictable family. We rarely touched, never talked plainly. And I became a writer who prefers implication to explanation. I used to call my story one of self-reliance and independence: I left home at sixteen, my father's predictions of disaster trailing me out the door, and made my way forward. But this story has a deeper theme: you have to take care of yourself, because no one else will. It is a story I have spent decades rewriting.

The psychoanalyst Donald P. Spence proposed that we carry two kinds of truths, one historical (verifiably true) and the other narrative (perhaps not true at all). For analysis, Spence thought, the latter is much more important. The many proponents of narrative theory today seem to assume that we are all sifting through debris to find the structure underneath—and not just that we do this, but that we *have* to do this, that sifting debris is a fundamental human need, that a self has to narrate to exist. But what if all the narration is a dream? We may know our history, the timeline of events, the key experiences, but many of us still seek a throughline. A unifying meaning or moral. We become both narrator and protagonist—because there has to be an explanation for all this. Doesn't there? The trick is that sooner or later you have to climb down from the cedar tree.

Many people have written detailed accounts of the past, without comment: Virginia Woolf, Jean Rhys, Isak Dinesen, John Steinbeck. A few admit to imperfect recall: Janet Malcolm, Howard Norman, early Mary McCarthy. Others explore it: John Updike, Zora Neale Hurston. Some say they don't care about the imperfections: late Mary McCarthy. Martha Gellhorn: "I forget places, people, events, and books as fast as I read them. . . . The situation is hopeless." She wrote copious memoirs anyway. John Berger thought the autobiographer was freer than a novelist. "What he omits, what he distorts, what he invents—everything, at least by the logic of the genre, is legitimate."

In her book on memoir, Mary Karr writes of McCarthy's *Memories of a Catholic Girlhood*, published in 1957, and of McCarthy's concern for the truth. To Karr, McCarthy pursued a standard appropriate for "histories and biographies and journalism." Perhaps people of her time "were more gullible or more secretive or the standards more rigorous." These days, the peculiar promise that memoir is true is more a wink and a nudge than a solemn handshake. "My own humble practices wholly oppose making stuff up," writes Karr, who then lists what she actually does: invent dialogue, change names and details, compress time, and describe details that she didn't observe in the moment. How Karr reconciles this dissonance is never clear. (It is not even explored.) The gap between my picky fact-checking and her pages of imaginary dialogue does not seem to me a matter of degree. I cannot remember what the adults milling around our ice cream socials said. I can guess, but a guess is all it is. Without it, I lose a little of the delicious intimacy of a scene, but otherwise, I am—and there is no way around it—making stuff up. Perhaps I am just as dissonant as Karr in the story I've come to tell. But I have tried to simply tell it, without adornment. Karr, seemingly at ease with the central conflict of our life's work, adds that "deceit in memoir irks me so badly."

If any one thing distinguishes current memoir from its progenitors (besides a concern with accuracy), it is the claiming of victimhood. In his study of American autobiography, Herbert Leibowitz proposes that its "grand theme . . . almost its fixation, is the quest for distinction." Today autobiography seems to be a litany of injury, the recounting of loss and harm caused by abuse, racism, abandonment, poverty, violence, rape, and struggle of a thousand kinds. The reasons for such a shift in focus, a shift we see in every layer of our social, cultural, and political landscapes, are beyond my scope. One of the pivotal purposes of memoir is to unveil the shades of meaning that exist in what we believe. This is the problem of memoir; this is the consolation of memoir. Scars are fine; I have written about scars; it is the focus on the unhealed wound that seems new.

William Gass at his most disenchanted said of the "vulgar copulation" of history and fiction that "nowhere would one find the blend better blended than in autobiography." To misuse history in this way "can only be to circumvent its aim, the truth, either because one wants to lie or now thinks lying doesn't matter." Or, he added, "because an enlivened life will sell better than a straightforward one." More even than the wink, I find a dismissal, as though none of this is worth noting. Of course, the writer seems to say, I don't *remember* this. But it's a good story and it *feels* true. Many writers no longer pretend otherwise: of course the story is manipulated. Our ordinary lives are pretty messy, with a lot of filler, so let's dispense with that. In which case, anything goes. Geoff Dyer: "Everything in this book really happened, but some of the things that happened only happened in my head."

Things have gone exactly as Gass feared: mundane history has gleefully mutated into a grand reveal, an almost genetic modification of memoir into autofiction. This is personal history as an imagined journey, a felt truth in a manipulated past. Is autofiction the opposite of memoir or its evil twin? Do they stretch in opposite directions until they meet? This is one of the fundamental excuses of the memoirist: it may be untrue, but that doesn't mean it isn't correct.

Amnesia, while annoying, is less interesting to me than the honest mistakes, the ones we don't even know we are making. I pulled out one of my own books recently, searching for a reference I could barely recall. Suddenly I was reading the story I was trying to write. I had forgotten that I'd written it already.

We swing between the poles of persistence and transience, and we all suffer from what one scientist refers to as a "proneness of memory to error." As soon as a memory is activated, it is suddenly fragile again, subject to interference. It must be reconsolidated every time. With each pass, tiny deformations appear. You can't tell what has changed, because each time you recall a memory it feels correct. Neruda: "Many of the things I remember have blurred as I recalled them, they have crumbled to dust, like irreparably shattered glass." The act of studying our own past—sorting family photos, trading stories with siblings, writing memoir—destroys it.

I wrote memoir when I was young. It didn't occur to me not to, that the events were too close. But of course all those stories are different now. That's the thing. The story never ends, it is retold and remade, over and over, minor characters stepping forward, a major aria fading out. And the gun lying on the table in the first act will inevitably go off toward the end.

Most wrong memories are accidental. The brain mixes things up, the way our cousin shows up in a dream about the office. Reaching for peach, it finds apricot. Both carry the peculiar tingle of the familiar, and most of the time either will do. Neuroimaging studies of the past few decades have shown a little success in distinguishing false memories from true, based on a faint neural sensory signature. But we don't live inside an MRI machine. The brain does not monitor itself for truth; once encoded, a memory is simply there, no matter how false it is, and a false memory can be as vivid, detailed, and laden with emotion as any other. The same neural networks are at play, and most of the time, we can't tell the difference.

Neuroscientists use the term "imagination inflation" to describe one way that falsehood creeps into memory. Simply imagining an event several times can create a memory in essentially the same way as having the experience. The same voltage spark, the same synaptic tinsel. Such inflation is strongest when a person questions the memory and then writes about it in detail. Add fake evidence and a little persuasion, and you have "false feedback." With relative ease, researchers have convinced people that they have had accidents, met famous people, nearly drowned, gotten lost, and committed crimes. In 2015, Elizabeth Loftus and Lawrence Patihis were able to convince more than 30 percent of research participants that they had seen a video of the crash of Flight 93 in Pennsylvania on 9/11. No such video exists. The participants maintained this false memory over time, even under rigorous questioning. The researchers concluded that "the misleading information has irrevocably replaced" the truth.

We can believe without recalling. But we can also recall without belief. A false memory can be undermined. With enough time, hard evidence, and supporting testimony, I could convince you that you have remembered an event wrongly. This is not easy to accomplish; people hold on tight. And I can't take the memory away. Perhaps the most important point I've absorbed from months of reading about memory is that even when a memory is proven wrong beyond all doubt, a person still remembers it.

Suggestive responses help to create false memories, and it gets easier if the suggestions come from an authority figure. Every time I am rewarded for a memory—*It's true*—I brighten the memory a bit. Every time I write about a memory, I am telling myself, *That's right. That's what happened.* Reassured, I strengthen the scene.

I used to think that I would be a good eyewitness. Now I no longer trust eyewitnesses at all. I am struck by how autobiographical memory is formed in the first place. Children live in a whirlwind of imagination inflation. Our parents and teachers have their own unreliable memories, their own constantly shifting contexts and biases, which they are only too happy to share. "You were so fussy when you were little. Don't you remember all those tantrums?" "Wasn't it exciting when Santa came last year?" All families have myths, and many families are fond of recalling them, passing stories about your childhood and your Uncle Joe and how Maria broke her leg around the dinner table like gems. Perhaps false memories feel true because of how often we visit them. Pillemer, among others, has studied how the ways parents reminisce with their children have "profound implications for the types of people that they will become."

My parents and grandparents weren't tale-tellers. We heard a few, the same ones told now and then: Grandpa driving a truck on the set of Errol Flynn's *The Adventures of Robin Hood*. Our Uncle Gus panning for gold up in the hills. But never a word about my father's service in the war. Not a word about how his father had died when he was just sixteen. I was endlessly curious, but too reserved (too proud) to ask questions; questions tended to be met with blank looks. Instead I explained things to myself and grew up to be a writer who likes to leave trails of breadcrumbs instead of explanations. Parental narration is not neutral. Parents make mistakes. Parents lie. *The policeman will get you if you don't behave. Boys don't cry*. We believe it all.

Since our memory is both true and false, so must be our memoir. Why not write the story that supports the inner truth—the narrative truth? Plenty of writers say that memoir is not about memory at all; that it is an attempt to explain oneself, to create coherence. To win an argument. I am casting shadow and light all the time; you have no idea what I've left out. But the rubble is what interests me, the fact that our pasts are unreliable. The fact that I am not sure and can never be sure. I want to explore what it means not to know, not to ever be able to know. Life is dead ends, conflict, dissonance, gaps, great clouds of confusion and misunderstanding. Do I tell a story, or do I tell you how it feels to have only the remains of one? The first is certainly a better *story*. But the second is better history. Which do I really want?

The philosopher Galen Strawson rejects the idea of life-as-story out of hand; he is antinarrative. Strawson, like me, doesn't believe in a pearl of self traveling intact through time. We are each watching what seems a ceaseless parade of selves. He doesn't experience his past or future as belonging to the self who is thinking about it. Saying *This happened to me* is a fallacy, and therefore *I am who I am because this happened to me* is a gross fallacy. The impulse to organize our lives into stories is "essentially a matter of bad faith, a radical (and typically irremediable) inauthenticity." If everything we remember changes each time we remember it, if our efforts to remember are influenced by every comment and story and photo we encounter, if all that effort of sorting and talking and writing about our pasts moves us ever more toward watching an imagined self, how can we know ourselves? It is difficult to find one's way about in this.

Did my father really throw the dog in the river that time? I think he did. I can see it happening, his meaty arms scooping up the shivering dog, the dog scrambling in the air, slamming into the water, climbing out onto the rocky beach. My father laughing. When I try to investigate this, when I question it—that beach wasn't rocky, it was sand—all I find is an old photograph of my father squatting beside the dog on the riverbank, watching the camera with a curiously sad gaze. All I find is an unhappy man, a cowed dog, and the tapestry of living with him, with his sorrow and anger and power, for sixteen years.

Dr. Welton, one of the most sober people I have ever known, remembered a window with a shiver of pain and desire. I expected him to give me a kind of mechanical explanation, yet he had nothing. What I remember decades later is his face, suddenly soft. His brisk speech slowing. His lambent nostalgia. It knocked me sideways somehow, to see his wistful, wishing glance at an empty corner that only he found full. In a very rich year of human anatomy and physiology, that moment taught me as much about being a human as anything he said in his lectures. The cedar tree, the shouting. Mere belief.

This writer's self can't stop telling stories, but I may never write memoir again. At least, I won't make the same promise. I can't. This doesn't feel like a loss or a change in the script; I am working on a book about the past right now. But the interrogation has changed. Lived life is past and present and future all receding at once. What we long to hold on to, we lose; what we remember is often what we would just as soon forget; the future is always bearing down, an endless distraction. I know myself as a glitter of synaptic activation, a flimsy thing easily swept aside. A ceaselessly increasing sum materializing out of nothingness, each integer instantly flung behind me. I am persistent. I am transient. Memory is not a fixed object, and neither am I.

JENNIFER SINOR

The Lives of Bryan

FROM *The American Scholar*

All that is not given is lost.
  —Indian proverb

"WE LOST BRYAN," my father says into the phone, his voice
breaking in the cavernous space between each word. He is talking
to an old friend of his, someone I knew as a child, one who also
lost his adult son. Sitting at a wooden table carried across the prairie in a wagon, my father cradles the phone with one hand and
his head with the other. His elbows rest on wood seeped in daili-
ness and grief. Silence fills my parents' kitchen as my father either
weeps or receives condolence. I don't remain to find out. I do not
stay to learn what can be said next.

Upstairs, I close the door to the guest bedroom. The walls have
been so recently repainted in Breezy Beach that the pictures have
not been rehung. They remain stacked against the baseboards.
That feels right to me. Tracts of emptiness. It is ten in the morning
on the second day after my forty-six-year-old brother died alone
in his bed. We are all new to the language of death. I have heard
my parents tell others that their son has died, or has passed away,
but this is the first time I hear my father say that we have *lost* my
brother. Like a sock or a wallet. He is not dead, only missing.

I had just handed the passports to the Delta agent when my other
brother, Scott, called. My husband, Michael, our two teenage children, and I were on our way to Costa Rica for ten days. For a moment, I considered not answering the phone, but Scott is often in
the mountains and out of service, so I took the call. Pragmatic and

a lawyer, Scott did not tell me to sit down. He did not lead with re-assurance and love. He did not tell me everything would be okay. "Bryan is dead," he said. Three words.

In the middle of the recently renovated Salt Lake City airport, where benches double as artwork and an iridescent glass sculpture cascades from the ceiling, I went to the floor. I just wanted to be near the ground, as if a tornado were in the area, or lightning on a mountain ridge, a grizzly on the trail—make yourself small, bring yourself low.

The black granite was cold, hard against my knees.

"Stop checking in," I sobbed to Michael. "Bryan's dead." The agent held our passports in her hand, suspended. The line of passengers pulsed to move forward, roller bags leaning hungrily against legs level with my eyes. I wanted out. This would become a familiar feeling over the next two weeks, the desire to step outside of my life, shed it like a jacket, leave it behind. But grief has no edges; it is only center. Surrounded by strangers all eager to be somewhere other than where they were, I stood up, the phone still to my ear, and threaded between bodies in search of an outside I would never find.

"I'm driving to Texas," Scott told me. He would be at our parents' house in forty-eight hours. The phone line was interrupted, and my mother's name appeared. Hold and Accept. End and Accept. Accept. Accept. Accept.

"Mom," I cried. "Mom, what's happened?"

My parents were stuck in traffic between Southlake and Denton, trying to get to their son to confirm he was dead. They sat gridlocked. I could hear my father in the background saying there shouldn't be traffic at this time of night. This was not right, made no sense, was not supposed to be. The friend who had found my brother—curled on his side, hand beneath chin, like a baby, Death, a mother rocking him to sleep, or was that a lie, wishful thinking, for we would never know, we would never see his body again, maybe contorted in pain, arms flung, legs bent, hand reaching for the phone, for help, for a way out—thought he was dead but wasn't sure.

Maybe he wasn't dead.

Maybe he would be found.

The first time we lost Bryan was at his birth. I was six but felt like sixty when my father, then a lieutenant commander in the navy,

called from the hospital to tell me that my baby brother wouldn't
be coming home. I had never heard my father cry before. It's a
sound a child does not want to hear, the sound that marks, like
a hatchet fall, the end of childhood. A negligent nurse, a human
being who made a mistake, the worst mistake, the kind that alters
another's life forever, had placed Bryan, minutes old, in a bassi-
net so that she could bathe him and then accidentally pressed the
pedal for scalding water before leaving the room. *Dear Lieutenant
Commander Sinor, I am writing to offer my sincere apologies for the most
unfortunate accident that occurred at this Medical Center in which your
son was injured. . . . After learning . . . I directed a new bathing routine for newborn infants . . . immediately . . . facts . . . evaluated . . .
investigating . . . perhaps . . . provide relief . . . such an event will not
recur . . . very much regret . . . sincere concern. . . . Rear Admiral Earl
Brown.* Bryan arrived in this world in a cauldron of boiling water.
Perhaps that is when he slipped from us, before I had ever held
him. I realize now that I never knew his original face. Only my
parents, the doctor, and the negligent nurse saw Bryan whole and
perfect before he was burned. For his first several winters, Bryan's
tiny feet would turn blue in the cold, the vessels unable to regulate
the blood flow, or maybe his skin was afraid of warmth. If flame is
what greets you as you enter the world, the smell of your own body
singed, how do you learn to trust?

The following day, I returned to the Salt Lake airport, alone. Bryan
was dead. The police had roped his home like a crime scene and
never allowed my parents to see him. Perhaps, a gift. As I made my
way to the plane, I wondered who grieved alongside me. That man
holding his phone to his chest like an oath? That woman yelling at
her children to keep up? Or maybe that man in front of me on the
escalator, muscled calves, wearing Nikes in pink? At first I felt angry
at all those rushing along the concourse to make their planes to
Bali or Disney or their lake house in the mountains. How dare they
be happy? But then I realized I was wearing the same clothing I had
worn the day before—before the call, before the news, before my
knees knew granite. Dressed for Costa Rica or dressed for death, I
looked the same. Tiny wheeled suitcases trundled behind everyone
in the terminal, holding what was important enough to carry on.
What could not be left behind.

At the moment of hearing that Bryan was dead, what I could

not carry was the knowledge that he had died by his own hand. Standing with my children, Aidan and Kellen, as Michael remained at the Delta counter trying to cancel our tickets, I begged the ceiling—face up, palms offered, out loud—that his death not have been by suicide, a possibility that had stalked him since his teens. Strangers avoided our tiny island of luggage, some of them checking in, some of them headed for security, some of them making sure they had their sweater or boarding pass or water bottle emptied, while I implored the ceiling, *Please, God, don't let it be suicide. Please, God. Please don't let it be suicide.* Perhaps another mother would have reassured her children that everything was okay. Perhaps another human would have contained that pain and saved it for later. But somehow, within seconds of hearing of Bryan's death, I realized that there were degrees of loss, and some versions would break us more than others. It was a strange kind of bargaining: I can accept this loss but not that loss.

But maybe lost is lost.

The second time we lost Bryan, it was not to fire but to water. Unwatched for a moment, he fell from the deck of our backyard pool and sank. Not yet two, barely talking, he lay face up at the bottom of the pool, just as I remembered seeing him for the first time in his crib, arms above his head, blond curls haloing his face. I hadn't even seen him fall. My mother was inside the house answering the telephone while Scott herded inner tubes toward me. I had been standing on the wooden deck, preparing to jump through that stack of inner tubes, when I saw Bryan's tiny body shimmering in a forest of sunlight on the floor of the pool. He wore only a diaper.

I had not known he was missing.

Were the crows in the oaks so loud that I could not hear the splash when he fell? Or was I too consumed with play to notice the residual waves lap at my feet following his descent? At the age of eight, I could stitch a sit-upon in Brownies, make my own cereal in the morning without spilling the milk, read books devoid of illustration, but I had not known he was gone.

Bryan died sometime before his friend found him, possibly up to two days before. He left the world, and I did not register his absence. I went to yoga. I ate a peanut-butter-and-honey sandwich. I slept in the June sun. Waves of loss met my body, but I failed to notice. Was he lost to me in those two days? Or only the moment

I found out? Did my brother die the moment Scott called, or did
he die two days earlier, alone in his bed, his dogs whining to be
let out?

He was dead when my mother pulled him from the water. It
never occurred to me to dive down and save him. Perhaps I recognized the limits of my reach. Or maybe I knew I couldn't carry him
to the surface. There are moments in your life that are ambered,
so ancient, that you are no longer sure that they happened to
the same person. I stood on the ground and watched my mother,
clad in shorts and a T-shirt that ran wet with chlorinated water, as
she begged God to save her baby. She offered my brother like a
sacrifice, his limp body resting on her forearms, her head thrown
back, the sounds coming from her mouth not words but sorrow
made manifest, serrated and raw. The terror of the moment was
complete. I could not move.

She placed Bryan on the deck and began to suck the water from
his lungs. His lips would have been cold but probably still soft. Baby
smell replaced by chemicals. Would his eyes have been open or
closed? Were they closed when his friend found him alone in bed?

I want them to be closed.

I did not see his original face.

I did not see his final face.

I ran to the neighbors for help because that is what she kept
yelling for me to do every time she came up from Bryan's mouth
to inhale.

When I returned, Bryan was alive.

I have always held that memory as one of horror and trauma,
and I have always felt alone in the experience. Scott was too young
to remember, and my mother carries a version all her own. What I
have never considered, until this moment, is the joy and relief my
mother must have felt when Bryan began to breathe again. I have
long thought that the happiest my mother has ever looked was when
I came home from school and she told me that my scalded baby
brother had come home from the hospital. That was the first time
I saw Bryan, the first night he slept outside an incubator. Her smile
that afternoon has forever remained with me because it revealed
the cloud of grief she had lived under for those many months. The
initial days of waiting for him to die, followed by the months of driving to the hospital every day to touch her baby through plastic. I
imagine that if I had been there at the moment she brought Bryan

back from the dead, the relief would have pulsed through the humid air. Instead, the second time we lost Bryan remains tangled in sorrow and silence. It feels like a story not of resurrection but rather of the frost of the future. My mother waited until my father came home from work to tell him what had happened that day in our back yard. I remember that he brought brand-new mask and snorkel sets for Scott and me and handed them to us before he went with my mother to the kitchen, where I heard her cry once again. The gift crumpled my stomach.

Although we lost Bryan, he never lost anything. He might not have been able to find things right away, but they were never lost. As a child, his room was always a disaster, Legos and books and clothes piled everywhere. By the time he reached high school, my mother had given up and asked only that he keep the door closed. Which means that when we walk out of the Texas sun and into the thin air-conditioning of Bryan's mobile home, two days after he has died, we arrive to a mess. The floor and the counters are covered with the remnants of his life. There is an entire room devoted solely to boxes inside boxes inside boxes inside boxes. Every piece of junk mail he has ever received, every single receipt, every bill, every matchbook, every card anyone has ever sent him, every letter, every present, every photograph, every school paper, every textbook, every movie ticket stub, every free gift from McDonald's, from Coca-Cola, from Home Depot, every plastic grocery sack, every empty Amy's burrito box, every pen, pencil, screwdriver, nail, every key to an unknown lock—all of it remains.

"Everyone take a room," Scott says, handing black contractor bags to each of us. The house smells of dogs, urine, and pot.

"Just decide what to keep, what to toss, what to give to Goodwill," he continues. "Use your best judgment. The dumpster will be here in a few hours." The concern is that Bryan's place will be looted if we don't clear it now. He lives in the north Texas countryside. Word travels fast. The following day a guy named Larry will stop by with his pickup and say he's heard that you can come here and take whatever you want. Worried about time, we set to work.

I stand on the dirty tile of the kitchen, the overhead light dimmed by grime. My brother was a private person. He never traveled, he never brought a girlfriend to my parents' house, he did not go to the dentist or the doctor, he had guns and knew how to use them. His dogs and his music and his cars made him happy. I do not want to go through his drawers.

The house stands as he left it before going to bed on whatever night it was that he went to bed and never woke up. This is only the second time I have been in his house since he graduated from high school. Before we are finished, I will know the brand of condoms he preferred as well as the greatest regret in his life, but the first time I open his cabinets with the contractor bag yawning at my feet, I can only whisper, "Please forgive me, Bryan." This becomes my mantra.

The third time we lost Bryan, it was to the earth. He was maybe thirteen years old—it was the summer we flew from Hawaii, where my father was stationed, to Colorado for our first backpacking trip. My uncle Jerry planned to take us into the Mount Zirkel Wilderness, though if he had known how unprepared we were for such a trip, he probably would have suggested car camping instead. Although we would come to embrace backpacking every summer as a family and learn to travel with lightness and economy, that August we might as well have been toting canned tuna and portable radios.

I wore blue jeans. Heavy denim with rivets that dug into my hip bones and grew ten pounds heavier every afternoon when the thunderstorms rolled through. We all carried neon-orange backpacks that had been salvaged from Goodwill, with belts that left our jeans-covered hips raw and cracked. None of us had waterproof hiking boots. We barely had hats. And it rained. Every day it rained. Some days the lightning sent us running for our tents.

But what hurt us the most was something we couldn't see: altitude sickness. Bryan threw up first, out the car window as we drove to the trailhead. He also threw up second and third. By the time we had loaded ourselves with weight, his face had lost its color. We all had headaches that stabbed the backs of our eyes. My throat was dry, and no amount of water could wet it. We no longer peed. Instead, we climbed the trail, dizzy with effort, cotton tube socks chafing our heels.

For whatever reason, Bryan was the sickest. Within a mile or so, he was sitting down on the trail. My uncle Jerry and cousin Shara, well acquainted with the rigors of backpacking, took weight from him. Soon my dad and Scott helped as well, so that Bryan carried an empty pack. Still, he kept stopping. Sometimes to throw up, more often to cry. He wanted to go home.

We trudged on. My uncle had probably chosen a short and easy trail for us, but it felt like climbing Everest. Our party of eight stretched along the mountainside, no one talking. My head throbbed in rhythm with my step. I slid my hands beneath my hip belt to protect my skin, but soon the backs of my hands were red and sore.

At some point, we realized we had lost Bryan. He had simply disappeared.

Taking our packs off, we called his name. A faraway hawk answered, then the wind, but not Bryan.

"What about the fork in the trail?" my dad asked.

"Did he take it?"

"Did anyone see him take it?"

"Who was hiking with him?"

"Bryan! Bryan!"

We made a plan. Some would go back on the trail and look for him; others would fan out into the alpine meadows to look amid the paintbrush and columbine, penstemon and yellow cinquefoil the color of the sun. Released from the weight of my pack, my legs seemed to float above the ground as I walked. Sweat soaked my shirt and made the denim grab my knees and thighs. It was late in the day. Thunderheads gathered overhead. The Mount Zirkel Wilderness stretches 160,000 acres.

I walked the meadows calling for my brother. Pikas chirped from rock piles, and vultures circled the trees. At the time, my ignorance protected me. I knew nothing of exposure or dehydration or lightning strikes. Still, I also understood that losing Bryan in the mountains was not the same as losing him at Safeway. I only had to look around at the glacially carved peaks and the seemingly endless swath of firs to know that the only ones who could find Bryan were the ones right here calling his name.

I don't remember who found him, my father maybe. Bryan had passed out in a meadow not unlike the one I had been searching. His body had been hidden by the tall grasses, so my father discovered him only when he came upon his sleeping form. Altitude sickness, for the most part, is a temporary condition. Your body acclimates. By the following morning, we were all feeling much better. By the end of the week, we were ready to do it all again.

And we would return every summer for the next ten years to back-pack as a family. Except for Bryan. He would remain home, where oxygen is not scarce and you can keep more than what you can carry.

By Sunday, my father is angry. On his way to Bryan's house, he calls from the road to tell us that we are to stop and do nothing until he arrives. Scott and I are sitting in the parking lot of Home Depot, two more giant boxes of contractor bags in the trunk, when we get the call. I can hear my father's anger from my place in the back seat. The car vibrates.

As does my father's body, a half hour later, when he arrives at Bryan's house. It is the kind of anger that consumed him when I was a child but has dimmed with age. I immediately become ten again, scared and full of shame. My father's anger has always been physical. Like fire, it takes the air from the room and sears what remains.

"Get in the house," he orders as he storms past my brother and me. At ten in the morning, it is already 100 degrees. Crickets saw in the scrub nearby, the sound electric and grating. Sweat soaks the waistband of my shorts, runs in drops down the sides of my face.

We gather in the room just off the kitchen, where the strongest air conditioner wraps cool tendrils around our sweaty bodies. My mom sits across from my father on a drum stool, my aunt on the floor, Scott and I in office chairs with blown-out backs, and my father in a ratty armchair.

"I have been talking with my brothers and sister," my father begins. His voice is quieter already. Something about being inside Bryan's house, or the cool, or the fact that we all did exactly what he said. Or maybe he's just so very tired that even his anger craves rest. "They all say we shouldn't be throwing anything away. We should have an auction. There is someone out there who is miss-ing an old issue of *Workbench* magazine and will want it. We can't just throw it away."

I was in charge of the shelves containing the magazines. He is speaking directly to me.

"I have Bryan's voice in my head," he continues. Now his words mix with tears. "Why are you letting them do this? Why are you letting them do this? Why don't you care?"

"But Dad—" I start.

He holds up his hand. "Every time we throw something away, we are throwing away a piece of your brother. Every. Single. Time."

The day before, I had cleared shelves and shelves of *Golf Digest, Forbes, National Geographic, Playboy, Workbench, Mother Earth News*, motocross magazines, dirt bike magazines, Mustang magazines, random car part catalogs, a Sunset guide to building a deck, another guide to building a tennis court, one dedicated to repairing quartz watches, Spanish textbooks, chemistry textbooks, pamphlets on succeeding as a student with ADHD, University of North Texas course catalogs from the early '90s, a McDonald's training manual. None of the magazines were addressed to Bryan except for a series on motorbiking. They were addressed to subscribers in Minnesota, Wisconsin, Iowa, Indiana. Bought, I would assume, in auction lots. Soon, Scott and I would discover that the most recent lots Bryan purchased were still wrapped in plastic in his giant workshop. It was so full that we could not get through the door. I had filled bag after bag with these heavy magazines and carried them to the dumpster. Tree to paper to earth, I said.

"You are throwing Bryan away," my father now says.

"Dad," I try again, this time kneeling in front of him on the floor, crying. "You have to move Bryan from your head to your heart."

I could be speaking Spanish. Auction has become the life preserver that my father will cling to amid the tsunami of grief. Auction will transmute Bryan's hoarding into treasure. Redeem him.

From that moment on, we decide that everything will pass through my father before being discarded. We designate "auction rooms." My father stands at the front of the dumpster. Very little gets past. I haul out torch lamps with broken bases and am told a screw is all that is required. A chair that sinks into itself just needs wood glue and clamps. After a few attempts, I take everything to the auction rooms. My father is right: the chair probably could be repaired and reupholstered. But we are doing triage, not plastic surgery, and there is simply no way we are going to find the one person on the planet who is seeking the June 1980 issue of *Workbench* in order to complete a set.

My dad suffers from the same illness that my brother did, a fear of losing, a fear that this AutoZone receipt from 2005 must be saved because bad things will happen if it is lost. A baby might get burned. A tiny body might plunge into the water, unwitnessed.

You cannot know what you might need in a world that is untrustworthy. Save everything. Save it all. Save it all. Save it all, save it, save it, saveit, saveit, saveit, savesavesavesavesavesavesavesavesave. We are going down.

Air took my brother the fourth time we lost him. Sixteen years old, Bryan was hanging out with a friend in Hawaii Kai while my parents worked downtown. Bored on a summer day, the two of them had decided to make Drano bombs and then throw them from the lava rock pier. Drano bombs require simple household items, specifically Drano, foil, and a container. Once trapped, the hydrogen chloride in the fluid mixes with the aluminum foil to create hydrogen gas. Quickly, often within seconds, the pressure builds to a point where the container burst, throwing lye everywhere.

Most Drano bombs are made in plastic bottles.

My brother and his friend chose glass.

The second before the bomb exploded in Bryan's hands, he realized the danger. That flit of understanding saved his life because he was in the midst of hurtling the bomb into the ocean when the Gallo wine jug exploded. The shrapnel entered the left side of his face, neck, shoulder, and chest. If he had held the container, it would have found his heart. When my father arrived at the ER, he says, he knew Bryan was dead. The blood alone was too much. Bryan's cheek flapped open. The tendons in his neck shone white amid the red. Bryan was not conscious, did not move, and my father began to mourn the death of his son once again.

By the time I saw Bryan a few weeks later, having flown home from college, his skin was starting to heal. Reconstructive surgery on his face would repair much of the damage, but angry red welts would populate his body for the rest of his life. For months, shards of glass worked their way to the surface, a strange kind of birth, where his skin would be pierced from within.

At the age of sixteen, Bryan retreated. Into the house. Into his body. Away from the world. He refused to have his picture taken. He walked with his head down and grew his hair long to curtain his scars. He assumed everyone was looking at him, mocking him, pointing to his disfigurement. Rather than trust another with his pain, he became a recluse. Held onto every piece of paper. Chose dogs for family because they never withheld their love.

It was like he vanished.

The night before my brother's backyard memorial, I sit with my father under the setting of the solstice sun. The longest day of the year, the longest day of my life. Ends that come too quickly or never come at all. He slumps in his chair, gazing at his hands in the growing darkness. For the first time in the day, being outside does not mean being sunburned. Winds play in the field behind my parents' house; airplanes, like far-off fireflies, make ready to land at DFW, their path across the sky reassuring in purpose.

"I'm so tired," my father says. These are words I have never heard him utter. He does not mean he needs to go to bed. He means he is tired of being alive.

"I thought he was dead," he continues, "when I came to the hospital. He was so bloody and pale. I didn't think there was any way he could be alive. I thought we lost him then."

"I know," I say, "that's why this is so hard. I think we all thought we had made it through."

"I worry about what the coroner's report will say. Maybe he was murdered?"

"No, Dad." I reach out for his hand. "It was a heart attack. Just a massive heart attack. There was nothing we could do."

The silence settles, and the summer sky darkens on the day we move toward fall.

"I love you so much," my father says. His voice is thready and thin.

"I know," I say. "And Bryan knew that, too."

"I don't know. I'm not sure."

We look across the field, empty of cows, empty of horses, full, though, of life we cannot see. Tomorrow a white tent will be erected, and we will set out fifty chairs. But that won't be enough. Because a hundred people will come to honor Bryan. Most of them I will not know. Other than my extended family, I will never have met any of the dozens who show up. I will open the door again and again to strangers who will say how much they loved my brother, how my brother would stop whatever he was doing to help them. They will speak of his generosity, his kindness, his love. "He helped me lift a door." "He fixed my car." "He fed my animals." They will stand up and bear witness to my brother's enormous heart. Many will cry. Poetry will be read, "Amazing Grace" sung. All under a sun that will beat down with a ferocity that most of us only want to flee. But we will remain, feeling a sun that never withholds.

The fifth time we lost Bryan it was to the ether, the space between the atoms. It might have been a Monday night, or possibly the Tuesday of June's full moon. Maybe his final moments were painful and scary. Possibly he knew that Death was coming for him. Or maybe he never woke from the dream he was having, a dream about my father driving the old Porsche Bryan bought for him, its engine finally rebuilt, every single part lovingly restored. Maybe he was sitting next to my father as they raced along a freeway unfamiliar with traffic. Nothing to stop them. Perhaps his last two dogs sat in the tiny back seat or maybe all six of his dogs gathered there, and Bryan could feel their hot breath as they panted over his shoulder, unwilling to miss a single second of the ride. The car speeds down the road, and Bryan looks over to my father with a smile that shows no teeth but lights his eyes, the hazel eyes he shares with my father, and with me. And they ride the road like they used to ride the waves at the beach, joyful in the moment, sun warming their skin, nothing in their hands. Carried.

JERALD WALKER

It's Hard Out Here
for a Memoirist

FROM *Prairie Schooner*

FOR LONGTIME MEMOIRISTS, there invariably comes a point
when the material runs a little thin, forcing them to make use of
their most guarded secrets and transgressions, as I shall do here.
To begin, then, once, many years ago, when I was seventeen, and
for a very brief period, merely seven weeks, to be exact, I was a
pimp. I am deeply ashamed of this. It helps to remind myself that
what mainly appealed to me about the profession were the fedoras
and Cadillacs as well as the possibility of having many girlfriends,
or at least one. And I especially liked the idea of not working,
or rather, as my older brother Tim used to say, not working for
"the man." Tim had worked for the man once and strongly advised
against it. There were much better options, he said, but the ones
he recommended, alas, were not those.

He would admit to having steered me wrong, I believe, if he
could. Tragically, he succumbed to some of the very vices he taught
me, his heart, overtaxed by the strains of street life and probably
regret, giving out at age forty-seven. The manner of his premature
demise could not have been predicted by anyone who knew him in
his youth: honors student, religious to the point of fanaticism, loving, witty, and kind. And then, overnight, it seemed, he was running
hustles and cons before dropping out of college and quitting his
part-time job as an accountant. But I do wonder, sometimes, if it was
not regret that played a role in his death. Maybe it was bitterness.

The idea to live outside the law, after all, could not have come to him on its own any more than it had come to me.

How it had come to me was this: I was engrossed in one of my sister's romance novels, fretting over the heroine's decision to elope with her fiancé's father, when Tim, nineteen, snatched the book from my hands. He had done this before. Romance novels, he suspected, were improper reading material for fourteen-year-old Black boys, and my friends had proved his suspicion to be true. They had recently discovered one on my dresser, my sister's feathered bookmark fanning from its pages, and the ensuing teasing was merciless. I never brought the novels to my bedroom again. Instead, I hid them in the garage where, every day after school, I would unearth one and sit on a blanket behind our parents' defunct station wagon to enter into faraway worlds of love and desire, always alert to the sound of approaching footsteps, which, on the day in question, escaped me. "Here," Tim said, dropping a book onto my lap. "Read *this*." I looked at the title. It was *Pimp: The Story of My Life*, by Iceberg Slim.

I returned it to him a few days later.

"What did you think?" he asked.

"I think," I said, "I should not have read that."

He disagreed. There was another author, he added, with whom I should also be familiar. His name was Donald Goines. Goines had been a pimp, too. He had also been a bootlegger, thief, addict, and inmate, so he had plenty of material at his disposal, enough to fill sixteen novels. I should not have read those either. And he probably should not have written them. It was believed that a number of the people on whom he had based his characters objected to their portrayal and rendered the harshest of critiques. Goines's body, along with his girlfriend's, was found in his apartment, full of bullets.

Some memoirists, in an effort to juice up the narrative tension, would exaggerate the gulf between their experiences and those of Donald Goines and Iceberg Slim, but the fact of the matter is if my avatar were an animal, it would have been, for the first eleven years of my life, Bambi. I knew nothing beyond church, Marvel Comics, the Three Stooges, and, when I turned twelve, but only in strict obedience to the demands of nature, the lingerie section of the Sears catalogue. Did I press my mouth upon the models' tiny faces? Did I rub my fingers along their miniature bosoms? Did I hold those pages up to the light, hoping to discover the mysteries beyond the discounted silks and satins? I did. Quite often. Obsessively, some might say. This, however, was hardly preparation for entering the worlds of Donald Goines and Iceberg Slim, although the worlds of Donald Goines and Iceberg Slim, in retrospect, would have been good preparation for entering the backyard of Rachel Jones. Rachel was a new girl on our block. Rumor had it she liked being felt up.

I provided a detailed account of my confirmation of this rumor in my second memoir, *The World in Flames*; suffice it here for the reader to picture Bambi getting his first whiff of smoke as the forest burns, for I, like that delicate creature, after willing my trembling, fourteen-year-old self beneath the raised deck where Rachel had lured me, was suddenly paralyzed with fear and indecision. She relieved me of both by taking control of my hands.

And yet that did not prepare me for the worlds of Donald Goines and Iceberg Slim either. Nor did the dirty magazine a classmate had pilfered from his father's stash and brought to school, nor the one I discovered while rummaging through my sister's bedroom, and certainly not her romance novels, though the one about the pilot and three stewardesses was helpful. In combination, however, these items awakened in me a strong curiosity about manhood and how I might enter into it. I read the books Tim gave me then, partially in search of answers. More often I found questions. I recall, in fact, after reading only the first paragraph of *Pimp*, asking my twin brother, "What's a 'hairy maw'?" He shrugged. I offered to show him the passage for context, but not being much of a reader, he declined. Besides, he was busy completing the homework Tim had assigned us, which was to roll joints with tree leaves. Once we mastered that, Tim had said, we could try it with actual marijuana.

When writing about certain subsets of American culture, one of the memoirist's great challenges is to draw a distinction between bad decisions and bad people. Tim was not a bad person. He had merely taken the pulse of our community, foresaw the swift demographic change from predominantly White, middle-class to Black, impoverished ghetto, and hoped to immunize his younger brothers against the coming surge of crime by injecting small amounts of it into our bloodstream. In a sense, this is similar to the practice I had heard of about wealthy people serving their underage children wine with dinner, as if in so doing the children, having surmised

Bordeaux is as innocuous as Ovaltine, would decide against becoming alcoholic. The unlucky among them, of course, are wrong, for something in their constitution awakens a craving for booze, all of which is to say that, after deducing the meaning of "hairy maw," I was curious to learn more.

Fortunately, this was the 1970s, the golden age of Black street cinema. A few classics still ran in theaters, but bootlegged copies were easy to find. My friends and I started with *The Mack* and *Sweet Sweetback's Baadasssss Song* before moving on to *Shaft*, *Trick Baby*, *Willie Dynamite*, and, of course, *Superfly*. *Superfly* was our favorite. We watched it again and again, each time our admiration growing for the main character, Youngblood Priest, as he snorted cocaine while winding through ghetto streets in his El Dorado, his pressed hair falling like silk from his fedora, his lush mustache curling down his upper lip in perpetual disdain of the shit that he, a Black man, had to overcome. Priest was a god to us all.

Others thought he was the devil. NAACP leader Junius Griffin, for instance, the man who coined the term "Blaxploitation," railed against the genre on the grounds that it perpetuated stereotypes of Blacks as criminals. Black men in particular, in the words of another objector, were celebrated for having "vast physical prowess but no cognitive skills." Protestors picketed theaters holding signs that read "Black Shame, White Profits" and "We Are Not All Pimps and Whores!" Cars in movie theater parking lots were firebombed. But there were advocates of the genre, too, who applauded African Americans' increased participation in the film industry and referred to the movies as mere action flicks. Gordon Parks Sr., director of *Shaft*, thought audiences should be given enough credit to know the difference between fantasy and reality. It was his son, however, Gordon Parks Jr., who offered the genre's best defense: "Blacks want to be entertained just like everyone else," he argued, "and if they enjoy superheroes with fast cars and fancy clothes, well, that's the American dream—*everyone's* American dream."

Right on. Because at that time on the South Side of Chicago, these superheroes felt vital for the heroic twist they put on the Black man's terrible plight. And what they perpetuated was our understanding that this plight could be transcended, which was to say it was possible to avoid selling out and working for the man. All we had to be was cunning. We had to be bold. We had to be ruthless. Above all, we had to look good.

I pressed my hair and bought a fedora. I perfected my stride and learned to talk with a toothpick balanced on my lower lip. I memorized the scripts of a dozen cons and hustles. When my Superfly avatar was fully formed, I hit the streets ready to lay claim to their riches, but the streets, I soon discovered, had scripts of their own. The one they wrote for me was of a fawn who masquerades as a buck and gets so in over his head that he ruins a decade of his life, and for this, years later, once I became a memoirist, I was grateful. So bountiful were my failings and misdeeds that when I wrote my first memoir, *Street Shadows*, I could pick and choose what to include without fear of depleting my material. I withheld enough, actually, to spruce up much of my second memoir and dozens of personal essays. And never once, in any of these accounts, for reasons of propriety and discretion, which were still good options for me then, did I mention Thelma Ellsworth.

I am tempted, in the common manner of memoirists, to cast myself in an exceedingly favorable light by describing Thelma as breathtakingly beautiful, like Pam Grier in *Foxy Brown*, or Tamara Hall in *Cleopatra Jones*, or Marki Bey in *Sugar Hill*, but it is important to note that no such woman would have had me. I leave it to the reader to imagine the woman who, at age thirty-one, would have had a seventeen-year-old high school dropout whose money, on the rare occasion he had it, was ill-gotten, who was a heavy consumer of drugs and alcohol, and who, incidentally, was high on both when he fell down a flight of stairs and ended up in an emergency room, thereby facilitating this chance encounter. Thelma was a nurse's aide. "I like your style," she said while bandaging my wrist.

I acknowledged the compliment with a slight adjustment to my fedora.

"What do you do," she asked, "sell dope?"

"Naw, *baby*," I said. "I'm a *pimp!*"

"Is that so?"

"Damn *right!*"

"Pimp," she said, smiling, "was my second guess."

"Really?"

"The toothpick gave you away. And your *smoothness*."

I adjusted my fedora again. A short while later, after I had, as we used to say, "spit my game," by which I mean repeated pickup lines I'd heard in various blaxploitation films, she gave me her number.

I had been chosen.

"Chosen?" Tim said, when I told him. "By who, and for what?"

"By this woman," I said, "to be her *pimp*."

"*Boy*, are you high?"

"Yes."

"Me, too," he said. "Tell me more."

I did, but first I reminded him of the scene in *The Mack* where the protagonist, Goldie, who had just been released from prison after a five-year stint, was at a bar when a female friend joined him for a drink. As they chatted, she revealed she had been working as a prostitute. The job was not optimal, she admitted, but the main drag was the harassment she received from pimps for being an independent contractor. "You know," she explained, "I'm an outlaw, and a lot of pimps are down on me because I won't choose. But Goldie, you know, I *need* a man. I *need* somebody in my corner. Somebody to *be* there. Help me, Goldie. I'm tired of being by myself."

"Thelma," I continued, "this woman I met, is tired of being by herself. She needs *somebody in her corner*."

"She said that?"

"More or less, after I told her I was a pimp."

"You *told her* you were a pimp?"

"It seemed the thing to do at the time."

"Then what?"

"I spit my game."

"And then?"

"She gave me her number."

"She chose you all right," Tim responded. "You know what to do now, don't you?"

"No," I said. "That's why I'm calling."

"Boy, didn't you read Donald Goines and Iceberg Slim?"

"That was a long time ago. And, to be honest, they were kind of confusing. Also, Thelma's not a *prostitute* prostitute, you know, other than working for the man."

"It's all the same. As long as she's making you that money!"

"Hell, yeah!"

"The main thing," he recommended, "is to play it cool."

"I did," I said. "I told her I'd have to *think* about calling her, just like Goldie told his lady friend."

"Good, good. The longer you play it cool, the better."

I played it cool for three days. When I called her, she invited me to her apartment for dinner. Two days later, I returned home to get my things.

Pimping was easy. All I did after driving Thelma to work was to pick up a few friends in her ten-year-old Pinto and head to the park to shoot hoops or get high. Sometimes we would simply grab a bottle of wine and go to her apartment to play Pong. Her shift ended at eleven p.m., so a little before then I would drive to the hospital to pick her up. She would be waiting for me outside the entrance with some of her female co-workers. They smiled and giggled as she got into the car.

A month into the life, she took me shopping for new clothes. Her fondness for floral shirts and tight slacks was not one I shared, but we were on the same page when it came to fedoras. She bought me seven, each a different color, one for every day of the week. Sometimes, because she had a good eye for these things, she would match one of the fedoras with one of the shirts she picked out for me to wear. My friends were impressed with my new look. Tim, however, was skeptical. But what got his approval was when I told him that Thelma finally agreed to call me "Daddy." "Daddy," she had said, "don't forget to pick up my dry cleaning."

"I won't," I'd responded.

"You forgot last week. And the week before that."

I took out my toothpick and said, "Don't hassle me, woman, about my *memory*."

"You got the grocery list?" she asked. I was driving her to work.

"Yes."

"Oh, we getting low on milk, too. I forget to add that."

"Okay."

"*Whole* milk, now. You know I don't like that two-percent shit you bought last time."

"I know, I know. Whole milk."

"And check the date."

"*Damn*, woman. You finished getting on *my case*?"

She smiled and asked, "You need any money, Daddy?"

It was only Wednesday, but I had just seven dollars left from the thirty she gave me each Monday. "I could use a little more," I said. She gave me a little more.

After dropping her off, I drove to Tim's apartment. He wasn't there, so I tracked down a few friends. We smoked a joint before heading to the liquor store to get a couple of forties. The liquor store was near the taverns where some bigtime pimps hung out. Their cars lined the street, Lincolns and Cadillacs but not the Rolls Royce that belonged to the legendary Magellan because, according to the grapevine, he was in intensive care after being stabbed by one of his women. Since it was unlikely that I would be stabbed by Thelma, I preferred my brand of pimping to his. It would have been nice, though, to have one of those slick rides.

I would get one in a few months, after I moved back home and started working for the man. Tim would say that I had sold out, which, technically, would be true, but it would not be like I'd had much of a choice. Thelma would throw me out after the last time I forgot her dry cleaning and fucked up the grocery shopping, as I was about to do that night. I remembered the dry cleaning at around nine, two hours after the cleaners had closed, but I still had time to make it to the grocery store. I hurried there after dropping off my friends. In the parking lot, before getting out of the car, I checked myself in the rearview mirror. I smiled. I looked good.

The store was busy, unusual for a Wednesday night. Maybe there was some kind of a sale, I thought, but I had not seen notice of one earlier while clipping the coupons that, I just realized, were still on the kitchen table. The grocery list was there, too. Now I would have to try to jog my memory by going down every aisle. That was how I ended up in the one with the magazines, which was also the one with the paperbacks, which happened to include the romance novels I used to borrow from my sister. They stopped me in my tracks.

Did I put six of them in the cart? Did I hide them beneath the dresser to read while Thelma was at work? Did I, overcome by nostalgia, and in sad recognition of an innocence long lost, bookmark the pages with a feather from one of my fedoras? And did I cry, on occasion, at the direction my life had taken and blame my poor, misguided brother? No. I did none of these things. But the urge was there. I would have acted on it, too, had I known I would become a memoirist. I could have used those scenes.

JONATHAN GLEASON

Proxemics

FROM *Colorado Review*

MY UNCLE IS AN ARCHITECT. From a prison in rural North Carolina, he sends letters stenciled with Corinthian columns, vaulted arcades, the stately domes of governmental buildings. Before his imprisonment he designed sets for local television productions, senior-living centers, and hotels. He lived for a year in Rome to study the masters of the golden proportion. He wrote back with stories about a melting church in Spain, which would take over one hundred years to complete and which was still in the process of being constructed—La Sagrada Familia—and how the builders spent their days in one of the spires, studying the plans from the original architect, Antonio Gaudí, trying to materialize them in the physical world. Some spaces must be imagined before they can be realized.

When my uncle used to visit our house, neighbors would come up to him in the yard and begin talking as if he were my father. There are almost twelve years between them, but they could be twins. All the men in my family look alike, me included—the strong gravity of genetics. I found my uncle's mug shot on the North Carolina prisoner database one afternoon. The blankness in his expression was the most startling, a pair of glassy eyes, a clenched jaw, an uncanny reflection: the same furrow chiseled into our brows, the same downturned corners of our eyes, my face, my father's face, but scooped clean of all affect.

If you asked my uncle why he is in prison, he would tell you it's for a crime he didn't commit. It is because his ex-wife is out to get him and his most recent ex-girlfriend, too. He would tell you about glitches in the ankle monitor he wore for a year while on probation, about the judge who, very suddenly, decided she didn't like him. He would tell you about flat tires and work appointments and engines shuddering to a halt: all the reasons he had to miss court dates or couldn't be home within the window of a certain hour. He might admit, after a while, to some of the lies he told, but he would say that they were told only out of necessity.

"My client is not in a hurry," Gaudí is said to have remarked of his cathedral. What was a century or two for God? Even before he was struck dead by a tram in the streets of Barcelona, he knew he would never see his life's work completed, and so he left behind schematics and models to guide the inheritors of his work through the process of creation—a process he found more sacred the longer he lived. Learning to construct the cathedral was like "learning another language," one of those inheritors later said. And it was not just "the vocabulary, but the grammar as well." Gaudí's work "expressed meaning not only through the sculpture and other decorations but through the architecture itself."

Once, on a date, a painter told me about a series he'd done based on the work of Edward T. Hall, the anthropologist, cross-cultural researcher, and accidental influencer of architecture. In the series, he painted intimate encounters at varying distances, so that each successive panel lost more and more of its resolution. The paintings had the effect of drifting away from someone while standing still or, if a viewer moved in the opposite direction, of cupping a person's face—skin and pores, stray hairs and musculature—into sharp focus.

Hall's early career was spent studying the ways people in different cultures communicate: the body language they used, the distances they maintained while talking. In 1966, he laid out in detail his theory for the field of proxemics: a branch of knowledge about the amount of space we keep between ourselves and others, and how that distance is encoded in culture and its institutions. "This is a frightening thought, in view of how very little is known about man," Hall wrote. "It also means that, in a very deep sense, our cities are creating different types of people in their slums, mental hospitals, prisons, and suburbs." He called his book *The Hidden Dimension*.

I'm thinking about *penitence* and *penitentiary*—two words knitted together by language and history, though their connection is easy to overlook. *Penitence*, the state of mind, and *penance*, the self-punishment that follows, now feel heavy with religious connotations, while *penitentiary* belongs in the brutal and bureaucratic world of courtrooms, parole boards, and lice powder. But the original Quaker penitentiaries were religious sites, founded on the belief that criminals could be redeemed through isolation and silence, and one of the first true penitentiaries was called Eastern State.

Eastern State was, as the sociologist Norman Johnston writes, "without a doubt the most influential prison that was ever built." Jails had existed for millennia. The idea of locking people up to await torture and execution or until they were able to repay their debts wasn't new. The innovation of Eastern State was conceptual: it took the confinement itself as the punishment. Quakers believed that through isolation and study whatever was lacking in the criminally minded could be reformed and filled.

Prisoners during the early years of Eastern State were given nothing to read but a Bible. Officers would escort prisoners, in black hoods, through the prison. And on Sundays ministers would shuffle down the halls, under shivering light, preaching sermons to the inmates. Cells contained nothing but a bed, a desk, and a doorway leading to a solitary courtyard. Even the architecture was shaped to reflect the notion of penance. While the exterior of Eastern State was built to intimidate, the long halls of its interior were vaulted like chapels, radial in design, and flooded at certain times of the day with great slabs of light. A skylight was chiseled into the roof of each cell—a narrow shaft of blue-white light meant to represent the eye of God. In the austerity of the prison, it must have glowed like something hot and numinous. Prisoners had another name for it, the Dead Eye.

Not everyone was convinced of Eastern State, its humanity or capacity for redemption. "In its intention, I am well convinced that it is kind, humane, and meant for reformation; but I am persuaded that those who devised this system of Prison Discipline, and those benevolent gentlemen who carry it into execution, do not know what it is that they are doing," wrote Charles Dickens in his 1842 travelogue, *American Notes for General Circulation.*

I saw the prison once by accident. My friend was living in the Fairmount neighborhood of Philadelphia. We'd gone for a walk and found ourselves suddenly next to an enormous stone wall, edged with ivy and boxwoods and little cherry trees. The structure even today is impossible to ignore, a Gothic fortress right in the middle of Philadelphia, complete with the beveled slivers of archer's windows, fake ramparts, and turrets. "The exterior of a solitary prison should exhibit as much as possible great strength and convey to the mind a cheerless blank indicative of the misery that awaits the unhappy being who enters," wrote the commissioners of Eastern State penitentiary. But by the time I saw it, there were foam gargoyles draped with chains flanking its entrance. It was Halloween, and in the half-century since the penitentiary closed, it had become a tourist attraction. For nineteen dollars, you could see the inside, visit Al Capone's cell, stand under ceilings ribbed with exposed beams. In the cold, bright morning, it was hard to imagine the place as exhibiting anything more than residual misery and outdated plumbing.

In a red folder on my father's desk, he saves every letter his brother sends. He arranges them by date and staples each envelope to the back of its letter. He drafts each return letter by hand—twice—with marginal notes and improvements, arrows indicating how paragraphs and sentences should be shuffled for maximum effect, before typing them up and photocopying a duplicate for himself. I wonder what he thinks as he writes these letters, if this is a distraction, or if he believes that there is a perfect arrangement of words that will "cure" his brother.

Their letters are written in the dialect of my childhood, with its small errors and eccentricities: *The car needs washed. I would of stayed. I didn't want the police called.* Errors, long ironed out of my speech, come rushing back to me with bitter clarity. My father and uncle wrestle over the label of victim, and who owns it. They talk about acceptance and making good out of a bad situation. They both mention "rock bottom" at some point, and they track the path of a prodigal son: sinner, repenter, returned, redeemed. My father sends books on self-improvement. He believes that prison, as painful as it may be, is the shock his brother needs. In one letter he writes, *I think you can change if you accept that you have made bad choices. . . . Right now you have the opportunity to focus on your physical and mental health without the burdens of work and family. I hope you will use this time to exercise and read as much as possible, and explore how you see the world and how you make decisions.* Once an altar boy, my father is no longer religious, so I am surprised how much his letters echo with the language of his Catholic upbringing, how neatly his thinking tracks the notions of the Quakers building the first penitentiaries. But it is easy to renounce a set of rituals, harder to give up a structure of thinking, especially one you have lived with for sixty years.

If you asked my father why his brother is in prison, he would say it is to learn a lesson. He would tell you that his brother is essentially a good man, a smart man who made bad choices, who become too arrogant and entitled. He would tell you about his brother's upbringing in a household with a single income, no mother, and an infrequent father, working long hours at an oil refinery. He would admit that his brother stalked his ex-girlfriend, broke his house arrest, and then made up a story about her brandishing a gun at him—a story later proven false in court. Despite the stalking and house arrest, his eventual charge was for perjury.

"Personal Distance: At this distance, one can hold or grasp the other person. Visual distortion of the other's features is no longer apparent. However, there is noticeable feedback from the muscles that control the eyes."

If animals have distances for hunting, hiding, and living together, why wouldn't we? Hall's proxemics range from intimate distances to public distances, and he uses somatics—the volume of our voices, the detail with which we perceive each other, the smells we can or cannot detect—to categorize these distances.

Cigarettes, soap bars, envelopes, stamps, SIM cards, cell phones, drugs (recreational), drugs (medicinal), needles, ink, messages, viruses, bodies: some of the items trafficked in and out of prison walls. Even our most strictly controlled prisons are porous, subject to leakage and contamination. In the case of disease, a community and its institutions are not separate, but interwoven. A community is only as healthy as its least healthy institution, and an institution is only as healthy as the community that surrounds it.

In Iowa, my roommate, Jay, works as a correctional officer at the prison in the adjacent town. His facility contains a rotating cast of prisoners. It functions as a type of holding unit, temporarily housing bodies until they can be slotted into their appropriate long-term facilities. The average stay is only ninety days, so prisoners are constantly being shuffled in and out of the facility, bringing with them whatever they've contracted on the outside. And because it is one of the few facilities with a hospital on campus, many of the prisoners are also patients, also sick.

One night, Jay describes watching a man swallow a pen in the cafeteria. "He just downed it like swallowing a vitamin," he says. Prisoners often swallow things to spend a few days in the hospital, he explains, a risky form of relief. One institution and its monotony swapped for another. Usually everything turns out all right in these instances, but sometimes there are catastrophic consequences: ruptured intestines, blocked colons, prisoners forced to haul around colostomy bags in unsanitary conditions. Another day Jay describes one of his duties: "guarding" prisoners with end-stage liver disease, renal failure, lung cancer. Prisoners who have been reduced, through confinement and illness, to no more than bodies, kept alive with nothing more than a dialysis machine and a ventilator. They are still shackled to their hospital beds. They are still guarded for the sake of being guarded. Kept alive for the sake of serving out their sentences. "Prison is not the place where you want to get sick," he finishes.

My father worries about his brother, though he rarely talks about it. I asked him once on a long drive from Ohio, where he lives, to Iowa, where I was moving. He became uncharacteristically silent, clenched the steering wheel, stared at the horizon with its burning bronze sun. In the past two years, I've seen his red hair lighten to white and his stamina fall. He is more haggard around the jowls now, and something in his eyes, bloodshot and in a perpetual squint, suggests a weariness sleep will not fix. My uncle was sentenced to twenty-one to thirty-five months beginning in 2019, just before the first wave of the pandemic. And so both his sentence and my father's worry have been compounded by this fear of sickness.

"Social Distance: Intimate visual detail in the face is not perceived, and nobody touches or expects to touch another person unless there is some special effort. Voice level is normal for Americans. . . . Conversations can be overheard at a distance of up to twenty feet."

In Eastern State, it was the solitude that prisoners feared most of all. When Alexis de Tocqueville interviewed the inmates there, they told him about the insects and animals—the crickets and butterflies and birds—that they had befriended, and about the terrible slowness of Sundays, the day when prisoners were not allowed to work. But solitude was also what kept inmates safe as the flu of 1918 swept through Philadelphia. Pennsylvania, with a population over a million, was an especially hard-hit state. In the first six months, the disease killed sixteen thousand Philadelphians, but the prison was miraculously spared. While the free were working in crowded, unhygienic conditions on factory assembly lines or in meat-processing facilities, prisoners were not only allowed but forced to keep their distance from others. Now the original purpose of penitentiaries, as ineffective as it was, has been abandoned. Even the pretense of rehabilitation and isolation are gone. Now it is the overcrowding, the doubled-up cells, and shared air that put this same population most at risk.

Facts and statistics: the average size of an American jail cell: 6 feet × 9 feet × 12 feet. Weekly turnover rate in a US jail: 55 percent. Percentage of prisoners awaiting trial: 75 percent. Percentage serving short sentences: 20 percent. Cases of COVID-19 documented in prisons as of September 2021: 661,000. The average co-pay for a doctor visit in prison: $4. The average hourly pay for the incarcerated: $.05. This would be the equivalent of someone making minimum wage on the outside paying approximately $580 for a co-pay.

My father comes from a large Irish Catholic family, seven siblings in total, though there are fewer of them now. His remaining brothers and sisters have made the drive down to North Carolina to visit their brother. Afterward, they bicker over gas mileage, takeout bills, and motel-room rentals. My father has never gone. He says he doesn't want to see his brother after years of being lied to. I suspect he also does not want to see his closest sibling and best friend reduced to those conditions.

Instead, my father pays for his brother's phone bill, even though he's not allowed to have a cell phone in prison, even though the two are no longer speaking. Someone (we suspect a girlfriend on the outside) burns through the data and minutes, and my father pays for more. I don't know how much money my father has sent to his brother. In fact, I don't know if he sends him any direct payments at all. What I do know is he also pays for a storage unit in Charlotte so that the few remaining objects tying his brother to a previous life—his mattress, his clothing, his collection of Precision watches—are not pawned or left out to be scavenged on the street. I know that he wants his brother to have some type of life to return to.

There is a saying that floats through my family, a kind of trite motto that I have believed in and rolled my eyes at by turns: *Your siblings are the people you'll be closest to in the world.* Your parents will likely die when you're middle age, your partner, if you have one, you'll meet later in life, but your siblings are a life sentence. My uncle has two sons a few years apart, and I heard this motto echoed again in his letter. *I try to remind them that their brother will likely become one of their best friends and biggest ally.*

I have one sibling, a sister three years younger than I. I see her most often in the house where we both grew up, for holidays and weddings, occasions when I fly home to Columbus, where she and my parents live. In their house, she is always shaking her head, complaining of all the things our parents have acquired over the years: an attic of stained mattresses and cracked box springs and discarded workout equipment, loose drawers of baby clothes, crushed paint tubes, melted crayons, and greening pennies—the detritus of life. It took me a long time to realize why this abundance bothers her so much. It's because she imagines a world without them, when there will be only the two of us, and all the stuff of their lives to sort through.

Facts and statistics II: the average amount of money spent on court fees and fines by the families of the incarcerated: $13,000. The average age of prisoners: 41, the same age as my uncle. The cost to send $200–$300 at the Avery/Mitchell Correctional Institute: $10.65. The cost to send up to $20: $3.45. JPay's annual revenue in 2014: 70.4 million dollars. Things not captured in these statistics: the cost of visitation, the cost of gas, the cost of motels. The cost of missed work and spent vacation days. The cost of lost sleep.

"Intimate Distance: At intimate distance, the presence of the other person is unmistakable and may at times be overwhelming because of the greatly stepped-up sensory inputs. Sight (often distorted), olfaction, heat from the other person's body, sound, smell, and feel of the breath all combine to signal unmistakable involvement with another body."

The truth is, at times I find it hard to feel bad for my uncle.

In his letters, there's a tone of persecution splashed across every other sentence, a persistent accusation smoldering under the surface of his prose. He spends pages defining his life in contrast to his brother. My father is allowed to visit his children, talk with them, touch them, while he is not. In places, he slips into an oddly formal mode, "appealing" my father's "policy" of isolation, and what it is doing to them both. And, at his worst, he couches his harshest accusations in rhetorical questions like what suffering would be enough for you? Maybe you've forgotten how to empathize?

Innocence appeals, with its purity and simplicity, to the dialectics of inside and outside, right and wrong, black and white. It is easy to believe in someone who is innocent, to advocate for their freedom and better treatment. But my uncle is not an innocent victim of a system; many people are not. He is both the guilty party and victim at once.

I remember once walking in on my father and my uncle sitting together on the couch after their father's funeral. They didn't see me from where I stood behind them in the doorway. I remember hearing the words *I can't remember her voice anymore* and my uncle crying. I knew that "her" referred to their mother, who had died when my father was twenty and his brother was nine. I'm skeptical of the past as a perfect cipher for making sense of the present. Dead mother to narcissistic personality disorder to disordered relationship with women to prison. What about all the people who turn out just fine? But I do believe in redemption. I believe people can change. I believe in second chances. And I believe we put people, the innocent and the guilty, in the worst situation imaginable and then act surprised when they become exactly what we fear.

Prisons are not just tools for punishment or rehabilitation. They are not just architecture and blank time. They are concrete experience, event, and sensation. They are the somatics of Hall's proxemics: razor wire, blacktop, steel, and cinder block. They are the smell of breaded fish frying in a cafeteria and the particular hardness of concrete, its leaching cold. They are the rattle and boom of cell doors closing in unison and the sudden muffle of sound. They are the unique frustration of waiting an hour for the phone only to have it break. They are fights over desks and call times. The sickening absence of visitors. The desperate boredom, always the boredom.

In his letters, my uncle describes his life as a series of absences: a year since he's driven a car or eaten a slice of pizza, a year since he's seen his two sons or chosen when to go to sleep and when to wake up. He mentions the pandemic only once, when he talks about the pain of losing visitors, the preciousness of a single fifteen-minute phone call each week. It makes sense why fights are breaking out. And it is all the more heartbreaking that this is what the pandemic means behind bars, not just the possibility of illness or death, but a robbery of one of the few joys many prisoners have left.

At one point, my uncle lays out in precise detail the process for sending a letter—you need his prisoner number and the facility's specific address. There are certain things you can't say without the letters being censored and, of course, a long list of items you can't send. As I read, I begin to notice all the places he's inserted his prisoner number into the letter—scrawled under his signature, floating above the top margin, in the return address of the envelope the letter came in—quiet requests to write.

My friend Colin is a landscape architect. One weekend, in Chicago, where I now live, we sit near the Belmont Harbor, and he tells me about the built world and how it influences us. How the spangling of light through planted trees lowers cortisol in the blood. How the "hardscaping" of the harbor where we sit—concrete steps that were once soft grass and huge stone breakers—was meant to prevent coastal erosion, but it also made it easier to banish the gay men who gathered here in the '90s. Another day, pointing to the mangy edge of a path stamped into a field, he says that architecture reveals our psychology, too, how the world we build can chafe against us and our natural impulses.

The work of artist James Casebere reimagines and rebuilds these spaces. His work consists mostly of intimate photographs of paper models he built to resemble public spaces: schools, amphitheaters, and asylums. Arcades of beveled arches. The branching tunnels of an underground. And of course penitentiaries. Sometimes his work is of the general—hallway, hospital, stacked beds, toilets. Other times it is specific. He has modeled Sing Sing, the tunnels and porticos of Bologna, and an entire neighborhood of Tripoli.

The photographs are dreamlike, toyish, and eerie in their austerity, too pure in their geometry, too smooth in their surfaces. They are photographs of a model, twice alienated from the real.

His work imagines, rather than describes, places of human occupation but wiped clean of humans. "I was thinking about the circulation of air, water and people, and the way that different plans for prisons developed out of those concerns," said Casebere in an interview with *Bomb* magazine. "Ventilation and clean air became a concern in the workplace, and in hospitals and other institutions like poorhouses and prisons, partly as a result of the new knowledge that germs are airborne."

Casebere had spent time at Eastern State in the '90s. He understood prisons as essentially a problem of management, and humans, even their emotions, as part of that managerial system. He wanted to make those systems visible; to force a viewer to confront the unsettling fact of a space designed for treatment, entertainment, transport, or confinement; and to propose, in doing so, a different future. As the novelist Rachel Kushner says, "Architecture shifts things away from the pieties of the liberal individual who is asked to extend their compassion to some incarcerated person they want to believe is innocent, rather than worthy of something better than prison, regardless of any axis of innocence and guilt. It suggests that maybe we, too, are worthy of something better, as a society. Or we should be."

"Public Distance: several important sensory shifts occur in the transition from the personal and social distances to public distance, which is well outside the circle of involvement."

I'm thinking about what it means to exit someone's "circle of involvement." For Hall this means no longer smelling someone, no longer registering the contracting of their eye muscles, perhaps no longer even seeing them. What else could it mean? That a person is so far removed, both physically and conceptually, that we no longer consider them. They disappear behind a wall, into a space we struggle to imagine.

For the most part, prisons don't look like Eastern State anymore. Prisons are now outside of the city, on campuses that might look as benign as high schools, hidden in a smoky landscape, nestled in rolling hills, nothing to suggest what they are except for the high cyclone fences and concertina wire.

One night, Jay comes home with a lemon-size welt throbbing on his bald head. He takes a bag of mixed vegetables out of the freezer and presses it against his temple, then sighs into an armchair. That afternoon, he was tasked with dragging a man out from under his cell bed, where the man was holed up, crouching and kicking at anyone who approached. The simple geometries, the open spaces, the flat surfaces—easy to search, easy to wipe clean—are all part of an architecture meant not only to manage prisoners, but to manage the fear of the people who work there. There should be nowhere to hide, no crevices to launch an attack, nothing unexpected that a correctional officer cannot account for. And yet: "It took three of us just to get him out," Jay tells me.

A friend once asked me how I could live with a correctional officer while being anti-prison. Didn't those two things negate each other? Didn't I live in a constant state of cognitive dissonance? As if we all don't live with our hypocrisies, our compromises.

My uncle's sentence was short, and he was let out early after a parole board deemed him a non-violent offender—a precious and specious designation. He left behind men much older than he, many of whom were sick, and equally "nonviolent."

My father and uncle are talking again—a fresh and uneasy armistice. They've landed in a strange place. My uncle has spent all his goodwill. He's overdrawn his credit, and then some. And yet, his brother, my dad, will never completely abandon him. They're stuck with each other, a painful, inescapable kind of stuck. Of memories between him and his brother, my uncle writes simply, *There are so many impactful ones.* Of forgiveness—for the brother he still believes abandoned him, for himself—he isn't sure, but he is open to the possibility.

It took 9 years to build Eastern State and 141 years for it to slide into disrepair. But it took only a few years after the site was abandoned for a forest—of mulberry bushes and maple saplings—to grow up around the architecture. It took just as long for the roofs and skylights to begin collapsing, for birds to roost in the watchtowers, for trees to begin unmooring the slabs of concrete in the foundation. In this strange purgatory between lives, I imagine a quiet place turned even quieter, one of Casebere's models flooded with water and light. A building lost in its own kind of penitence. Even as prisons were being built en masse across the country, Eastern State was a reminder that nothing is irrevocable. Everything can be redone and remade, and some things can be forgiven.

BROCK CLARKE

Woodstove

FROM *Five Points*

> For some time now the impression has been growing upon me
> that everyone is dead.
> —Walker Percy, *The Moviegoer*

MY DOG JUST DIED. Her name was Maude. It is not necessary
to tell you how wonderful she was, since all dogs are wonderful,
even the ones you know would be more wonderful if they were
someone else's dog. She was six years old and died of cancer. I had
friends who told me, helpfully, that six years old seemed awfully
young for a dog to die of cancer, but then they'd looked it up and
discovered that it's common for Bernese Mountain dogs—Maude
was a Bernese Mountain dog (Some people intentionally call Bernese
Mountain dogs "Berners" and other people mistakenly call them
"Burmese Mountain Dogs." I like it better when people mistakenly
call them "Burmese Mountain Dogs.")—to die young, of cancer. It
is supposed to be comforting when someone dies when and how
they're expected to.

I wasn't there when Maude died: I was out of state, a time zone
away, visiting my older son. There was no one in the house but
Maude and the dog sitter. Maude was supposed to have at least
another month to live. I swear I wouldn't have left her with a dog
sitter if I thought she was going to die so soon. But I did, and she
did: the dog sitter woke up on the second day of my absence and
found Maude dead in the kitchen. I wonder if it's more terrible
to wake up to your own dead dog, or to someone else's. In any
case, it was pretty terrible—emotionally, sure, but also logistically:
the dog sitter was a one-hundred-pound person who suddenly had

to figure out what to do with someone else's one-hundred-pound dead dog. I told her that it wasn't her job to do anything, and that it wasn't her fault, and that she should get the hell out of the house immediately before she was further traumatized, and I'd feel obliged to pay for her therapy. I then called a friend of mine, who is a traveling vet. A traveling vet is someone who goes to people's houses to, more often than not, euthanize their pets. I wasn't necessarily looking for her to do anything in particular. I was just looking for advice. I'd had dogs before, and they had all died and you will hear about how they all died, but none of them had died like this.

"I'll take care of her," the traveling vet said. "Take care of her" turned out to mean that she and her husband would come get Maude and bring her to the place where they stored dead animals on their way to being cremated. Which they would also take care of. I was grateful for this, until I got home later that night. Before Maude and I been taken care of, I'd imagined how awful it would be to come home and find Maude, dead for those many hours, still on the kitchen floor. But now the house was empty and that was more awful. It was like Maude had never been there at all.

This is not a story about cancer. This is a story about death, and since all stories about death are also stories about greed, and since all stories about greed are also stories about futility, it is a story about greed and futility, too. But it's true that someone else I loved—my friend Rupert—also died of cancer in the past year. It is necessary for me to tell you how wonderful Rupert was, because unlike dogs, all people are not wonderful, and even friends tend to be wonderful only a quarter of the time. But Rupert was a great guy, 100 percent heaven material. What people don't tell you about friends is that you can learn something from them. And one of the many things I learned from Rupert is that if you're not a surly asshole, then strangers in bars will want to talk to you and buy you drinks. For instance: Rupert and I were in a bar in Rochester, New York—this was probably 1992—and had been for some time, and I'd sort of lost track of where Rupert was, and in fact I'd probably lost track of where I was, when I heard someone call my name. I looked over, and it was Rupert, arm in arm with a stranger, a middle-age guy who looked kind of familiar. They were both waving at me. Later on, I asked Rupert who in the hell that was, and he told me that it was Tug McGraw, an All-Star pitcher for the Philadelphia Phillies from when we were in high school. Rupert had just met him and already they were hugging each other.

Anyway, Rupert died. Unlike Maude, who died quickly, and inexpensively, Rupert was sick for a long time, and it cost him a lot of money. After Rupert was diagnosed, he called me up and told me about his meeting with his oncologist, who wanted Rupert to try an experimental treatment the oncologist called "The Radical." The Radical was going to be very expensive, and it very well might prolong Rupert's life, but there was no guarantee for how long, and at what physical and financial cost. But Rupert was going to do it, he was game, and that was another thing about Rupert: he was always game, and if he was game, then the oncologist was game, too. "Oh yeah," the oncologist had told Rupert. "You gotta go with the Radical."

"It was," Rupert said to me on the phone, "like he was a salesman at the Kia lot across the street, trying to sell me a Sorento."

I told this story at Rupert's memorial service, which was attended by the many people who loved him, and also the oncologist. I'd pictured him as a burly guy with a huge head of hair, a college football player gone to surgery instead of seed. Instead, he was a small, tidy, mild-looking man who bore a strong resemblance to Harry Truman. After giving my little speech, I wandered over to the bar. The oncologist was standing there. He smiled at me; it didn't seem like I'd hurt his feelings, but I apologized anyway. He waved me off. "It works, you know," he said. "The Radical works."

I didn't know what to say to that. What could he possibly mean? We were at Rupert's *memorial service*. Did he mean that the Radical had allowed Rupert a few years longer than he otherwise might have? That was not proof that something had *worked*, not as far as I was concerned. Rupert was dead. The Radical hadn't saved his life, and my little speech hadn't brought him back to life, either. Neither had worked.

Rupert's memorial service took place in Fairfield County, Connecticut, which is the home, or one of the homes, of Keith Richards. Keith Richards shares the same exact birthday with my father, and I've always wanted to have Keith show up to my father's house on their birthday dressed as my father, in loafers and khaki pants and a tucked-in, button-down shirt and a fleece vest, and, if Keith really wanted to go for it, a wig of white thinning hair, combed to the side. Although really that would be more a present for me than for my father.

My father's sister, my aunt Penny, teaches in Weston, Connecticut, which is the town where Keith Richards lives. In fact, she taught Keith Richards's children, a fact, which, as I write it, seems more like something I've repeated, or made up, as opposed to something that is true and that I've verified. I'm not going to verify it. It sounds like something my aunt would have done. She is a remarkable person, a woman who last year retired as a kindergarten teacher at age seventy-nine, only to return this year as a substitute teacher. She will teach, I've heard her say, until she dies. I don't like the sound of that. I also don't like it when my aunt tells supposedly charming stories of things I did and said when I was young, but she tells them anyway. Apparently, when I was four years old, I liked to talk to her while she was in the bathtub, and also that I liked to brush her hair. My aunt had little wooden Christmas figurines of the holy family, and she would let me throw them down the stairs. "There goes Mary," she has said I said as the things tumbled from the second story of her house to the first "there goes Joseph, there goes baby Jesus."

Like Jesus, my aunt is also a worker of miracles. Once, while holding a full glass of white wine, she walked through a closed screen door. I don't mean she passed through it, like a spirit; I mean she charged through it, not paying attention, thinking that it was open, knocked the thing down, and then staggered through the wreckage of frame and screen, saying, repeatedly, "Oh shit!" but not falling and not spilling a drop of wine, either.

Not everyone in this essay is dead. My aunt is alive, for instance, I hope she stays that way for a long time, and that I have the chance to tell many more stories about her, but for now, this one: my father and my aunt own a lake house—they inherited it from their parents—and two summers ago, at that house, I was using a shot glass to make a Manhattan, until my father told me not to. When I asked him why, he said, "That's not a shot glass, that's an eye wash glass." An eye wash glass, he said, was the glass you used to rinse your eye when something was in it. I didn't know there was a glass specific to that purpose, and I didn't know why this eye wash glass, which looked like a shot glass, was stored among the other shot glasses if it was in fact not a shot glass but an eye wash glass. But before I could say this, my father said, "It's also the glass your aunt uses to clean her fake tooth."

I've told this story to my fiction writing students, under the principle that if something is in your story, then it must have multiple purposes. It seems like good advice, to me, but my students seem to have no use for it. That's fine. I'm used to them ignoring me. I sometimes even ignore my own advice. For instance, for years I've been telling my students that they're not allowed to write about their dead dogs.

I grew up in the country. That can mean a lot of things, but for me it meant that we had to be constantly mindful of our septic tank and our well. We had rhymes to help us to remember when to flush, or not; long showers were discouraged; normal-length showers were also discouraged. Then there were the dishes, which had to be washed, and you were in trouble if it was your turn and you forgot. But if the dishwasher was loaded and running, and there were still dishes in the sink that needed to be washed, well, you were not allowed to hand-wash them, not while the dishwasher was running, because that put a strain on the well, and was also bad for the septic tank.

So I learned to worry about water. Likewise, the cold. This was in upstate New York, and it was cold all the time. Our house was heated by oil, and oil, as everyone knows, tends to run out; we also had a woodstove, just in case the oil ran out, but you can run out of wood, too. Although we never ran out of either. Regardless, my brothers and I learned to be vigilant about the thermostat. We were constantly being asked by our father, first thing in the morning, "Who fiddled with the thermostat?" None of us had ever fiddled with the thermostat. But apparently that was a lie, and someone was always fiddling with the thermostat.

Occasionally, these worries about the water and the cold intersected, and became truly scary. For a short time, our water was somehow hooked up to the town system. I never learned how, or why, and it's possible that the hook up was illegal and in fact we were stealing town water. My father insists that wasn't so, but of course you'd expect someone who was stealing town water to say that.

One late winter, though, something went wrong, and we suddenly didn't have water. My father trudged up the hill. There, at the top of our property, was a metal grate. My father lifted the grate and plunged into the hole, which was filled with icy water, and where he fiddled with the pipe that connected our house to town water. This took a terrifyingly long time. When my father finally emerged from the hole his face was fire red and his lips were arctic blue and he couldn't stop shaking and I prayed to the God I then believed in to please save my father's life and if he did I'd never again try to take a long shower or fiddle with the thermostat or gripe about how we couldn't get cable TV because we lived too far out in the country to get cable TV.

I had friends who lived in town, and occasionally I would go to their houses after school and we would watch their cable TV and they would run the water longer than strictly necessary and flush their toilets whenever they used them and the thermostat was turned high and it was hot enough to take off your sweatshirt and I felt so free, but I also felt, or felt obliged to feel, that that kind of freedom was cheap, and a sign of laziness, and weakness. I now wonder what kind of person I would have been had I grown up in town, and not in the country.

My dogs might have died differently, too. My first dog, Rosie—a high-strung, untrainable, or at least untrained, English Setter—was struck and killed by a car. This was her fault, because she chased cars. This was also our fault, though, because we let her run free. But then, we lived in the country, and what was the point of living in the country if you didn't let your dogs run free?

Rosie spent most of her life covered in burdocks. That is what I remember second most clearly about her: that she would be gone for hours, and no amount of calling would bring her back. No, she would only come back when she was tired of being away, and suddenly there she was, tongue hanging out, a wild look in her eyes, her fur matted with burdocks. My parents would then chastise her, and one would restrain her while the other cut the burdocks off with scissors. No wonder she didn't like to come back.

The thing I remember most clearly about Rosie was how she died. We lived on a steep hill, and the road going down that steep hill had a thirty-mile-per-hour speed limit, but no one paid any attention to it. On this day I was outside, with my middle brother, away from the road, doing whatever we usually did. One of the things we usually did was rip up weeds with long, thick, water-filled stems and big root balls, and twirl them over our heads like bolos before flinging them at each other. Let's say we were doing that, away from the road. My father was doing something closer to the road. Rosie was chasing cars. From where my brother and I were throwing weeds at each other I could hear a car roaring down the hill; I could hear my father call Rosie's name; I could hear the car hit Rosie. What kind of sound does a car hitting a dog at fifty-five miles per hour make? It makes a thick, wet sound. It was the kind of sound my brother and I wanted to be making when we hit each other with those weeds.

Rosie died on impact. I remember my parents saying that it was a good thing she died immediately, that she didn't suffer, but that's only the kind of thing you say in retrospect, when you're trying to remember something good about the dog, something other than the way she died, and the sound of her dying.

Earlier I said that all my dogs are dead, and that you'll hear about them. Likewise my grandparents. The first to die was my father's father. He, like Rupert, was a wonderful man, and a large part of his wonderfulness was his absolute predictability. For instance, no matter how early you woke up, he'd have already been up for hours and he would say to you "Good afternoon!" even though it was in fact eight in the morning. And what had he been doing during the hours he'd he been awake, and you hadn't? As far as I could tell, not a lot. He'd made his eggs and toast, and then he'd eaten then. While he ate, he read the newspaper, the Springfield *Republican*, cover to cover, including the comics, which he referred to as "the editorials." God, I loved that man.

And he loved me, too, and liked people in general, although there were exceptions. For instance Nazis, and the Mafia, whose long a's he made short to express how much he hated them. That'll show 'em. My grandfather also hated hunters. I don't know what he had against them, except that they made sudden loud noises, and left their empty beer cans in the woods, and he viewed them as violent, whereas he viewed himself as pacific. Whenever he received news of one hunter drunkenly and/or accidentally shooting another, my grandfather would mutter, "Good," which of course had the effect of making him seem more violent, and less pacific. Also, he was made thoughtful by fat people. My grandfather was a thin man, and like a lot of thin people he viewed obesity as a character flaw. But unlike a lot of thin people, he was aware of his prejudice. "I know it's not their fault," he said, on multiple occasions. "I know I'm lucky that I can eat whatever I want and not gain weight." But then, an hour later, while watching Wheel of Fortune and seeing an overweight contestant in her little cubicle, he would say, "How does she *fit* in that thing?"

Are you like me? When, say, someone's grandfather dies of a stroke at age eighty, do you think—but not say—*Well, yeah, so what, of course, he was old?* My grandfather had a stroke when he was eighty. I was in my early twenties. My parents were out of the country. I was staying with my youngest brother—not the one I'd thrown weeds at—while they were away. My aunt had called with the news. My grandfather was unconscious. He wasn't dead yet, but he would be soon. My aunt and I agreed that I wouldn't call my parents; they'd be home soon enough, and there was nothing they could do anyway, and there was no sense in ruining what was left of their vacation. I'd told my brother—who was only thirteen years old—about our grandfather, and he took the news like the little soldier he was. But I didn't tell him not to tell our parents. I didn't figure there was any need to. My parents rarely went on vacation, but when they did, they never called home just to check in. But this time, my father did, when I was out of the house, and my brother answered the phone, and told our father what had happened to our grandfather.

"What did he say?" I asked my brother.

"He cried," my brother said.

"Goddammit!" I said, of course being mad at myself and not at my brother. He cried anyway, which is another thing I wish I could forget, another thing I wish some other, happier memory would come along and displace.

Anyway, my parents came home, and my grandfather never regained consciousness and died soon after. Occasionally, when I'm at the lake house, I'll open a book and there, on the first page, I'll see his handwriting: his name—P. H. Clarke—and the year when he read the book. When that happens, do I feel my grandfather's presence? Does it feel like my grandfather is still with me? No, but I fucking wish.

My second dog, Daisy, also an English Setter, was somewhat better trained than Rosie. That is, she would come eventually if you called her for long enough. But she also chased cars and was also hit by one. I wasn't there to see it or hear it, and she survived the blow and lived for a few more years before we had to put her to sleep because of the arthritis in her back legs, which was where she'd been hit by the car those years earlier. When we talk about her death, we always talk about how she'd been run over by a car, not that we'd had her euthanized. This isn't to say that we were wrong to euthanize her; I think we had to do it, just as we have to say, about her dying, that she was run over by a car.

We've long blamed Daisy's car-chasing on the bad influence of another dog, Buffy. Buffy was my mother's parents' cocker spaniel. Buffy came to live with us when she got older. "Came to live with us" is a lovely way of putting it. A less lovely way of putting it is that my grandparents moved into a condo and didn't really have room for a dog and couldn't really take care of a dog anymore and really didn't want to take care of Buffy anymore—Buffy, who, like many cocker spaniels was the genetic victim of many nonlethal but still really gross ailments, halitosis being the most gross and the most omnipresent. Buffy weighed thirty pounds and had the breath of a dragon. It was hard to love her. My grandparents had tried and now they were tired of trying and it my parents' turn.

And Buffy chased cars. Daisy was a puppy when we got Buffy, and as I said, we've long blamed Buffy for teaching her to chase cars. Never mind that Daisy could have learned all by herself. And never mind that while Daisy died after being hit by a car, Buffy died of something else entirely.

My brothers and I called my mother's parents Noni and Nono. Nono had a proper name, but everyone who was not his child or grandchild called him Stutz, because when he was young his favorite car was a Stutz Bearcat. What a wonderful name for a car, and what a wonderful nickname for a person. I wish I were a different person, who lived in a different time, and owned a different car. Because who could ever fall in love with, and want themselves nicknamed for, the Toyota Camry?

So Nono had an interesting nickname. He lived an interesting life, too. He, like my noni, was the child of Italian immigrants. Like many children of immigrants, he was encouraged to forsake his old language in order to become expert in his new one. He did that, became expert enough to become a lawyer, a lawyer who represented many clients whose first language was Italian.

So, he relearned Italian to better represent them. He did this, by all accounts, effortlessly, and in fact he was a great appreciator of difficult things done effortlessly. When he did a difficult thing effortlessly, my nono advertised his accomplishment by saying, "Just like New York!" even though he'd lived his entire life in Massachusetts.

And then, of course, he died. His death wasn't that awful compared to most of the other deaths in this essay: in his late eighties he had a heart attack, briefly rallied, then died. It's not a death that I like to think about, but it's not one I have to try hard to forget, either. But one of the many terrible things about someone dying is that sooner or later a memory of them, one you'd rather not have, will appear and then it's pretty impossible to dislodge it. Here's this one: when I was an early teenager I was at the beach with my extended family—my parents and brothers, my noni and nono, my aunt and uncle and my cousins. My nono was a stocky guy, an amateur boxer in his heyday, but he was no longer in his heyday and like many men past their heydays his chest had fallen and gone to flab. Nothing unusual about that. He wasn't ashamed of it, certainly, and was always bare-chested at the beach. He was bare-chested this day. One of my older cousins and I were standing, also shirtless, talking to Nono, who was slumped down in his beach chair in a way that made his breasts look like they were reaching for his stomach. I noticed, and I know my cousin did, too. Because when Nono turned to talk to someone else, my cousin leaned over and whispered in my ear, "Nono has tits."

A remarkable sentence. Too remarkable. Because whenever I try to remember my nono, and all his many triumphs and kindnesses and eccentricities, that sentence—"Nono has tits"—keeps getting in the way.

We often talk about someone dying a dignified death. But by that I think we mean not that death is dignified, but that life, which is often undignified, is over.

For instance, Marley, the Dalmatian my parents got to replace Daisy. Dalmatians are beautiful dogs, but they are also terrifyingly twitchy. This is why they are among the most popular dogs to get, and also among the dogs mostly likely to given away or abandoned. My mother in particular loved Marley, but she also was convinced that Marley was going to, for no reason, out of nowhere, bite someone right in the face.

Marley never did. But she did put a ball that was too big in her mouth, and that gave her TMJ, bad. That diagnosis made me laugh when I heard it. I had never heard of a dog getting TMJ. It was like a dog having ADHD. Which Marley might have also had.

Anyway, it wasn't funny. It hurt Marley to eat, and her jaw sometimes got stuck in the open position, making her look like she was gobsmacked by something. Is it ethically wrong to project human emotions onto animals, or is it wrong not to? I always forget. Let's just say it's wrong not to. Marley was embarrassed by her TMJ, and her slack jaw. Who could blame her? It was undignified.

This was why, I think, my noni found her such good company. Noni was a dignified woman: large, but not fat (she would have fit comfortably inside the Wheel of Fortune contestant cubicle, but, being dignified, she would never have allowed that to happen), and regal, with a bemused superior look on her face and with large rings bejeweling her arthritically gnarled knuckles and fingers. I loved her, as I loved all my grandparents, but I never felt that I knew her all that well. Unknowability being the price you pay for dignity. Unknowability being the way you remain dignified.

As I said, my nono died when he was in his late eighties. Noni was a few years younger. But soon after her husband died, my noni's health failed, and then kept failing, and after a few years she ended up having to move in with my parents. It is impossible to remain dignified when, as an adult, you have to move in with your children. You could tell it embarrassed my noni. It diminished her. Literally, she seemed to shrink. Her right leg weakened, and she started walking with a serious list. She lost much of her hearing, too. It became impossible to watch television with her, so loud did the set have to be turned up for her to hear. Finally, my parents bought her a set of headphones that could be plugged into the TV. The headphones were huge, covering not just her ears but much of her head. She looked ridiculous. Absolutely without dignity.

But Marley loved her. Around everyone else, the dog acted nervous—not as though Marley was unsure what people might do to her, but as though she was unsure of what she might do to them, of what bad things she might be capable of. But around my noni Marley was calm, calm. She clearly had no intention of biting my noni in the face. They would sit there—Noni with her huge headphones, Marley with her messed-up jaw—Noni lightly petting Marley's head and Marley *letting* her while they watched *Jag*. It was possible to look at them and feel hopeful. Even when we get old and have lost almost everything that makes us feel good, there is someone for us, someone like us, someone to make us feel less alone.

I won't tell you how my noni died. It was not dramatic; it was grinding and familiar and forever-seeming, and it was exactly the kind of death people envision when they say that they want to die before they get old. Marley, in contrast, died when she was poisoned by a neighbor. Or she died after eating poison that a neighbor had, for some reason, left outside his house. Either way, she ate poison, and from that, almost immediately, horribly, painfully, she died.

I keep talking about "my dogs" but most of those dogs were in fact my parents' dogs. Only two were mine. Maude was the second, Hannah the first. Hannah was a German short-haired pointer, as twitchy and unruly as Rosie and Daisy. I don't know if we're doomed to make our parents' mistakes, but most of the time we make them anyway. But one difference was that Hannah was a city dog. The only time she was ever in the country was when I took her to visit my parents, and in fact one of those times she was clipped by a car and nearly had her tail ripped off. But she didn't die from that, not even close. Unlike Maude, she lived to a ripe old dog age; like Maude, she died of cancer. That is to say, she had cancer, and lived with it for several months longer than I probably should have let her, until I finally had her put to sleep. I was with her in the examining room petting her head when the vet put the needle in, and then Hannah died. And then I wept. It was a roaring kind of weeping, the noise rising and rising, like a hurricane, and the vet tried to console me, but I would not be consoled. I bet my grief was heard in the other examining rooms and in the waiting room, and in the kennels, and throughout the entire veterinary complex. Speaking of being undignified. The vet finally said that I should go, and not to worry about the bill, they'd just mail it to me.

I hate stories of how sad people were when their pets died. It makes them seem heroic for doing something as basic as being sad. So let me also tell you this story, also involving Hannah, and also set in Rochester. Hannah was a year or so old. I was walking her. I'd just gotten her to the point where I could walk her, on a leash, without her trying to tear my arm out of its socket. I was feeling good about that. As I walked her, a dog from across the street came charging out of its house. It was a smallish dog, a terrier kind of thing. It was barking viciously at us. Which is to say, at Hannah. But it was barking from the sidewalk. That it is, from the sidewalk on the opposite side of the street. I always assume that other people's dogs are better trained than my dogs, and so I assumed the dog would stay on the other side of the street. After all, it had so far. Hannah and I stopped and watched that dog bark and bark. It was an athletic barker, too: it sort of levitated, briefly, each time it woofed. "Look at that fucking dog," I said to Hannah. Some people think it's important to talk to your dogs, but I think it's important to swear to them, too. That sounds like a piece of wisdom. Here's another one: if you and your dog stand too long, watching an unleashed dog bark at you from across the street, then sooner or later that dog will run across the street to get at you.

That dog did, and it was hit by a car. The car wasn't moving as fast as the one that had hit Rosie, but the sound was the same. The dog's owner apparently had not heard his dog barking, but he heard his dog being hit by the car. He ran out of the house and into the street and scooped his dog up and ran back into the house. I don't know if he'd noticed me and Hannah standing there. I wonder now, when he tells the story, if he tells the story, if he knows that there's someone else besides himself and his dog to blame.

There is one more dead person left in this essay, and one more dead dog, too. That sounds terrible, but once you set up the rules for a story, you can't just change them because they're depressing. That's another thing I teach my students, another thing they're smart, probably, to ignore.

My father's mother lived the longest, and probably the best, of all my grandparents. I have been lucky enough to have been loved by all my grandparents, and to have had grandparents who gave their grandchildren many reasons to love them, and very few reasons to not. But I think I loved my grandmother the most because for the longest time she was moderately healthy, and so for the longest time she was allowed to remain herself, and so I had more time as an adult to get to know her, and to learn all the things there were about her to love. I've had a chance to write elsewhere about my grandmother, and so let me tell you only a very short story about her here. I was sitting with my grandmother and my aunt Penny in the living room at the lake house. There was something on the TV. It might have been the Miss America Pageant. My aunt and my grandmother liked to watch the Miss America Pageant. No, they liked to have the Miss America Pageant playing in the background, like a song you only had to pay attention to when it was really bad, or surprisingly not. The TV was tiny and was nestled among the books on the bookshelves, the books signed and dated by my grandfather, the shelves built by my father.

My grandmother was eighty-five. Her husband had been dead now for five years. My grandmother had lived alone all this time, and loved when people came over, and I think people loved to come over. I know I did, and my aunt did, too, even though inevitably, when people came over, my grandmother would, apropos nothing, start worrying about her money running out.

"In fifteen years I don't think I'll have any money left at all," my grandmother said, in her high warbly voice that always reminded me of Big Bird's.

I did the math. I am bad at math, but not so bad that I couldn't add fifteen to eighty-five. I looked at Aunt Penny. She looked back at me, over the top of her glass of white wine. She choked a little on the wine, swallowed it, and then started laughing. Which gave me permission to laugh, too.

"I don't think that's something you're going to have to worry about, Mother," my aunt said.

My grandmother didn't say anything. She just sat there, smirking, like she knew something we didn't.

And she almost made it! My grandmother died just before her ninety-eighth birthday. How does that make me feel? It makes me feel like she and I got fucking robbed. I wonder if I'd feel differently if she'd actually lived until she was one hundred, or if even that wouldn't have been enough.

The winter Buffy came to live with my parents was frigid, even more so than usual. There were days and days of snow, days and days where we didn't see the sun, days and days when the temperature never got above zero. It is hard now to imagine. I wish we didn't have to.

At the time, it would have been hard to imagine that I would think back to those days with wonder and longing. At the time, I just felt abused by the weather.

The dogs, Buffy and Daisy, seemed to like it well enough, though. They treated the snow like people treat sand at the beach. They frolicked in it, and then they rested on it. One day the snow had stopped falling just long enough for my father to snowblow the driveway. He and my mother had plans to go out that night, and he needed to clear the driveway so he could go pick up the sitter. The dogs were running around, chasing the snowblower as though it was just a smaller car. I was watching this from our house's front window. Finally, Buffy seemed to get tired of running, and lay down on the stretch of driveway that my father had already cleared. Daisy, the younger dog, the dog that would be hit by a car, and years later die of it, continued to sprint around and my father continued to snowblow the driveway. All seemed normal. But then Daisy stopped running and sniffed Buffy. I didn't think anything of it, but my father did. He cut the snowblower, walked over to Buffy, kneeled; it seemed like he was saying something to her. Then he scooped up the dog in his arms—the way the man two hundred miles away and twenty years later would to his car-struck dog on that street in Rochester—and walked out of my line of vision, and into the cellar. I ran down to meet him.

There was an enormous woodstove in the cellar, always raging, never making as much heat in the rest of the house as I wanted it to. My father had put a blanket next to the woodstove, and he gently placed Buffy on that blanket. Buffy looked wrong. By which I mean that she looked dead, but I didn't want to think that. Neither did my father.

"I think she's just really cold," my father said. There was something teary in his voice. He disliked that dog, but he wasn't ready for her to go. I love my father, and I'm not ready for him to go, either. Recently he got pneumonia, bad, and I thought, Please, I'm not ready for you to go, and he didn't go, and I was so relieved, but the relief was temporary, and stupid, and futile, because I'll never be ready, no one is ever ready, and nothing, no amount of time, is ever enough.

Anyway, my father wasn't ready for Buffy to go, but he was late: He had to shower and get dressed and pick up the sitter and bring her back to the house, and in the midst of all that he somehow forgot that there was a thawing dead dog down by the woodstove in our cellar. He somehow forgot to tell the babysitter, too. But my middle brother and I did. We'd admitted the truth to ourselves by now: Buffy was dead, not just frozen. We told the babysitter that there was a dead dog in the cellar. She didn't believe us. So we showed her. We showed her Buffy, lying there, next to the wood-stove. The babysitter wasn't horrified. She wasn't disgusted. She was confused. I could see it on her face. What, she wanted to know, am I looking at here? Here's what she was looking at: she was look-ing at a dead dog that had been loved too early, or too late, or not enough, or not in the proper way, and she was also looking at the woodstove, the thing that had no chance, no chance at all, of bringing the dead back to life.

MICHAEL W. CLUNE

The Anatomy of Panic

FROM *Harper's Magazine*

I HAD MY FIRST PANIC ATTACK when I was fifteen, in the middle of January, while I was sitting in geometry class. Winter in Illinois, flesh comes off the bones—what did we need geometry for? We could look at the naked angles of the trees, the circles in the sky at night. At noon we could look at our own faces. All the basic shapes were there, in bone. Bright winter sun turns kids skinless. Skins them. But there we were in geometry class. The teacher also taught physics. He was grotesquely tall. Thin. He'd demonstrate the angles with his bones.

This was Catholic school. The blackboard was useless. A gray swamp dense with half-drowned numbers. Mr. Streeling would bend a leg in midair: 90 degrees, cleaner than a protractor. He'd stand and tilt his impossibly flat torso: 45 degrees. He could lift his pant leg, unbundle new levels of bone like a spider: 15 degrees, 55, 100.

I was sitting under the fluorescence when it happened. The first time, technically. Though I could tell it was the first time only in retrospect, looking back from the third time. My right hand on my desk, my left hand fiddling with a pencil in the air.

Mr. Streeling's voice booms: Open the textbook, page 96. The textbook lies next to my hand on the desk. Next to the textbook is a large blue rubber eraser. Hand, textbook, eraser. Desktop bright in the fake light.

My hand, I realize slowly, it's a . . . *thing.*

My hand is a thing. Hand, textbook, eraser. Three things.

Oh.

That's when I forgot how to breathe. Ty saw it happen. He was sitting across the room. But he saw me, and he gave me a look like *what the hell*. Watching me trying to remember how to breathe. It wasn't going well. I was sucking in too much air, or I wasn't breathing enough out. The rhythm was all wrong.

Darkness at the edge of vision . . .

Two seconds blotted out. When I came back my lungs had picked up the tune. The old in-and-out, the tune you hear all the time. If it ever stops, try to remember it. You can't. Breathe in, breathe out, breathe in, breathe out. It never stops. But if it does, it's hard to remember how it goes. Ask dead people. Ask me. I gave Ty a weak smile, like I'd been joking, my face probably red or maybe white or even a little blue. Ty turned slowly back to his textbook, shaking his head like I was crazy.

The second time it happened was in a movie theater. My dad had taken me to see *The Godfather Part III*. It was a Tuesday night. Late January. The theater was basically deserted. Kind of depressing, this father-son outing on a school night. Kind of cool, too. Like we didn't give a fuck about school nights.

I think the show started around ten p.m. Everything was fine. The film was pretty good. Until halfway through, when the Al Pacino character says he has diabetes. As he said that word, *diabetes*, I could feel gas rising in my blood. The gas started to rise maybe a minute before *diabetes*. Like I knew he was going to say it. Like I prophesized it.

This time what I forgot was how to move blood through my body. My blood stopped. When your blood stops, the gas rises. That's my experience. Gas rising in the blood. Dad snored beside me. I woke him up, said we have to go. He looked at me. Okay.

As soon as we got up my blood started to move again. I was still in shock or something. Walking like I was about to fall over. When we got to the car I lay back in the passenger seat and pressed my forehead to the cold glass and Dad asked me if I was okay and I said yes, which he knew was a lie, but there was nothing else I could say.

I couldn't tell him that my blood had stopped. I couldn't tell him about the gas in my blood. Those were inside symptoms, not outside symptoms. I knew on some intuitive level that my blood stopping at the word *diabetes* wasn't a symptom Dad could work with. There'd be questions. Plus my blood actually stopped about a minute before the word. Hard to explain.

In fact there was nothing that could be said between myself and Dad about what had happened to me in the theater. So it was the same as nothing happening. That was the second time.

The third time was two weeks later. A Sunday night in February. I climbed into my narrow bed in my narrow room at Dad's place. I was reading *Ivanhoe*. The old Signet Classic paperback. There was a painting of a joust on the cover. A lot of red in the painting, I remember that. But not from bleeding knights like you'd expect. The knights were whole. The red was in the atmosphere. I sat up in my bed with my pillow propped against the wall and opened the book and started to read. It was probably ten fifteen or so. I usually read for a little while before falling asleep.

At a certain point early in the first chapter I became aware that I was having or was about to have a heart attack. As long as I kept reading I didn't have to think about this too much. When you're reading, the words of the book borrow the voice in your head. Words need a voice. The voice they use when you read is your voice. It's the voice your thoughts talk in. So if you give the voice to the book, your thoughts have no voice. They have to wait for paragraphs to end. They have to hold their breath until the chapter breaks.

So the lords and ladies went to the joust, and the Saxon guy threw meat to his dog in his hall, and the other Saxon guy ran away, and the Jewish guy spoke to his daughter, and I was having a heart attack, and the Knight Templar looked down from atop his war horse. He had an evil look in his eye.

I read at a medium pace. Too fast and the voice in your head can't keep up with the words. That's what your thoughts are waiting for. They catch the voice and flood your head with news of the catastrophe unfolding in your body.

But if you read too slow then it's not just the chapter breaks you have to watch out for. Now you've got holes and gaps between the words. Maybe in some situations that's a good thing. You can savor the words. The words come swaddled with silence, like expensive truffles, each one separate, while cheap chocolates are packed next to one another with their sides touching.

In a reading situation like mine you want the words packed

together with their sides touching. Because silence isn't delicate truffle-swaddling in that situation. It's heart-attack holes. It's not even silence. Every second the book isn't talking your thoughts are talking, urgently, telling you about this heart attack you're either having or about to have.

So I read at a medium pace. A constant, medium pace. I developed a technique where I'd read over the chapter breaks, and run the paragraphs together. I didn't pause. Sometimes I'd feel myself speeding up—the voice in my head began slipping on words. But I didn't lose it. I slowed down. Not too much. I kept the pace medium.

By chapter three I had it down cold. I was a genius at reading *Ivanhoe* by chapter three. I doubt it's ever been read so well. It had a voice all to itself, with no interruptions, and no breaks, for the entire length of the book. How often has that happened in the history of *Ivanhoe*? The whole time I was reading I never even found out whether I was actually having the heart attack or just about to have it. That's how good an *Ivanhoe* reader I got to be. The very next thought would have told me. But the next thought never came.

I suspended the heart attack in *Ivanhoe*. Like when you shake a solution of oil and vinegar. As long as you shake it, the oil and vinegar are suspended in one another. When you stop, they separate. So long as I read *Ivanhoe* my heart attack stayed suspended in the story.

I didn't stop reading. I didn't go to the bathroom. I didn't change my position. I didn't look at the clock. We went through the hours like that. Me, the Saxon lord, the Jewish guy, the heart attack, and the Knight Templar. We moved through eleven p.m. like that. In suspension. Midnight. one a.m. two a.m. three a.m. And then the legendary, unseen hour. four a.m.

I heard Dad get up. The end of the story was very close now. Richard Coeur-de-Lion has come home. The news of his return spreads. Dad moves behind the thin wall that separates my room from his. Ivanhoe, Rowena. The sound of the shower. Rebecca! Rebecca. . . . Dad goes down the stairs and I can hear the clink of silverware. The sound of the fridge opening.

> Ivanhoe distinguished himself in the service of Richard, and
> was graced with farther marks of the royal favour. He might

have risen still higher but for the premature death of the heroic Coeur-de-Lion, before the Castle of Chaluz, near Limoges.

At 4:35 a.m. *Ivanhoe* ended. I put down the book. I put on my
pants and pulled on my sweater. Then I walked downstairs and
told Dad that I was having a heart attack.

At the emergency room they told me what I was actually having
was a panic attack.

"A panic attack?" I repeated.

The bright fluorescence of the hospital room shone on red and
black medical devices. Shone on my hands, which were crossed on
my lap. They looked more like things than ever.

Dad welcomed the news.

"A panic attack," he said. "Nothing to worry about, thank God."

The emergency room doctor nodded.

"People often think they're having a heart attack when they first
have a panic attack."

Actually it was the third time, I realized. It took three tries for
it to learn how to mimic recognizable symptoms, to make itself
public.

"What am I panicking about?" I asked.

They didn't find it easy to answer that question. To tell the
truth they didn't find it a very compelling question. In the emergency room they deal with organ failure, stab wounds. Things of
that nature. Philosophical questions about quasi-diseases give way
to the urgency of actual vivid outside-the-body blood, in large
amounts. Pulseless wrists, severed legs. Prestigious, respectable
conditions with absolutely unfakeable symptoms.

"Probably nothing," Dad ventured after a few seconds, looking
hesitantly at the doctor.

"Could be anything," said the doctor. "If it happens again,
breathe into a paper bag."

"What?"

"A paper bag," he repeated.

He explained, as best as I could understand him, that what
happens when you have a panic attack is you hyperventilate. You
breathe more and more quickly. So you have more oxygen than
carbon dioxide, and your blood vessels constrict, which causes you
to feel lightheaded. You get tingling in the extremities, and other

symptoms which can easily mimic an ignorant person's impression of what a heart attack is like.

He looked at me compassionately.

"But if you breathe into a paper bag, that will restore the carbon dioxide."

"So a paper bag cures panic attacks?" Dad asked.

The doctor paused. His beeper started to go off.

"Yes," he said. "Please excuse me."

On the way back from the hospital, Dad stopped at the grocery store to buy some paper bags. He gave me two to stuff into my backpack. Then he dropped me off at school.

"Wait," he yelled from the car as I was walking away.

I hurried back. He thrust something at me through the open window.

"Better take one more bag," he said. "In case one of them gets wet."

"My mouth's dry," I said.

"What," he said.

"It's not wet," I said. "There's no way the bag can get wet."

"What," he said.

"Okay," I said, taking the bag.

"Have a good day," he said, rolling up the window and driving off.

The regular entrance, where the bus dropped us off, was locked. So I had to go in through the main entrance. I'd never used it before. Plainly it was designed for adults. The door swung open into a corridor with what looked like a real marble floor. Expensive-looking dark-green tiles on the walls.

I crept through silently. The right side of the wall had about a hundred framed black-and-white photographs hung on it. Priests. All smiling. Facing the camera with the confidence of men who know they won't have faces for long. Now they'd all stepped out of their faces. That's what black-and-white photographs mean.

The faces hung there like rows of empty sneakers in a shop window. The priests had stepped out. Into the air, I thought. Breathing out, never breathing in. Maybe that's what it's like when you step out of your face at the end. Like the opposite of a panic attack. You breathe out more than you breathe in. Then you're out. Free.

I fingered my paper bag. What had the doctor said? A paper

bag is a device for breathing out more than you breathe in? Was that it? I wondered if other people used them. I stared at the wall of priests. Huffing their own carbon dioxide in a paper bag right before the shutter clicked. Maybe that's how they practiced for not having a face anymore.

I was sweating in my winter coat.

Pull yourself together, I thought. I hurried down the corridor.

When I was about ten feet from the end, the door swung open. A nun I'd never seen before stepped through, glaring.

"What are you doing here?"

I blinked guiltily. Sweating in my coat, still holding the empty paper bag Dad had given me. I hadn't had a shower that morning. Greasy hair plastered my forehead.

"Get to class," she said.

She held the door open, pointing. I stuffed the bag in my pocket and shuffled forward. When I got close she stopped me. Put her long white hand on my shoulder.

"What's in your pocket?"

I gulped.

"Nothing," I said.

"Show me."

I dug the bags out.

"Just some paper bags," I said.

She squinted down through her spectacles.

"That's trash," she observed. "What are you carrying trash around in your pockets for? Throw it out."

She pointed. For a second I didn't realize what she was pointing at. It looked like a model of a spaceship. That opening on top . . . a garbage can! I clutched my bags tighter.

"I can't *throw them out*," I said. "The doctor gave them to me. I mean he prescribed them." The nun opened her mouth. She stared at me incredulously. Then she closed her mouth.

"You're planning to steal something," she said at last.

"No!" I said.

"Those bags won't be empty when you leave," she said. "Because you're going to steal something to put in them."

"No way," I said.

"I'm right, aren't I?"

"No."

"What are you going to steal?"

I didn't know how to respond.

"Three items," mused the nun. "Three items smaller than a paper lunch bag . . ."

"They aren't lunch bags," I insisted. "They're medical bags."

She ignored this.

"When you leave today," she said, stepping aside, still holding the door open, "come this way. I want to see you before you try to leave."

She made a brushing motion with her free hand, moving me along.

I walked through the door.

"Actually," she snapped at the last second, "don't come this way when you leave. Don't come through here again."

The door swung shut. I looked down at the bags, clutched in my sweating hand.

They were wet. They were soaking wet.

I went into the first bathroom I saw and tried to dry out one of the bags under a hand dryer.

Dry, I thought. *Dry, you bastard.*

An attack could spring at any second. The damn bag felt like it was shrinking under the heat. When the dryer sound died I looked at what remained in my hand. A soft warm wrinkled tan skein. Like a monkey's nut sack, I thought. I held it up. The neck was all ragged. It was going to be really difficult to get a good seal.

I began to experience a strong sensation that my body was a thing. Suddenly I felt very strongly that I had no more in common with my own body than with the gray walls of the bathroom.

Panic attack.

As soon as I put the bag to my mouth it started blowing in and out like an accordion, making an incredible sound, like a monkey was standing up and crouching down and standing up in it.

This is my breath, I thought. This invisible spastic monkey is my breath.

I got you in the bag, I thought. Trapped you. I see you now, you little monkey. Look at you jump.

After a while the monkey started to jump a little less frantically. This is what the phrase *got it in the bag* means, I reflected.

I got it in the bag.

I looked at my hand, wrapped around the neck of the bag. It

had ceased to resemble the hand of a mannequin. It felt like mine again.

Another thirty seconds and my breath was bobbing gently in the bag, as tame as you please.

Gingerly, I took the bag away from my lips. It went limp. My breath, out of the bag. Free.

I waited to see what it would do.

I took in a big gulp of air and tensed, feeling the air expanding my chest, wondering if the exhale would be normal or whether it would be just a constipated little gasp.

A good long slow breath out. I felt my shoulders relax. Looked at the deflated bag in my palm with relief, and something like affection.

It works, I thought. It's no problem.

Two days later, at lunch, I sat at my usual table with Ty and Nicole and the others. I was intensely aware of Lisa, who was sitting three tables behind me. I wondered if she was watching my back, guessing the movements of my hands as I ate my sandwich. I sat straight, tried to give my motions an unstudied insouciance.

"You have food on your face," Nicole observed.

That was when I had a false prophecy. I suddenly felt absolutely certain that Nicole was about to say *diabetes*. I stared at her. The air went into prediabetic stillness. The seconds flattened and stretched.

I stared straight at Nicole's face, waiting.

She looked back at me. "What. The fuck. Are you staring at?" she said.

Misfire. No diabetes. But I couldn't blink. Neither did she. A feeling of unbearable intimacy developed. Staring at each other, our intertwined gazes like a sliver of ice, sliced off the social glacier, floating.

"Staring contest," Ty said.

I somehow unscrewed my gaze from Nicole's spiral eyes. We both blinked. She looked at me with quick, darting glances, like her eyes were sore.

"Weirdo," she said.

"I'm zoned out," I said. "I haven't been sleeping too good."

"You should drink cough syrup for that," Ty said.

"That's your answer for everything," Nicole said.

"My dad's a doctor."

"Does he prescribe cough syrup for everything?"

"No," he said.

Nicole laughed.

"He's a bad doctor," Ty finished.

Ty was covering for me. He'd noticed the weirdness, and he was spraying the table with the small-arms fire of a stupid joke to provide cover so I could pull it together. That was the kind of thing that made you love him.

"Ty's right," I told Nicole. "Cough syrup will cure any disease."

"It's just a question," he said, "of the right dosage."

"Two tablespoons to fall asleep," I said.

"Half a bottle cures a fever," Ty said.

"And ten bottles," said Nicole, joining in, "cures diabetes."

My smile vanished.

"Cures it permanent," said Ty.

I put the smile back on my face. I got up and walked across the cafeteria toward the bathroom. The fluorescent lights were too bright. I was having trouble with my eyes. They would get stuck, as I was walking. Looking at a spot of tiled wall in front of me, I got stuck in it. Like staring at Nicole, but generalized. Inorganic surfaces became porous to my looking.

I felt my gaze vibrating inside my face. I became excruciatingly aware of the socket of my face, the socket that held my looking: the little fringe of my long hair, the faint brown circles of the frames of my glasses, the flesh-colored shadow of my nose.

My gaze turned in its socket. I couldn't control it. It spiraled into that circle of yellow tile wall. Blinking didn't cut it off. The blinks passed through it like bullets through a column of water.

It started to affect my walk. I was being pulled toward the spot of wall while I was aiming for the door twenty feet to the right. My head was turned one way, my body another. People will notice, I thought.

I fumbled for the paper bag in my pocket. Somehow I got my gaze free and pointed the right way. Quick glances, I thought. That's the key. That's the secret. Quick fast glances and the serious stare doesn't develop, the gaze doesn't get stuck.

And now I was worrying about whether it was real, whether the gaze-getting-stuck thing was even real, whether anything real had happened between me and Nicole, whether it was a weirdness that had a name, or whether it didn't have a name and would disappear on its own.

Fuck diabetes, I thought.

I made it to the bathroom. Dull mirrors and drab metal stalls passed sickly fluorescence between them. Thankfully one was empty. I kicked the seat down, then kicked the toilet paper roller hard with my foot so it sounded like I was getting a whole lot of toilet paper, masking the sound of me unwrinkling my paper bag. If people were listening, I thought, they could think I needed a lot of toilet paper. They could think I had diarrhea.

Then I had the bag to my face and the carbon dioxide was expanding my lungs and my thoughts were slowing. I forgot that my gaze was lodged in a socket of flesh, a socket of thingly substance. The frames of my glasses no longer stood out against my vision as alien.

It's just a reaction, I thought. Everyone has words that are bad for them.

My breath came slower now. The bag de- and reflated calmly and regularly, with the unurgency of a domestic machine. A lawn mower, a vacuum cleaner. I lowered the bag.

I sat on the closed toilet seat with the paper bag loose in my right hand, breathing slowly, a smile growing on my face.

After a few weeks I'd learned how to deal with the panic attacks pretty well. Just having a paper bag, knowing it was the ten-bottles-of-cough-syrup cure for panic—that gave me confidence. Plus I began to learn some little tricks. When I felt the looking getting heavy and bright in my head—when I felt the first sudden flicker of awareness at the *weirdness* of my face and skull being a *thing* that had somehow trapped this thinking-looking that was thinking *this very thought*, that was *looking* at this very *thing*, that was burrowing *out* of my head *into* something else—when I felt that, I started to move my look around.

Quick fast glances, not lingering on any object—and especially not on any face. Linger for no more than a second. That was my rule. Keep it moving. The panic would dissipate after a few minutes of that.

I wondered a little about why and how it worked. I'd wonder—what the hell is wrong with me, anyway? Who or what am I? Why, in certain moods, when my gaze rested too long on a single object, did I physically feel as if I was starting to come out of my head? Like my head was a diving board. My thinking and looking standing on the diving board. Starting to bounce a little. Blue water below. Or yellow tile wall. Or Nicole's eyes. Or a carpet, or the dull metal of a bathroom stall. The diving board: a stray strand of my dark hair, the flesh-colored outline of my nose, the frames of my glasses. My looking stood on this, started to bounce a little, testing . . .

Like I could dive out of my face, leave the empty vibrating board of my head behind. Like my looking could drip onto the porous yellow tile of the lunchroom wall, or pour into Nicole's eyes, into the capacious strangeness of her thoughts, the rooms she knew, her instinctive movements. And I'd be out there in that—gone.

I wondered if the panic was my head clenching down on my looking. The way you bite down to keep from throwing up. I wondered—but not for long, because thoughts could start the panic. Thinking about panic could turn into panic. I wasn't even sure if thinking about panic was different from panic. A philosophical question. I was a pragmatist. I kept my eyes moving. I kept a paper bag in my pocket. I was good. The majority of the time I felt fine.

The first person I told about it—besides my dad and the ER doctor—was Lisa. I'd finally gotten up the nerve to speak to her, and we got friendly. One day she asked me over to her house. I rode my bike. We were in her brother's room—he was at college—looking at records, talking about the old song "More Than a Feeling," and somehow I ended up telling her about my panic attacks. She didn't freak out or anything. She seemed interested, curious. Her questions made me realize I didn't know anything about panic attacks.

The next day I went to the library to see what I could find out. I rode my bike all the way into downtown Libertyville, a thirty-minute trip. When I got inside, I found that, as usual, the library was mostly inhabited by kids and their mothers. They were concentrated in the children's book section, which was separated from the rest of the library by soundproof glass.

As I walked by, kids pressed themselves against the glass, making horrific faces, showing what they'd do to me if they ever got loose. Their mothers hovered in the background, dim, harassed figures.

Once in a while a really little kid would streak by, half naked, waving a book, a stick, or a diaper.

I watched for a little while. It was strangely soothing. Viewed from the outside, the children's book section was more like an aquarium than a zoo, with the soupy undersea light, and the differing velocities, altitudes, and sizes of the inhabitants. Also like an aquarium, it was totally silent.

Inside the children's book section, as you were reminded whenever the door opened, it was more like a zoo.

I walked into the adult section. The inhabitants intrigued me. Furtive, awkward individuals, carrying books. I didn't know many adults who read books, except for Ty's mom, who was a feminist. I certainly didn't know any adults who went to the library.

What did the adults who came here do? What did they read? Where did they come from?

I saw a medium-size woman, of middle age, with glasses. Someone who would have been unremarkable if she'd appeared at the supermarket, or in the children's book section. But here she was carrying what appeared to be an adult book, of appropriate size and thickness, through the adult section of the Libertyville library on a Sunday.

I went to the card catalogue to look up *Panic*. There were four subjects starting with that word:

Panic Attack Prevention
Panic Disorders Chemotherapy
Panic Political Aspects
Panic Finance

I wrote down the numbers for the books and began searching the stacks. The single book the catalogue listed under the first heading was missing, perhaps checked out.

The single book under the second heading was very technical, and concerned panic disorders as a side effect of chemotherapy. It didn't really say much more about panic attacks than what the ER doctor had told me. It was mostly about different medications that seemed to prevent cancer patients from getting panic attacks, plus speculation about which parts of the brain would be affected. It didn't mention paper bags, oddly, which made me think that maybe chemotherapy panic attacks were different from the ones I had.

There were no books at all under the third heading.

There were six books under the last heading, about financial panics.

I read a little from the introductions to the two least thick financial panic books. Maybe, I thought, they called them financial panics because they're somehow like panic attacks. Or maybe the financial panics came first, and they named the other kind, the kind I had, after the financial panics, because of how they resembled them.

These books turned out to be much more illuminating and relevant than the chemotherapy book. The basic idea of a financial panic is that the stock market starts to fall, and then people start to panic. In an extraordinary passage, the author of the second book seemed to suggest that sometimes people just *thought* that the stock market was about to fall, so they panicked, and only then did the stock market actually fall.

This seemed to have potential application to my own case.

Perhaps when I felt the possibility of leaving my face and head—the possibility of falling out of my head, so to speak—I started to panic. Or was it the panic itself that caused me to feel like I was about to fall out of my head? I couldn't be sure.

Regardless, there was one important difference between my condition and financial panics. The stock market did in fact fall. But I had never fallen out of my head.

So far, I reminded myself. I hadn't fallen out *so far*. In the financial panics, the stock market always fell. "The bottom dropped out," is how one author put it. The market fell catastrophically. This was how you knew it was a panic. It was how you diagnosed the panic.

Perhaps, I thought, I hadn't actually had a real panic attack yet. Maybe I was just continually being brought to the edge of panic, suspended at a prepanic stage. Maybe the paper bags, and the other tricks I'd found—like moving my eyes around—prevented the actual panic. Real panic was falling. Catastrophic falling.

All this was suggestive, and more than a little anxiety-inducing, but it left me with more questions than answers. My condition was obviously related to financial panics, but I needed to find information about my specific kind of panic. I didn't know where else to look. I had the vague sense that the Libertyville public library had significant gaps. But surely something as important as panic attacks would be discussed somewhere, probably under some other heading altogether.

I scoured the medical section of the stacks. It wasn't easy. There was diabetes everywhere in those books. Every page was a minefield. And there was cancer, a word which was making me increasingly uncomfortable.

I was tired of standing in the stacks holding heavy reference volumes, tired of avoiding *diabetes*, cringing at *cancer*. I was about to call it a day when the non-descript woman suddenly got up from her chair.

She'd been reading from two different books. I'd surreptitiously observed her while doing my own research. Now she got up, gathered her things, and prepared to leave. I risked a searching glance as she passed. She was holding only one of the two books she'd been reading. I waited, pretending to peruse the medical book in my hand, until she'd gone through the checkout line, under the unsmiling eyes of the librarian, and out the front door.

Then I slowly, casually made my way to the chair she'd vacated. Making sure the librarian wasn't watching, I picked up the book the woman had left lying there.

The book was very old. On the spine was the title: *The Complete Works of Oscar Wilde.*

The name meant nothing to me. I opened the book. The font was a style I'd never seen before. It was quite legible, but it had a certain airy quality. The pages smelled ancient. Not ancient like old people. But not the scentless timelessness of a rock or a stone either. A third kind of oldness.

I looked at the table of contents. Then I picked a title in the middle: *Salome.* I turned to its page. Under the play's name was an ornate image of a thin woman holding a man's head on a plate.

I began to read.

The language was like nothing I'd ever encountered. A little like the Bible, maybe. But only a little. By the end of the first page, I felt excitement rising in me.

Or was it panic?

I stopped reading. I looked around—the stacks, the white walls, the lights, the distant checkout counter with the librarian laughing gaily with a patron.

Panic, I thought. Or prepanic. Whatever it was, I felt it clearly now. On the diving . . .

I looked back down at the book, and now I could see the shadow of my thought . . . the warp across the page. But then the part of the page I was looking at resolved into a word, the word dissolved into a sentence. Then I was inside the book: "You are always looking at her. You look at her too much. It is dangerous to look at people in such fashion. Something terrible may happen."

My scalp started to tingle. *Dangerous to look at people too much.* I understood! I kept reading.

"Ah! I have kissed thy mouth, Jokanaan, I have kissed thy mouth. There was a bitter taste on thy lips. Was it the taste of blood? . . . Nay; but perchance it is the taste of love . . ."

I read. I didn't stop. The play wasn't very long, but it was long enough. When I looked up again, the lights in the children's section were off. The librarian was standing behind the checkout counter, glaring at me. The clock read ten to four. The library closed at four on Sundays.

I couldn't think about that.

I thought about *Ivanhoe*, about how I'd suspended a panic attack in that book, too.

I thought about Salome. Salome dancing. I thought about Herod. I thought about Jokanaan. The man. Her lover. The headless lover.

The meaning of the play was completely clear to me. It wasn't clear to Herod, who, when Salome kisses the decapitated head, orders her killed. He thinks she's a pervert. The play's meaning probably, I thought, wasn't clear to other people who read it.

Today I am older, I have done the research, and I know that none of the many people who have written about that play have understood it.

I understood it at once.

Salome had committed no crime by having Jokanaan's head cut off. Jokanaan wasn't in that head. The play isn't the story of a beautiful woman and a man who dies. It's the story of the love between a beautiful woman and a living, headless man. A true story.

I remembered what Lisa had said, talking about my panic: "Would your head suddenly be empty? Would I be sitting here with you, and suddenly your head would like—roll back—and your tongue would loll out? Would you be out there in the air . . . *headless?*"

Prophecy, I thought.

My mouth was dry.

I went into the stacks and didn't come out until I had every book by Oscar Wilde the library possessed. I even found a biography of him.

The biography of Oscar Wilde was mostly useless. The author didn't understand *Salome*. Not one mention of panic.

But it wasn't entirely useless. It described Oscar Wilde's fascination with ancient Greece. When I mentioned this to Lisa the next day at school, she grew thoughtful. She wondered if the word *panic* had anything to do with the Greek god Pan. Then she conceived the idea of going to the school library during lunch and looking up both *Pan* and *panic* in the encyclopedia, something that had never occurred to me.

The encyclopedia entry on *panic* confirmed Lisa's intuition: the word panic is derived from the Greek *panikos*, meaning of the god Pan, and originally referred to the sudden fear aroused by the presence of the god.

We thought about this in silence.

The day was overcast; the high library windows held thin blocks of undifferentiated light. I leaned against a shelf, looking absently at the solemn, terse titles of reference works. On the spine of the *L* volume, an enormous fly moved slowly.

Lisa sat cross-legged on the narrow tile floor between the stacks, the big *P* volume spread open in her lap. Now she was reading the entry for *Pan*. Her lips moved silently. Her eyes widened.

"What?" I asked.

Disturbed by the unintentionally high volume of my voice, I peeked out nervously, glancing down the central hall to confirm what I knew I'd find: the nun at the checkout glowering in our direction. We were the only kids in the library. It was technically legal for students to be there during lunch. But it was strange. The nun's suspicions had been aroused.

Lisa gestured at the page.

"It says here that Pan was generally a happy and playful god.

But he would sometimes like let out a great *yell* that would scare everyone."

"Everyone?" I asked.

She looked up blinking.

"The shepherds, I guess, or the animals. Pan is the god of the wild."

"The wild?" I whispered.

That's when she grinned. Years later, when I was in college, I saw in a history book a picture of Stalin's daughter, Svetlana, sitting on Beria's lap and grinning exactly like Lisa did then.

Look it up. Google "Stalin's daughter Beria photograph."

Beria's eyes are obscured by the glare on his round glasses. His face is expressionless. Stalin works at a table in the background. Only Svetlana shows emotion.

She's grinning. And it's as if the entire horror and mystery of that scene—millions of people killed for no reason; Stalin probably working on a list of enemies in the background; Beria, the head of the secret police—the entire emotional range of that terrifying world is compressed into Svetlana's grin. A thousand tons of pressure per inch.

That grin is just about the only expression of human emotion from the heart of Stalinist Russia ever captured on film.

Human?

The look in Svetlana's eyes—it's not *in* her eyes, the look leaps *out* of her eyes. It's loose, free, in the air.

The expression of a wild animal. Her grin is the expression of a wild animal. Wild animals, when trapped, when caged, often frown, sometimes grin. All animals grin, if they have the right lips. The ones with the right lips grin constantly. Tigers. Apes. Hippos.

The wildness of Svetlana's grin is . . . obscene. No one could ever understand it. That's what *wild* means. I first saw that image almost exactly seven years after that afternoon with Lisa in the Carmel Catholic High School library. And I recognized it. When I said the word *wild,* Lisa lifted her head from the entry on *Pan* and grinned at me like Svetlana.

"Pan is the god," she whispered, grinning, "of the wild. Of, like, shepherds. Of wild music, and . . ." Her smile opened wider. "The Greeks considered him also to be the god of *theatrical criticism.*"

I literally fell over. I fell against the stacks and then slid to the ground, knocking half a dozen volumes down with me.

"No," I said.

"Look," she said. She was laughing now. She held the *P* volume to me, finger pointing. I was collapsed on the floor amid a heap of books. When she lifted the *P* volume from her lap I saw her white panties, a curl of dark hair at the edge.

I tore my eyes away, stared at the sentence she pointed to, not understanding. Over a slow second it resolved: "In addition, the Greeks considered Pan to be the patron god of theatrical criticism."

"*Salome*'s a play," Lisa said slowly. "You interpreted the *meaning* of the play, which is the meaning of *panic*. You did *theatrical criticism* on *Salome* to understand *panic*, which comes from the god *Pan*, and *Pan* is the *god* of *theatrical criticism*."

"What are you two doing on the floor?" said the nun.

We looked up, into the light. The camera clicked. Lisa, with her wild smile, me with my round glasses full of blank light, my face like a mask.

When I got home, I got out my unused geometry notebook and began writing down the characteristics of panic. They were fresh in my mind:

1. Light too bright.
2. Something's wrong.
3. Tingling in the fingers and toes.
4. Faster heartbeat.
5. Faster breathing.
6. Eyes moving around a lot.
7. The feeling that everything is strange.
8. The feeling that material objects are strange. And alien. They've always been horribly strange and alien, but only now am I really seeing it. Now is the *first time* I'm really seeing it, and it doesn't feel like it's just me, it doesn't feel like it's just a feeling, it's more than a feeling. These . . . *things.*
9. The conviction that my body is a thing. My hands. My nose.
10. Eyes starting to stick in things.
11. The fringe of body around my looking getting very bright.
12. Very alien.
13. The feeling that I could come out of my body. My head, in particular.
14. That my looking/thinking could pour or leap out.

15. Wonder where thoughts come from.
16. Wonder what looking is.
17. Afraid of what's next.

What is it? I wondered, looking at the list. Is this a disease? It felt strange to think of panic as a disease. Because each panic attack gave me the very clear sense that I was *seeing* and *understanding* things for the first time, things I'd never seen or understood before. This was symptom number seven on my list.

Of course, part of me always knew this was wrong. *I've felt this way before*, part of me knew, *this is just another panic attack, time to get out the paper bag.* With déjà vu, you feel like something has happened before, but you rationally know it hasn't. A panic attack is the opposite. Even today, when one strikes, I rationally know it has happened before, but it doesn't feel like it. It takes a little while, and sometimes a long while, for me to accept that what's happening isn't happening for the first time.

And it is taking me a *very* long while to accept that what the panic attack is showing me isn't real, that there isn't something basically strange and magic and horrible and impossible about being here, being in *this*.

Because a panic attack doesn't feel like a panic attack. It feels like insight.

If/Then

FROM *New Letters*

I

We hear the horse before we see her. At the echo of hooves on packed dirt, we turn to glimpse a brown and cream mare galloping toward the split rail fence separating corral from pasture. She moves with the recklessness of the untethered and of the spooked. Although we can't be sure, we sense that none of this should be happening. It is the first day of the new decade, and our thoughts are about the future, about what will happen, what could happen, and most especially of what we want to happen. The horse jumps, and we stop marking the seconds. When she leaps, it is in defiance of gravity. She becomes suspended in time. At this moment, she will jump/is jumping/has jumped.

II

The year I turned four Mt. St. Helens came alive. To the rest of the country, the eruption spanned a day, but to those of us who lived within sight of the volcano, the earthquakes and ashy expulsions lasted most of the year, from early spring to late fall of 1980. My siblings and I tried to make snowballs from the ash that periodically fell from the sky. Our father stored water in milk jugs and bought a second shotgun. He called a family meeting and showed us the space underneath the staircase where we should go if the mountain had a second cataclysmic explosion. We practiced getting there quickly—at first in the daytime, later after being woken from sleep, and later still blindfolded and crawling.

I sometimes joke that this was my first apocalypse. In truth, it is the first memory I have of my father's particular fixation on the end of the world. In the years to come, he will make preparations for our family to survive a number of potential apocalypses: Halley's comet, planet X, the new world order, Y2K, and others. It's taken me most of my adult life to understand that my father sees the collapse of civilization as a game he can win. He turned seventy-four this year and he still talks about the world ending like my husband talks about the Mets winning another pennant. It hasn't happened yet, but it will.

III

The horse's name is Scar, and she hasn't yet jumped. It's late December and my family is at the Southern Cross Ranch in Georgia because we want to give our two teenagers an adventure—a way to get them out of their routines and off their electronics. I'm trying to create memories of a childhood I wished I'd had. We're also here because it's affordable and half a day's drive from our home in Tennessee.

We arrive during a daylong downpour. The depressions along the property's fence line have filled with water, and the oversize puddles attract ducks, geese, and other small birds. They are surrounded by the horses, some of whom are tucked under the handful of trees in the pasture. Most of them appear indifferent to the weather and are grazing or galloping.

"Look at all the horsies," I say, as if my children are still toddlers.

The sixteen-year-old rolls her eyes. The fourteen-year-old takes his headphones out and says, "What?"

Sometimes I think it is the only word he knows.

"We're here," my husband says, putting the car in park.

The hotel is fronted by four Doric columns and a large brick staircase. It is located just east of Atlanta and bills itself as a "dude ranch experience wrapped in southern hospitality." The seventeen guest rooms lean heavily into accouterments of the mythologized American west. We're staying in the Iroquois room. There is no room dedicated to the Muscogee, who inhabited this bit of land in Madison, Georgia, before the colonizers arrived.

Although most of us learn about the history of the Wild West and Reconstruction as two separate social studies units, they cover roughly the same period in time: 1865 through 1900. This hotel is the only place I've seen them mashed together. It is a bit like seeing what other countries market as American food (in the Philippines spaghetti is served with diced hot dogs).

At Southern Cross, this means putting the Cattle Baron–themed room across the hall from one called Mint Julep. This hybrid approach is intentional, at least according to the brochures. The current iteration of the ranch was born in 1991 when Inge Wendling, a German woman with experience in horse breeding for the European market, decided to open a bed and breakfast/dude ranch.

We check in and then head to the stables for our first ride. Our experience with horses is limited to a handful of guided rides and, in my case, a week at a similar ranch in Arizona. Each of us is sized for a horse, outfitted with a saddle and the necessary riding gear, before being shown how to properly groom our horses.

All of us are given older mares to ride. We will keep the same horse for the duration of our five-day stay. While the guide teaches my son how to saddle his horse, Cheyenne, I brush, and then braid my horse's mane. Her name is Lovebug and she is chatty offering whinnies and snorts at the other horses around her. My son's horse answers back.

The riding trails crisscross the more than 200 acres of woods and pastures that make up the ranch. The trail guide tells us that because it's muddy we won't be able to canter, but that if we show strong horsemanship we'll be able to go out without a guide for the rest of our stay. It feels like a dangerous idea—to let four people who've barely ridden out on their own. I mention something about maybe getting lost and our guide laughs.

"Let the horse lead and she'll take you right back to the barn."

Behind me, my son is singing. His voice has started to change and it makes me think about how close we are to having raised adults. They are capable of surviving without me.

IV

The key to surviving an apocalypse is to see it coming. The volcano was my first lesson in the language of end times. My second came several years later when I was in fourth grade. For most of my childhood, my father worked in elevator maintenance. He never brought his work home with him, but on some weekends he was on-call. This meant that if someone got stuck on an elevator, or the moving sidewalk stopped moving on a busy Saturday at the airport, he'd be called to come and fix it. When this happened, he'd often take one of us older kids with him. It was called "keeping him company."

Most of my memories of these times with my father are images: playing in the clothing racks at department stores, the particular smell of hospital basements, the rudeness of airport travelers when inconvenienced. Other memories are mere impressions: the chill of the night air and the empty parking garage as I sort through the tools in the back of my father's pickup truck, or how small he looked at the bottom of a machine pit in his gray work uniform.

The only trip I recall with any accuracy is one we took to Montgomery Park during winter break. The building had an atrium with a view of the sky, and despite the light pollution and the glare, you could see the night sky and the moon. I saw it on that trip, and again years later when I was there for my senior prom. Space took up much of my imagination that year—in school, we were following Sharon Christa McAuliffe's journey to becoming the first teacher/astronaut and learning about Halley's comet, which would arrive in October of that year.

I asked him why the moon had seemed to follow us as we drove along the Willamette River that night. I don't think he answered me. Instead he started to talk about his belief that what happens in the sky will tell us if the end of the world is close. His exact words are mixed up in my memory with all the conversations that came after it, and my own ideas of the stars in motion. That year I'd been to the planetarium and seen Sagittarius come alive and shoot his arrow at the bright red heart of the scorpion. And so, as he talked, I pictured the planets, the moon, and the stars as animated figures moving across the sky.

While he worked on the escalators in the upper machine pit, he continued to explain how planets, solar eclipses, and comets had foretold the end of every great civilization. I handed him wrenches, screwdrivers, and machine oil. At one point he brought up the moon, telling me that when it turned to blood we would know it was the beginning of the end. For the rest of the night I stared through the glass atrium at the moon and pictured it lique-fying. I closed my eyes and saw it drip down the night sky as if it were a painting.

When I returned to school that January, my class watched the spaceship Challenger, with our teacher/astronaut aboard, explode into smoke. Our teacher unplugged the television and rolled it out the classroom door without mentioning what we'd seen. I closed my eyes and saw the moon streak the sky with blood.

V

The rain lifts on our third day at the ranch. We arrive at the barn to find a large gray cat perched on one of the hitching posts. She is swishing her tail and watching a red foal run the circumference of the paddock in front of where we saddle the horses. From inside the barn we hear a great commotion—a horse moving angrily around whinnying loudly. We retrieve our assigned horses from the corral and tether them. My horse, Ladybug, talks to the foal as I use the curry comb to brush the dirt from her neck, back, sides and hindquarters. I watch my children and husband do the same for their horses.

My daughter is smitten with the foal, who runs as if he's just discovered he has legs. He throws his head back and then stops mid gallop. He looks wet. From inside the barn we hear the sound of hooves stomping the ground and kicking at the stall door. My son and I exchange glances, as if to say somebody's in trouble. A moment later, one of the trail guides comes around the corner and we ask about the commotion.

"Separation anxiety," she says, and checks the cinch on my hus-band's horse.

"What's the horse's name?" my daughter asks, indicating the foal in the paddock.

"That's Spartan," the guide says, and then tells us that the horse is three months old.

I ask if it is his mother in the barn—the horse making all of the noise.

"Not exactly," she says, as she finishes with my husband's horse and moves on to help my son. She explains the story as we mount our horses in preparation for our ride.

Spartan's mother had come to the ranch as a surrender. She was an older mare who hadn't been well cared for, and so the owners of the ranch put her in one of the far pastures to fatten up. At the time no one had any idea she was pregnant. A few months later they found her with the red foal. The mother ignored him and refused to feed him, and so the workers brought the foal back. Peaches, who'd never given birth, had immediately adopted him. They'd been staying in the same stall ever since.

My husband says it didn't seem like they should be apart. The guide agrees and tells us that they were worried Spartan was running a fever because he was all sweaty, but when they took him out and took his temperature, they saw that he'd just peed all over himself. They were letting him run around while they cleaned the stall.

Even after our horses are saddled and ready for the trail, we stay and watch Spartan frolic. Our horses are patient, occasionally flicking their tails at the flies that have come out with the sun. Peaches never stops protesting her adopted foal's absence from her stall. I think about the way that baby horses arrive in the world ready to run. Years later, I hear our poet laureate, Ada Limón, read about the phenomenon in "What I Didn't Know Before." It is a poem about love and recognition, and in it she observes that a newborn horse does not exist in liminal spaces, like a baby, but is a "beast hellbent on walking, scrambling after/the mother."

Children are not horses. They arrive and require you to keep them alive for longer than you think is possible. Not only do they inhabit liminal spaces, but they drag the whole family in with them—all of us existing in stairways, doorways, bridges.

VI

I spent much of my adolescence waiting for the moon to turn to blood while watching my father stockpile food, fuel, bullets, and medicine. As a family, we learned to start a fire without matches, to purify water with iodine, to snare a rabbit, and dozens of other survival skills. I didn't take to it, but I see now that it was his way of keeping us safe. My father isn't a hugger. He gave us his love by making sure we had the skills needed to survive without him. He bought a 500-gallon propane tank so we'd have heat. He bought a 500-gallon water tank so we wouldn't go thirsty. When we survived the end of the world, then we would know we were loved.

In addition to survival supplies, my father also collected books about all the potential ways the world could end. This was before the internet, and so I have memories of scouring flea markets, Powell's used bookstore, and garage sales for titles that held prophecy, speculation, and research about the end times. He collected omens from these books and traded them as if they were stock tips. It was harder to do before the internet, but there were plenty of people who shared his interest. It is quite human to want to know the future. Prediction is a hedge against failure, pain, and loss. When faced with uncertainty, our natural response is to seek knowledge.

Consider that many of our earliest texts are attempts to know not only what an event or incident means, but also what it predicts. *The Compendia of Ominous Phenomena*, an early Babylonian text preserved in archives and libraries throughout Mesopotamia, is an encyclopedia of predictions that ascribe meaning to observable experiences in our universe. These texts, written in Sumerian, apply the if/then construction to an exhaustive list of omens. For instance: if a pig carries a reed and enters a man's house, the owner will become rich, or when the moon disappears, evil will befall the land.

These are the types of omens my father collected. They could be categorized: signs from dreams, signs from the sky, signs as natural disasters, signs divined from animal behavior, and so on. Over the years, the catalyst for the apocalypse has changed, but my father's list of omens has remained the same.

Consider the moon turning red. A so-called blood moon happens when the earth passes in front of the sun. Our planet, acting like an umbrella, casts a shadow over the moon. If this happens during the full lunar phase, it will appear to us as if a red shadow is overtaking the normally white-appearing moon. The most recent one, in November 2022, was the last of a series of four consecutive blood moons known as the tetrad, which became the subject of a number of end of the world predictions.

During my teenage years, I fought with my father about his omens. I pushed back against learning to can the garden tomatoes and how to butcher a chicken. I refused to participate in his middle of the night emergency drills. Whenever he'd try to start a conversation with me about planet X, I'd yell at him and leave the room. It took me a long time to figure out why his fascination with the end of the world made me so angry.

The year I graduated from college, *Deep Impact* came out. It's one of two late 1990s movies about an asteroid hitting (and potentially destroying) the Earth. In the movie, they refer to the threat as an Extinction Level Event or E.L.E. I won't defend the film as an artistic masterpiece, but I will say that it's pretty great for a movie meant to entertain. What makes it great to me is a scene near the end of the movie when everyone thinks all hope is lost. The news anchor (Tea Leoni) who'd broken the story to the public and been the face of efforts to save the earth rushes to be with her estranged father. As the asteroid is hurtling toward them, they reconcile and then walk out and watch as part of the space rock impacts off the coast of Maryland. The last thing they see, the camera sees, is a flash and then a wall of water. The scene cuts away and we're left with the impression that they were obliterated.

I've watched the movie a dozen times. Each time I relive the relief I experienced when I saw it on the big screen. I don't have to survive the end of the world. If I know when and how the world will end, then I can plan for obliteration. For a long time, at least until I had my own children, I found the thought comforting. Having children complicated my feelings about survival, and the obligations we have to those we bring into this world.

VII

It is the last night of 2019 and we're gathered around a gas fireplace on one of the ranch's many porches. This is part of my plan—to sit under the stars and talk with our children about the future. Earlier that night we'd watched Baz Luhrmann's *The Great Gatsby* because I wanted them to be thinking about the 1920s as one way the world could be. Luhrmann's version of Fitzgerald's book lays bare the pain of that great American tragedy of wanting to move beyond the life you'd been born into. It works. On this night, our teenagers have come up for air from their long turmoil of hormones and inexplicable rage against us to offer thoughts about the next decade. We've raised these children on promises about living in a better world than we had. They speak of college, of careers, of relationships. I wish these wants—expressed with such tentativeness—into the world for them, ahead of them.

Above us is a sky bright with stars. I think about how the name of the ranch is also the name of a constellation. It can't be seen from where we are, but if we were in the Southern Hemisphere, we'd be able to see the cross shape and the two stars that form a line that points to the South Pole. I tell them this and about using the sky as navigation. They've grown cold.

The walk back to our rooms takes us along the fenced horse pasture. In the light given off from the hotel, we make out their shapes. Another family has made a fire in a pit and is roasting marshmallows. We hear the horses out in the dark, breathing and talking to one another. They're unsaddled and have the choice of who to be near and where to stand as they nibble on grass and swish their tails. The flies have gone to bed. My husband makes a joke about them being off the clock.

I tell the kids and my husband to pick out a star and make a wish for the next ten years. There are so many stars. This type of wishing is my version of prayer now that I do not pray. I look for a star to send my wish. There is a bright red one near the dipper. I choose it because I think I will be able to find it easily in the years to come. Of course, what I ask of it is not one wish but a decade's worth of wishes. I am searching for signs that my anxious daughter will overcome her anxiety. That my son, queer in a part of the country where it is dangerous to be out, will be safe and find happiness in a relationship. That I keep writing. That I will stop writing. That I go back to church or find faith again. That my marriage is okay. That I'm saving enough money. That the world will get better.

VIII

As a parent, I continue my father's tradition of collecting omens. There exists in my brain an entire filing cabinet of if/then events. The Babylonians eventually ran out of existing omens to compile. In an effort of preparation that my father would admire, the diviners began to list all possible omens and their subsequent meanings. One report of the text describes the process as "discovering pre-existent information written into the fabric of the world by the gods." The results feel exhaustive in the best sort of way: If a pig carries a palm frond, then a storm will rise. If a pig carries a string plaited from date palm fibers, then there will be famine in the land. If a pig carries a large reed bundle and plays with it, then there will be a storm, and so on.

My own omen making is a form of magical thinking. If there is a double rainbow at my daughter's soccer game, then she will score a goal. If a tree limb falls in my driveway, then I should cancel the day's events. If I wake with a headache, then someone in my family will be sick. If I say the thing I want aloud, then I will never get it.

There have been forty-five blood moons since I was born. The next one will be in late March. The idea of these omens happening over and over again makes me think that although one lunar eclipse might eventually herald the end of civilization, what it portends is more likely to be smaller in nature. What if each blood moon were a sign of someone's personal apocalypse: a divorce, a job loss, sickness? One of the many multitudes within ourselves ending and making way for the next iteration. Our understanding of the word apocalypse as belief in an imminent end of the present world dates only to 1858. Before that, the word meant to uncover, disclose, reveal.

IX

Scar jumps on New Year's Day. It is busy at the ranch—in addition to the handful of us staying there, about twenty people have arrived just for the horse ride. It surprises me when I see these day visitors. The pace of our stay had been leisurely, and now there is a frantic energy in the barn. We had started that morning with our own frantic energy: my daughter woke with a stomach bug. To keep our day from going awry, we've left her in her room to sleep and coerced our son into riding without earbuds.

We check in and then start the work of retrieving our horses and getting them ready for a ride. All of us are in the process of saddling our horses when we hear the beating of hooves against packed dirt. We watch as Scar clears the fence. She takes two more strides and then falls onto her side. It is a long moment before anyone moves. The trail guide helping us with our saddles reties the reins of my husband's horse to the hitching post and runs inside the barn.

My horse and my son's horse strain against their tethers. They are talking to each other and to the horse who has fallen. On several occasions she tries to get on her feet, but each time she collapses before she stands. Two of the trail guides kneel and speak to the horse. We all are waiting to be told what to do. The horse lies directly next to the entryway into the woods.

The owner's son arrives on a golf cart. We've seen him intermittently throughout the week—he'd broken his leg in a horse-related accident and had not done much hands-on work with us or our horses. He has his wife with him and soon the two of them have helped saddle the rest of the horses and are moving the nearly thirty riders to the pasture next to the ranch.

A step stool appears and we use it to mount our horses. While we are waiting for my husband to mount, a woman arrives in a small hatchback. Through the murmurs of the crowd we learn this is the veterinarian. She and the owner's son take the golf cart to the fallen horse. While this happens, we are told by the wife to take the long way around to the wooded path.

Our family regroups and the three of us explore the side yard. We guide the horses along the fence line and then up and over several small mounds at the far edge of the property. There are unsaddled horses who gallop past us and once or twice one of our horses starts to canter. The dogs, small blue heelers, follow and try to move the horses to where they think they should go.

As we take the back path to the wooded trails, my horse pricks her ears. She tenses and starts to move quicker. I don't know if she's seen the barn and is done with me and done with riding, or if there is another reason, but she moves quickly from a jog to a canter. My ineffectual yelling and pulling on the reins does nothing. I think about how much it would hurt to fall, so I lower my head and try to move my body with hers. I figure she is old and will stop running soon.

After five or so minutes, we round the bend to the barn and she finally slows. I catch my breath and get her to stop so I can get off. As I land on the ground, she lifts her head and lets out a long snort and then shakes her head before whinnying. I see what she has seen. The horse who had jumped the fence lies still. Scar is dead.

My horse continues to talk to her as if she were not.

A few minutes later, my husband and son arrive. They are bewildered by my sudden swift ride and have followed me at a much slower pace. We agree to be done riding for the day and because my hands are still shaking, my husband helps me with my horse. As he leaves us to put the horses away, I stand facing my son, telling him about the adventure of riding an almost galloping horse. Over my son's shoulder, I see a forklift trundle past. At first I don't register what it is doing, but then my eyes see that Scar hangs limp across the machine's tines. Her head lolls and her back legs hang uneven.

"Don't look," I say to my son.

He looks. Our memories will be linked by this image. He will make meaning from it, and I will make meaning. We watch until the machine and horse have moved beyond our line of sight. I try to find a way to tell him how to navigate this moment, this image, this omen.

X

Most people don't know that in addition to rotating once every twenty-four hours, the earth rotates along another axis every 26,000 years. This "precision of the equinoxes" as it was called for centuries means that we do not see the same night sky as our ancestors. When the ancient Greeks looked at the sky, they could see the stars that made up the Southern Cross or Crux constellation. Today nobody above the equator can see those particular stars. But in the year 30,000 should this ranch still stand, should the land it is on not be under water or ice or laid to waste by earthquakes or tornados, visitors will be able to look up into the sky and see the Southern Cross.

XI

Later that afternoon, we return to the barn. My daughter is feeling better and wants to visit the mini horses and the foal. She and my son bring carrots. While they move around the barn and talk to the horses in their stalls, I talk with the groom about the dead horse. She tells me the vet who put the horse down said that a toxin had traveled from her liver to her brain. The diagnosis explained the suddenness and the violence of her escape from the corral.

It's taken me a long time to write this story. As I look over my notes from our conversation, I am surprised to find that Scar is the horse who had given birth in the field and abandoned her foal. I think that can't be right. It is too neat. And maybe it isn't right. It is entirely possible that in the years between then and now and the various notes I jotted on paper and in my phone that the truth of the story became garbled.

We talk for a while longer and then she suggests that the children might like to get closer to Spartan and Peaches. She lets the foal out and my children help feed her. Except for the dead horse, it has been a good trip. My daughter learned to play pool after dinners in the game room. She has taken to riding, like she takes to everything with ease and competence. Scrolling through the pictures of her from that week, I see that on the back of her horse, Payday, she looks as if she belongs in a Ralph Lauren ad. She and her brother smile without even knowing it as they pet the red foal. My husband takes their photos and smiles at me. I consider that the omen might be the foal and its adopted mother and not the dead horse.

XII

The world shuts down less than three months after we leave the ranch. The image of the horse being carried to her burial ground by a forklift is behind my eyes more often than I would like. I see it in my dreams—suspended in air as it jumps, then hanging limply from the tines of the forklift. The hope we had for this new decade dissipates as if it were alcohol rubbed across every surface touched by a stranger.

During those long weeks in March 2020, I look at the night sky and find the star I sent my decade's worth of dreams to, then use an app on my phone to find its name: Arcturus. It is the brightest star in the northern celestial hemisphere and takes its name from a Greek word (Arktouros) which means bear guard. The mythology says that Zeus created the star to protect the nearby constellations, Arcas and Callisto (Ursa Major and Ursa Minor).

In April a wren makes a nest in a bike helmet in our garage.

There are deals I make with myself. If all of the eggs become baby birds, if all of the birds fly away, if. Lately I've been dreaming of the apocalypse, but instead of four horsemen, four bears arrive to herald the end of times. They argue about which one is minor and who is major.

In this new decade time has lost all meaning. One year has become three and all of it seemed to happen all at once. Our world will end/is ending/has ended.

JENNIFER SENIOR

The Ones We Sent Away

FROM *The Atlantic*

THIS STORY STARTS, of all things, with a viral tweet. It's the summer of 2021. My husband wanders into the kitchen and asks whether I've seen the post from the English theater director that has been whipping around Twitter, the one featuring a photograph of his nonverbal son. I have not. I head up the stairs to my computer. "How will I find it?" I shout.

"You'll find it," he tells me.

I do, within a matter of seconds: a picture of Joey Unwin, smiling gently for the camera, his bare calves and sandaled toes a few steps from an inlet by the sea. Perhaps you, too, have seen this photo? His father, Stephen, surely did not intend it to become the sensation it did—he wasn't being political, wasn't playing to the groundlings. "Joey is 25 today," he wrote. "He's never said a word in his life, but has taught me so much more than I've ever taught him."

That this earnest, heartfelt tweet has been liked some 80,000 times and retweeted more than 2,600 is already striking. But even more so is the cascade of replies: scores of photographs from parents of non- and minimally verbal children from all over the world. Some of the kids are young and some are old; some hold pets and some sit on swings; some grin broadly and some affect a more serious, thoughtful air. One is proudly holding a tray of Yorkshire pudding he's baked. Another is spooning his mom on a picnic blanket.

I spend nearly an hour, just scrolling. I am only partway through when I realize my husband hasn't steered me toward this outpouring simply because it's an atypical Twitter moment, suffused with the sincere and the personal. It's because he recognizes that to me, the tweet and downrush of replies *are* personal.

He knows that I have an aunt whom no one speaks about and who herself barely speaks. She is, at the time of this tweet, seventeen years old and living in a group home in upstate New York. I have met her just once. Before this very moment, in fact, I have forgotten she exists at all.

It is extraordinary what we hide from ourselves—and even more extraordinary that we once hid her, my mother's *sister,* and so many like her from everyone. Here are all these pictures of nonverbal children, so pulsingly alive—their parents describing their pleasures, their passions, their strengths and styles and tastes—while I know nothing, absolutely nothing, of my aunt's life at all. She is a thinning shadow, an aging ghost.

When I first discovered that my mother had a younger sister, I reacted as if I'd been told about the existence of a new planet. This fact at once astonished me and made an eerie kind of sense, suddenly explaining the gravitational force that had invisibly arranged my family's movements and behaviors for years. Now I understood why my grandfather spent so many hours in retirement as a volunteer at the Westchester Association for Retarded Citizens. Now I understood my grandmother's annual trips to the local department store to buy Christmas presents, although we were Jewish. (At the time, my aunt lived in a group home where the residents were taken to church every Sunday.)

I now even understood, perhaps, the flickers of melancholy I would see in my grandmother, an otherwise buoyant and intrepid personality, charming and sly and full of wit.

And my mom: Where do you start with my mom? For almost two years, she had a sister. Then, at the age of six and a half, she watched as her only sibling, almost five years younger, was spirited away. It would be forty years before she saw her again.

Strange how seldom we think about who our parents were as people before we made their acquaintance—all the dynamics and influences that shaped them, the defining traumas and triumphs of their early lives. Yet how are we to know them, really, if we don't? And show them compassion and understanding as they age?

I was twelve when I learned. My mother and I were sitting at the kitchen table when I wondered aloud what I'd do if I ever had a disabled child. This provided her with an opening.

Her name is Adele.

She had red hair, I was told. Weird: Who in our family had red hair? (Actually, my great-grandmother, but I knew her only as a white-haired battle-ax dedicated in equal measure to her soap operas and cigarettes.) She is *profoundly retarded*, my mother explained. There had been no language revolution back then. This was the proper descriptor, found in textbooks and doctors' charts. My mother elaborated that the bones in Adele's head had knitted together far too early when she was a baby. So, a smaller brain. It was only when I met her sixteen years later that I understood the physical implications of this: a markedly smaller head.

It was staggering to meet someone who looked just like my mother, but with red hair and a much smaller head.

My grandmother told my mother that she instantly knew something was different when Adele was born. Her cry wasn't like other babies'. She was inconsolable, had to be carried everywhere. Her family doctor said nonsense, Adele was fine. For an entire year, he maintained that she was fine, even though, at the age of one, she couldn't hold a bottle and didn't respond to the stimuli that other toddlers do. I can't imagine what this casual brush-off must have done to my grandmother, who knew, in some back cavern of her heart, that her daughter was not the same as other children. But it was 1952, the summer that Adele turned one. What male doctor took a working-class woman without a college education seriously in 1952?

Only when my mother and her family went to the Catskills that same summer did a doctor finally offer a very different diagnosis. My grandmother had gone to see this local fellow not because Adele was sick, but because *she* was; Adele had merely come along. But whatever ailed my grandmother didn't capture this man's attention. Her daughter did. He took one look at her and demanded to know whether my aunt was getting the care she required.

What did he mean?

"That child is a microcephalic idiot."

My grandmother told this story to my mother, word for word, more than four decades later.

In March of 1953, my grandparents took Adele, all of twenty-one months, to Willowbrook State School. It would be many years before I learned exactly what that name meant, years before I learned what kind of gothic mansion of horrors it was. And my mother, who didn't know how to explain what on earth had happened, began telling people that she was an only child.

It is the fall of 2021. My aunt lives in a uniquely unlovely part of upstate New York, a dreary grayscape of strip malls and Pizza Huts and liquor stores. But her group home is a snuggery of overstuffed furniture, flowers, family photos; the outside is framed by an actual white picket fence. It is precisely the kind of home you would hope that your aunt, abandoned to an institution through a cruel accident of timing and gravely misplaced ideas, would find herself in as she ages. When my mother and I arrive to see her, she is waiting for us at the door.

The drive to this house was ninety minutes from where my folks live in northern Westchester. Yet the car ride yielded just twenty-nine minutes and fifteen seconds of recorded conversation with my mother. This could partly be explained by the unfamiliar directions in her GPS, but still: Here she was, visiting the sister she hadn't seen since 1998—and then only twice before that, in 1993, shortly after her father died—and she had almost nothing to say about where we were headed or what the weather was like inside her head. She seemed far more interested in telling me about the necklaces she was making and selling to support Hadassah, one of her favorite charities. Whether this was out of anxiety or enthusiasm, I didn't know.

"Are you feeling nervous about seeing her?" I finally asked.

"No."

"Really? Why not? *I'm* nervous."

"Why are you nervous?"

"Why are you *not* nervous?"

"Because I made peace with my separation from her many, many years ago."

My grandparents, for their part, had visited my aunt almost every week, at least when she was young. Even after my grandmother moved to Florida, she made an effort to visit once a year. When I was in my late teens or early twenties, I remember my mother telling me that Adele never knew or understood who my grandmother was, not ever. This fact stuck with me—and hit me especially hard when I became a mother myself. As we were humming along the Taconic State Parkway, I reconfirmed: Adele didn't recognize her own mother?

"No," she said. "She didn't know her. She didn't understand the concept of a mother."

But when my mother last saw her sister, in 1998, it wasn't my grandmother who accompanied her. It was me. The whole trip had been at my instigation, just like this one. I'd mentioned that I was interested in meeting my aunt, and my mother had stunned me then, just as she'd stunned me now, by saying, "Why don't we go together?"

And what do I remember of that singular day? How uncharacteristically animated and affectionate my mother was when she saw Adele, for one thing. You could almost discern the outlines of the little girl she'd been, the one who would circle Adele's crib and play a made-up game she called "Here, Baby." Also, how petite my aunt was—4 foot 8, dumpling-shaped—and how slack the musculature was around her jaw, which may have had something to do with the fact that my aunt had no teeth. She had supposedly taken a medication that had made them decay, though there's really no way to know.

But what stayed with me most from that day—what I thought about for years afterward—were the needlepoint canvases marching along the walls in Adele's bedroom. My mother and I both gasped when we saw them. My mother, too, was an avid needlepointer in those years, undertaking almost comically ambitious projects—the Chagall windows, the Unicorn Tapestries. Adele's handiwork was simpler, cruder, but there it was, betokening the same passion, the same obsession.

One other thing: my mother and I discovered that day that Adele could carry a tune—and when she sang, she suddenly had hundreds of words at her disposal, not just *yes* and *no,* the only two words we heard her speak. Again, we were amazed. For years, my mother was a pianist and studied opera; her technical skills were impeccable, her sight-reading was impeccable, her ear was impeccable. She could pick up the telephone and tell you that the dial tone was a major third.

My mother couldn't get over it—the needlepoints, the singing.

I felt like I was staring at some kind of photonegative of a twin study.

So here we are, twenty-three years later, and Adele is greeting us at the door. She is wearing a bright-red sweater. There is my mother at the door. She, too, is wearing a bright-red sweater. Adele is wearing a long, chunky beaded necklace she has recently made at her day program. And my mother, like her sister, is wearing a long, chunky beaded necklace she has recently made—not at a day program, obviously, but for Hadassah. It turns out that Adele loves making necklaces and has whole drawers of them. As, lately, does my mother.

I have a picture of the two of them standing side by side that day. I cannot stop looking at it.

Carmen Ayala, Adele's extraordinary seventy-nine-year-old care-taker, has instructed Adele to say "Hello, Rona, I love you" to my mother, a gesture that's both sweet and awkward—Adele doesn't know my mother by sight, much less by name. Still, it catches my mother by surprise, not least because it suggests that her sister's vocabulary has expanded considerably since we last saw her, when she was living in a different group home. They embrace and take seats on the couch in the living room. We try, for a time, to ask Adele basic questions about her day, without much success, though when we ask if she knows any Christmas carols—the holiday is coming up—she sings "Santa Claus Is Coming to Town" for us, and my mother replies in kind with "Silent Night." Then Adele zones out, staring at her hands. She can spend hours staring at her hands.

My mother and I start to ask Carmen and her youngest child, Evelyn—she lives nearby and knows well all three residents in her parents' home—the customary questions: How did Carmen get into this line of work? What is Adele's routine? How did Adele handle the transition to Carmen's house twenty-two years ago, after her previous caretaker retired? And although I'm interested in the answers, I find myself growing restless, thoughts of that Twitter thread pluck-ing at my consciousness. I finally blurt out: What is my aunt *like*?

Evelyn replies first. "Very meticulous," she says. "She needs things a certain way, and she will correct you the minute you do something wrong."

I stare at my mother, who says nothing. I turn back to Evelyn and Carmen and prompt them. Such as?

Her clothes have to match, they say, down to the underwear. She keeps her bed pin-neat.

"She knows where everything is at," Evelyn continues. "If we"—meaning her or any of her family members—"come here and we are washing a dish and we put it in the wrong place, she will tell us, *Nope.*"

I stare at my mother expectantly. Still nothing.

"Like, *That doesn't go there,*" Evelyn explains.

At this point, my mother pipes up. "I don't let anyone else load the dishwasher."

Finally.

"That's Adele," Evelyn says.

Arthur Miller's youngest son, Daniel, was institutionalized. He was born with Down syndrome in 1966 and sent to Southbury Training School, in Connecticut, when he was about four years old. Miller never once mentioned him in his memoir *Timebends*, and Miller's *New York Times* obituary said not one word about him, naming three children, rather than four.

Erik Erikson, the storied developmental psychologist, also put his son with Down syndrome in an institution. He and his wife, Joan, told their other three children that their brother died shortly after he was born in 1944. They eventually told all three the truth, but not at the same time. Their oldest son learned first. That must have been quite a secret to keep.

Pearl S. Buck, the Nobel Prize winner for literature and author of *The Good Earth*, institutionalized her nine-year-old daughter, Carol, likely in 1929. But Buck was different: she regularly visited her daughter, and twenty-one years later had the courage to write about her experience in *The Child Who Never Grew*.

It is remarkable how many Americans have relations who were, at some point during the past century, sequestered from public view. They were warehoused, disappeared, roughly shorn from the family tree. "Delineated" is how the Georgetown disability-studies scholar Jennifer Natalya Fink puts it, meaning denied their proper place in their ancestral lineage.

With time, we would learn the terrible toll that institutionalization took on those individuals. But they weren't the only ones who paid a price, Fink argues. So did their parents, their siblings, future generations. In hiding our disabled relations, she writes in her book *All Our Families*, we as a culture came to view disability "as an individual trauma to a singular family, rather than a common, collective, and normal experience of all families."

This is precisely what happened to Fink. When her daughter was diagnosed with autism at two and a half, Fink was devastated, despite her liberal politics and enlightened attitude toward neuro-diversity. Then she realized that the only disabled person she knew about in her family was a relative who'd been institutionalized in the early '70s. This sent her on a journey to learn more about him—and in so doing, she discovered yet another disabled family member, in Scotland. Had she known far more about them—had they been an integral part of family discussions and photo albums (and, in the case of the American relative, family events)—she would have had a far richer, more expansive understanding of her ancestry; her own child's disability would have seemed like "part of the warp and woof of our lineage," as she writes, rather than an exception.

It occurred to me that this may have been one of my uncon-scious motives in trying to get to know Adele at such a late stage of my own life, in addition to simple curiosity about a lost relative. It would be a minor act of restitution, of relineation. Without any malevolent intent, we'd all colluded in one woman's erasure. And our entire family had been the poorer for it.

Mass institutionalization wasn't always the norm in the United States. During the colonial era, people with developmental and intellectual disabilities were integrated into most communities; in the early 1800s, with the advent of asylums and special schools, American educators hoped some could be cured and quickly returned to mainstream society.

But by the late nineteenth century, it became clear that in-tellectual disabilities couldn't be vanquished simply by sending people to the right schools or asylums, and once the eugen-ics movement captured the public's imagination, the fate of the country's intellectually and developmentally disabled was sealed. "Undesirables" and "defectives" weren't just institution-alized; they became the involuntary subjects of medical exper-iments, waking from mysterious surgeries to discover that they could no longer have children.

Cue the line from *Buck v. Bell*, the infamous 1927 Supreme Court case that upheld a Virginia statute permitting the sterilization of the so-called intellectually unfit: "Three generations of imbeciles are enough."

Then the postwar era came along, with its apron-clad mothers and gray-flanneled fathers and all-around emphasis on a certain species of Americanness, a certain norm. "I'm speaking in huge generalities here," says Kim E. Nielsen, the author of *A Disability History of the United States*, "but I think that push for social conformity exacerbated the incredible shame folks had about family members with intellectual and physical disabilities." Institutionalizing such family members often became the most attractive—or viable—option. The stigma associated with having a different sort of child was too great; too often, schools wouldn't have them, state-subsidized therapies weren't available to them, and churches wouldn't come to their aid. "There were no support structures at all," Nielsen told me. "It was almost the opposite. There were *anti*-support structures."

My aunt was born in that postwar period. But I don't think my grandparents were capitulating to social pressure when they institutionalized Adele. They were simply listening to the advice of their doctors, authoritative men with white coats and granite faces who told them there was no point in keeping their daughter at home. According to my mother, my grandparents ferried Adele from one specialist to another, each declaring that she would never walk, never talk, never outgrow her diapers.

Which raised a question, on further reflection: Did my aunt's condition have a name? As we were driving along, my mother told me she didn't know; Adele had never had genetic testing.

Really? I asked. Even now? In the 2020s?

Really.

My grandparents are no longer with us. I know little of what they were told or how they felt when they were advised to send their second child away. But I imagine the script sounded similar to what a physician told Pearl S. Buck when she took Carol to the Mayo Clinic. "This child will be a burden on you all your life," he said, according to Buck's memoir. "Do not let her absorb you. Find a place where she can be happy and leave her there and live your own life." She did as she was told. But it violated every ounce of her maternal intuition. "Perhaps the best way to put it," she wrote, "is that I felt as though I were bleeding inwardly and desperately."

"The parents who institutionalized their children—they, too, are survivors of institutionalization and victims of it," Fink told me.

"They were broken by this. It was not presented as a choice, for the most part. And even when it was, the medical establishment made it seem like institutionalization was the *best* choice."

That applied to my grandmother, a tower of resilience, a woman who survived her father's suicide, a brutal knife attack by a madman in a public restroom, and breast cancer at a relatively young age. She, like Buck, bled inwardly and desperately, in the most literal sense, developing an ulcer when my mom was eleven or twelve. "Before Grandma died, she started talking about Adele, and for the first time that I can remember, she admitted that she felt terrible institutionalizing her," my mother told me as we drove. "When I reminded her that if she had not institutionalized her, nobody in the family would've had a normal life, she said, 'Yes, but she would've been with people who loved her.'"

One of the beneficiaries of that so-called normal life was, ostensibly, my mother. In his magisterial *Far from the Tree*, the writer Andrew Solomon notes that the most commonly cited rationale for institutionalization in those years was that neurotypical siblings would suffer—from shame, from attention starvation—if their disabled siblings were kept at home.

But it's more complicated than that, isn't it? My mother has never in her life uttered a cross word about her parents' decision, and she's hardly the sort to play the victim—she may have been trained as an opera singer, but she's the least divalike person I know. Yet when I asked her what it was like when Adele left the house, she reflexively confirmed Fink's hypothesis: She suffered. "It was like I lost an arm or a leg," she said.

In his second memoir, *Twin*, the composer and pianist Allen Shawn writes about the trauma of losing his twin sister, Mary, to an institution when they were eight years old. He describes her absence as "an unmourned death," which closely matches my mother's experience; he writes, too, that when she was sent away, it felt to him like a form of punishment, "an expulsion, an exile," which my mother has also recounted in melancholy detail.

But what most captured my attention was Shawn's analysis of how his sister affected his personality. "From an early age," he writes, "I intuited that there were tensions surrounding Mary and instinctively took it upon myself to continue to be the easier child and avoid worrying my parents."

That was my mother: the peerless good girl. High-achieving, rule-abiding, perfection-seeking. She skipped a grade. Until junior high, she chose practicing piano over playing with friends. In high school, she sang with the all-city chorus at Carnegie Hall.

Did she ever rebel? I asked her.

"Nah," she said. "I was a goody-goody."

To this day, my mother is the good girl. Buttoned-up, always reasonable, always in control. When hotter tempers flare around her, she defaults to a cool 66 degrees.

My mother was thrilled when her parents brought her newborn sister home. She remembers Adele scooching to different corners of her playpen to follow her as she ran in circles around it. She remembers sitting on the kitchen counter and watching my grandmother prepare bottles. She remembers my grandmother asking her to go on tiptoe into my grandparents' room to see if Adele was asleep in her crib or still fussing. When my grandmother and grandfather began their frantic circuit of New York City's specialists, wondering what could be done to help Adele, my mother had no clue that anything was the matter. Why would she? She was six years old. She'd always wanted a sibling and now she'd been gifted one. Adele was marvelous. Adele was perfect. Adele was her sister.

When my grandparents left to take Adele to Willowbrook in March of 1953, they had no idea what to tell my mother, settling eventually on the story that they were taking her sister to "walking school." My mom thought little of it. But for weeks, months, years, she kept expecting Adele to return. *When is she coming back?* she would regularly ask. *We don't know*, my grandparents would reply.

At eight, my mother one day had a sudden meltdown—became unstrung, hysterical—and demanded much more loudly to know when Adele would be returning, pointing out that it was taking her an awfully long time to learn how to walk. That was the first time she saw my grandmother cry.

I don't know, she still answered.

That same year, my great-grandmother, recently widowed, moved in with my grandparents. More specifically, she moved into my mother's room, into the twin bed that Adele was supposed to occupy. My mother was furious about having to move her things, furious that she was losing her privacy, furious that her grandmother was moving into Adele's bed. (Now she modified the question she regularly asked her parents: *Where will Adele sleep when she comes home?*

And they would always reply: *We'll figure it out when the time comes*.)
Adele never did come home, and my grandparents would never try
to have another child to fill that bed. My great-grandmother was
there to stay.

My great-grandmother: Lord. She meant well, I suppose. But
she had only a grade-school education and all the subtlety of a
flyswatter. When my mother was thirteen, my great-grandmother
told her that she had to be good enough for two children, smart
enough for two children. "She kept emphasizing that my parents
had lost a child," my mother said. The pressure was awful.

By thirteen, of course, my mother had already figured out that
something was different about her sister—and that Adele was never
coming home. She'd heard the neighborhood kids whisper. One
cruelly declared she'd heard Adele was in reform school. Con-
sciously or unconsciously, my mother began handling the situation
in her own way, volunteering in classrooms for kids with intellectual
disabilities. Two liked her so much that she started tutoring them
privately.

Yet throughout my mother's childhood, my grandparents never
once invited her to come with them to visit Adele. At first she was
told no children were allowed; by the time her parents did ask her
to join them, my mother, at that point an adult with children of
her own, said no. She felt too raw, too tender about it. She didn't
want to unloose a current of ancient hurts. My grandparents never
raised it again.

I asked if she ever sat around and just thought about Adele. "Oh,
sure," she told me. "I wonder what she would've been like if she
weren't disabled. I wonder what kind of relationship we would've
had. I wonder whether I would've had nieces and nephews. Whether
she would've had a husband, whether she would've had a good marriage, whether we would've been close, whether we would've lived
near each other . . ."

And what ran through her mind, I asked, when she set eyes on
Adele for the first time in forty years, back in 1993? "I got deprived
of having a real sibling," she said.

For weeks afterward, I thought long and hard about this particular regret. Because my aunt *was* a real sibling. But no one of my
mother's generation was told to think this way. The disabled were
dramatically underestimated and therefore criminally undercul-
tivated: hidden in institutions, treated interchangeably, decanted

of all humanity—spectral figures at best, relegated to the margins of society and memory. Even their closest family members were trained to forget them. After my mother came home from that visit, she scribbled six pages of impressions titled "I Have a Sister." As if she were finally allowing it to register. To acknowledge this clandestine part of herself.

It is painful, almost too painful, to think about how differently my mother might have felt—how different her life and my aunt's might have been—if they had been born today.

It's June 2022. I've just asked Adele how many pictures are sitting in front of me. My mother is skeptical. I ask again. "How many pictures? One . . ."

"One," she repeats.

"Two . . ." I say.

"Two, three," she finishes.

I look triumphantly at my mother.

My mother is now somewhere between skeptical and delighted. She tries herself. "How many fingers?" she asks, holding up her hand.

"Five."

There are five.

"She understands," I tell my mother.

"Well, either that or she memorized it."

I show Adele two fingers and ask how many.

"Two."

There's a reason my mother is surprised. When we visited Adele in 1998, she barely spoke at all, much less showed that she had a notional sense of quantity. (She will today show us that she can count to twelve before she starts skipping around.) She wasn't agitated back then when we saw her, not exactly. But she wasn't relaxed. A transfixing report about Adele, sent to my mother not that long ago, suggests that one of the reasons she may be more alert now—and possesses a larger vocabulary—is because she's on a better, less sedating regimen of medications.

But there's another reason, I think, for my mother's skepticism. Her whole life, she'd been given to understand that Adele's condition was fixed—that her sister was consigned to a life without any deepening or growth. As she put it to me during that first car ride: "There would be no reason for her to get any more cognizant or any smarter." That's how everyone thought about disability back in my mother's day. It's my own generation—and the ones following—that came to see the brain as a miracle of plasticity, teachable and retrainable right into old age.

Yet Adele exceeded the expectations of all the specialists who gave dire predictions to my grandparents. She did learn to talk. She did become toilet-trained. Not only can she walk, but she dances a mean salsa, which she shows us now—and where she gets her sense of rhythm, I don't know, but it's great. (I personally dance like Elaine on *Seinfeld*.) Carmen and her husband, Juan, both from Puerto Rico, often play Latin music, and Adele jumps right in, with one hand on her belly and the other high and outward-facing, as if on the shoulder of an imaginary partner, all while shaking her hips and waggling her rear. Juan, whom she calls "Daddy," often joins her.

I ask Carmen (whom she calls "Mommy") whether Adele knows any Spanish, given that she and Juan speak it around the house. She says yes.

"*¡Mamá!*" Carmen calls to Adele.

"What?"

"*¿Tú quieres a papi?*" Do you love Daddy?

"What?"

"*¿Tú quieres mucho a papi?*" Do you love Daddy a lot?

Adele nods emphatically.

"How much?" Carmen asks, switching to English. "How much you love Daddy? Let me see how much."

"Four dollars."

"Four dollars!" Carmen exclaims. "Oh my God." Juan cracks up.

This kind of confusion is also typical of what we see in Adele throughout this, our second visit to the Ayala home. The report sent to my mother, which contains assessments of the institutions she's inhabited and the day programs she's attended throughout her life, continually notes that she has trouble grasping concepts—that she "can name various objects, but become[s] confused when long sentences are used." It adds that she "often mumbles and is difficult to understand. If she does not understand what is being said to her, she simply says, 'Yeah.'"

And we do have a hard time understanding her, and she does say "Yeah" to a number of our basic questions about her day, which can make getting to know her frustrating. But not when she becomes animated about things she likes. Summer is approaching, for instance, which means Adele will shortly be going to camp. She adores camp. I ask what she does there. "A game! And color." Coloring, she means.

Other things Adele loves: *Care Bears*, stuffed animals, blingy baseball hats, shopping at Walmart, wearing perfume, preparing Juan's nightclothes, tucking in her roommate each night.

Camp is the only time Carmen truly gets a break from caring for Adele and her two housemates—"I don't like to leave them with nobody," she explains to me—and even when she does go out, she generally doesn't travel very far.

I stare at Carmen, now eighty, and realize I already live in fear of the moment when she won't be able to look after my aunt anymore. She has pulmonary hypertension and requires oxygen every night, and sometimes during the day. Yet she still cares for her three charges, whose pictures populate her photo albums right alongside those of her biological kids and grandkids. (My favorite: Adele standing next to a life-size Angry Bird.) Every day, she helps bathe them; makes their beds; shops for them; manages their various doctor appointments; takes them on outings; and, with Juan, prepares their breakfast, lunch, and dinner. Five out of seven days, this means rising at five a.m. In my aunt's specific case, it means doing her hair each morning just the way she likes, putting in her earrings, and pureeing her food—Adele refuses to wear her dentures.

"When I was raising my kids, you know—it's something that you miss," Carmen explains.

Adele's transition to the Ayala home wasn't easy. Change is hard for her; she likes order. And when she arrived at Carmen's house twenty-three years ago, she had scabies, which—in addition to raising questions about how well cared for she'd been in her previous home—meant that Carmen had to throw out everything she owned: her beloved stuffed animals, her clothes, her sheets. The adjustment became that much more traumatic; now my aunt truly had nothing. She threw tantrums. She once called Carmen "the B-word" (as Carmen puts it). Carmen phoned the home liaison. "And she says, 'Carmen, easy. She's a very good lady.'"

I ask how she earned my aunt's trust. "I used to sit down with her and, you know, I used to talk to her a lot," she says. "Talking, talking, talking to her. I'm telling her, 'Come here, help me with this' or 'Help me with that.'"

Now, Carmen says, Adele can recite all of her grandchildren's names and knows them by sight. She demonstrates, asking Adele to name everyone in her son Edgar's family. "J.J., Lucas, Janet, Jessica . . ." Adele says. Neither of her housemates can do this. "It doesn't matter how long she hasn't seen them," Evelyn, Carmen's daughter, later tells me. "She knows who they are. She has a memory that she'll meet somebody and she'll remember their name. That's her gift."

Her gift? I am incredulous when I hear this. I keep thinking about what I've been told my whole adult life: that Adele never even recognized her own mother, at least as far as my mom understood it. Was this some kind of misapprehension? Maybe Adele *had* known my grandmother? Or maybe she hadn't, but only because she'd been so aggressively narcotized?

As Carmen is talking with us, Adele gently rests her head on my mother's shoulder and keeps it there. My mother, ordinarily a coil of discipline and control (always correct, always the good girl), looks so blissed out, so happy. When our visit is over, she tells me that this was her favorite part, Adele burrowing into her—and that she's already thinking about when she can next see her again.

November 22, 1977: *On medication due to head banging behaviors . . . She stares off into space, fixates on her hands, or hair and has the compulsion to smell people's hair* (Wassaic State School, Amenia, New York).

This is from the report sent to my mother, the one containing assessments of Adele from the different institutions she's lived in and day programs she's been a part of. I had a closer look at it maybe a week or two after our second visit.

February 11, 1986: *(Psychotropic) Meds originally prescribed for screaming, hitting others, hitting self, extreme irritability* (case-worker report from a day-treatment program, Ulster County, New York). It is noted that she is taking 150 milligrams daily of Mellaril, a first-generation antipsychotic.

October 1991: *Outbursts look like psychosis . . . yell[s] out statements such as "Adele. Stop that!" or . . . "Leave me alone!"* (summary of a report from a day program, Kingston, New York).

Late 2006: *Psychiatry providers now recognize that there is psychosis present and Zyprexa is effectively treating this* (summary of various evaluations).

The report is eight pages long. But you get the idea. The dear woman who nestled into my mother's shoulder, waved at us until our car pulled out of sight, and recently wandered into Carmen's room when she intuited that something was the matter (Carmen was unwell) also had an unremitting history, until not that long ago, of violent outbursts, self-harm, and psychosis.

Far be it from me to quarrel with those who evaluated her, including the esteemed men in white coats. But "psychosis" seemed, when I read this report, like an incomplete story, carrying with it the stench of laziness and *One Flew Over the Cuckoo's Nest* reductivism—*This person is difficult; let's sedate her.*

I could have been totally wrong. Based on this report, Adele certainly seemed, at times, to pose a danger to herself and others. But I found it curious that nowhere in this document did it say anything about a behavior that even my untrained eye detected immediately during our visits: My aunt does tons of harmless stimming, the repetitive motions frequently associated with autism. (She is especially fond of wiggling her fingers in front of her eyes.) In all the years of observational data about her—at least from what I saw here—there wasn't a word about this, or the word *autism* itself. And autistic individuals, when frustrated or confronted with change or responding to excessive stimuli, can sometimes behave aggressively—or in ways that could be misread as psychotic.

And so, for that matter, can traumatized people.

It is December 2022. A visiting nurse, Emane, whom Adele calls Batman, is swabbing Adele's cheek. My aunt is being sweet and obedient; Emane, tender yet efficient. The sample will go to a lab in Marshfield, Wisconsin, that will sequence Adele's genes.

Wendy Chung, the Boston Children's Hospital geneticist with whom my mother and I are working, has warned us that there is only a one-in-three chance that Adele's genetic test will come back with a condition or syndrome that has an actual name. But Chung has told me, as have a number of other experts, that there's no other way to know for sure what Adele has. Dozens of things can cause microcephaly.

"But if you can find out exactly what she has," Chung says, "then you can find a family—"

"—with a child who has it now," I say.

Exactly, she says. And then I can compare how children with this syndrome fare today, versus how they fared in the 1950s.

My mother, Adele's medical proxy, had to sign the forms to do this genetic test. My aunt was incapable of giving her own consent. And it occurs to me, as I sit here watching her so docilely allow Emane to rake her cheek with a Q-tip, that Adele has never been able to give her consent for anything, good or bad, her whole life. Not for the medications she has taken, which may or may not have helped her; not for mammograms, which, given our family history, are indisputably a good idea. Not for any of the things that were done to her while she was institutionalized until the age of twenty-eight; not for a trip to the mall to get ice cream.

She cannot consent to this profile, I suddenly realize with some alarm.

I spend quite a few weeks fretting about this. Only after speaking with Rosemarie Garland-Thomson, a renowned bioethicist and disability scholar, do I understand exactly why this is so. The last thing I want to do is hurt Adele. So *not* writing about her would be consistent with this wish, in keeping with the benevolent spirit of the Hippocratic oath: I'd be doing no harm. Whereas I am trying to do good, a much riskier proposition. "The problem with trying to do good," she tells me, "is you don't know how it's going to come out."

"I don't have a *legal* right to know anything about my relatives who were disappeared," says Jennifer Natalya Fink, who faced a similar ethical predicament when she wrote *All Our Families.* "But I have a *moral* right. And it's a moral wrong, what was done to them. For us not to keep perpetuating those wrongs, we have to integrate knowledge of our disabled forebears."

There remains a school of thought that privileges the privacy of people with intellectual disabilities above all else, particularly when it comes to something as delicate as divulging their medical history. And this argument may be right. I don't know. But I ultimately decide, in the weeks after that swab, that integrating Adele means saying her name, and that understanding Adele—and her needs, and her potential, and whether she's been treated with the appropriate care and dignity her whole life—means knowing and naming whatever syndrome she has. To refrain from doing so would simply mean more erasure. Worse: it would imply that her condition is shameful, and there's been more than enough of that in my family.

To hell with shame.

I don't know why this is, but I keep coming back to my mother's deep desire for order. I had always assumed, I suppose, that it was a response to early trauma—a natural reaction to helplessly watching her sister get shipped away. But then I spent time with Adele and discovered that she shared the same trait, as if it were inscribed in the family genes.

I mention this one day to Evelyn, Carmen's daughter, on the phone. She mulls it over. "But maybe it comes from the same place in Adele," she says. "She was taken from her mother. She's been controlled *her whole life*. You don't know what she's gone through, where she's been."

I sit in chastened silence for several seconds. She is absolutely right. Of course it could come from the same place. Adele no doubt also experienced savage trauma in her life. It was just less legible, because she had no clear way to convey it. For all I know, my aunt is a *matryoshka* doll of buried pain.

In January 1972, Michael Wilkins met in a Staten Island diner with a young television journalist named Geraldo Rivera and discreetly handed him a key. It opened the doors to Building No. 6 at Willowbrook State School, from which Wilkins, a doctor, had recently been fired. He'd been encouraging the parents of the children in that ward—and others, from the sound of it—to organize for better living conditions. The administration didn't like that very much.

In February of that year, Rivera's half-hour exposé, "Willowbrook: The Last Great Disgrace," aired on WABC-TV. It was sickening. To this day, it remains one of the most powerful testaments to the horrors and moral degeneracy of institutionalization. You can easily find it on YouTube.

Rivera was by no means the first to visit Willowbrook. Robert F. Kennedy had toured the place in 1965 and called it "a snake pit." But because Rivera suddenly had access to one of the ghastliest dorms on campus, he and his camera crew could storm the premises unannounced. What he found—and what his viewers saw—was the

kind of suffering one associates with early-Renaissance depictions
of hell. The room was dark and bare. The children were naked,
wailing, and rocking on the floor. Some were caked in their own
feces. "How can I tell you about the way it smelled?" Rivera asked. "It
smelled of filth, it smelled of disease, and it smelled of death." He
went on to interview Wilkins, who made it clear that Willowbrook
wasn't a "school" at all. "Their life is just hours and hours of endless
nothing to do," he said of the patients, adding that 100 percent of
them contracted hepatitis within the first six months of moving in.

Actually, doctors were deliberately giving some of those children
hepatitis. Even into the 1970s, the intellectually disabled were the
subjects of government-funded medical experiments.

"Trauma is severe," Wilkins told Rivera, "because these patients are
left together on a ward—70 retarded people, basically unattended,
fighting for a small scrap of paper on the floor to play with, fighting
for the attention of the attendants."

"Can the children be trained?" Rivera asked at one point.

"Yes," the doctor said. "Every child can be trained. There's no
effort. We don't know what these kids are capable of doing."

This was where my aunt spent the formative period of her
youth, from the time she was a toddler until she was twelve or
thirteen years old. Though she left eight years before Rivera and
his crew arrived, it's hard to imagine that the conditions were any
better in her day. As Kim E. Nielsen writes in *A Disability History
of the United States*, World War II was devastating for these institutions, which were hardly exemplary to begin with. The young
men who worked there were shipped off to war, and most of the
other employees found better-paying jobs and superior conditions
in defense plants. These state facilities remained dreadfully poor-
paying and understaffed from then on, their budgets forever in
governors' crosshairs.

"It was horrible," Diana McCourt told me. She placed her daughter, Nina, born with severe autism, in Willowbrook in 1971. "She
always smelled of urine. Everything smelled of urine. It's like it was
in the bricks and mortar."

Diana and her husband, Malachy McCourt—the memoirist,
actor, radio host, and famous New York pub owner—soon became
outspoken activists and got involved in a class-action lawsuit against
the institution. "I can't quite tell you how much they didn't want
us to witness what was going on inside," Malachy told me. When

children were presented to their parents, they were taken to the entranceway of their dorm after being hastily dressed by attendants. "The clothes were never her clothes," Diana said. "She was wearing whatever they could find in the pile."

But most chilling of all was an offhand comment Diana made about the reports she received about her daughter. They were vague, she said, or demonstrably untrue, or maddeningly pedestrian—that she'd just gone to see the dentist, for instance. "The dentist," Diana said, "was notorious for pulling people's teeth."

Wait, I said. Repeat that?

"Instead of dental care, they pulled the teeth out."

Is *that* how my aunt lost her teeth?

Rivera noted in his special that the wards contained no toothbrushes that he could see.

I'd like to think that Adele's life improved when she went to Wassaic State School in 1964. But New York produced, at that moment in time, nothing but hellholes. (Rivera also visited Letchworth Village in his documentary, an institution so awful that the McCourts steered clear of it, opting for Willowbrook instead.) Wassaic, too, had a reputation for being grim. At least one note from the report sent to my mother indicated that my aunt was very keen on leaving it. The date was January 18, 1980. Adele was by then twenty-eight years old and had enough of a vocabulary to get her point across. "Clothes and suitcase?" she asked one of the clinicians.

Even when my aunt finally transferred to residential care, living in private homes and attending local programs in upstate New York, her treatment, until the '90s, seemed less than ideal. In March of 1980, my aunt attended a day facility in an old factory that still had very loud electric and pneumatic machines, and the result was disastrous—"agitated, violent outbursts." She was frequently taken to the "Quiet Room," quilted with actual padded walls, where the staff would physically restrain her. This practice, the report notes, is no longer used in New York.

It took seven years and nine months before her team realized that the industrial cacophony was causing a good deal of the problem.

It is mid-December 2022. Adele's genetic test has come back.

Her disorder does indeed have a name. Remarkably, it would not have had a name if we'd tested her just four years ago. But in

2020, a group of fifty-plus researchers announced their discovery of Coffin-Siris syndrome 12, the "12" signifying a rare subtype within an already rare disorder. At the time they made this discovery, they could identify just twelve people in the world whose intellectual disability was caused by a mutation in this particular gene. Since then, says Scott Barish, the lead author of the paper announcing the finding, the number has climbed to somewhere between thirty and fifty. So now, with my aunt, it's that number plus one.

I immediately join a Facebook group for people with Coffin-Siris syndrome. I find only a few parents with children who have the same subtype as Adele. One couple lives in Moscow; another, Italy. But as soon as I post something about my aunt, there's a flurry of replies from mothers and fathers of kids across the Coffin-Siris spectrum, most of them focused on the same thing: Adele's age. Seventy-one! How thrilling that someone with Coffin-Siris syndrome could live that long! They want to know all about her, and what kind of health she is in. (Robust, I reply.)

Because Coffin-Siris syndrome, first described in 1970, can be caused by mutations in any one of a variety of genes, its manifestations vary. As a rule, though, the disorder involves some level of intellectual disability and developmental delays. Many people with Coffin-Siris syndrome also have "coarse facial features," a phrase I've come to absolutely loathe; trouble with different organ systems; and underdeveloped pinkie fingers or toes (which is how, before genetic testing came along, a specialist might suspect a patient had it). Some, though by no means all, have microcephaly.

As far as I know, my aunt's fingers and toes are all fully developed—Coffin-Siris syndrome 12 doesn't seem to affect pinkies as much—and she doesn't appear to have any organ trouble. She does, however, have microcephaly, as did four of the twelve subjects in the breakthrough paper about her specific subtype. But what really stood out to me in that study—and I mean really shone in a hue all its own—was this: five of the dozen subjects displayed autistic traits.

In fact, the sparse literature on this subject suggests that a substantial portion of people with Coffin-Siris syndrome, no matter what genetic variant they've got, have a diagnosis of autism spectrum disorder as well.

Which is what I've suspected my aunt has had all along.

Knowing what I now do, I'm that much keener to find a family with a child who has Coffin-Siris syndrome 12 that would be willing to welcome me into their home. I call Barish, the lead author of the breakthrough paper, who heroically refers me to two. But one suddenly becomes shy and the other lives in Ireland. I start making my way through the other fifty co–first authors, co–corresponding authors, and just plain coauthors listed in the study. For a long while, I get nothing—turns out I'm talking to lab people, mostly—though I learn a lot about protein complexes and gene expression.

Then I reach Isabelle Thiffault, a molecular geneticist at Children's Mercy Kansas City. By some extraordinary fluke, she has, in her database, *four* children with my aunt's subtype. Two have microcephaly. One of those two is a seven-year-old girl named Emma, who lives in the Kansas City area.

I call her mom, Grace Feist. Would she mind if I paid a visit? She would not.

Grace and her husband, Jerry, took Emma in at seven months old and adopted her at a year and a half, knowing she had significant intellectual and developmental delays. They were prepared. They had fallen in love.

They also had ample state resources at their disposal, heavily subsidized or even free. More still: they had a rich universe of support groups to draw from, a sophisticated public school in their backyard, and the benefit of a culture that's come a long way toward appreciating neurodiversity.

They were able to actively choose Emma. Whereas my grandparents—pressured by doctors, stamped by stigma, broken by exhaustion and confusion and pain—felt like they had no choice but to give their daughter away.

"So this is the best thing, because it will keep your hair nice and neat, and it doesn't have any tingles."

Tingles? I ask. It's late February 2023. We're sitting in Emma's bedroom in Lee's Summit, Missouri, and she's waving a new silk pillowcase at me.

"They're like big stuff in your hair." She gestures at her thick brown ponytail.

Tingles . . . oh, tangles!

She nods. "Guess what? Tangles will get in your hair. If Mommy's brushing, I will be so mad."

A few feet from her is a mounted poster that says FOR LIKE EVER. As in: *We've embraced this little girl for life—for, like, ever.* Grace got it at T.J. Maxx shortly after Emma's adoption became official.

Every time I hear Emma speak, I find it hard to believe that she and my aunt have a mutation in the same gene. She chatters merrily in full sentences, talks about her friends, and can express how she feels, often in ways that are surprising or quite poignant.

"Emma, are you the same as other kids or different?" Grace asks when we pick her up at school the next day.

"Different."

"Why?" she asks.

"Because I'm the only one doing coloring. Not the other kids."

"Do you like being different?" I ask her.

"No."

"Why?" I ask.

"Because I want to be like other people."

But what I'm stuck on is all the ways that Emma *started out* like my aunt. When Grace and Jerry (a very involved father, just shy around reporters) first took her in at seven months to foster her, "she just lay there like a two-month-old baby," Grace says. "We thought she was blind." She didn't make eye contact; she couldn't roll. But in Bismarck, North Dakota, where Grace and Jerry were living at the time, Emma was entitled to all kinds of state-funded early intervention, as she is in Missouri. By nine months old, she was sitting unsupported, thanks to hours spent in a special tube swing to help her develop her core muscles.

Emma wasn't as late to walk as Adele, but she didn't take her first wobbly step until sixteen months, and because it was 2016, rather than the early 1950s, physical therapists again intervened, having her toddle on uneven surfaces—pillows, cushions—to bolster muscle tone. She developed a smoother gait at about two, but it took a couple more years for her to have the balance and coordination to walk normally, or to climb the stairs without help.

And speech! A huge surprise. Emma may be a bubbly ingenue, telling me all about indoor recess and her BFFs at school, but that's hardly how she started. When she was four years old, she had only one hundred words in her vocabulary, and that's a generous estimate. "The way it was described was: she's not deaf, but it's almost the speech of someone who can't hear," Grace says. But

Emma was working with state-funded speech therapists at the time, and they determined that she had auditory-processing disorder. When she got to her public school in Lee's Summit—which gives extra speech and occupational therapy to those who need it, plus additional reading and math instruction—her vocabulary started to grow, slowly at first, and then in a rush. "I don't know what it was," Grace says.

Well. I have some idea. It was having a supportive school. It was having several hours a week of occupational, physical, and speech therapy from the time Emma was an infant. And it was Grace herself.

If you're going to have an intellectual disability, who you really want as your mother is Grace Feist. Thirty-three, forever in flip-flops, and brimming with opinions—she has the concentrated energy of a honeybee—Grace has gone to exceptional lengths to tend to Emma's education and psychological well-being. She's decorated the basement playroom in pastels and muted colors. ("With visual-processing disorder, which Emma has, it's not as overwhelming," Grace explains.) Once a week, she takes Emma to vision therapy; she picks Emma up at school early every day to focus even more on her reading and math at home, without distraction. Grace is the queen of resourcefulness when it comes to all things pedagogical.

"I had a developmental pediatrician tell me: 'There is no rock you haven't looked under. This is what you have, and that's okay,'" she says. "And he came from the best of intentions. But let me tell you, there were, like, fifty rocks I hadn't looked under."

As Grace and Emma give me a tour of Emma's in-home classroom, all I can think is, *My God, the effort.* It contains a bucket of at least eighty fidget toys, many of them simple household items repurposed for anxious hands (silicone sink scrubbers, sewing bobbins). Emma sits on a purple wobble disk—it looks like a whoopee cushion the size of a satellite dish—to continue developing her core muscles. The walls are lined with giant flash cards from Secret Stories, a phonics-based reading program that makes intuitive sense and seems kind of *fun*, which is a good thing, because almost nothing demoralizes Emma more than trying to read. She can barely do it, though she's trying.

"How does reading feel?" Grace asks.

"Mad," Emma says. She's wearing a resplendent lavender shirt with daisies on it. "Because if Mommy say, 'Read this now,' I would be super grumpy. Because they have hard words." She's pointing to a rudimentary book she's been struggling with. "But some people say, 'This is easy!'"

"How does that make you feel?" Grace asks.

"Mad. Sad."

We move on to look at the shelves on the wall. They're stocked with tactile learning tools: numbers made of sandpaper. Montessori cubes showing multiples of ten. Wax Wikki Stix to make letter shapes.

"If you change the approach to everything being multisensory—you see it, you hear it, you taste it, you touch it, you smell it—then you learn it," Grace says. "Because you're using all these neural pathways for the same information. Then everyone can learn."

Perhaps I shouldn't be surprised by Grace's tenacity. She was raised in Florida, near Orlando, and had her first daughter, Chloe, at sixteen. She joined the Navy as a reservist in 2010 and worked for a time as a military police officer; then she worked security in an oil field in North Dakota, where she made great money and got to see the northern lights, as long as she was willing to put up with temperatures 20 degrees below zero. She met Jerry, then an information technologist, on the website Plenty of Fish. Today, he's a professional YouTuber, with an inspirational-Christian channel that has 2.6 million subscribers. On December 28, 2016, they adopted Emma. In 2018, Grace gave birth to another daughter, Anna.

"Having Anna was the best thing for Emma," Grace says, "because it really taught her how to play—with other kids, even with toys. That mimicking, that seeing what to do. Because when you would buy Emma toys, she would just line them up."

Grace and Jerry have made enormous sacrifices on Emma's behalf. The whole family has. They don't travel, because Emma needs structure and control. They seldom go to restaurants, but when they do, they bring along her purple noise-canceling headphones—shooting earmuffs, purchased at Walmart—in case the sound overwhelms her; she needs to leave the restaurant several times a meal in any event, just to ground herself. "That's how we live our life," Grace says.

Their life used to be even more difficult. When she was younger, Emma, like my aunt, was inclined toward self-harm. When I first mention to Grace that Adele has no teeth—and that I fear they were removed at Willowbrook or Wassaic—Grace cuts me off: "Because she would bite herself until she bled?"

Sweet Jesus. I hadn't even thought of that.

"Because Emma did," Grace says. "I have pictures of it."

She doesn't show me those pictures. But she does show me a picture of four-year-old Emma with a giant green-and-purple Frankenstein bruise bulging from her forehead. "She'd hit herself in the face," Grace says. "She would bang her head on the floor, like, hard."

And why does she think Emma did that? "She's trapped in this mind where she knows what she wants, she knows what she needs, but *you* don't know, and she doesn't know how to tell you," Grace says. "Is she aggressive? Yeah. I would be pissed, too."

I haven't noticed any aggression in Emma—just a lot of sass, a gal who wants to show off her dance moves and introduce me to her stuffies. But again, this may be in part due to early-childhood interventions: Armies of occupational and speech therapists taught her how to be gentle, demonstrating how to talk kindly to dolls, and they encouraged Grace to teach Emma sign language, which she did, so that Emma could better express her wishes. As Emma got older, Grace read tons of books about emotional self-regulation, teaching her daughter to externalize her frustration. "We'd be in the middle of Walmart and she'd be stomping her feet," Grace says. "But you know what? She wasn't punching herself in the head."

Today, Emma is flourishing. She may not yet know her phone number or address. She may not be able to tell you the names of the months or all the days of the week. But she's making great strides, especially now that she's learning at home. When I left her house in late February, she could count to twelve; four months later, she was adding and subtracting. "Emma is going to thrive in her life," Grace says. "Is she going to work at McDonald's? Maybe. Is she gonna bag groceries? Maybe. But she's gonna be okay." Grace's goal, she says, is to make sure that Emma's mental health always comes first. "I have never met anyone more resilient or determined," she adds.

As I prepare to leave, Grace gives me two gifts she's purchased for my aunt. They're things Emma likes: a lavender-scented unicorn Warmie (a stuffed animal you can safely heat in the microwave) and Pinch Me therapy dough that smells like oranges. "Anything scented is always really calming for Emma," she explains.

Then Emma hands me a picture she's drawn of me and Adele. Grace asks if she remembers why she drew it. "Yeah!" Emma says. "Because she has a hard time going to school."

"Like you," Grace says. Then: "You know what her aunt has?"

I assume she is going to say something about Coffin-Siris syndrome 12, but in a way that's comprehensible to a child who has it, too. But that isn't where Grace is headed. "She has a woman who loves her and takes care of her because her mommy wasn't able to. Just like you. Did you know that?"

Emma shakes her head.

I thank Grace and Emma for the gifts and head out to my rental car. I last maybe thirty seconds before losing it.

Is it a fair or genuine comparison, lining up my aunt and Emma side by side? Using Emma's life story thus far as some kind of counterfactual history? To ask *What if*?

Yes and no, obviously.

There's variability in all genetic disorders, including Coffin-Siris syndrome, even among those with mutations in the same gene. The original paper looking at my aunt's specific subtype found that four out of the twelve individuals had microcephaly, for example, but one had macrocephaly; go figure. My aunt and Emma, though they both have subtype 12, clearly have different manifestations of it, a phenomenon one can observe just from looking at them: Emma is big for her age while my aunt is tiny; my aunt's microcephaly is unignorable, because her sutures—the flexible material between a baby's skull bones—closed prematurely, while Emma's didn't, making her microcephaly harder to detect. Her doctor says it may be easier to see as she gets older, though.

"If your aunt had had the treatments available today, I suspect her life would be very different," says Bonnie Sullivan, the clinical geneticist at Children's Mercy Kansas City who treats Emma. We're speaking just days after I return home. She has looked at both Adele's and Emma's specific gene mutations. "She may not have been as high-functioning as Emma, but she could have maximized her potential, and her quality of life would've been a lot better."

It seems impossible to quarrel with this assessment. The literature on disability is bursting with stories—heartening or depressing, depending on your point of view—about the advances made by people with intellectual disabilities once they were liberated from the medieval torments of their institutions. Studies as far back as the 1960s showed that children with Down syndrome begin to speak earlier and have higher IQs if they're kept in home settings rather than institutional ones. Judith Scott, warehoused with Down syndrome in 1950 at the age of seven, famously became an artist once her twin sister established herself as her legal guardian thirty-five years later; her handsome fiber-art sculptures are now part of the permanent collections of the Museum of Modern Art and the Centre Pompidou.

But perhaps the best-known example of what happens to underloved, under-stimulated children are the orphans from Nicolae Ceaușescu's Romania, where "child gulags" warehoused some 170,000 kids in appalling conditions. These children became tragic, unwilling conscripts in an inadvertent mass experiment in institutional neglect. When, eleven years after Ceaușescu's execution, American researchers finally began to study 136 of them, putting half in foster settings and monitoring their development, the findings were bleak. Only 18 percent of those still in orphanages showed secure attachments by age three and a half, versus almost 50 percent of those who'd been transferred to family settings. By the time the kids still in orphanages had reached sixteen, more than 60 percent suffered from a psychiatric condition.

Which brings me back to my aunt's repeated diagnoses, over the years, of psychosis. Maybe the condition was inevitable; maybe my aunt would have been psychotic no matter what kind of life she'd led. But when I watched those gruesome spools of footage from Willowbrook, all I could think was: *Who wouldn't be driven mad by such a place?* After she left Willowbrook, Adele would abruptly shout "Stop hurting me!" for no apparent reason. Her care team assumed she was having hallucinations, a plausible postulate. But isn't it equally plausible to theorize that she was reliving some unspeakable abuse from her past? Or, as the Georgetown philosopher and disability-studies professor Joel Michael Reynolds puts it (speaking my thoughts aloud): "Why isn't that a completely reasonable response to PTSD?"

I'll never know how Adele's life could have turned out if she'd been born in 2015, as Emma was. All I have is a plague of questions.

What if a task force of occupational, speech, and physical therapists had shown up at my grandparents' home each week, teaching
Adele to walk, talk, and gently play with dolls?

What if she had spent her formative years not rotting in her
own diapers or staring at the walls, but engaging in organized
play, attending school, and basking in the company of adults who
loved her?

What if she'd had caretakers who inhaled book after book about
emotional self-regulation and encouraged her to stomp her feet in
department stores, rather than hit herself in the head?

And what if—*what if*—Adele had had a sister to play with?

It's possible that all the interventions in the world would have
done nothing, or next to it. Sullivan says she's seen families re-
cruit every imaginable expert and pour their energies into every
conceivable intervention, yet with depressingly little to show for
it. "There are some individuals with such severe manifestations
of certain disorders that aggressive interventions don't seem to
change the outcome very much," she says. "And it kills me. I truly
grieve that result. Because the parents are trying everything."

Similarly, there are children who wind up in residential care in
spite of their parents' best and most valiant efforts, because their
risk of self-harm or of harming others remains too great. Parents
are not, nor should they be expected to be, saints.

But my mind keeps looping back to that eight-page report my
mother was sent about Adele's history. The notes from Willowbrook,
what few there are, tell a story all their own.

*March 19, 1953: 21-month-old girl, quite small for her age . . . able to
sit without support, to imitate movements, and is reported to be able to say
"mama."* Adele's IQ is measured at 52.

*February 1, 1960: Microcephalic child of 8 1/2 years with limited
speech and partial echolalia. She is disoriented, and her acquaintance with
simple objects in her surroundings is rather poor even for her overall mental
level . . . Rate of development has markedly slowed down since the last eval-
uation 7 years ago. The consequent drop in IQ is considerable.* This time
it is measured at 27.

In her seven years of staring at those walls and rocking naked
on the floor and never once, I assume, being shown a particle of
love apart from those brief visits from my grandparents, Adele's
IQ dropped by almost half, startling even those who evaluated her.

And yes, maybe this was destined to happen; maybe her smaller brain had less noticeable consequences in a toddler than in an eight-year-old.

But if my aunt could expand her vocabulary simply by going off a useless antipsychotic and onto Zyprexa—in middle age!—imagine what else she might have been capable of over the course of her life, if only she'd been given a half, a quarter, a hundredth of a chance.

It's a sunny day in May of this year. I'm working on the back deck, nearing the end of writing this story. My cellphone rings. It's Evelyn, Carmen's daughter. She apologizes for calling me on a Sunday, but something serious has happened. Adele has collapsed; she's in the hospital; it's looking bad. Can I please locate my mom?

I leave messages everywhere and call Adele's nurse, Emane, who I've been told is in the hospital with her. Emane is upset. No one will tell her anything. She's been banished to the waiting room. They really need my mother, my aunt's medical proxy.

A few minutes later, my mother phones them. A few minutes after that, my father conveys the news to me: Adele has died.

A heart attack, apparently. Just after breakfast.

I call Evelyn. She is crying. I stammer my way through this conversation, also crying, but mainly because we barely got to know my aunt, because this was supposed to be the beginning of something and not the end, because I know the grief I feel in no way matches Evelyn's or Carmen's or Juan's. I am fluttering with an awkward mixture of shame, regret, sadness. "She was loved," Evelyn keeps saying, over and over.

I know, I say. I just wish more by us.

"You came at exactly the right time," Evelyn assures me. "I truly believe that."

I hang up. God, they're so gracious, this family. "We don't judge," Evelyn told us the first time we went up to see Adele at the Ayalas'. She meant it.

I phone my mother. She has lurched into administrative mode, planning the funeral. This is peak Mom, organizing things, surmounting the tough stuff by finding footholds in the small details. I wait a bit and call Carmen, though with some trepidation. My mother says she was unhelmed—bawling—when they first spoke. Carmen, calmer but still sobbing throughout our talk, tells me it's true. "I broke down. I didn't expect it to happen like that."

We bury Adele three days later. It's a gorgeous afternoon, perfect really, but the incongruities and dissonances of the hour are hard to ignore. Here we are, having a Jewish funeral for a woman who was never exposed to the Jewish tradition her whole life, while those whose lives have been most brutally upended—those who have spent the past twenty-four years loving and caring for Adele—are Catholics. My aunt will be buried next to her mother, forever reunited, while the woman whom she called "Mommy"—who just four nights ago rubbed Vicks VapoRub on her back and brought her tea because she had a cough—will go back to a house with an empty twin bed.

I'd like to think that in the afterlife, my grandmother's heart will mend. That she will never again be told to send Adele away, that God will say to her: *It's okay, she's lovely as she is; she's my child, too.*

Problem is, I'm not much of a believer. I wish I was.

But the rabbi, Lisa Rubin, is brilliant, making something seamless out of the chaotic threads of my aunt's life and the untidy grief of this motley group, managing to acknowledge the trauma of my mother, the trauma of my aunt, and the trauma of my grandparents, showing them the compassion they deserved their whole lives but probably never got and certainly never gave to themselves. And she honors the Ayala family in the most beautiful way, invoking the Jewish legend of the *Lamed Vavniks*, or thirty-six individuals in every generation who are the most righteous of all humanity. "They're often called the hidden saints among us," she says. "The people who do God's work faithfully and humbly and whose virtue keeps the world spinning. They pour compassion and love on those around them with no desire for recognition." To my family, she says, Carmen, Juan, and Evelyn are the *Lamed Vavniks*—"the hidden saints of Adele's life."

The Ayalas are all discreetly weeping. Carmen will later tell me: *I will miss Adele so much.*

My mother is invited to speak next. Evelyn will speak after her, then one of Adele's housemates, then Adele's psychologist, then her case manager—it's wonderful that they've turned up.

But my mother . . . I'm not quite prepared. She starts with a version of something I've heard before—that losing Adele was a trauma that took decades to heal. But then she elaborates in a way she hasn't even in our most intimate discussions: The three times she saw Adele back in the '90s, she still felt disconnected from her. Adele's previous caretakers had left my mom and my grandmother (and in one case, my mom and me) all alone with my aunt in their living room; they hadn't said a thing about who Adele was or what her place was in their home. That changed, my mother says, when she saw Adele at the Ayalas', discovering the charming, idiosyncratic character of her baby sister—and how very much she was loved, how she fit into a family.

"Those visits changed everything for me," she says. "I opened my heart to Adele after shutting her out for nearly seventy years, and I found myself loving her again the same way I did as a six-year-old child." I hear a catch in her voice. She pauses, then regains her composure. "Now," she continues, "I've lost Adele for the second time. And it hurts in a way I never expected. But I would not trade those visits for anything, because my life is so much richer. Adele has taught me to love in a whole new way."

She finishes. And then, without warning, she rushes into the arms of my dad and starts crying in deep, seismic sobs. "I lost all those years," she says into his shirt. I can barely make it out.

I've never seen her sense of control desert her in this way.

My mind wanders back to the last time I saw Adele. It was December, when Emane swabbed her cheek. I was alone then, just me and my recording device; my mother was in Florida. Carmen reminded Adele that I was her niece, her sister's daughter. "Do you remember Rona?" she asked. "Yeah," Adele said, but it wasn't a convincing "yeah"—more like one of the blank ones she uttered when she didn't understand.

We collected Adele's DNA, and then I stuck around, curious to see how my aunt passed her afternoons and evenings. Spending that brief stretch with her meant experiencing time in a sensual way, almost, just feeling the thickness of the hours as they passed. We sat for a while together in the kitchen. Then we went upstairs to her bedroom, a warm, delightful space, her dresser tumbling with stuffed animals and her bed popping with a pink Disney-princess blanket. Adele carefully selected her outfit for the next day, matching every item of clothing, down to her socks.

There are many different shades of periwinkle blue. I had no idea.

Then she undressed, put on a plush lavender bathrobe, and headed into the shower to slowly bathe herself and wash her hair. Carmen supervised, but left her alone. After she'd dried herself off, Adele headed back into her room, closed all of the blinds ("for night"), and settled into her rocking chair. She spent the next half an hour, at least, just rocking. She often wiggled her fingers in front of her eyes. Occasionally she broke into a smile or chanted the same words to herself ("paint, pepper") or gave a little laugh. She seemed content.

But in the shower—and I'll never forget this, not for as long as my battered memory is intact—she babbled much more coherently. "Sister. Rona. Janet. Mirna. Rrrrrrrona"—she rolled the *R*—"A doll. A teddy bear."

I've listened to that wisp of audio dozens of times, just to make sure I didn't wish those words into existence.

Sister. Rona. She was already committing my mother's name to memory, and to her own family tree, along with Carmen's daughter and daughter-in-law, Mirna and Janet. Her ability to sweep in such things was, as Evelyn said, her gift. And now, we in our family will finally be committing her name to ours, which for so long—so pointlessly long—had a phantom bough.

Adele Halperin. Daughter, sister, aunt. June 30, 1951–May 7, 2023.

If Not Now, Later

FROM *The New Yorker*

"IT'S RATHER VEXING, isn't it, not to know what flowers will come up next year?" I said to my friend Brigid, in a voice that sounded more like a character's in a novel than my own. It was November 2017, and my family had just moved into our house in Princeton. The trees were shedding their leaves, in a theatrical manner that was new to us—we had relocated from California to the East Coast four months earlier.

"There are some roses," Brigid said. "Those look like lilies."

"And those are hostas."

There were six or seven rosebushes, with residual flowers, fuchsia-colored, shivering on top of the near-leafless branches. Lilies and hostas, their leaves already paled and half rotted by the cold autumn rain, remained recognizable. The rest of the garden was a wilted mystery, buried under fallen leaves.

I was not a character, but I was speaking like one for a reason: I was pondering a set of characters. I went on and told Brigid about a moment in *The Saga of the Century Trilogy*, by Rebecca West, about a British family living in London in the first half of the twentieth century. The eldest daughter in the family, Cordelia, newly wed, has moved into a pretty house in Kensington; when she has her two younger sisters over for a visit, she frets, with the leisure of a young woman married into respectability and stability, about not knowing whether the hawthorn tree in her garden will bear white, pink, or red flowers in the spring.

A few chapters later, the hawthorn tree blooms. By then, the little brother of the family, Richard Quin, still a teenager, has been killed in the Great War, ten days after arriving in France. "Killed, not missing?" Cordelia cries out in agony when she's told the news. The hawthorn tree outside reveals the answer to the riddle from the winter before: the flowers are red.

It is a quick stroke in a trilogy. The first time I read it, I did not fully register the weight of the detail. But, moving into a house in the fall, studying a garden that would remain unknowable for the moment, I went back and reread the few paragraphs about the tree.

Richard Quin, in West's trilogy, is killed in the same manner that one imagines Andrew Ramsay is killed in *To the Lighthouse*: "[A shell exploded. Twenty or thirty young men were blown up in France, among them Andrew Ramsay, whose death, mercifully, was instantaneous.]"

For all we know, Richard Quin might have died next to Andrew Ramsay, in a pair of Virginia Woolf brackets.

Some days, that pair of brackets of Woolf's continue to baffle me. Other days, they feel just right. The predicament when writing about a sudden, untimely death: the more you remember, the more elusive that death becomes. A sudden, untimely death is a black hole, absorbing all that you can give, not really clamoring for more. Though is a black hole ever to be fully filled so that it can cease to be one? Has anyone been able to define, capture, or even get close to a black hole?

[In September 2017, our older son, Vincent, died by suicide, at sixteen.]

[On that day, we put down the deposit for the house. Deposit, death, in that order, four hours apart.]

In a novel, I would never have put the two happenings on the same day. In writing fiction, one avoids coincidences like that, which offer unearned drama, shoddy poignancy, convenient metaphor, predictable spectacle. Life, however, does not follow a novelist's discipline. Fiction, one suspects, is often tamer than life.

Some fiction is tamer than some life, I should amend. And I confess that this is only a variation of a statement made by another character in *The Saga of the Century Trilogy*, who, upon discovering her husband's extramarital affair, reads *Madame Bovary* and exclaims, "But art is so much more real than life. Some art is much more real than some life, I mean."

A couple of months after Vincent died, a colleague asked me where I was "in the process of grieving," assuming, I supposed, that there would be, and should be, a conclusion of mourning at some point. That phrase struck me as inaccurate; she might as well have asked me where I was "in the process of living."

There is, alas, not a normal course of life, against which deviations can be measured and, hopefully, corrected. Only changed courses, altered lives. One can look longingly at the alternatives: Vincent graduating from high school (as our younger son did this summer) or graduating from college (as Vincent's old school friends will next year), but alternatives belong to the realm of fiction. To paraphrase Elizabeth Bowen, the great Anglo-Irish writer, good fiction is good because it offers "the palpable presence of the alternatives." In life, that presence can be palpably felt, but too much preoccupation with the alternatives may lead to a dilemma of either/or; even, neither here nor there. "Dilemma," from its Greek etymology, means two lemmas: double assumptions, double propositions. But death is definitive; death does not lead to a dilemma.

I think about the alternative lives of my characters all the time. But, as I did not live in fiction, I decided, soon after Vincent's death, to stop pondering the alternatives. *What if* belongs to fiction; *what now*, to this real life.

What now, in the last months of 2017: I could not read fiction. It was not a problem of mental focus. I spent hours every day reading Shakespeare's plays and Wallace Stevens's poems—all of a sudden, those words were the only ones that made sense to me. But if I stopped reading fiction would I ever be able to write fiction again? I was in the middle of a long novel. Forging ahead or scrapping the project felt equally impossible. Anguished, I looked up "anguish" in the OED, to make sure that I was using the right word to describe my situation, and, indeed, it was an apt word choice. Etymologically, "anguish" comes to us from the Latin *angustia*—narrowness, lack of space, narrow space, narrow passage, strait, limitations, restrictions, confinement, imprisonment, restrictedness, shortage, scantiness, critical situation, narrowmindedness, pettiness.

A black hole takes all and gives back naught. The anguish from a sudden, untimely death has a narrowing effect: alternatives are lost; space in the mind, too.

On her next visit, Brigid brought me two books. The first was *Onward and Upward in the Garden,* a collection of fourteen essays by the former *New Yorker* fiction editor Katharine S. White. The essays were originally published, in a span of twelve years, in the magazine, ostensibly as reviews of nursery catalogues. The other book was *Two Gardeners: A Friendship in Letters,* a collection of correspondence between White and Elizabeth Lawrence. Lawrence was a gardener and a gardening writer in North Carolina, and the friendship began when Lawrence wrote a fan letter to White after reading her first essay, "A Romp in the Catalogues," in the March 1, 1958, issue of *The New Yorker.* For a year, they were "Mrs. White" and "Miss Lawrence" to each other, and then they became "Katharine" and "Elizabeth." They would write to each other for the next nineteen years, until White's death, in 1977.

Through the winter, I read the two books, very slowly. There was no reason to hurry, as that first winter was a long one; cold, snowy—cold and snowy for recent transplants from California, in any case. Day after day, I looked at the bare limbs of the trees, brownish gray, and the stale snow covering the garden, grayish white. I thought one afternoon, What if spring never returns? Right away I recognized the illogic and the melodrama of that thought. I had at my hand the words of two gardeners of yesteryear, books that had taken years to be written. Were these words not enough evidence that spring always comes, if not now, later?

[That winter, I often returned to Marianne Moore's words: "If nothing charms or sustains us (and we are getting food and fresh air) it is for us to say, 'If not now, later,' and not mope." Incidentally, it was Moore who may have first suggested that White should collect her reviews of garden catalogues into a book.]

Not to mope, I thought, was a proper goal: It would take all my energy and all my vigilance, and it was attainable. White's essays and the letters between White and Lawrence were just right for that aspiration. The two women (and likely some of the gardens and many of the plants that they had written about) were no more, and yet their words remained and sustained, offering facts and opinions, gardening tales and personal woes, seasons and years, illnesses and deaths—all there, ready to distract me.

For instance, there were the names of plants to learn. In both books, I encountered many names, some familiar, others unfamiliar, and every one of them—even the most common, like "peony" or "lotus" or "fuchsia"—required investigation. Unlike Lawrence, I'm not a purist when it comes to botany, and I don't always look up the

Latin names for the plants. But I do like to know the etymology of
their English names. And what one can learn just by going to the
dictionary! "Peony" goes all the way back to ancient Greek: Paieon,
or Paeon, was the physician of the gods. (What afflicts the gods?
Possibly what afflicts us mortals.) "Lotus" comes from the Greek
lōtos, a mythical plant bringing forgetfulness to those who eat its
fruits. (I have eaten my share of lotus seeds, a delicacy in Chinese
cuisine, without achieving oblivion.) "Fuchsia," a word I often
misspelled as "fuschia"—what mythical story accompanies thee? It
turns out that fuchsia was named for the sixteenth-century German
physician and botanist Leonhard Fuchs, whose name gave birth
not only to that of the flower and that of the color but also to the
nickname, Fuchsienstadt, for his hometown of Wemding, where
there is a pyramid made of as many as seven hundred fuchsia
plants. And yet Fuchs never saw the flower fuchsia in his lifetime:
It was discovered in the Caribbean and named by the French botanist and monk Charles Plumier, who was born 145 years after
Fuchs. What led Plumier to name the flower for Fuchs? One can
ask the question, but any speculation would be closer to fiction,
just as peony was once the physician of the gods and lotus would
bring forgetfulness.

Nearer our time—nearer than Fuchs and Plumier—were the
horticulturists, seedsmen, growers, some older than White, others
her contemporaries, behind those nursery catalogues which
were once scrutinized by her. "They are as individualistic . . . as
any Faulkner or Hemingway, and they can be just as frustrating
or rewarding," White wrote. And what a great joy to get to know
the Faulkners and Hemingways of the nursery world through her
words. Signing off for the catalogue of White Flower Farm was one
Amos Pettingill. "I have no idea whether Amos Pettingill is a real
person—the name sounds like an ill-advised fabrication," White
observed. Real or not, the name alone, I thought, was enough to
send one's imagination on a detour to Dickens-land. In the catalogue of White Flower Farm, Mr. Pettingill claimed that its French
Pussy Willow was "not the unreliable wild Pussy Willow," which
led White to protest, "What is unreliable, pray, about the native
wild pussies? I have found them trustworthy in every respect." David
Burpee, the president of the W. Atlee Burpee & Company, cam-
paigned to have the marigold recognized as the national flower
of the United States. White, describing "David Burpee's one-man

lobby," noted, "I was also pleased as well as entertained, a couple of years back, when Mr. Burpee in person went to Washington, bearing marigold boutonnieres for the legislators, and, at a Congressional hearing on naming a national flower, faced down the Senatorial proponents of grass, the corn tassel, the rose, and the carnation." (Mr. Burpee did not succeed; the rose prevailed to become the national flower.)

To catch a glimpse, in White's essays, of these men and women who once lived in their gardens, cultivating, hybridizing, dreaming of colors and shapes and scents that would catch their fancy, and then turning their obsessions into words, hoping that their catalogues would catch the fancy of many gardeners' hearts: There is nothing narrowing in the world of roses, dahlias, marigolds, tulips, daylilies, and chrysanthemums. They were not black holes but rabbit holes.

And, of course, there were White and Lawrence, knowledgeable, opinionated, delighting in miscellanies. In her first letter, Lawrence recommended that White write about Cecil Houdyshel's catalogues (which always opened with "Dear Floral Friends"): "I think he is in his nineties now, so you had better hurry." In reply, White confessed, "I am always nervous when I write about old people." Both women saw a garden writer in Lewis Carroll. In her first *New Yorker* review of nursery catalogues, referring to the card gardeners painting roses in *Alice's Adventures in Wonderland*, White wrote, "Lewis Carroll was prophetic; today the garden men are quite as busy changing the colors of flowers as they are changing their size and shape." A year later, Lawrence wrote in a letter, "If I have to hear flowers talk, I would rather read *Through the Looking-Glass*, which *is* my favorite garden book."

[Their conversation led me to reread *Alice's Adventures in Wonderland* and *Through the Looking-Glass*, the first fiction I read after Vincent's death. The books, of course, have less to do with the missed or lost alternatives; instead, they make perfect nonsense out of the alternatives.]

After we moved into the house, I ordered twenty-five hyacinth bulbs (Delft Blue) and buried them haphazardly in the corners where I was certain that they would not interfere with any existing plants. Twenty-five, in retrospect, was a touchingly small number—a gesture rather than a plan, a prelude to a dream rather than a dream realized. But a gardener, like a writer, must start somewhere. (Last fall, I planted eight hundred bulbs; the fall before, seven hundred.)

Because of those twenty-five bulbs, garden catalogues began to arrive. One could be realistic: it had taken little time for one's address to be shared among the nurseries. One could also be romantic: imagine that tentative order of bulbs as a small bugle, announcing a budding gardener. The catalogues, though radically improved graphically from the ones reviewed by White, still bore the same names: White Flower Farm, Wayside Gardens, Park Seed Company, W. Atlee Burpee & Company, and several more. I perused the catalogues as I imagined White and Lawrence had done; although new to this literature, I had yet to cultivate my tastes and form my opinions.

It occurred to me one day that no one had made a catalogue of gardeners: professional gardeners, who might be like important cultivars, bearing poetic or eccentric names; amateurs, akin to common carnations and cornflowers; and those, like me, who were gardeners only in their fantasies. Such a catalogue, abundant with human stories, would be amusing to read, no? I then realized that I was, true to my profession, fictioneering again.

When I was growing up, in Beijing, my family lived on the ground floor of an apartment block, so we were lucky to have a tiny lot, about 2 meters by 1.5 meters. My father, who had come from poor peasant stock, gardened judiciously: a grapevine that produced very sweet grapes (often pillaged by the wasps), our favorite green beans (which bore the name "pig ears"), loofahs (good for soup when the gourds were young and tender; when they were old and fibrous, they made the best kitchen scrubs), a honeysuckle plant (dried honeysuckle flowers can be used as medicinal tea). One year, when I was four or five, he planted some potatoes and described to me the unforgettable flavor of new potatoes. The only other time I have heard such a rapturous description of new potatoes was from an Irish poet in Cork.

My father did not garden for beauty. Some years, he would plant a cluster of impatiens, which he called "fingernail flowers" because, in the old days, the pink and red petals had been used when painting girls' fingernails. The only constant floral decorations in our garden were the morning glories, self-seeding and wildly vivacious. Once, two women laughed at our garden to my face, dismissing my father as a lazy gardener who grew flowers that were no more than weeds. I was too young and too intimidated to defend him: he was a nuclear physicist, but he also did all the grocery shopping and most of the housework, cooked three meals a day for the family, and gardened in his spare time.

People who cultivated peonies and roses and orchids were not necessarily kind, which was not a surprise. I had learned from Chinese history that cold-blooded dictators—Chairman Mao, for instance—had also written heartrending poetry, and that capricious dynastic tyrants had often been supreme calligraphers and painters. On the other hand, people who were cruel to garden plants could easily extend that cruelty to human beings. One day, my mother uprooted the honeysuckle for no other reason than that she could—so she would—inflict pain. My father mourned, and I seethed, though we both did so quietly.

When the spring of 2018 arrived, I, the daughter of my pragmatic father, started by growing vegetables in containers—I was still waiting for the flowers in the garden to emerge and show themselves to me. In the next two years, I grew Chinese celtuce, baby bok choy, green beans, eggplants, tomatoes, sweet peppers, okra, and a variety of herbs, and ended up having plenty of opportunities to observe at close hand birds and squirrels, snails and slugs, aphids and spider mites, and all the other archenemies of a garden. Various campaigns were carried out: I ordered live ladybugs, hundreds at a time, and released them in the evenings after it rained, hoping that they would not fly away; I hung up birdhouses, waiting for wrens to move in and feed their chicks with my garden's offering of bugs; fake snakes were strategically placed to ward off rodents, and they did little but frighten me every time I stepped on their rubbery bodies.

And then there is the problem without any solution: the bigger animals. Deer graze undiscriminatingly (but luckily, in my case, only in the front yard, for the backyard is fenced). The fence, of course, does nothing to deter rabbits. (On a visit I paid to the Irish writer William Trevor, at his house in Devon, he pointed out rolls of metal mesh, to be buried at a certain depth—inches? feet? I forgot how much—into the ground as a rabbit fence. I have yet to be so enterprising.) The rabbits show up in late May or early June, fist-size fluffs, and a month later they can stand on their hind feet and stretch more than a foot tall. They chomp down everything and turn me into a maddened Mrs. McGregor. (I will never believe any catalogue if it dares label a plant rabbit-resistant.) Next comes our resident groundhog. Perhaps there is more than one, but they all look the same to me: giant and comical. The groundhogs are the most effective destroyers of a garden. I named ours for an infamous politician, although a friend, quite sensibly, pointed out that calling the groundhog by the politician's name was an insult to the animal: the groundhog is doing only what he's supposed to do, tramping and feasting in what he considers his garden.

One early summer morning, I looked out the window and saw two deer and a rabbit in my front garden, eating up some hydrangea bushes I had planted a few weeks earlier. It occurred to me that, had I been able to go back to my childhood self and tell her that one day I would live in a place where rabbits and deer eat side by side peacefully, the child would be incredulous: Certainly no real people could live in a fairy tale like that?

"I am sure that if you had been told when you were a child about all the things that you were going to have to do, you would have thought you had better die at once, you would not have believed you could ever have the strength to do them." In West's trilogy, Richard Quin says this to his mother before he leaves to be killed in France. Had I been able to go back to my childhood self and tell her that one day I would live as a mother who has lost a son, the child would be equally incredulous: Surely such things happen only in fiction, to characters who are much more interesting and tragic?

My garden this spring looks a little different from the garden that came back to life in spring 2018. For two years in a row, it was razed by an endless army of rabbits, and, by late summer, it looked like a sad head suffering irregular hair loss, with large bald patches and some surviving stalks of flowers. But this, I had learned from White and Lawrence, is only part of a garden's fate. In a letter from the spring of 1960, Lawrence reported to White about her magnolia, "We had a real frost last night (almost unheard of for mid-April) and *Magnolia Lennei* is covered with brown rags. I am going to chop it down, for this happens too often." In her reply, White wrote, "I called home and learned that mice had eaten and destroyed nine of my old-fashioned rose bushes, so I am extra sympathetic about the magnolia."

Anything can happen in a garden, nothing lasts, and yet something can always be made out of the soil, even with the most
destructive weather, even when rabbits and groundhogs and Japanese beetles join forces, greedy and ruthless. All things in the
garden, just as in life, are provisional and impermanent. One
gardens with the same unblinded hope and the same willingness
to concede as one lives, always ready to say, If not now, later; if
not this year, next year.

But these sentiments would have sounded preachy had I said
them to Vincent when he was alive. (The truth is, I would not
have been able to, since I had not yet learned them myself.) A few
weeks before his death, when we were touring the house with real
estate agents, he said to me, "This garden needs improvement. I
can't wait to garden with you."

One can linger in that memory, but there is no reason to attach
too much meaning to it. A garden is not a shrine. Living is not
metaphorizing. I don't always think about Vincent's plan to work
alongside me when I potter in the garden. A garden is trustworthy
only at this moment, in this now: the past is irrevocable, the future
unpredictable.

[Though I did plant a special patch of tulips for Vincent last
fall: Tulipa Vincent van Gogh, dark and mysterious, and Tulipa
Ballerina, golden and elegant.]

Five years later, I still consider myself a beginning gardener.
I'm avid, but always ready to surrender to disappointments, to
setbacks, to failures and deaths. Unlike White and Lawrence, I
garden without a design. (From E. B. White's introduction to the
essay collection, one gathers that Katharine's garden provided
the right colors, shapes, and scents throughout the year.) Much
of the planting and growing delights me because of the connections I can make.

The blooming of the Vanessa Bell, one of my favorite roses
from the David Austin catalogue, reminds me of one of the last
public readings that William Trevor gave, in 2008; I had flown
from California to England to attend the event, which took place
in Charleston, Vanessa Bell and Duncan Grant's house in East
Sussex. Emily Brontë, another of my favorite David Austin roses,
blooms with what I call "a wuthering tenderness," and when the
Emily Brontës are blooming I always think of my first reading of

Wuthering Heights, as a teenager in Beijing. Mystified and electri-
fied, I held on to the book as though it offered a refuge for my
mind, but I now suspect that I was only pretending to understand
the passion and the drama in the story. A few Roald Dahls from
David Austin were planted because Dahl was among my children's
favorite authors when they were young. The Lady of Shalott and
Tess of the d'Urbervilles for poetry and fiction. The Lady Gardener
as a self-mocking gesture.

Over the past few years, I've added a dozen hydrangea bushes
to the garden, because one of my characters, Lilia—who, like me,
lost a child at the age of forty-four—has grown hydrangeas all
her life with a passion. [It was the novel I was working on when
Vincent died. I had already written about the death of Lilia's child
when I encountered the same loss.]

Daylilies are not really my favorite, but I grow them because in
my father's village in southern China the soil is the meagerest type,
and the only crops my father's family could grow were yams and
daylilies; the flowers were harvested for culinary use—a delicacy
for other people.

Some flowers in my garden have been inherited from the previous owners: astilbes, baptisias, azaleas, and buddleias. When
the astilbes bloom, their white flowers make a shimmering mass
in the sun, countering the meaning of their name, in Greek, as
something that does not shimmer. The baptisias have indigo flowers, and the name comes from the Greek: to dip, to immerse, to
dye (which shares the root with "baptism"). Azaleas' name, too,
comes from the Greek, meaning "dry," but there is nothing dry
about these flowers. Buddleias, however, were simply named for
an English botanist, Adam Buddle.

Primroses bloom early, before the roses. Anemones (ancient
Greek's daughters of the wind) wave their strikingly colorful
and delicate flowers in the spring breeze. Geraniums (from the
Greek: cranes) expand long-leggedly. Campanulas (from the
Latin: little bells) produce bell-shaped flowers without making a
cacophony. These and other varieties I have added to the garden.
Some have stayed and prospered. Others have proved to be a
trustworthy food supply for rabbits. Delphiniums, I have learned,
can never stay in the garden for more than a few days. Dianthus
and phlox are a game of statistics, which is possibly just like fate;

if they survive the raids of the rabbits, they have neither themselves nor me to credit.

When Vincent was in the eighth grade, I drove him and a friend,
a girl, back from a birthday party, and, like all mothers, I eaves-
dropped on their conversation. They were discussing the girl's
decision not to participate in a poetry contest. She had read the
previous winners, she said, and they were composed of words such
as "injustice," "inequality," "empowerment," "action." "What I don't
understand," the girl said, "is why can't we write about flowers anymore."

"Of course we can," Vincent said. "But . . ."

He did not finish the sentence. I wondered if he was asking: Is
there still a place for Emily Dickinson these days?

Every spring, when the first flush of David Austin roses bloom,
there is always a moment when I turn, in my mind, to Vincent.
"Here's something you haven't seen: these roses." The line is
offered as a fact, not as an argument, for a rose is never an argument. There is no such thing as an angry rose or a moping rose
or an empowered rose; only a realistic rose, a matter-of-fact rose,
a transient rose.

A garden is a place full of random, diverting, and irrelevant
happenings, and a garden, as good as a rabbit hole, serves also
as an antidote to a black hole. These days, I often get up early.
Every flower seems to require an individual greeting from me. In
the Buddhist tradition, one encounters sayings like "A flower is a
world, a grass leaf is a paradise." But I, not quite a believer in any
kind of religion or metaphor, would rather think that each flower
in my garden holds some concrete space, a physical one as well as
a temporal one. A flower, like a thought, a sentence, a book, is but a
placeholder.

AMY MARGOLIS

1978

FROM *The Iowa Review*

Insurance. Kansas City. *1978*.

In the photo, my father and I sit at the dining room table—a repurposed card table that belonged to crazy Aunt Pearl in her apartment on the Country Club Plaza.

I'm seventeen. My father is sixty-one. We are a long people, and in Aunt Pearl's low, spindly, card-table chairs, my father's torso is colossal. It might be the Belvedere Torso, if the Belvedere Torso wore a herringbone sports jacket and had a head.

In our house, everything is out of scale. The palatial, valanced drapes are too heavy for the room. Aunt Pearl's enormous baroque breakfront occupies nearly an entire wall.

It's 1978. I'm wearing a long-sleeved black leotard, Lee jeans, and platform sandals with nude knee-high nylons. A suffusion of eerie light, the kind of light spaceships arrive in, softens the edges of my bony frame. It's possible I'm dematerializing.

On the wall, between the palatial drapes and the enormous breakfront, hangs the sand-cast sculpture my uncle Harry made of the tablets Moses brought down from Sinai. The crooked tablets pitch forward, eager to be hurled.

Today, I leave this place and fly to New York City, with a suitcase full of leotards and tights, to begin my formal training as a dancer. I'm going to my older sister, an actress, a shattering beauty I barely know, and to Hell's Kitchen, my new neighborhood, and to the

Martha Graham School of Contemporary Dance, and to the men who will teach me how to be a woman.

Across the table, my father instructs me in the ways of health insurance in case I crack my head. He turns the pages of a fat booklet that is my personal policy. Between us, the tall tapers my parents are too anxious to light steady themselves in their miniature holders.

My father looks over his reading glasses, which he calls his half-asses, and says, "Don't crack your head."

In the corner, a crushed laundry basket piled high with sheets is ready to erupt.

Egg Salad. New York. 1978.

We decided we'd make egg salad. It required all three of us: Paul and Philip—giants both, with prodigious appetites—and me, a line drawing of a girl with turned-out feet and a bun so taut and so trained that my hairline strained to hold fast to my face. At seventeen, it already receded to my ears. I didn't know how to roast a chicken, even, nor had I learned, in the sure, sinister style of Betty Crocker, how to make an egg behave. I didn't cook. I barely ate, less still in the company of men. There was much I didn't do in the company of men. It didn't matter how gay they were.

Which came first, the chicken or the egg?

Paul said, "We'll add a little mustard. A little mustard gives it a flavor."

"I'd like to try Sister's version tonight, thank you," Philip said. He'd had an audition that afternoon for a commercial. Something humiliating. Bodily. Already he guessed he wouldn't get a callback. Philip was a dear, a great big lovey, but he could turn on a dime, like a husband. What did I know of husbands? I knew this much: they could turn on a dime.

"I prefer to have the egg salad Little Sister's way."

Paul shrank with a miniscule grief. He was easy to wound. It was easy to see exactly where, usually at the base of his broad, bony sternum, two fingers above his xiphoid process, where you would sink the heel of your hand to revive him.

Paul was long and lean and attenuated, like a dying note.

"Gawd. I'm suggesting a little mustard for a flavor, merely," he said. "But if it *hurts* you, if it causes you some sort of *injury*, well, banish the thought." Paul returned the yellow tin of dry mustard to the cupboard. I was rather hoping to get a closer look at it, this mustard that had a life beyond the refrigerator door. Paul was my first Canadian, and I was curious to know what other new shapes his condiments might take. I wanted some time in that spice cabinet.

Paul instructed me: "Philip's a delicate flower in the flavor department, darling. He's highly olfactory."

I took note of this fact re: Philip. I asked Paul to spell olfactory, please, and he did, slowly and distinctly, while I copied it out on the inside of my forearm. I would look it up when I got back to our apartment, my sister's and mine.

"What's your secret, hon?" Paul asked. "What do you like to use in your egg salad?"

Probably he sensed I was stricken by the question. Beyond the obvious, egg salad might comprise just about anything. It was a head-scratcher, egg salad. Why did they call it that, even? It was no longer an egg, never a salad.

I stood in Paul and Philip's kitchen noodling this mystery until Paul took my elbow and walked me to the refrigerator. We perused its contents arm in arm.

"Pickles?" I hazarded.

"Splendid," Paul said.

It was the year my whole life started.

I Do Not Wish to Go into the Volcano. New York. 1978.

The night Paul and I had agreed to have sex, he arrived with a branch of yellow freesia that smelled like Juicy Fruit, a package of Tiparillos, and a Charleston Chew.

"I come in peace," he said, and smiled.

I plucked the Charleston Chew from his hand. I looked into the hallway—to the right, to the left—and made sure he wasn't spotted, and I nodded him silently into the apartment, as if it were a speakeasy. I bolted the door behind him. Then chained it.

I appraised the Charleston Chew in my two palms. Who knew you could find them here. Who knew where to look, even. I closed my eyes and turned it around in my fingers, and when the paper wrapper crackled and exhaled its fumes, I thought I might actually faint. I wanted badly to bury my face in it.

"You said you used to like those, back when you ate candy, like a regular person."

"I love them," I said.

"Super!" Paul said. "When was that exactly? How old were you then, when you ate the candies?"

I abandoned Paul to the foyer. I guessed he supposed he should ask all these personal questions now that we were going to have sex. It was a courtesy, this line of inquiry, that I knew straight fellows affected, but I wondered where Paul had heard of it. The movies, I guessed. Or maybe Canada.

I retired to my fainting couch with my Tiparillos and my Charleston Chew, and I tried not to weep with the joy of it.

"Can I come in?" Paul asked, still standing in the foyer, holding the branch of freesia.

Mornings on the Upper West Side, the ballerinas, pared down like eels, stretch and bend into the long light. At the barre, their slender arms draw arcs. They reach absently for something far, far away; they don't much hunger for it. A ballet mistress floats in on tiptoe, a little skirt just concealing her rump. She claps her tiny hands, which flutter around her like a fan, and sings, "People, people," and they all glide to attention.

On the East Side, at the Martha Graham School of Contemporary Dance, we throw a virgin into a volcano to start the day.

I am an affront to Armgard von Bardeleben, who leads our class at Martha Graham. Armgard is a towering, Aryan monster-woman whose name has limbs in it. It is impossible for me to disguise how frightened I am of her. It is there in the mirror for the entire room to see, and from every angle.

She gives us the combination and the pianist begins to play. He is a furious Jamaican with long dreadlocks, and he shakes his head no—no, no, no—when he plays and when he pauses. He resides in a state of refusal. From across the room, Armgard eyes me suspiciously. I'm already off tempo. I am, as a rule, too much in my own head, in my own world. I'm too dependent on the mirror. I don't listen to the music. I am an adolescent girl given to abstraction, and no matter how hard I try to hold fast to my body, it escapes me. It's quicker and nimbler than I am. Years from now, when I am

in college, I'll learn to blame the Gnostics for starting this argument. I'll shake my fist to high heaven and call them fuckers. Why
did you do it, you fuckers! But today, I am a head chasing after a
body on Sixty-Third Street and Second Avenue, and this spectacle
infuriates Armgard von Bardeleben.

"Ach, du lieber Gott!" she screams. The Jamaican accompanist
rears up like a horse and lands back on the keys. "You, you . . . !"
Armgard starts, and in the mirror I watch her pull off her ballet
slipper to fight me.

Paul's body is so attenuated and refined, I might pulverize him. I
am such a galoot, such an irredeemable oaf. Outside the studio,
I'm a sprawling mess of errant parts, only outside the studio they
haven't removed all the furniture. I walk two fingers up the rungs
of Paul's sternum and balance them on his clavicle. "I'm gonna
jump!" I say, with quavering finger-knees, and in a second, distant
voice I call back, "Do it! Do it!" I enact this small suicide one time
after another.

"We're not getting anywhere with this," Paul says.

Paul has come here to do me this favor. There is nothing for him
in it except the opportunity for convention, which is a novelty. Paul
is a faggot. "Say it, darling," he tells me. "With *gusto*." I cannot say
it. Nor can I say what I am—a virgin—but I don't have to because
it's there for all the world to see, like a giant pineapple growing out
of my head. Every week my virginity sprouts a new, garish fruit, and
soon I will labor under the weight of a headdress as high as Carmen
Miranda's. I want it off me.

The night we made our date with convention, Paul said, "Say I'm
a faggot, or I won't sleep with you."

Between the bed and the wall, where I have wedged myself, it's soft
and warm on one side, cool and hard on the other. I am perfectly
balanced on the equator. "My darling," Paul says, "this can't work.
Not with you over there and me over here. What's happening?"

"I love it here," I say.

"You love it," Paul says. "How fabulous for you. But you're hiding from me, and that makes me feel lonely. That makes me feel
like a crumb."

"Why?" I ask. "You're not supposed to care. The point was that
you don't care."

Paul stands and pulls the bed from the wall. I drop from the equator straight to the floor. "Okay," he says, "that was mean," and he lies down. "That was a mean thing to say, and you said it."

This is why I must never speak.

I lie under the bed, my palms on the box spring where I imagine Paul's body should be.

"Paul?" I say, in a voice so small it's nearly a whisper. "Paul, I love you."

"You don't have to say that," he says.

"It's true," I say.

"You don't have to mean it, either."

Armgard von Bardeleben has stopped class to make me turn across the floor until I am able to locate the music in my body. "We have all the day, yes?" she asks the class. The class agrees we do. I begin on a clean diagonal, but after several passes, I pick up speed and start to veer. "Don't you stop, you!" she shouts. "Don't you *dream* to stop." The Jamaican accompanist sees I'm headed for him and stretches both arms across his keyboard. As I reach him, he bolts off the bench and takes hold of me by my bun. He walks me backward into the waist of the grand piano, like a tango. He brings his face to my ear.

"Girl," he says, his breath hot on my neck. "This is my home. You've come into my house now."

"Better," says Armgard, and she waves the class back to the center.

Alone in my bed at night, the furious Jamaican pianist and I dance. In our dance, we run circles around each other. I circle once, twice. The third time I run and throw myself into his arms. He winds up like a hammer thrower, the sweat flying from his dreads. He turns and turns and hurls me across the music, and somehow he's catching me on the other side.

Men Among Men. New York. 1978.

Tonight, Paul and Philip and I are going to a club in the old Meatpacking District, a neighborhood I haven't been to.

"What should I wear?" I ask Paul. When we go to clubs, Paul has something to say about my outfit. Mostly we go to Studio 54, where you have to be chosen to get in, where a crush of people strains against a red velvet rope—straight people in tube tops and chinos.

"What you have on works," Paul says. "Your cheekbones could use some light."

At Studio 54 there is a gatekeeper. For some reason that no one has explained, we have a privileged status. For us the gatekeeper unhooks the red velvet rope, the waters part, and we pass like the Jews out of Egypt. The passage is terrifying. I lower my head and make myself small, and I hold tight to Paul's hand or to the edge of Philip's giant cape. I hurry through and hope to God I'm not plucked out and left to stand on Fifty-Fourth Street alone at midnight with the straight people in chinos.

Tonight, for the club in the Meatpacking District, I wear a shiny black leotard—a dress-up leotard—and Lee jeans. Lee has just started making a special cut for ladies. The flaps of fabric at the sides would be for my hips, if I had hips. On me, the ladies' jeans have an equestrian flair.

"You could put on a different pair of jeans," Paul says.

The Meatpacking District is an abandoned civilization in the teeming city. We get in a cab and Philip gives the driver directions, but it's as if he says, "Take us to nowhere," and the driver knows exactly where nowhere is.

In New York, I am always afraid, but never with Paul and Philip. Paul and Philip are men, especially Philip. They're towering figures both, and unabashed, and at home in their skin. They're older than me and they know everything. In Manhattan Plaza, the apartment complex where we live, Paul dresses me up like a doll and powders me with sparkle dust and Philip pulls me onto his lap and reads me the stories I missed in childhood, like the story of Babar, who is an elephant, and also French.

There is no traffic in the Meatpacking District. There are no storefronts, no homeless, no garbage cans or human detritus. Sometimes, in Midtown or in the Village, Philip opens his giant cape and throws it around me like Dracula. Together we walk, my arms around his waist. I close my eyes and go where he takes me.

Tonight, in the Meatpacking District, we're bare, we're too much exposed.

"Where's the meat?" I ask.

"The meat!" Paul screams, and laughs. When Paul laughs, he throws his head back like a starlet. He has a flexible neck for a man.

"The butcher shops," I say. "The slaughterhouses. Where are they?"

I'm from Kansas City, a cow town, but I don't like to think about slaughterhouses. Still, I wish there were one here now.

"Long gone," Philip says. "The meatpackers packed up and left years and years ago."

"Where's the meat!" Paul sings. His voice rolls like smoke along the barren streets to the river.

The bar is in a narrow street behind a door with no sign. The music is so loud and percussive, it makes the long, low building's tenuous roof jump. Outside, the cracked sidewalk trembles underfoot.

Paul and Philip install me on a stool at the bar. Men in leather pants and white muscle shirts, the shirts we call wifebeaters where I grew up, rush to pet and embrace me. I'm the only woman here. I wish I had taken more care with my outfit, with my face. The men stroke my hair. One leans in close and says, "You're flawless." He gives me the softest kiss on my forehead, like the kiss Glinda the Good Witch gives Dorothy.

The men lock elbows with Paul and Philip and dance them away, into the crowd of other men.

I'm so painfully shy, it's a misery for me to speak, but here I'm not expected to. The bare-chested bartender brings me sweet drinks—the kind no real drinker drinks—and I perch demurely, fishing for cherries and pineapple chunks in my frosted glass. I nod along to the music. I enjoy my rich interior life.

My life with Paul and Philip asks practically nothing of me. I'm content to wait for them outside the dim rooms at the backs of bars that don't have signs, and to avert my eyes—this is easy for me—from the doings of men among men in the absence of women. I'm a dancer. I spend my days with men in leotards, like me. We're shapes in a mirror. I spend my days with women who starve themselves pitilessly. They want badly to escape gravity. I want to hold fast to the floor. I want to feel something like weight. I want to land.

In the dim light of the room that separates the bar from the bathrooms, the men pulse and bend, their lithe shadows fading.

I am the only lady in the ladies' room. The ladies' room is full of men. Men making out against the walls, at the sinks, in the stalls. Somehow I imagine that when they understand I'm here, the men will stop and file out in an orderly fashion. They'll wash their hands first, of course. It doesn't work this way. I bend down and look under the stalls, hoping for one without feet. There are so many feet facing every which way, some in odd numbers.

"At the end, Cookie," one of the men says, tipping his head in the direction of the last stall.

I enter the stall and lock the door. I take stock. I cannot urinate in a room full of men. This is a fact. This is a hard truth. I hang my purse on the hook on the stall door and walk out. "Excuse me," I say. "Pardon me, please," I say, and I turn on every faucet at every sink. I return to my stall and get to work. I should not have worn a leotard to a bar in the Meatpacking District.

From the toilet, the gush of water from so many faucets softens the sounds the men make with one another. I'm peaceful enough now and pleased with myself for my easiness in a bathroom full of men. Here I am, I think, in a bathroom full of men, going to the bathroom.

From a hole in the stall wall between me and my neighbor, near the toilet paper holder, an engorged penis advances. It stops. In the garish fluorescent bathroom light, it's unmistakable. Also, impossible. It's the color of a new brick. It's mapped with fat blue veins. It has the merest bend, toward me.

I study it, the errant penis. It throbs with life.

If I were a mother, I'd wrap it in soft cloths and place it in a basket among the bulrushes and float it down the river to safety like baby Moses. But I'm not a mother. I'm barely a woman. This is what I'm here to learn. This is what I hope Paul and Philip will, somehow, teach me.

Teach me how to be a woman in a body.

I take a length of toilet paper and drape it over the penis. I'm at a loss for a social convention in this particular situation. I'm sure there is something one does in this instance, but I understand I'm not the one to do it. The penis is not intended for me.

Because it's never inappropriate to say thank you, I say it.

"Thank you," I say.

Through the hole the penis leaves behind: the swish of coarse denim, a metal belt buckle, a shoe dropped to the floor, and dropped again. My neighbor is putting himself together in such a hurry, he's lost his balance. He careens from wall to wall. I cover the hole with my palm.

"Shhh," I want to whisper. "I'm not the authorities. I'm not the

Gestapo." In my mind, I'm Anne Frank and my anonymous neighbor is also Anne Frank. We must stay perfectly still. But I say nothing. I understand that it's a kindness to say nothing. It's a kindness to flush the toilet and upset this silence. It's a kindness to let the anonymous man anonymously take his leave of me.

This is the first goodbye.

NICOLE GRAEV LIPSON

As They Like It:
Learning to Follow My Child's Lead

FROM *Virginia Quarterly Review*

Act I

I want my students to fall madly in love with Rosalind. She's my favorite of all Shakespeare's heroines, I tell them, pressing my hand to my heart, pretending to swoon. They watch me gamely from their desks—the boys with their 2009 Justin Bieber bowl cuts, the girls in their UGGs, all of them the sort of ambitious student who would actually choose a course on Shakespearean comedy for their senior English elective.

It's my first time teaching *As You Like It*, a play rarely included on high school syllabi, though I've never understood why. There's no Shakespeare tale more attuned to the restless yearning of the teenage heart than that of Rosalind, who disguises herself as a shepherd named Ganymede and flees her uncle's oppressive court for the lush and embracing Forest of Arden. There, she and her cousin Celia, posing as Ganymede's sister, consort with the local rustics and engage in the sorts of activities that high schoolers love: flouting conventions, philosophizing, pursuing their crushes, cracking dirty jokes. Plus, it's in *As You Like It* that the famous "All the world's a stage" speech appears, and who better to contemplate this notion than teenagers, just now realizing that everyone is walking around pretending?

Over the following weeks, I'll introduce my students to the five-act structure and the themes of pastoral drama and the main divergence between comedy and tragedy (in the former, things go awry and all is mended; in the latter, things go awry and everyone dies). But my true goal—the goal that keeps me awake at night tinkering with lesson plans, the goal that makes me feel the work that I've chosen matters—is to use this play to convince these future custodians of the world they must all be feminists.

I start by passing around a handout: three Elizabethan men of letters extolling the womanly virtues. "There is nothing that becommeth a maid better than soberness, silence, shamefastness, and chastitie," we're informed by Thomas Bentley, compiler of a 1,500-page women's prayer book—and it doesn't take long for my students to conclude that this line of thinking persists. I take volunteers to act out Rosalind's first scene: "Look," I say, "how she shatters this absurd standard with her wit and eloquence!" and then watch with satisfaction as they scribble in their books. I share with them a fact I love, which is that Rosalind speaks more lines than any other Shakespearean heroine—"Quantitative proof," I nearly shout, "of her refusal to be silent."

If this baby turns out to be a girl, I say, resting my palm on my middle, five months round with my first child, then I will name her Rosalind and pray that she grows to be as brilliant and brave as her namesake.

Teaching is always personal, but now I'm possessed by the personal. What does it mean, I ask my students, that Rosalind can only feel safe in the forest dressed as a boy? (I want no daughter of mine to feel, as I have, the cold-veined terror of walking alone in a female body down a shadowed alley.) What does it mean, I ask, that Rosalind can only voice her romantic needs to her crush, Orlando, when she's duped him into thinking she's a boy? (I want no daughter of mine to know, as I have, the cramped, mute pain of censoring herself to please a man.)

One day, I have a terrific idea for a homework assignment. Go home, I say, and write a one-page description of your day: what you did, thought, felt. Then, turn your paper over and describe this same day, but imagining you're the opposite sex. It isn't enough for us to traffic in abstractions: I want these girls to feel the daily ways their femaleness constrains them, so that they might be moved to fight these constraints. I want these boys to feel what their female classmates feel, so that they might be moved to become allies in this fight.

There are few greater joys, when you're a teacher, than discovering the key that unlocks what you've been trying to pry open. But in the final minutes of class the next day, as one student, and then another, reads their homework aloud, time slows and the desks tilt and I understand without knowing how to stop it that everything is going wrong. The boys, in the form of girls, giggle and sway their hips and put on lip gloss. The girls, in the form of boys, play football and hit on chicks. Instead of dissolving stereotypes, what we're doing, in this excruciating semicircle, is reifying them.

And then things get worse.

I move through the room, collecting the homework. When I get to Lucas, he keeps his eyes down, shifts some papers around.

"Did you leave it at home, Lucas?"

"No," he says.

"Did you forget to do it?"

"No," he says.

Lucas is one of the most diligent students I've ever had, and in the best of ways, because his diligence has nothing to do with college applications or compliance but with a deep and driving desire to really get things. He has never, in the two years I've been his teacher, failed to turn in work.

The room has emptied and it's just the two of us. Silence. Fluorescent light. Something is wrong. Something raw and beating hangs in the space between us. I do not know what this thing is or how to draw it out so that I can tend to it.

"Can you help me out a little?" I try.

He looks at me. There are freckles on his nose, curtains of hair across his forehead. Behind his glasses, his eyes are two hazel pools. "It was just too hard," he says, "to write about this topic."

I am not understanding. The air is thick with my lack of understanding.

"Too hard?"

He looks up at the ceiling, takes a breath. "Too hard," he goes on, "because I think about it every day of my life. All I want is for my brain to stop fucking thinking about it."

His words pool in my ears and linger there. And because it is the first decade of the new century—because Caitlyn Jenner is not yet Caitlyn Jenner and public bathrooms are not yet the focus of op-eds and pronouns are only on my radar when I'm planning grammar lessons; because my softness pleases me and my curves please me and the secret sinuous parts of me please me and I've had no reason to imagine what my life would be like if they didn't; and because it has never once occurred to me, inside the tunnel of my own agenda, that Rosalind might yearn for something other than equality when she slips into the clothes of a man—it takes far longer than it should for me to grasp what he is telling me.

"I see, Lucas," I say. "I see."

But the truth is, I was only just then beginning to see.

I had no idea how hard it would be to see.

Act II

When our daughter is born, my husband, Paul, and I do not name her Rosalind—but she takes after my favorite heroine nonetheless. She announces her needs with muscular cries, grabs onto the world with determined fists. Like Rosalind, she delights in humor, grinning as she bites her toes on the changing table, toppling with laughter when we pretend to drink from her bottle. And she loves, like Rosalind, to talk: in coos, in words, in paragraphs—in romping soliloquies delivered from the back of the car. She is sprightly and clever, can keep up with the quickest of clowns.

So we're a little confused, when Leah starts kindergarten, that she seems to have such trouble making friends. She hunkers beside me on the playground bench as her classmates gallop by, grows sullen when I suggest she join a couple of girls on the swings. The scene before her beckons, joyous and wheeling, but something is keeping her watching, trapped in the wings.

When she finally makes a friend, I'm deeply relieved. Zeke loves Han Solo and the Beast Quest fantasy series like her, and when they joust with their homemade lightsabers in our kitchen, their laughs are indistinguishable. Through Zeke, Leah becomes friends with Miles, and then with Daniel and Jinhai, Tobias and Max, and before long, she has a true and proper crew. She looks forward to school, and her face shines, and she is happy.

I've never been a fan of the label *tomboy*—the way it suggests there's only one real way to be a girl. And yet, can we ever fully escape the language we've been handed to map our world? My daughter becomes, before my eyes, a tomboy, for this is the most familiar way I have to see her. And in truth, I take a little pride in her tomboyishness—have maybe even encouraged it, careful not to read her books like *Fancy Nancy* and *Pinkalicious,* careful not to ooh and aah over the way her skirt twirls. Unlike the beribboned Nancy in her dress-up heels, a girl who can run with the boys is slightly renegade, like the gutsy heroines from my favorite children's classics: Jo March, getting into "scrapes" and sullying her petticoats; Scout in her overalls, rolling in tires. She's a girl who has dared to cast off the limits imposed on her.

Rosalind goes a step further than these tomboy heroines when she decides not simply to act like a boy but to impersonate one. By the end of *As You Like It's* first act, her ruthless uncle has usurped her father's throne, sent him into hiding, and banished her from his court: Rosalind, in other words, has been completely undone by patriarchy. Despondent, she speaks in listless monosyllables as she and Celia plan their escape to Arden—until she has an invigorating idea: Wouldn't it be wonderful, she suggests, her phrases lengthening, her imagery gathering energy, "That I did suit me all points like a man? / A gallant curtle-axe upon my thigh, / A boar-spear in my hand." No matter how terrified she is on their journey, she proclaims, she'll project "a swashing and a martial outside, / As many other mannish cowards have / That do outface it with their semblances." Centuries before Judith Butler, here is Rosalind, surmising in her own whimsical way that gender is a performance.

But once she's actually in costume, traveling through the forest, something interesting happens: Her emotional landscape shifts to align with her male attire. "I could find it in my heart to disgrace my man's apparel and to cry like a woman," she announces to Celia when they arrive, exhausted, in Arden. "But," she goes on, "I must comfort the weaker vessel, as doublet and hose ought to show itself courageous to petticoat." Her masculine clothing rouses something in her, and she rises above her own distress to encourage her cousin onward. This might seem like a moment of virtuoso acting on Rosalind's part—the consummate Butlerian performance. But is it really? The inner strength she summons is, after all, her strength. Freed from the corsets and costumery of womanhood, it isn't manhood Rosalind steps into, but her truest self.

This is the version of Rosalind that lives in me as I watch Leah on the playground one fall afternoon in first grade. She and a throng of classmates have organized a chasing game, boys against girls—and she is on the boys' team. She rockets through leaves, shouting commands to her teammates, shins streaked with dirt, ponytail whipping in the wind. On the boys' team, my daughter scales slides like mountains and stretches her limbs to her soul's horizons. On the boys' team, she's the powerful girl she is.

This is the Rosalind I carry in my heart one year later, when Leah comes down to breakfast in her little brother's clothes: cargo shorts and button-down shirt, shark-tooth necklace and baseball cap. Seconds later, Jacob comes trailing behind in her clothes: a gold headband and dotted leggings and the yellow eyelet skirt my mother bought her for special occasions. He spins and prances, howls with laughter—there isn't room in his body to contain how hilarious this is. But Leah, in the hallway mirror, does not laugh. She narrows her eyes, turns her hat backward. In boys' clothes, she is the cool, slick girl she is.

And when my daughter starts third grade, this is the Rosalind I see her through, like a transparent overlay, as we wander through Target looking for back-to-school clothes. She walks down the bubblegum pink aisles of the girls' section, past sequined T-shirts and ruffled sweatshirts—circling and circling, scanning, searching—and then drifts into the rugged outback of the boys' section, where she pulls item after item from the shelves until her arms are loaded. In the boys' section, my daughter claims what hasn't been offered to her. In the boys' section, she's the dissident girl she is.

I know this plot so well and I'm a sucker for it—the one about the girl who finds, in the trappings of boyhood, her ticket to autonomy. Rosalind is hardly the only fictional maiden who cross-dresses her way to emancipation. She isn't even the only one conceived by Shakespeare, who also gave us Imogen and Julia, Viola in her servant's livery and Portia in her lawyer's robes. Centuries before Rosalind, there was Athena, who appeared in male guise to assist Odysseus, and Ovid's Iphis, whose mother raised her as a boy to save her from infanticide. And centuries later came her many film successors, like Mulan, who poses as a soldier to save her father from conscription in the army; and Terry from the '80s teen flick *Just One of the Guys*, who masquerades as a boy to get an edge in a high school internship competition; and Viola of the *Twelfth Night*—inspired comedy *She's the Man*, who impersonates her brother so she can play college soccer after her team's been cut.

This storyline, like the conditions that give rise to it, isn't just the stuff of fiction. Think of the female authors—the Brontë sisters and George Eliot and George Sand and Isak Dinesen and P. L. Travers and P. D. James—who've assumed masculine pen names to get their voices heard. The Victorian surgeon Margaret Ann Bulkley lived for years as Dr. James Barry so she could practice medicine. Kathrine Switzer became the first woman to register and run in the Boston Marathon, using just her first and middle initials to sneak past the ban on female athletes. Rachel Balkovec broke into the male-dominated dugouts of professional baseball by using the name "Rae" on her résumé, eventually becoming the first female manager in the history of the minor leagues.

When we get home from Target, Leah spills her new clothes onto the breakfast table. And then, right there in our kitchen, she tugs and shimmies her way into them one by one: the stove-pipe jeans; the pocket T-shirt; the baggy hoodie; the navy parka. As she zips and snaps herself in, her cheeks pinkening, her eyes brightening, I see a girl who is doing what she can to unleash her powers and hold tight to her fate. This is a story that makes sense to me, a story I can get behind.

And like Switzer, Mulan, Rosalind, and all the other cross-dressing heroines who've captured my imagination, my daughter, too, I assume, will one day reach the part of the story when her disguise has served its purpose. Her courage revealed, her ambitions realized, she will slough off her costume like a rumpled cocoon. And then, true to the tomboy canon, she will stand, plain and proud, in the truth of who she is—the beautiful, flesh-and-blood girl I birthed into the world.

Act III

In 1599, the year Shakespeare wrote *As You Like It*, wearing male clothing was becoming something of a trend among urban English women. Emboldened by the increased social mobility that accompanied the earliest stirrings of capitalism, many appeared in public donning cloaks, doublets, feathered hats, and other mannish trappings—a practice that didn't go over well with England's ruling class, who understood how this threatened their patriarchal authority. Ministers, under the order of James I, invoked Deuteronomy as they warned their parishioners that "The woman shall not wear that which pertaineth unto a man . . . for all that do so are an abomination unto the Lord thy God." Those who violated this command risked being whipped or pilloried by London's magistrates.

In fourth grade, my daughter does not abandon her costume. As she enters fifth grade, she does not abandon her costume. At what age, had she lived in early modern England, would she have been old enough to be punished for her transgression?

I'm grateful to live in a decade and country where we can clothe ourselves as we like with less chance of arrest. But as Leah's tomboy phase stretches into early adolescence, my pride becomes more measured. I'm unsettled to notice how the "girl" things of this world she's simply done without have become, over time, the targets of her snarkiest derision. She snorts at her little sister's hair bows, says "Ewww . . ." when she ends up with the pink mug at breakfast. Where's the line, I begin to wonder, between a healthy rejection of female stereotypes and misogyny absorbed and turned inward? This thought nags at me, making me long to see my daughter find strength and vitality inside her girlhood rather than on the lam from it.

Rosalind, too, is in no rush to give up her masculine presentation, pretending to be Ganymede long after her disguise has served its purpose. She's made it to Arden unscathed, ingratiated herself with the locals, and settled happily into country living— and still she maintains the ruse. And who could blame her? Not only does her costume unleash her buried courage and powers of expression, but it enables her to do the unthinkable for a woman at the time and acquire her own property, a working farm she buys from a local shepherd.

Rosalind decides to prolong her performance even further when she discovers that the dashing Orlando, whom she recently met at court, is also in the forest, where he's come to escape his murderous brother. Though she's spoken with Orlando only once, the encounter was enough to leave her besotted. And she's thrilled to learn—as she stumbles upon the love poems he's penned in her honor and strewn from Arden's trees—that their conversation left him just as smitten. "Alas the day! what shall I do with my doublet and hose?" she exclaims to Celia when she learns Orlando is close by. Resuming their flirtation, she realizes, will mean relinquishing her disguise.

But when Orlando wanders onto the scene moments later, she makes the split-second decision to stay in character. "I will speak to him like a saucy lackey," she whispers to Celia, "and under that habit play the knave with him." As Ganymede, Rosalind can be her most audacious self with Orlando, and her agile mind is on peak display in their verbal jousting that follows. By the time the two part, she's come up with an idea that will allow her to enjoy both the freedom of her male persona and the romantic energy between her and Orlando. What he must do, Rosalind-as-Ganymede tells him, is submit to her no-fail remedy for lovesickness, which turns out to be a sort of rudimentary form of psychodrama therapy: she can "cure" him, she says, if he agrees to call her Rosalind and visit her daily, pretending to woo her.

As the pair carry out this plan, we see a near-total reversal of the conventional dynamics of courtship. Orlando may seem, in their role-play, to be the pursuer, but it's Rosalind who truly holds the power, prescribing for Orlando the moves he should make, the words he should utter. As Ganymede, Rosalind slowly shapes him into the lover she wishes him to be—a little less melodramatic, a little more clear-sighted. Her schooling makes him worthy, by the play's end, of the restoration of her female identity and her hand in marriage.

I remember watching a 2008 performance of *As You Like It* on the Boston Common, pre-motherhood, grinning in the summer dusk as the actress playing Rosalind embodied, superbly, her character's fiendish thrill at upending the gender norms of romance. But I think if I were to attend this same production now, I might be even more compelled by the brief scene that follows, in which Celia lays into Rosalind for the sexist jokes she's been making to Orlando "man-to-man." "You have simply misused our sex in your love-prate," she exclaims, berating her treasonous cousin for what she's "done to her own nest."

These are the words I would hang on now, from my blanket on the grass, for there would be—if not in the flesh, then in my thoughts—my daughter sitting beside me, with her lanky legs and enormous high tops, her rounding hips and boxy track shorts, leaving me doubting whether freedom based on a double standard is freedom at all. And there would be, underneath this, a far less abstract fear: that in trying to stop the world from turning my daughter into the girl it wants her to be, I've sent the message there's something wrong with being a girl altogether.

If you've known the corrosive burden of second-guessing the lessons you've imparted as a parent, maybe you'll understand my relief when, in the fall of fifth grade, Leah makes friends with a group of girls she adores. Maybe you'll understand how my entire body lightens when these girls come to our house for a sleepover, where they paint squish toys shaped like ice cream cones and stir up brimming bowls of rainbow slime. Maybe you'll understand the absolution I feel when I open my email, one day, to find a link to a floral romper Leah hopes I will buy her.

Let me describe what I feel when my daughter appears in my doorway asking, for the first time ever, if I'll French braid her hair. We sit down on my rug, and I run my hands through her waves, feeling them tumble, thick and silky, between my fingers. I weave one section over another, gathering in more strands, smoothing down my work. And as I do, I am flooded by a memory of sitting in front of my own mother at her dressing table, feeling her slip barrettes into place behind my temples. The air is fragrant from her shower and warm from her rollers and I feel cared for and anointed in a way that is distinctly feminine, that has everything to do with the tending of one female body by another. I have returned, on this rug, to my own lived version of maidenhood, familiar and comforting as my mother's touch. I take in the pale curve of Leah's neck, the smooth edge of her shoulder, and am seized by possessive wonder at this miracle of a girl, in whose lineaments I recognize my own.

I have no idea that, just three months later, Leah will give away her floral romper to her little sister, though Nora is half a decade away from fitting into it. I have no idea that I will sit behind her at the barbershop she has begged me to bring her to, watching her hair drop in long, dark sheaves to the floor.

Act IV

"All the world's a stage, / And all the men and women merely players," observes Jaques, the secondary character who utters *As You Like It's* most renowned words. The summer of 2021, when Leah crops her hair an inch from her head, is the summer a curtain opens, and she steps out onto the set a different character.

The entire theater we inhabit, in fact, has been transformed. It seems to me that the world until this moment followed one set of logic, and now it follows a different logic, as if I've been transported in the dark of night to an upside-down realm.

The summer Leah cuts off nearly all her hair is the summer she asks me what my favorite boys' names are. It's the summer a friend's nephew starts to go by *she* and Cora from around the corner starts to go by *he* and a classmate of Leah's starts to go by *she* some days and *he* others. It's the summer I can no longer keep Leah's friends' names straight, for Caroline has become Cal and then Cody, and when April arrives at our house for dinner, I learn that he's Aiden. Our days become a pageant of exits and entrances, everyone coming and going playing different parts.

It's during this summer—the one before sixth grade—that Leah teaches me about Bitmojis, the cute digital avatars you can customize. She shows me how they work, scrolling through the selection categories: There are options for gender and options for age, options for skin tone and options for body type, options for pants and skirts and shoes and hats and scarves and belts and gloves and glasses and rings and watches. She helps me make my own Bitmoji, and I get a little window into the fun of it, this limitless choose-your-own adventure of personal identity. "Want to see mine?" Leah asks, and with a touch of a finger here she is: a rakish mop-headed kid in a striped rugby shirt, sneakers planted firmly on the ground.

The summer of Leah's haircut marks the start of a perpetual season of mistaken identity. "What can I get for you, buddy?" a Starbucks barista asks her that August. "Morning, sir," says the friendly crossing guard that fall. One Saturday the following winter, our family walks to a nearby synagogue to attend a bat mitzvah. As Leah climbs the steps in her boots and bulky parka, the security guard gives her a thumbs-up: "You keeping everyone protected, Muscles?" he says. Nothing in her expression helps me understand how she feels about these greetings.

Do I consider, as my daughter's body reshapes itself under her winter layers into woman form, that perhaps this isn't a passing phase at all? Do I wonder, when I behold her avatar, what deeper, unspoken longings it might contain? I do—more and more every day, I do—for in 2021, discussions of gender identity are everywhere: in curricula and lectures and PTA meetings and

appendix

board meetings and broadcasts and podcasts and the pages of celebrity magazines, where Demi Lovato has revealed she's non-binary and Elliot Page has opened up about stepping into his male identity.

I think often, during this cultural efflorescence, of my student Lucas—the caged pain in his eyes, the courage it must have taken him to break the silence between us—and how much easier his teen years could have been had he been born just one decade later. I wonder where Lucas is now, and whether he's found his way to comfort and wholeness. My hopes for Lucas's happiness are surprisingly strong given how long it's been since I knew him—and far simpler than the mix of emotions that churns in me as I watch my daughter's spirit converge with the fervors of her era.

Leah is my child, yes: It's natural that my relationship to her identity would be more complicated. But my preoccupations are more specific than this. I can't stop thinking, for instance, about a particular Slate article reporting that, between 2006 and 2013, trans-youth clinics in North America and Europe saw more female-assigned patients seeking treatment than vice versa—a significant change from prior years. Researchers offer various possible explanations for this shift, but one thing I think about as I read, which the piece doesn't mention, is the difference between what it means to live as a man and to live as a woman—a difference that, since 2016, has only become grimmer for women. "How gender identities are constituted and how specific brands of sexuality are formed," writes scholar Keith Thomas in a reissued 1994 *New York Review of Books* essay I come across about queer undercurrents in Renaissance texts, "are issues that are inseparably connected with the structure of power and the working of society in all its dimensions." Changing gender is never a power-neutral conversion—a truth my friend Mira hinted at, less eloquently, after the reversal of *Roe v. Wade*, when she said, "I never doubt the depth of trans women's dysphoria, because why the hell else would someone choose to become a woman in our fucked-up patriarchy?"

I laughed loud and hard at this comment, not only because I found it funny, but also because I understood it to be the sort of thing we aren't supposed to say as well-meaning liberals in a well-meaning liberal Boston suburb. I'm no longer certain what I can and cannot say, but more and more, I suspect that what I'm thinking falls in the latter category. I should not wonder aloud—as Paul and I have in private—whether the drastic uptick in transgender youth might in part reflect a rising preference for gender-bending as the particular teen reinvention mode du jour, the way I briefly became a goth in 1992, or speculate that all these name changes must be hard for teachers to keep track of.

When I'm helping a gallery curator friend write a press release for an exhibit of art by mothers—all of whom, including me, are cisgender women—and she sheepishly suggests we omit the word "woman," I don't object. Like her, I understand that to claim my native womanhood as something distinguishable from trans-womanhood—and my motherhood as something inseverable from my womanhood—is to risk being branded a "transphobe" or "TERF," no matter how fully I support trans rights.

I should not mention to anyone outside my closest circle my discomfort reading the *Self* magazine story titled "6 Things You Should Know Before Having Top Surgery," as if it were dishing out tips for a kettlebell workout.

When the third mother in a two-month span tells me that her own teenage child has had, or will be having, top surgery—which is another way of saying they have had, or will be having, their breasts cut off—I should respond with a gentle head tilt and supportive nod. I must not let on, as I am nodding, the visceral sorrow this image has stirred in me, and how I can't disentangle it from all the violences perpetrated on the bodies of girls, and which girls, far too often, turn on themselves. Nodding at this mother, I wonder for an instant if I might have cut off my breasts had this option been commonly available when I was in the throes of adolescence, the new and unruly markers of my femaleness filling me with such humiliation that I starved myself down to an amenorrheic androgyny. I knew nothing at all, in those days, of the powers lying dormant in my breasts—the pleasure of them cupped in the hands of a lover, the miracle of them nourishing new life.

I keep these thoughts silent, too—not just now, but always. I keep silent as I watch my daughter out of the corner of my eye, my reservations building in me like a sinister subplot.

I don't know what to say when Leah is greeted as a boy, for I haven't figured out what to do with my uncertainty, or what kind of mother to be in this upside-down theater. And so I say nothing as we leave Starbucks, nothing on the far side of the crosswalk, nothing after we've passed the temple security guard—because to say something feels like stepping into a thicket I don't know how to beat a path through. To say something is to name, and to name is to turn the intangible into something real and solid and corporeal that must be reckoned with.

One day, without warning, Paul steps right into this thicket. Our family has just arrived at a tropical-themed family party at a restaurant, where a smiling waiter distributes leis of orchids to the female guests and cowrie-bead necklaces to the male ones. As Leah pulls over her head the beads that she's been handed, Paul turns to her: "Do you want us to correct people," he asks, "when they assume you're a boy?" My breath catches behind my ribs. From where I stand, ruminating and paralyzed, even this simple question seems reckless. Leah is quiet for a moment, and then she shrugs a little.

"I guess I don't really care either way," she says.

It makes sense that Paul, a less tentative human than me generally, would be less tentative about entering this territory. But I wonder, sometimes, if his comparative ease when we discuss the changes in Leah behind closed doors has anything to do with the fact that the version of selfhood our daughter is migrating toward is his version of selfhood, original and familiar to him. Every day that passes feels like one more mile she's drifted from me, her native homeland, to a foreign harbor. There's pain for me in this parting, a pain it's difficult for me to give voice to, though I hear it, from time to time, in my barbed attempts at lightness. "If she is going to dress like a guy," I say to Paul one day after Leah leaves the house in a Hawaiian shirt and chinos, "must it be a middle-aged insurance salesman?" A little gallows humor to temper my grief.

Maybe, in this way, my story isn't a new story, though its details are particular to our era. Maybe it's the story shared by parents everywhere, since time immemorial, who've had to accept, as their children grow, that they are not them. Maybe I've reached that turning point all parents, in their individual ways, must someday reach, when the world, it feels, has spun out from under our feet, taking our children with it toward a future we can't catch up to.

One spring afternoon, I pick up Leah at school, and she slides into the passenger seat beside me. She opens a bag of potato chips and fiddles with the radio buttons, stopping when she gets to KISS FM. Dove Cameron's "Boyfriend" is on again. *I could be a better boyfriend than him,* crows Cameron in her sultry soprano to the implied female love interest she's trying to steal. Leah hums and bops along with her shoulders for a bit, and then pauses: "Just pretend you don't notice the bad language, Mom," she says.

"What bad language?"

"You didn't hear that?"

I listen closer. "Beyond the boyfriend part I can barely make out the words."

"Huh," Leah says. She crunches a potato chip, takes a sip from her water bottle. "Maybe it's like how there are certain frequencies people can't hear anymore once they're old," she jokes.

Maybe so, I think, as we speed through stands of oak trees thickening with leaves—for I am no longer certain whether my years allow me to see more than my oldest child, or whether they keep me from seeing the things that she sees at all.

Act V

As far as I know, Rosalind is the only Shakespearean character to be the subject of a biography. On the surface, this concept makes no sense at all, since biographies are about real, not made-up, people. But theater scholar Angela Thirlwell pulls the conceit off beautifully in *Rosalind: Shakespeare's Immortal Heroine,* which I discover one afternoon at my town library. From the moment I could read, my favorite characters have often felt more real to me than living people—and here, according to the flap copy, was someone as taken by Rosalind as I was.

In bed that night, I skip ahead to the chapter "Call Me Ganymede—Rosalind Crosses the Border," hoping, as my daughter drifts into her own borderlands across the hall, it might contain something helpful. As I read, I'm reminded that, in Shakespeare's time, male actors performed all female roles, since women were barred from the stage. This means that by the middle of *As You Like It,* Rosalind contains not two or even three but four layers of gender: She's a man (the actor), who plays a woman (Rosalind), pretending to be a man (Ganymede), who impersonates a woman (Rosalind). You'd think all this switching back and forth would confuse audiences. But as I think back to the productions of the play that I've seen—from that outdoor staging on Boston Common, to the BBC film version with Helen Mirren, to the Kenneth Branagh adaptation set in Japan—I can't remember ever losing grasp of which Rosalind I was watching. Or, more accurately, it didn't so much matter which Rosalind I was watching, because her layers had melded into a single, cohesive character whose moods and fluctuations made perfect sense. At one moment, this character might be more masculine, and at another, more feminine—but she was always, always Rosalind.

In my first teaching job, in my twenties, I co-taught eleventh-grade English with another new teacher, who would become one of the most treasured friends of my life. Sara and I pored over *Frankenstein* and *The Bluest Eye* together, planned lessons after school together, graded essays over sangria together, becoming, over time, such a constant and mutually adoring unit that another teacher, Brian, took to calling us the Married Couple. In the faculty room one day, he posed to us a very heteronormative and possibly flirtatious question: "So, which one of you is the husband, and which one the wife?"

It was a puzzle that depended entirely on superficial stereotypes—and therefore a puzzle unworthy of being solved. And yet, against our better judgment, we found ourselves thinking about it. I'm demurer than Sara, we decided, but also more practical. Sara is bolder than me, but also more emotional. I'm daintier than Sara, but also more thick-skinned. She's sturdier than me, but also more porous. No matter how many times we went over it, the traits culturally marked as "male" and "female" seemed to exist in us more or less equally—just as they do in the rational and irrational, sensible and romantic, courageous and cautious Rosalind, whose power lies not, I've come to believe, in her assumption of maleness, but in her ability to transcend the categories of gender altogether.

When I'm with Leah and we run into people we haven't seen in a while, I can see how they struggle with her in-betweenness. Their eyes stay on her a second too long; their weight shifts. *What is she?* they seem to be thinking. I'm as susceptible to the urge to classify as anyone, but I've begun to notice, in these moments, a protective impulse flare in me. I want to warn them to step back. Leave her be. I cannot tell these people what my daughter is: when I look at her, I see only my child.

On the last day of sixth grade, I take Leah for lunch to celebrate. The sun shines on our outdoor table, and while I haven't planned to have with her a Serious Talk About Identity, something about the gentle air of this day prompts me to dip a toe in. I mention a child at Leah's Hebrew school who has started going by *they/them* pronouns, marveling aloud at how far the world has come since I was her age, how much more sophisticatedly her generation thinks about gender. Leah's eyes dance; her whole body seems to buzz to life. And then she begins to talk to me—volubly and gleefully, like an eager scholar—about all she knows and feels and thinks on this subject.

A silence opens up. "Leah," I say, smoothing out the napkin on my lap, "I've been curious how you think about your gender."

She looks at me, surprised and a little delighted. She smiles a bit. She thinks for a moment. And then she claps her head in her hands in a pantomime of confusion. "I don't know!" she says. "I never know what to say when teachers ask us to go around and say what our pronouns are."

She falls quiet, sips from her glass. I can see she has said all she will.

Before I know it, I am articulating things to my daughter that I haven't, until this very moment, known I've thought. Things about how rapidly the world is moving, and how insistently it seems to want its children to catch up. Things about the beauty and truth that can bloom in the taking of time. Leah listens, almost certainly not fully understanding my ramblings, but happily spooning up her pasta nonetheless, and then after a while we drift to another topic, and she orders another Sprite, and I eat another piece of bread. From the outside, it looks like nothing at this table has changed, but on this dappled patio of the Cheesecake Factory, there's a lightness between us I haven't felt in ages.

As You Like It is very much a play about lightness. When its characters flee the court, they trade rigidity and convention for open-endedness and improvisation: In Arden's pastures, they can follow their curiosities, test out alternatives, reverse course, live "as they like." This flexibility is what separates Shakespeare's comic heroes from his tragic ones—like Lear, or Macbeth, or Othello, whose single-minded need for certainty sends them hurtling toward death, the ultimate final conclusion. I remember being totally fascinated to learn, from my college Shakespeare professor, that the conditional word *if* appears more often in *As You Like It* than in any other Shakespeare play—nearly 150 times. Most of these appearances occur while the characters are in Arden, its spirit of possibility alive even at the sentence level. Touchstone, the court jester who's tagged along with Rosalind and Celia to the forest, delivers a lengthy ode to the swinging-door magic of this little conjunction, which can make anything provisional. "Your If is the only peacemaker," he proclaims. "Much virtue in If."

Much virtue in If. I've been returning to this phrase lately, revolving it in my mind, holding it up as a sort of mantra. So often, as a mother, I'm either being a gatekeeper, barring my children from going where I feel they shouldn't, or a cheerleader, speeding them to where I feel they should. But between these poles lies another way—which is to be Arden, a neutral witness to my children's wanderings, a shaded wood where they can play out their possible selves. It isn't easy for me to linger in semidarkness. Maybe it's hard for all of us. We want our clear outlines, our firm contours. We want our drawers and our shelves, our slots and compartments. We want our ten steps, our seven stages, our five acts, our three acts. We want our introductions and conclusions— and here, before I bid adieu, is mine.

That night, before she goes to sleep, Leah calls to me from her room. "You coming, Mom?" I'm certain that, any day now, she'll decide she's too old for this ritual, and I'll be dispatched for good. But for now, I'm still wanted here, on this bed cluttered with stuffed animals, under a poster of Harry Styles—a perfectly composed tableau of human becoming. I curl my arm around my daughter, tucking it under her side. As we lie in the quiet, I think for a second that I should probably seize this opportunity to pick up our conversation from lunch, probe a bit more, help Leah get to the bottom of what it is that she is and how she wants to be seen.

Is loving the same thing as seeing? In this moment, I feel that it's not.

I reach out across the chasm of my blindness, taking my child's hand in the dark.

KATHLEEN ALCOTT

Trapdoor

TOWARD THE END of my life in New York, a decade and change I would dispense with as casually as I'd begun it, came a season of psychic misery that felt as vertiginous, as alarming and noiseless, as a winding drive along a cliff—the windows sealed shut against a danger still visible. My acupuncturist, Christina,* might have been the only person who knew how truly I had wanted to stop living. Six months into treating me, a period in which my than-atotic impulses could alight on certain objects as glistering and totemic, she moved offices, taking up in an unremarkable office building on Union Square. It was December 2021 when I first visited her there, on a half-vacant ninth floor, and an elevator opened to reveal the most unusual door I had ever seen. Isolated at one end of the hall, it left me succored, almost beatific. On glass painted black, unsteadily at the edges, was a prim gold-leaf heading: OFFICE OF THE ESTATE OF SAMUEL KLEIN, DECEASED. Under that, six names were printed in the same serif—the text DEC'D appended, with a baffling kind of menace, to three. I felt convinced that the knob had not been turned in recent history: whoever was responsible had declared themselves bereaved, a few times over, then vanished.

I've always been bored by the prospect of ghosts—I spend my fear on what life may contain, not what death might imperfectly silence—but I do like to feel in conversation with the decades that made my life possible. At the outset I believed this explained

---

* Her name has been changed to protect her privacy.

my feeling for the door. I imagined what decay and pestilence lay behind it—Dictaphones and hatboxes, green Tiffany desk lamps, ossifying mimeographs—but I was more fascinated by what it was than by what it might conceal, its silence nonpareil in a New York that had become, in the pandemic, operatic with a very American chaos. Its hush seemed to repudiate the shrieking city beyond, but it also forgave my darker contortions, my thoughts of vanishing that had not seemed fit for the lissome fountains or eager traffic, the pregnant clouds discoursing with great buildings outside.

I would die, I later texted someone, joking and certainly not, with a photo of the door, *to work in peace*. It was true that I'd been having a difficult time working, a problem that was more troubling for the fact that working—writing—was all I'd ever been capable of doing. The peculiar velocity of the fiction writer is to race head-to-head with what you've repressed until it overtakes you—whether to leave you tailing in interest, or overturned on the pavement of your real life, bloodied where the truth has cut you off. I was too young when I sold my first novel, twenty-two, to consider what it would mean to keep this kind of big-data cloud on my subconscious. Three books and a careerist, monomaniacal decade later, that record became the officious appendix to the jagged, episodic, spiritual crisis into which I fell.

When I had first gone to see Chris, it was ostensibly for a physical ailment, a startling pain at the base of my neck that physicians and chiropractors had not helped. It had come on with no inciting event, keeping me from turning a lock without a bolt of agony. I was single, thirty-two, living alone in pre-vaccine isolation, and I shattered three glasses in a week trying to lift them, and the injury felt tantamount to a judgment—if I had made different choices, if I'd had different priorities, when I would not have been trapped there, in the dark that was coming early and total, sliding toward me like water: someone loving would have risen to turn on a light. I had always felt my work was more important than I was—who cared whom I hurt, where I lived, or for how long—and I had mostly avoided the slow grade of real partnership, anyone who might reliably appear with a bag of vegetables or expect me to do the same, opting instead for obvious shows of smoke: relationships that took place suddenly in other countries or pressurized seasons, with remote people who flickered into oceans to surf or mountains to climb or wars to report, sending exquisite letters and allowing me, in their distance, mine. What I needed from any relationship, I would say, haughtily, was privacy: to be able to shut the door.

Until the inexplicable injury, I had been a zealous exerciser, demonstrably or hideously vain—too thin, the content and zaftig and married people in my life felt comfortable announcing. I had taken great care of my body, running bridges in balaclavas when winter slipped ruthless, because my mind was somewhere I didn't want to be left idle. I speculated that the pain might have something to do with the unusual position in which I slept, on which most people I'd been with had commented. *Mangled*, one man I loved said, seeming relieved I was finally awake. The reasons for my tendencies, waking and sleeping, had been hidden in my books and stories all along, but I had refused the pattern, and then my body had revolted.

When I mentioned the macabre, bituminous door to Chris, whose demeanor is something like a time-lapse of spring—brutality and kindness cycling in rapturous color—she did not have much to say. She had ministered to me while I lay in so many different kinds of crises, her face said; she had tried to help me in so many ways. Cupping and moxibustion; lancing and needling; something experimental called battlefield acupuncture, which involved her piercing my auricular cartilage with needles that stayed there for a week. Had I forgotten the months I felt hunted—by thoughts of death and risk, illness and drowning, accident and suicide, and by a particular secret of my childhood, which I had confessed to her as though I had just learned it? Chris, whose belief in qi had so often embarrassed me—*there!* she would shout, hearing what she claimed was my blood finding motive force—wanted me moving in the direction of life.

It was as if she understood that the door would magnetize that dark dimension of my thinking, the death drive that had made me alternately brave (or pathologically reckless) and clinically sad, and which I had always explained, perhaps a little too easily, with a constituent history: when I was young, before my brain had quite finished forming, my family died. I had struggled with how prominently, on the hierarchy of personal identifiers, this fact was meant to sit, even as I bitterly understood, and wished others would understand, its separative effect. The door, in its static defeat, was a palliative: proclaiming a past that would always be happening to those who had experienced it, as well as the sovereign right never to discuss it.

Writing fiction is a recursive disavowal, a psychic chase that requires moving between what is known about the self and where you vanish when you refuse to know it. It didn't occur to me until recently that I learned to dissociate early. As a reedy adolescent, spotlit onstage in adult repertory theater, I was already fleeing—reality in general, or the sound of my father's portable oxygen tank, which followed him around like a pet. It didn't occur to me until I heard one again, by chance, in public, and immediately moved to find an exit, how its once-a-minute hiss was the rhythm and ghoul of my childhood, or how a minute, to a child, is just long enough to disappear into it—lie to herself that something menacing isn't coming, feel frightened anew when it does. If the sound of my father reached me at all from where he was a faithful member of the darkened audience, I would look deeper into the lie of the play, spreading my shoulders in the clothes that weren't mine, enjoying conversations that always swung along the same hinge in another fixed time.

My first mingy paycheck as an artist came that way, a four-hundred-dollar stipend the year I was thirteen, a season in which I was the only child at rehearsals, and enraptured by the prospect of psychologies that weren't mine. All spring the sweatered director preached the Meisner technique—the same line, spoken a hundred times—and I watched divorcing, middle-age actors, sitting in folding chairs under stage lights, come to weeping by how the same words could transfigure, or blacken, if you repeated them continuously, if they were the only words you had. I remember the relief of reading about myself in a newspaper for the first time, a review of my performance that made me feel realer than I ever had (I was not anyone's daughter, I was not my life but a fact in print), and then the anxiety when I understood it might be some time before I was real again.

Maybe the Meisner method's tacky circularity intrigued me because it told me there was more I could learn, on my own, about things I could not really speak about. I was already turning over the same peculiarities of my childhood, the years my father had worked out an arrangement, after a period of living in his car, in which he would squat in a desiccated barn in the backyard of some neighbors of my mother's. My parents had met at the *Oakland Tribune* in 1987—he forty-six to her thirty-four—but by the time she was pregnant were both mysteriously unemployed and uninsured, perhaps due to involvement with substances that made life easier.

They married, packed up for a folksy town of forty thousand people one hour north, and two years later were divorced. There was only one house between ours and the lot with the barn: that of Martha and Peter, a one-dimensional pinnacle of happy whiteness— a dalmatian named Pepper, a baby on the way. I would sometimes hitch myself up the meager fence that bordered my mother's rental to peer over their groomed backyard, spying in order to catch a glimpse of my father's aggressive misery. He could usually be seen, through a gap that had once held a hay door, on the upper level, and it shamed me that he had no privacy. Their emerald lawn, his orange piss pot; their shining deck, his dewy sleeping bag; their white gazebo, his brown liquor.

There's no one left to ask why this seemed like a fine idea, allowing that laughably horrific aperture onto his dysfunction. My mother, in those years, was on public assistance and nursing to death her brother, who was in his mid-thirties and vanishing of AIDS—an extravagantly beautiful chef who insisted on cooking what he could no longer eat. She'd moved him into her bedroom and herself into mine, onto a mattress where it calmed me, from the vantage of my loft bed, to watch her sleep. I seem to remember my father's argument was for proximity, and that I was meant to understand his homelessness as a sacrifice undertaken on my behalf—his talents were too big for that small town, and if it weren't for me, he would have been elsewhere. Once a leftist of some volition and a journalist of some promise, though not of the fame or importance he insinuated and taught me to insinuate, he spent the last five years of his life an imperious gas station cashier, friendless and malignant, picking shouting matches with customers he believed had condescended to him. When this happened in my vicinity, I would pass out back to the station's garage, studying oil spills in the concrete as though they were clouds in the sky. I stopped acting when he finally died, the year I was fifteen, maybe because I no longer had the practical need. The years in between his dying and my beginning to publish—fifteen to twenty-two—are more or less lost to me. I was a bright girl in handcuffs, in and out of school, drinking opium in a narrow lace dress, falling from one level of a staggered roof to another in the middle of some brownout, barbacking for a season in Arkansas, dreamily pregnant in an alpine river and putting off the abortion, asking for trouble, trouble itself.

My cosplay of the past started at twenty in San Francisco, where all of my friends and lovers were in or orbiting bands like Thee Oh Sees or Ty Segall or Girls, Sic Alps or Royal Baths, who had digested polyphonic sixties psychedelia or melodic seventies hedonism to critical darling reception. California is a great preservationist of these decades, in part because the weather is less destructive to old things, and in part because its children, raised on the records and films that go on describing the twentieth century, harbor a magical belief that they invented it. We took all the same drugs, among the same trees, in the same clothes, that the culture we worshipped had directed us toward. We had Chelsea boots or winklepickers that clasped to one side, minidresses with accordion sleeves, shrug coats in jacquard chenille, and we smoked on marble stoops with a vague but animating revanchism that was not, in the peculiar blush of the first Obama Administration, altogether political— mostly a cruel scorn that might be directed at anyone who did not belong. This was the eve of the Google Bus, Google Glass, the bros in high-tech performance fabrics, but recession-desperate landlords were already throwing startups cheap leases in art deco buildings downtown. The end of our lotus-eating era would be particularly devastating to those who stayed to resist it, and the cautionary tales, later, were the people we had all known who in the space of a decade went from appearing in the pages of fashion magazines or *Rolling Stone* to sleeping in ATM vestibules, moving in with their mothers, or busking on Haight. I would remember one of them, how back then he'd seemed gentle to all the world, as tender with the crabs at a tidal pool where we might drive at dusk as he was with the cocaine on a gilt mirror, forever parting his long honey hair to one side or another, arranging fresh ranunculi on his mantel. I spent a week or three sleeping in that bedroom, under those cherub cornices. Though I can recall with him, with many of these people, that beneath the pretty images they projected it was hard to locate the there there, it didn't occur to me there was a reason I liked to be around that, or that I couldn't find their suffering because I didn't want to look for it. It didn't occur to me I was becoming a paper lantern myself.

As a writer among the musicians I was something of an interloper, watching for some egress I would know when it came, and I got out before the city emptied of culture in earnest. My real life began, or that was the way I put it to myself later, when I published a lugubrious piece of hagiography about my father, repurposing his own vainglorious phrases. *[My father] was almost killed once looking down the barrel of a machine gun in occupied Czechoslovakia while working for Radio Free Europe, once by an erupting volcano he stood on the rim of in Hawaii for the sake of reporting on it.* The piece enumerated his achievements, tidily summing up the sorry end of his life as some honorable consequence of the spectacle of Cold War decades in which he'd been so heroic. It gained me an agent, and I moved to New York, where she sold my first novel, and I started to associate with a different kind of person, Waspy, educated, rule-following. Very few people dressed the way I did, and no one knew about the ways I'd behaved, and then I stopped thinking of my father.

(My mother's life ended much more suddenly and politely than my father's had, soon after I left California. In March, she turned yellow as the daffodils just risen. In April, it seemed like all in one Sunday, she received the terminal pancreatic cancer diagnosis, decided she had better file a tax extension in case, showed me a meteor shower she had hallucinated, asked to use the bathroom, and died.)

Though I had long since drifted off the stage, my habits as a New Yorker must have appeared to others as eccentric or narcissistic theater. I had stepped, wittingly and not, into a new image: a distraction in pale green sequins, passing out of the revolving doors of midtown buildings with the last dinosaurs of publishing, old white men who taught me how to order a martini and from whose fiction mine seemed descended as they touched my knees. I did or could not think much about why my life had to look the way it did, whether snobbery was a response to trauma, appearance a layering response to unwelcome depths. I had stalked thrift stores and flea markets, becoming a manipulative, garrulous haggler. I had taught myself what World War II had done to women's wear, what certain epidemics had done to ideas about décor and furniture. At various points, I owned a celadon silk ball gown from the twenties, a framed original advertisement of Kenneth Noland's first show in a New York gallery, a Swiss art nouveau catalogue of mountain flowers, a coffee table book that bragged about the 1966 destructive flood of Florence, an original double-breasted

Rudi Gernreich bikini in impractical blue wool, a seventy-pound brutalist copper headboard marbled tawny and psychedelic, and a russet 1975 Volvo 164E. The car had no airbags, and, for the first year I owned it, a faulty brake booster, and it inspired at least a few dreams of my dying in flames.

What I loved about New York was not just how many eras went on simultaneously—the eighties in the chunky Memphis Group shapes for sale in the bleary lighting district along the Bowery, the sixties on uptown corners where you might see hats like wedding cakes disappearing into a yellow taxi. It was a breeding ground for a kind of temporal irredentism, creating small countries of people who had not kept up, and could survive by finding others among the eight million who had also, however obliviously or resolutely, refused the zeitgeist. My cultural intake had always been skewed toward music and paintings and films already canonized, and maybe I was happiest in the warstruck chiaroscuro of Marcel Carné, or the tilted feelings of the fauves for the woods, because I had read the theory, understood the trajectory of the movements. I knew which questions these pieces would ask of me, and if my horizons were low, spangled with spontaneous, sense-driven interactions and transactions, they offered me a kind of control I could never enjoy in my life with people. I gave little thought to the remark those behaviors out in the world made about my life in my mind—that perhaps, in order to avoid thinking of my past, what I had cultivated was a very obvious presence.

I hadn't known I was intent on transforming upward, but I remember reading pieces in the *New York Observer* and the *Daily Telegraph*, out of London, that described my appearance when there was no need to describe my appearance—"more Madison Avenue than Bedford Avenue with her bright blond hair, pocketbook and well-cut pastel outfit . . . too put-together to be at a party with $3 drink specials," "she dresses like a cross between a 1930s lady librarian and Diane Keaton in *Annie Hall*, all raffia clutch bag, sensible heels and mustard and beige tones"—and understanding I had pulled off a trick without really meaning to, that the feminine silhouettes that had yawned with some ironic bite in drug-smeared parties in the Mission and the Tenderloin scanned very differently elsewhere.

As the decade floated down, I populated my life with lucky, wealthy people, whose troubles I privately, selfishly, never saw as quite real, and whom I always started to resent after enough time had unwound. Why was I angry with them for seeing me as one of them, I wondered later, when for years I had contorted myself in order to pass, donning the correct wool blazer, living in the $3 million brownstone of a much older boyfriend, teaching at the right universities, learning to eat from atop the convexity of my down-turned fork tines, excusing myself to the restroom if the topic of my early life went afield of the slogans I'd devised, doing whatever I could to belong there and then, and not to the places and times I had left.

New York was the most hospitable environment for the way I needed to live, the paintings and buildings and cinemas and gardens a companionate supervening of relationships where I never really told the truth. I paid for cold borscht in private, traceless cash at B&H Dairy on Second Avenue; developed a psychosexual, contentious codependency with a gifted Russian cobbler named Gregor; bought braids of sweetgrass at the one Indian health food store that carried it; regularly spent twenty minutes in line at Film Forum, making conversation; met a stranger on a C train stalled for half an hour and spent a summer in bed with him; went without notice, as was later largely impossible, into museums and galleries. But still I couldn't manage the city without taking seasons, sometimes contiguous, away, meaning that people started asking *where* are you instead of *how*, which I must, in retrospect, have preferred. I loved my clothes packed into grids of color, the wheels of my suitcases slowly grinding into teeth. As my twenties dwindled, I shuttered my social-media accounts one by one, relishing the vanishing silence, the insistence that real life was sensory. My tastes were a locating religion, and my absences made it easier to icily break with many of the people of rarefied privilege with whom I'd become closest, and I observed my life with quiet righteousness as I whittled it down, as if I were not the one who would have to survive it.

Pessoa writes, in *The Book of Disquiet*, about an aesthetic being the saving grace of a secular life, describing a necessity in the vacuum left by the church, who had architected one's very subconscious. One has to live her waking hours understanding their influence on dreams, the book entreats, to prize the dreams above all else. This is, in fact, no way to live, though it is a way to sleep.

It's hard to remember exactly what I said to Chris, sobbing on her table in the winter of 2021, and easier to picture how she touched my face when that was a public health risk, and spoke my name while drawing breath from the same air. "It's going to get better," she had said, covering my bare body in medical paper, placing needles between my eyes, along my tibia and scapula, between my metatarsals. I was stunned to have found her, Christina, whose intake was two hours, who spoke to my insurance company to get me further care, who took notes with the dedicated focus of a professional interpreter.

But I guess that came later, her assertion that I would want to live my life rather than end it, as my mind had begun to obsessively threaten, once she had begun to treat me in earnest. I must still want to skip over the conversations we had at the outset, which I still cringe to recall, talking about the way I slept—on my stomach, left knee craned up, face screwed way right, arms cactussed in opposition.

Why did I sleep that way?

I wasn't sure, I answered, perhaps angrily, bothered by her bluntness. I had for as long as I could remember. But that was nothing I could help, and I had come so she would help me.

Why did I sleep that way?

I guess, I hemmed, because I'd had to share a bed with my father, when he'd had a bed, until I was about twelve, and because I'd kept my head away as so not to see him. Because I'd despised it.

Why did I despise it?

The answer was not, exactly, that my father had raped me, although the effects—namely, that he had made me feel soiled for eternity, separate from other people and so intent on avoiding commitments to them—were similar. My issues with intimacy were written not just all over me, but by me, in the fiction that knew me better. *That's what passed for paternity*, I had written in a short story, in the voice of a woman describing her father. *Making your daughter your little wife.* In every novel I'd written there was some kind of sexual disassociation or abuse, some kind of trauma experienced by a child who later fails to enter their own maturity, their own consequences, so exposed have they been to the intimacies and failures of the adults around them. There are some writers who keep copies of their own books on display, but I had always kept mine in boxes, hidden in closets and storage units and under where I slept.

And though I had always had trouble sleeping, I hadn't ever had trouble getting out of bed until, in the silence of the pandemic and the cage of my injury, I remembered what I must never have really forgotten about my father. It was not just how he threw glasses and screamed, or would floor the gas as a way of inciting fear until I spoke the apology he demanded, but how there'd been a sexual and romantic skein over almost everything he said and did. Rather than pay child support, he would send me what could only be called love letters, particularly after some episode of violence; rather than drive me to school, he would manically spend his little money on what could only be categorized as extravagant dates. Trips up in a single-prop plane, out on the bay to whale watch among the Farallon Islands, into some tacky open-air market to get a henna tattoo on my exposed shoulder, all the while taking photos, a roll of film in an afternoon, for all of my childhood asking that I pose against hill or ocean, edging closer on his knees to get the right angle. He would speak to me about the women he was sleeping with, and, by the time I was about ten, after he was firmly isolated by his illness or his dysfunction, graphically about the bodies of those he would like to, how long it had been since he'd been touched, what that did to a person psychologically, there were studies, there were essays, I should read them, he had left me something to read. My appearance was often the subject of letters he mailed to me at my mother's, a fixation that drove all the thin-strapped dresses he bought me when he had no place to live, then the portraits he paid photographers to take.

I had been in therapy on and off for ten years, mostly, I thought, to deal with being orphaned by early adulthood—but somehow I'd avoided the topic of my father's behavior, perhaps because of how much I'd needed the story of his life, as he'd related it to me, as a cornerstone of my own myth, and in part because I felt my traumas would have been illegible. When I went to see Chris, she had done me the intuitive favor of treating the maladies coming off my childhood as though I remained the child experiencing them, asking questions so facile, so sincere, I could not condescend to them. Do you know there's no way he's coming to get you? she had asked, and I buckled and I wept, scorning the sincerity of the exercise at the same time it unzipped me. There was nothing as humiliating or as painful as being an adult confined to childhood, I thought, then how that enclosure was just the other side of the

trapdoor you fell through after being a child confined to adulthood. I could locate no memories of my father assaulting me, only
a childhood and adolescence enduring physical transgressions just
at the threshold—his fingers in my mouth some sixish years later
than I was teething, shirtless massages I could only manage with
my eyes boiled shut, mysterious detours to other people's guest
rooms for solemn conversation—expecting subconsciously or not,
that someday he would.* It explained an anxiety that had always
followed me, the hollow curiosity about suicide that my mind
would surface as a narcotic, and the distinct, irrational suspicion
I'd always tendered: I would die young. When I looked into the
consequences of being sexually abused as a child, this was buried
among them: *the sense of a foreshortened future.* Coupled with that
sense was this fact: victims were much more likely to suffer a premature death.

My clearest memory of that season of recognition is calling an
ex who'd been hideously abused in his own childhood. It had been
years since we were together, but we still addressed each other
as *baby,* and I was walking through Central Park in a white wool
trench coat wondering why that was, thinking we were perhaps
both the kind of people who needed that infantilizing illusion—
someday, our sleep would be protected by somebody else. Maybe
I had called him hoping to be told how different my experience
had been, but as I qualified the ways perhaps my father's behavior
didn't constitute abuse, he giggled wickedly, lovingly, the way you
might at a child's insistence of some unreality. Soon, I might as
well have told him, I will open the first vegetarian restaurant on
the moon. Why vegetarian, you must ask the child, before you tell
her: honey, it's never going to happen on the moon.

What I had experienced, a new therapist told me soon after,
with no equivocation or doubt, was called *covert incest,* and I went
mute and wondered if I was going to black out. I had conceived
of the chaotic years after my father died as grief, but half my life

---

* In the process of fact-checking this essay, I reached out to my father's sister, from
whom he had been intermittently estranged. Not knowing the subject matter of the
piece, she said there was something she had always wanted to ask: Had my father
molested me? When she was twenty, and my father thirty-two, he had suggested he
sleep in her bed; her mother had not believed her. She had always had a feeling
about his behavior toward me, and relayed an anecdote, from the year I was three,
that to me all but confirmed it.

later it was clear: that was time lived not with the negative outline of someone whose care I'd lost, but in the ragged shape of a
weapon that someone damaged, or evil, had cut me. I had made
the lie about who he was so foundational that the truth was like
some illimitable gossip, reaching back into everything I'd achieved
or owned or planned—the five hundred thousand words I had
published, the brown tweed suit with mother-of-pearl buttons, the
people I had cared for and the reasons I had cared for them, the
vacations I had taken in ancient cities, or dense South American
rainforest, where I thought I had been happy. It made the rest of
my life seem like a deception, too, and then, for the first time I
could recall, I could not recall my reasons for getting out of bed.

I asked Chris to take a photo of me on her table that spring,
during a session when I was so obscured by paper and needles that
there was almost nothing to identify me except the horrific bevels
of my hip bones, and when she sent it to me later I could see what
people had been saying about my body, the concerning and total
lack of adipose tissue. But I also felt relief in what the image would
have suggested to anyone: I had been the subject of some experiment, and I had finally, mercifully, perhaps honorably, died.

I scuttled like a roach beneath the surface of a year and a half,
on Zoloft and Ambien, Lexapro and Adderall, Wellbutrin and
clonazepam and Gabapentin, temporizing, knowing dimly that
Christina was correct about some change I needed to make to
my life. I remember not that much—sobbing phone calls I took
in the snowy park. The paper bags from the pharmacy that cluttered the bottoms of my purses, the wheezing, vanishing, blue-
gray people who sat in the peeling vinyl chairs by the pickup
window, resigned to whichever delay of the pill that wouldn't
help them much. A month I was pulled between someone male
and cis-het and someone trans and nonbinary, both of whom, in
the rapidly unfurled and accepted umbrella of vanilla S and M
that had entered even the lexicon of advertising—you could see
buses advertising products for "every single submissive"—wanted
to be called *sir*. It was sort of funny, an old friend and I laughed,
how making love had become the subversive sexual act, though
when I thought about this alone it wasn't funny at all.

During this period I flickered in and out of aesthetic anonymity,
cutting off the waving hair that had kissed my waist, wearing fish-
ermen's wool and rubber boots, wondering blankly, newly, if I was

meant to be a woman, if I was meant to be a writer, what, most plainly, I was for. Judith Butler describes gender as an imitation without an original, and while it is true that I had always imagined my femininity first as how it would be photographed, I had not realized that the imitation I had come to perfect was of a woman who would have been company to my father in his glorious past—passenger, perhaps, in the car crash in a Spanish olive grove. He bragged that he survived it, under Franco's regime, with Afghan heroin in his pocket.

When I came to, vaguely stabilized, when I watched someone career down the sidewalk on one of the electric scooters that were suddenly ubiquitous, when I noticed their full-face monoglass that was protection against both COVID-19 and the sun, it was spring 2022, and I could no longer really locate the past I'd haunted. I'd spend an afternoon at the gym and thirty minutes after in the sauna, suppurating with impressions of the altered world outside, how on most blocks you saw the newly installed freestanding public touch screens—which looked and functioned like a phone but at a 1,000 percent scale, suggesting that if their own devices died, people would only accept help from something that looked like a bigger, permanent phone. The height of the pandemic had diseased the internet with a warty banality of white centrist think pieces about virtual office culture and virtual friendship culture and "the new normal," but I read nothing about how it actually felt to drag a physical self through a city that seemed insistent upon its new irrelevance. Even in the sauna, which I needed to be a final bodily refuge, people were on TikTok, texting and vaping, were wearing their gym clothes and putting their sneakers up on the wood and sniping at each other, as I seemed to hear all the time—the period of nearly socialist solidarity, the messaging on the subway directing us to protect one another, had fallen. Everyone understood, Americanly, that no one was coming to save them: it was every man for himself.

I claimed that the way New York made me feel now had to do with this era of selfishness and neoliberal technologies, with the blue light that seemed more preponderant than sun—I asked friends whether it did not seem like two years had elapsed but twenty—but I also knew that the way the city had seemed to transform was painful because of how obviously it insisted that the years of my blithe denial were over. After the city's reopening, I could operate again in some of the ways I preferred, but I couldn't even squint and fool myself that around the corner was some restaurant where I'd repeat the lines about my early life, about my father, and be believed, because I no longer believed them myself. My father, I used to say in interviews, made me into a writer, insisting I memorize words out of the dictionary. It was my greatest casuist pirouette—taking the fact that he had put words in my mouth, imbuing it with a flourish of moral worthiness.

In the summer I left the city to travel for a few months, sensing I would leave it permanently after returning in October. Christina was characteristically forceful; tucked in her blunt approval of my leaving was her criticism of the fact that I had stayed. On my way out of her office, I passed the door I had first seen the year before, the list of its dead. I hadn't told Christina that the door had become the last point of interest in a city that I had long stopped feeling curiosity for, and which, I selfishly and insanely felt, had long stopped feeling curiosity for me. I never mentioned how, during on-and-off bouts of insomnia, I'd gotten out of bed and googled the door with the thin, rote hope of someone putting on a kettle. During the sifting, spiking silences of two and three in the morning, I'd learned that the fourth person named on the door had also died; that the Klein family business, a discount clothing store, had in the thirties been the largest women's wear store in the world. I had felt a real longing, imagining the riches to be had for a steal—Klein, an erstwhile tailor with famous taste, claimed never to stock fewer than two hundred thousand pieces, and the prices hovered so low that the racks were befouled by riots. To those who had an eye, S. Klein's became an apparatus of upward mobility, but then the wealthy started shopping there for sport. It was the same story of class ascension I understood, building a life of costume and stage sets, the same threat that someone of means might slip around the back of the facade and knock at its flimsy supports.

The door seemed to suggest the present had never outpaced the past, as mine had not, that then and now lived alongside each other in a gentle custody agreement. Chris would have shaken her head if I mentioned this, turned her back to wash her hands. Perhaps, in the silence of her dismissal, I might have considered why this dissonant comity granted me such relief—how it demonstrated that life could contain two versions, and they need not contradict, speak to, or comment on each other.

At the base of the Pyrenees, in an economically bereft Catalonian village of a hundred people, I spent the afternoons after I'd written hiking into dry mountains, swimming in deep gorges, filching hot, wild peaches from the gnarled vestiges of an orchard abandoned some decades before. This had been a habit a long time, leaving the city for more and more remote solitude, and I had always needed to face trouble this way—alone above the tree line, down among a littoral cave system, when it could easily be said that no one knew exactly where I was, or gliding through a river or sea at night, where I could see my body as the same color as everything that surrounded it. Just as my fiction had hidden the more painful truths about my unhappiness, it had suggested a certain answer to it—the characters in it often disappeared to land, were last seen with a newly high, newly distant third-person narration, desperate then peaceful, passing into desert, vanishing into water or trees. *Is this safe?* friends had asked, over the years, the kind of familied people who cling to rocks and peer at distances. A death wish always has a brighter part to it, and this was mine, that I would climb high and swim deep, go alone and go far.

Toward the end of September, late at night in Madrid, hearing the susurrus of the very drunk meandering under the balcony, I witnessed myself email about a rental in northern California. The house sat on a hill in an unincorporated community of one thousand on the borders of Hitchcock country, far removed from any major freeways, where the pale belfries and golden hills are largely preserved by the burden of getting to them. I assumed it was an emotional coin toss I'd volley before myself, that I'd never live anywhere close to where I'd come from, that I'd back out once the possibility was real. I'd always looked down upon those who lived within driving distance of their nativities, believing that the point of life was lapidary, not continuous. But soon after I was taking a video tour, sending money across time zones, and then I was in New York packing up a decade of my life. Twice I called the number listed for the Klein estate, which never rang and went straight to voicemail. Wanting and not wanting a voice to answer, I was filled with the kind of shimmering dread that comes for the hallucinating, whose frangible place between worlds is the more frightening thing than the delusion itself.

Once the floors of my apartment were swept and all my possessions had been loaded onto a truck, I made a plan to say good-bye to Christina. When the time came and the elevator doors opened, I saw that the door was gone. It had been replaced with another—galvanized steel, the fodder of heist canon, absent of text or any other human indication. Pulling up a photo of the door on my phone, touching the steel, touching the other doors, zooming in on the photo to be sure I had the office number right, I was convinced the image was correct and the world was not, and I paced the hall, believing, as I tend to when confronted with some unquestionable fact, as I had for seventeen years, that I was not the one mistaken.

Standing outside Christina's office, we hugged a long time, and when I brought up the door's disappearance, she answered that the executors had moved offices, from the ninth to the third floor. When I passed down to see it—the 900 that no longer made sense, with direct neighbors on its left and right, much more visible than where it had been for eight decades—I found details I had missed when mistaking it for a monument. Around the gold-leaf letters, outlined with a fine brush in black paint much glossier than the matte that surrounded it, were the imprecise stitches of what appeared to be permanent marker: someone, trying to em-phasize the names of the dead, in the places where the original outline had faded, had left tiny claw marks of another black, and the chamfered wood framing the glass seemed recently repainted gold.

Staring at that glass which reflected nothing, my last night in the city, the last weeks before the clocks would abbreviate life into winter, I was galled by my long misconception—that the executors had baldly enunciated their grievances, then kept as far from their past as I had from mine. Instead, it turned out they'd always kept vigil, making small annotations to the boundary between life and their losses, to memory as they stood before it, leaving flowers, however stray and ragged.

In my last moments by the door, I scrawled a note to the two remaining executors, both likely in their eighties or nineties, slip-ping it through the mail slot's brass tongue, telling them I was fascinated, asking whether they'd speak to me. And just as they would not to the message I finally left on their answering machine, no one ever responded. I admired their evasion, for the right they were exercising was not so different than that of which I had availed myself. To live in furtive independence, however isolating or unpopular—to accept few messages, despite having left some, blatant, alarming, for others to read.

I arrived in California after dark, taking serpentine roads through fog, relieved to discover how frequently I had no service. Signs were everywhere, indicating distance and direction, insisting that the body went on without a digital shadow, unsynced and unreachable. I sat much of the week on my forested deck, surrounded by old-growth redwoods and lacy buckeyes and winding, mossy oaks and spritely palms, everywhere I looked another kind of green—sylvan, olive, that bluish juniper, an emerald glossed almost to black. Maybe I had come to witness some ending, the state as it buckled and myself as I molted, to pay penance for all the years I had not come home. I might last six months, I might make it a year, but now it was fire season, and it was easy to picture, foolish not to imagine, what those trees would look like gone orange and red: how I'd run out through the smoke, taking close to blind those same roads I had taken in, hurtling unknowing past gulches dry so long new life had begun to grow on their floors.

A few days in I hiked to the highest place I could find, winding toward the smell of ocean, coming across crowds of quail who moved like beads of the same necklace, elk that looked like shadows printed on the loamy distance. Rising six hundred feet, through verdant copses and others where burned trees looked like knives, I finally sat to cry. I bawled because I had escaped or finally knew I never would entirely, not my hometown or my class or my adopted city, but an idea that had stalked me since I was born my father's daughter: that my life was not really mine, but something he'd authored, and which belonged to him. So much of my life as a woman had been an assertion of my elemental separateness, living and dressing so I would not be mistaken for anybody, itself an orchestration of my wish never to be mistaken for anybody else's.

I thought then of the first time he got me high, when I must have been eleven, coughing hot smoke. We were lying on top of the covers in his rented room, amid the meager possessions of his life—a carved wooden box full of foreign coins and gold cuff links, the curling photo of Gandhi and printed Pete Seeger lyrics he had pinned up above his typewriter—and he asked in the pleasant, curious tone of a philosopher whether, if he could find a scientist who would halt my aging so I'd remain his little daughter forever, I would consent. That's where the memory precipitously stops, at the moment I knew that my answer was meant to be yes, that my subjugation would appease the great injustices he felt had been done to him.

It bores me, it shatters me to understand it, how much of our behavior is just a rejoinder to an old question, like something shouted down the hall at some delay, the hall being all the time we hurried down, the shout being the noise we make once we think we're safe.

From the distance of age I could nearly see it from above—how, when I was a child desperate to be alone, I had sometimes scrambled along the gossip of a creek. It made me dolorous now, to see those beds of stone where water no longer confided, and in the absence of that sound I listened to others. The tender owl at night, the anxious donkey afternoons. The red rufous hummingbirds who dove blaring through morning, tracing the shape of a *j* at such speed that their path downward could be mistaken for suicide, and the whir of their wings for some man-made weapon.

JAMES WHORTON JR.

An Upset Place

FROM *The Gettysburg Review*

1. Solo Male Goes West

Around 1840, Isaac Love left North Carolina on a borrowed horse. He was a young man with reddish hair. He could read. He had borrowed the horse without permission.

He crossed Tennessee longways, a trip that today takes six and a half hours by car, not counting gas stops. Isaac Love made the trip shortly after the forced removal of the Five Civilized Tribes across approximately the same ground. The tribes were called "civilized" because they wore cloth instead of skins, ate pork instead of game, and farmed with draft animals instead of hand tools. For the Cherokee, Chickasaw, Choctaw, Creek, and Seminole people—driven off in large groups that included the young, old, and sick—the trip took three to four months. Thousands died along the way. Isaac Love, a solo male on a horse, might have done it in a month.

How was his trip? I don't know. The kind of clothes he wore, the kind of hat, how often he got rained on, what knife he carried, what gun—unknown. Sometimes, it is safe to assume, dogs ran out barking at him as he passed a farm. Did he have a plan? Was he angry at his father? He must have talked to the horse. Among the things he saw that do not exist in Tennessee anymore were chestnut trees with trunks four feet across.

At the far edge of Tennessee, he came to a wide river of brown

water. The Mississippi River. It had a medley of smells and con-
tained whole trees, human waste, rotting vegetation, also living
vegetation, whiskered catfish, wedding rings, pencil shavings. . . .
Anything that could be lost or rinsed away was liable to join this
drainage channel to the south end of the continent. Today, driving
Interstate 40, travelers cross it on the Hernando de Soto Bridge.
Around the middle, they pass under a sign saying, Welcome to
Arkansas.

Love and his horse stepped onto a raft. Or maybe, in Memphis,
he sold the stolen horse and boarded a steamboat. From Memphis,
he would have floated down the river through a dozen U-shaped
bends. He'd have had the sun in his eyes one way, then the river
would twist, and the sun would be at his back. To one side a high
bank crumbled into the water, leaving bluffs topped with stands of
cane tall enough to hide a house, while on the other side, in some
places, the river had no visible bank—trees emerged directly out of
the water into a forest he could cross by canoe.

Shortly past Island 73, the river bent left, toward the town of
Rosedale, Mississippi.

At Island 74, the river cut right. That's where another big river,
the Arkansas, empties into the Mississippi. In the angle of those two
rivers was the doomed town of Napoleon, Arkansas.

Samuel Clemens, a frequent visitor to Napoleon, wrote that it
was a "town of innumerable fights—an inquest every day" in *Life on
the Mississippi*. The best hotel was a dismantled steamboat. Beyond
the town: swamp. The place was notorious for its mosquitoes,
"or muschetos," as Supreme Court Justice Peter Daniel described
them in a letter to his daughter, remarking also on "the Buffalo
Gnat, an insect so fierce & so insatiate that it kills the horses &
mules, bleeding them to death." The naturalist Thomas Nuttall,
passing through this part of Arkansas a few years earlier than Love,
described picking from his skin and clothes "more than fifty ticks
(*Acarus sanguisugas*), which are here more troublesome than in any
other part of America in which I have been."

Where Isaac Love spent his first night in Arkansas—in a bed, in
the steamboat that had been dragged up on shore in Napoleon, or
on a high piece of ground beside a horse tied to a tree—is unknown.

The mosquito may have been the deadliest animal in the Arkansas
swamps, but the panther got more respect. In *A Journal of Travels*

into the Arkansa Territory During the Year 1819, Nuttall recorded "a somewhat curious anecdote" his guide had told him about a dog, a wolf, and a deer found mangled under a tree. "It appeared that the panther, having killed a deer, and eat his fill, got into a tree to watch the remainder, and had, in his own defense, successively fallen upon the wolf and the dog as intruders on his provision."

Lesson: when you find a partly eaten deer in Arkansas, leave it alone.

A person did not see a panther every day. Even a panther did not see a panther every day. They traveled solo. People called them "painters," "lions," or "catamounts." A grown one with its tail stretched out was six or eight feet long. Its fur was the color of dry cane, except for some black at the end of its tail. When not hiding in trees, they sometimes hid in canebrakes.

Enormous woodpeckers hammered on branches overhead with their long, bone-white beaks. They were often seen in pairs, a black-crested female with a red-crested male. From this bird's perspective, a big cypress, oak, or water tupelo wasn't ripe for sixty or a hundred years, when its branches softened enough for the woodpecker to flake the bark off and probe for the white grubs fattening themselves to finger size. The pairs of woodpeckers hollowed out nests in these ripening branches, and from the ground, a person could watch them ducking in and out through a round opening, calling to each other in notes that sounded like someone learning to play the clarinet.

It was an upset place, the forested lowlands in this part of Arkansas. Boys were on the loose with sharp tools. One recalled the thrill of being permitted to hack down as many trees as he wanted: "Like a ruthless youth with latent destructive propensities, I found an extraordinary pleasure in laying low with a keen axe the broad pines. I welcomed with a savage delight the apparent agony, the portentous shiver which ran from foot to topmost plume, the thunderous fall, and the wild recoil of its neighbors, as it rebounded and quivered before it lay its still strength."

Like Isaac Love, that boy was a new arrival, a Welsh orphan going by the name William Stanley. Unlike Love, Stanley left a memoir that provides some crisp impressions of that churned-up time. After murdering twenty conifers, he turned his attention to the gangs of enslaved men who cut the felled trunks into pieces and hauled them into piles for burning. They chanted as they worked. "I became infected with their spirit and assisted at the log-rolling, or lent a hand at the toting," Stanley wrote. "I waxed so enthusiastic over this manly work, which demanded the exertion of every ounce of muscle, that it is a marvel I did not suffer from the strain."

He didn't really have time to suffer from the strain. An incident soon caused him to walk off the job. The problem was the overseer, whose whip, meant for a man named Jim, happened to brush uncomfortably close:

> He flicked at his naked shoulders with his whip, and the lash, flying unexpectedly near me, caused us both to drop our spikes. Unassisted by us, the weight of the log was too great for the others, and it fell to the ground crushing the foot of one of them. Meantime, furious at the indignity, I had engaged him in a wordy contest: hot words, even threats, were exchanged, and had it not been for the cries of the wounded man who was held fast by the log, we should probably have fought.

Stanley complained to the plantation owner, who smiled at Stanley's innocence. He was not about to involve himself in the details of which slave had been whipped and why. "Fieldwork" was the overseer's business.

Unlike Jim and the man whose foot was crushed, Stanley was free to leave, so he packed his things and stalked off into the woods, a solo Welsh boy with a head full of thoughts in Arkansas. "My eyes traveled through the far-reaching colonnades of tapering pine and flourishing oak, and for a great part of the time I lost consciousness of my circumstances, while my mind was absorbed in interminable imaginings of impossible discoveries and incidents." Had the "patty-rollers"—also known as the "paterolls" or the "patrollers"—come upon him during his hike, they would not have questioned him. His hair was straight, combed loosely across his forehead, and his eyes were light. Most importantly, he was light skinned; his color was his pass. Instead of thinking about evasion, he hoped to surprise some large predator and kill it with his walking stick. "I saw myself as the hero of many a thrilling surprise," he wrote. But he was telling himself a story and knew it. "Brought to a proper sense of the scenes, and my real condition, I recognized how helpless I was against a snarling catamount, or couchant panther; I was devoutly thankful that Arkansas was so civilized that my courage was in no fear of being tested."

Isaac Love also had light eyes. In this upset place, a solo male, free and unencumbered, could walk into the woods, clear some land he liked, and stay there. Brush could be cut and stumps dug out and burned. Where the ground was too wet to plow, ditches could be scraped out. The work was hard. To join up with others, though, meant giving up some part of the independence he had claimed by leaving the other place.

It was a trade-off: Freedom versus attachment. Solohood versus encumbrance. At this time in the Arkansas Delta, wild parakeets colored green, yellow, and red moved between the trees in flocks of hundreds. They lived their lives that way, nervously bunched. The panther, in contrast, was a solitary creature. It remained still for hours at a time, and when it moved, it went quietly, guarding its solitude until something prompted it to let out a cry that carried half a mile. The cry has been likened to a human scream, but it was designed by nature to sound like nothing other than a panther in heat. It is the signal these normally unsociable predators use, during a strange period in their lives, to find each other and make new panthers.

Isaac Love married a woman named Elizabeth Ferrell. Her parents, like Isaac, were immigrants from the East, but they had been there long enough to establish a farm in Desha County (pronounced de-SHAY), twenty miles outside Napoleon. No slaves on this farm; the family did the work of remaking the humpy forest with its old complexities—its black snakes drooping from branches or swimming on top of slow-moving water, its swarming and stinging flies, its mosquitos—into acres of flat, dark, alluvial soil drained by straight ditches. The steamboats burned wood, and in 1840, Desha County sold enough cut and split cordwood to form a pile four feet by four feet by fifteen miles long. On days when he was cutting trees, Isaac Love would have carried a whetstone in his pocket, bringing it out often to sharpen the axe. Over time, the flat surface of the stone became dished, and that was a record of his work.

Isaac and Elizabeth were not married long. The seventh US census recorded the causes of death for one year in Desha County:

Fever, Cholera, Rheumatism, Cholera, Inf. of Lungs, Inf. of
Bowels, Cholera, Cholera, Cholera, Cholera, Cholera, Con-
sumption, Consumption, Cholera, Cholera, Cholera, Cholera,
Cholera, Consumption, Consumption, Cholera, Cholera, Un-
known, Cholera, Cholera, Fever, Cholera, Worms, Inflam. of
Bowels, Cholera, Cholera, Unknown, Consumption, Whoop-
ing Cough, Whooping Cough, Whooping Cough, Whooping
Cough, Cholera, Drowned, Apoplexy, Fever, Fever, Flux, Flux,
Flux, Consumption, Flux, Flux, Croup, Croup, Unknown,
Unknown, Shot in Duel, Dropsy, Consumption, Flux, Flux,
Flux, Unknown, Pneumonia, Croup, Dropsy, Cholera, Fever,
Fit, Fever, Fever, Old Age, Scrofula, Fever, Cholera, Consump-
tion, Fever, Smallpox, Smallpox, Unknown, Cholera, Cholera,
Smallpox, Consumption, Fever, Pleurisy, Frozen, Croup, Fever,
Fever, Unknown, Unknown, Inflam. of Lungs, Liver Com-
plaint, Inflam. of Bowels, Inflam. of Brain, Fever, Fever, Chol-
era, Cholera, Cholera, Fever, Fever, Croup, Cholera, Fever,
Cholera, Fever, Worms, Scrofula, Cholera, Unknown, Worms,
Fever, Sudden, Unknown, Paralysis, Fever, Fever, Fever, Fever,
Cholera, Cholera, Fever, Fever, Fever, Fever, Fever, Inflam. of
Lungs, Worms, Fever, Fever, Fever, Consumption, Fever, Fever,
Sudden, Drowned, Unknown, Smallpox, Smallpox

In Elizabeth's case, the cause was likely related to the birth of
her first child.

Which is more astonishing: that people die or that they are born?

Regardless, the baby posed a serious problem for Isaac. A new
foal is up on its legs and looking for milk right away. Within a few
hours, its hooves are hard, and it is hopping up and down the paddock. The baby's feet, weeks into life, were still soft, and the toes
unfolded in a confused way, not like anything that would be useful
for walking. Its head was too big for its neck, its screaming was painful to hear, and the person with the milk was gone.

In Desha County at this time, men outnumbered women two
to one.

2. Arkansas

The state flag of Arkansas has four stars, symbolizing four sover-
eignties that have governed there: Spain, France, the Confederate

States, and the United States. In 2019, the Arkansas House of Representatives considered a bill to redesignate the Confederate star (it's the one on top—they look alike, though) to represent the people who lived there before the Europeans came. The *Arkansas Democrat-Gazette* quoted Robert Freeman of Hot Springs, who told the House State Agencies and Government Affairs Committee that "the tribes that lived in the state at the time of its settling 'contributed actually nothing' to the founding of the state."

He is correct, unless you consider leaving to be a contribution. By the time the State of Arkansas became a thing, the Quapaw people had already been pushed onto reservations farther west. The Quapaw Nation is today based in Oklahoma.

The earliest recorded immigrant from the East, first forerunner of Isaac Love, was the Spaniard after whom the I-40 bridge is named: Hernando de Soto. He appeared at the place called "Arcanças"—or "Akansea," or "Alkansas," or "Akanças"—on June 18, 1541, accompanied by a few hundred men, some horses, and a herd of Spanish pigs. They had been tramping through the pre-upset eastern woodlands of North America for two years. Their clothes having come apart, they wore combinations of hide and fur under their steel armor. The people they met in what would later be called "Arkansaw," or "Arkanzas," received them differently from place to place. One town welcomed them with pecans, fish, and persimmons. Another did not welcome them at all—when the Spaniards tramped into that village, it was empty.

De Soto was looking for gold. He died of fever—malaria from a mosquito bite, maybe. His body was added to the Mississippi, and the Spaniards moved on.

The French arrived 140 years later and by a more efficient route, floating down from what is now called Canada. The leader of this expedition was René-Robert Cavelier, Sieur de La Salle, and his object was not gold but real estate. On reaching the Gulf of Mexico in April 1682, La Salle sank a pole in the ground and read out a proclamation claiming the entire Mississippi River, along with all rivers emptying into it and all the country drained by those rivers, in the name of King Louis XIV.

The French called the place Louisiana. They established a few posts and did business with the people who lived there, trading knives, beads, and guns for furs and skins to be shipped back to

Europe. Natives and immigrants married, and the names of their towns were also mixed—Kaskaskia, Sainte Genevieve.

Thomas Nuttall, the man who picked fifty ticks from his clothes, found these French Americans to be a not very industrious group. They enjoyed dancing at their backwoods balls. The men dressed in leather pants like Indians. The village near Arkansas Post had no hatmaker, and the people wore handkerchiefs on their heads. They seemed content to grow a little corn and eat a lot of pork. Some kept slaves, but Nuttall considered them underutilized: "With a little industry, surely every person in possession of slaves might have, at least, a kitchen garden! But these Canadian descendants, so long nurtured amidst savages, have become strangers to civilized comforts and regular industry."

A girl named Julia lived on one of these farms. She was around twelve at the time of Nuttall's visit, a brown-eyed speaker of French and English. She had lived her whole life in Arkansas, in a house with no glass in the windows. She would have learned to cook over coals—cornbread, bacon, peas, beans, and sweet potatoes. She made butter. She looked after the younger children, and there were a lot in this household—Félicité, Jean-Baptiste, Pierre, Louis, Caliste, Mannet, Virginia, Reges, Israel, Arsene, Athenais. They were Catholic, and the priest noted their names as he baptized them. Eventually, Julia had a baby, too, a daughter baptized Mary Ann. There was a place in the register for the father to be listed, but the priest left that blank. The only clue, if it was a clue, was the note by Julia's name: "Slave of Mr. Dumont."

Physics says a block of wood is mostly empty space, and the story of Julia will have to be that way, too. The facts are widely separated. But the block of wood is real, and so is she. After Mr. Dumont's death, Julia had a second daughter, baptized Louisanna. The father was Sam, no last name.

There is a story that, one day, Marquis de Lafayette visited. This is the same Lafayette who spent a winter with George Washington at Valley Forge and who later consulted with Jefferson while drafting the Declaration of the Rights of Man and of the Citizen. When he stopped at Arkansas Post, the French Arkansans threw a ball in his honor, and at this ball, Lafayette danced with Virginia Dumont. Virginia would have been no more than three at the time. It's possible that this story is not true.

What's certain is that the household of the Dumonts—or the "Dumos," or "Dumonds," as they finally agreed to spell it—was a large and complicated one, with babies arriving all the time: siblings, half-siblings, cousins, stepchildren. Mr. Dumond's widow was now the head of it, Julia was in the middle of it, Virginia grew up in it, and it became more complicated again when Virginia married Isaac Love, the six-foot-tall immigrant with light eyes, reddish hair, and an infant son.

In the fall of 1850, a census enumerator stopped at the Dumond farm, just north of the Arkansas River, not far from Arkansas Post and the town of Napoleon. He counted eight cows, five horses, twenty sheep, two oxen, and twenty-two humans, including seven he labeled "mulatto" and four he called "black." For the other eleven, he did not indicate a race. Children numbered thirteen, a couple having joined the household by marriage, others bought or inherited. Of the nine adults, only two were men: Isaac, in his mid-twenties now, and Virginia's brother Caliste. Their forty acres of cleared bottomland yielded six hundred bushels of corn that year, and the sheep produced forty pounds of wool. It was enough.

Their neighbors the Menards had a sixty-foot mound in their field. If you dug into the side of it, the mound yielded curious contents such as matted corn husks, pieces of bone, and clay pots with attractive patterns etched into them. Beyond the fields in every direction were the dark, busy forests thick with mosquitoes and parakeets, deer and deer ticks, black snakes and cottonmouths, occasional shy panthers, and lean, erect, magenta-headed turkeys. The turkeys, when alarmed, would turn and run for fifteen yards before leaping implausibly into flight. The oak and cypress trees were in all states of vigor, new ones coming up and old ones dying in parts. Throughout the day, but especially in the morning, the white-billed woodpeckers hammered on the trunks of trees. The quality of the sound depended on the tree. Where the wood was dry and hollow, the drumming rang. If the trunk was tall, the drumming carried, often answered seconds later by another bird hammering on another trunk.

A forest with dying trees is a rich and regal place. An ailing tree cannot creep off and hide, like a sick animal; it dies standing where it grew. When a trunk falls, sometimes it's so tied up with vines it does not hit the ground. If caught in the V of another tree, it remains there, its fall prolonged for another year. The woodpeckers keep hammering. Beetles dig into the tissue of the tree and deposit their eggs, from which the white larvae or grubs emerge. Snakes, squirrels, raccoons, possums, spiders, mosses, ferns, and fungi also live in the hollows of the dead trees. When the trunk eventually touches ground, no crew arrives with orange cones and chain saws to cut it up and remove the pieces. It lays there, pointing whatever direction.

Most years in spring, the river swelled into the forest, flooding it with every kind of flotsam—branches, leaves, feathers, hair, the mixed scat of various species. When the forest drained, random body parts and dirt and debris would stay dammed up behind this or that fallen trunk, creating a low trash pile with silt mixed in, which softened and blackened and was crossed another year by another falling trunk and another dammed-up pile of random waste. But it wasn't really random. There was a deep pattern. The soft floor of the forest was crossed by narrow black paths deer had cut with their hooves. Turkeys used the same paths, also bobcats, any group of hogs straying through, rabbits, and any girl or boy out walking through the woods for any reason or for no reason at all.

The disruption that was taking place—a disruption that would overwhelm not just lives but an ecosystem, as well as shape the identities of broad classes of people—would not have happened except for an earlier one, four thousand miles away. A German named Friedrich Engels, visiting northwestern England in the 1840s, saw "a country which, a hundred years ago chiefly swamp land, thinly populated, is now sown with towns and villages, and is the most densely populated strip of country in England." Coal, the buried residue of another interrupted age, was plentiful enough to fuel a hundred textile mills in the city of Manchester.

Engels had been sent there by his father, who owned cotton mills on the Rhine and had opened a branch in Manchester. Walking in the city, Engels got lost in the dense, winding lanes where the mill workers lived. In a neighborhood called Little Ireland, he wrote, "masses of refuse, offal and sickening filth lie among standing pools in all directions; the atmosphere is poisoned by the effluvia from these, and laden and darkened by the smoke of a dozen tall factory chimneys. A horde of ragged women and children swarm about here, as filthy as the swine that thrive upon the garbage heaps and in the puddles." He quit the family business, partnering with Karl Marx instead to write *The Communist Manifesto*.

Manchester, England, had nothing to do with the soaked woods of southeast Arkansas. Two rivers and an ocean separated them. Looked at another way, though, the two rivers and an ocean connected them. And Manchester, though it was full of coal-fired cotton mills, did not grow cotton.

This connection had a mighty effect on what the Arkansas Delta would become. It's visible on maps, in the property lines. The old French farms at Arkansas Post stretched back from the Arkansas River in irregular strips, sometimes wedge-shaped, following the terrain. The US Land Office took a different approach, more like cutting up a sheet cake. Surveyors gridded the land into townships (a misleading name, since they were not towns but checkerboard squares). Each township was divided into thirty-six sections, and the sections were split into halves, quarters, and half-quarters. In this way, the land was apportioned so that the organic wealth deposited there over a couple of million years could be more thoroughly extracted.

In 1850, Isaac Love bought 135 acres in Desha County on a bend in the Arkansas River. The ground was low-mounded, dark, vulnerable, soft, and rich, and in the language of the seventh US census, it was "unimproved." In other words, it was full of massive living, dying, and dead hardwood trees, snapping turtles, poison ivy, and armadillos, among countless other things. Bones were buried in it, and the ground that wasn't flooded bore tracks. Love closed the deal at the land office in Helena, sixty miles north of the Dumond farm. Where did he get the cash? Unknown, but he was a young man in charge of himself, so he might have gotten it anywhere. Maybe he sold some hogs, or a colt, or ninety loads of cordwood, or maybe he borrowed it from his mother-in-law. It was also at this point in his life that Isaac Love first acquired the title to another man.

The man's name is not recorded. Possibly Love bought him at a slave market in Memphis or New Orleans. He may have traded with a neighbor or someone in Napoleon.

In what way, with what words, did Isaac Love introduce himself to the man he bought? Unknown. They were close in age, both physically in the strongest years of life. One was encumbered by choice; the other was portable property. The county clerk would have recorded the sale in a stilted form of English—"The party of the first part for and in consideration of a sum of lawful money having bargained, granted and sold unto the party of the second part . . ." Was there a handshake? Who'd have shaken hands with whom?

The investment must have paid off, because Isaac and Virginia Love took on more slaves. They hired an overseer—John B. West Jr., an emigrant from Alabama—and they put up two shelters for the new people to sleep in. Slowly, another sixty acres of forest were smoothed into fields. In 1860, their small plantation shipped thirty bales of cotton down the Mississippi to New Orleans, where it would then be shipped across the Atlantic and up the Mersey to the steam mills of Manchester.

Soon after that, a surprise. Eight years into their marriage, Virginia had a child. She named him Louis, after her father, and they chose Edward, after Isaac's father, as a middle name. This happens to be my middle name, too.

I know Louis Edward Love's face well because my grandmother kept his picture in a small oval frame on the desktop of a secretary that had belonged to him. He was her father. In the picture, he wears a goatee and small wire-framed glasses. He was a doctor in Dardanelle for many years, and, perhaps for this reason, he had married late. He was sixty when my grandmother was born.

My grandmother told me a little about him—only a little—when I was eleven. She was not a freewheeling storyteller. She remembered the Dumond name—they were French and had come down from Canada, she explained—and she smiled when she told me that her father was born at a place called Arkansas Post, an early town that had been of some importance once. Later, I tried to look it up on one of those folding road maps that service stations used to give out for free. Our Arkansas visits were long car trips. I did not find Arkansas Post on the map, which made me wonder.

She never knew her grandfather, Isaac Love, and did not know much about him except that he had showed up in Arkansas rather suspiciously, without connections. Her mother was the one who had passed down the story about the stolen horse.

That story had two opposite effects for me: stimulating, then lulling. It pleased my eleven-year-old self to think I had come from a person who might have been hung for horse stealing but got away. It was a story to fall asleep to and dream about. My parents, aunts, and uncles included five teachers, one banker, and one airplane salesman. No felons; no horse thieves.

It is strange to be a child. As children, we sense at some point that we came from somewhere—we did not give birth to ourselves after all—but have no means of seeing our origins. By the time we think to look around or ask questions, we're already in the middle of something else. Even our parents—for me, the people who rode in the front seat of the Pontiac for twenty-one hours on the drive to Arkansas—are not the people who made us anymore. Those people were younger, and our names were not constantly on their lips. Maybe I should say it is strange to be a person.

My grandmother must have known about Isaac Love's plantation and the people who were enslaved there, but she never spoke about them. At least, not to me.

Had she told me, what would she have said?

It was a different time. True, but so was five minutes ago. The time when slavery was legal is not all that remote. There are people alive today who knew and can recall the faces and voices of people who were enslaved.

It made sense at the time. No, it didn't. But also yes, it did—which shows how marvelously flexible the human capacity for making sense is. Sense is made out of sentences, and a sentence is a little story. Believing stories is easy, especially when they are the stimulating-then-lulling kind.

Twenty years ago in Abingdon, Virginia, at an event called the Virginia Creeper Festival, I had a weird conversation with a man who was selling some pamphlets he had authored. He had convinced himself that no American slave was ever beaten by, or on behalf of, an owner. His logic was this: Would you purposely dent your own truck? No. So why would you purposely damage your slave?

We were standing in the street, which had been closed for the festival. He was dressed in a gray Confederate Army uniform. I admit, at the time, I did not know how to argue with him. Should I point out that a person is not a truck? But he knew that. What he needed was not another argument but a larger world of facts.

In the late 1930s, when it was almost too late, the Works Progress Administration sent writers knocking on doors around Arkansas. They were looking for people who could speak from experience about being enslaved. Peter Brown of Helena was eighty-six when he spoke to Miss Irene Robertson. She had no tape recorder but tried to write his words as she heard them.

> My remembrance of slavery is not at tall favorable. I heard
> the master and overseers whooping the slaves b'fore day. They
> had stakes fixed in the ground and tied them down on their
> stomachs stretched out and they beat them with a bull whoop
> (cowhide woven). They would break the blisters on them with
> white oak paddles that had holes in it so it would suck. They
> be saying, "Oh pray, master." He'd say, "Better pray for your-
> self." I heard that going on when I was a child.

That phrase, "Oh pray"—the cry of one person in complete
subordination to another—is remembered more than once in the
WPA's Arkansas narratives. Mary Brown recalled the stripes on her
grandmother's back. Mattie Fennen saw her mother beaten. Sallie
Crane wore a gag in her mouth for three days after trying to run
away.

Leonard Franklin's mother knocked an overseer down and beat
him in his face until he needed a doctor.

Peter Brown told the following:

> Ma had to work when she wasn't able. Pa stole her out and
> one night a small panther smelled them and come on a log up
> over where they slept in a canebrake. Pa killed it with a bowie
> knife. Ma had a baby out there in the canebrake. Pa had stole
> her out. They went back and they never made her work no
> more. She was a fast breeder; she had three sets of twins. They
> told him if he would stay out of the woods they wouldn't make
> her work no more, take care of her children. They prized fast
> breeders. They would come to see her and bring her things
> then. She had ten children, three pairs of twins. Jona and
> Sofa, Peter and Alice, Isaac and Jacob.

Silas Dothram did not know where he was born or when, and he
had never met his father or known his mother. He guessed he was
eighty-two or eighty-three. "When I found myself the white people
had me," he said.

The Dumond and Love households had always included babies
from various mothers, in various stages of helplessness—siblings
and half-siblings nursing, then drinking from a cup, then eating
mush made from boiled cornmeal; children being hauled on
someone's hip, then set down to walk, all while learning to speak a

mixed idiom with roots in French, English, Native American, and African languages. The offspring were understood variously as free and slave, boy and girl, black, white, and mulatto. *Mulatto* comes from *mule*, of course. A mule is a cross between two species, horse and donkey.

All humans are one species. We're an interesting species, but there are many ways in which we are not special. Songbirds are said to have dialects, and otters use tools. Calves cry when they are separated from their mothers. Like all animals, humans are without chlorophyll, which means we have to eat plants to live or else eat other animals.

In 1862, Thomas Wentworth Higginson asked Emily Dickinson why she did not get out and mix with people more. The problem with men and women, she wrote back, is that "they talk of Hallowed things, aloud—and embarrass my dog."

Dogs are dishonest sometimes, but they don't preach, and they don't *explain*. Explaining is a human thing. We do it idly, obsessively, professionally, and habitually—for entertainment but also to get our children to sleep and to make the knowledge of our choices bearable. I'm explaining right now. There are people who, after a full day spent explaining themselves to others at work, will spend the entire drive home explaining themselves out loud to nobody.

Virginia Dumond, like most humans, grew up in a house full of stories, and there was surely a story to explain why some in the house were owned while others owned themselves. Born owned, born free: the bare facts did not make sense without the story. Later, after she married Isaac Love, there must have been another story to explain why these owned people would be removed from the house and moved into separate shelters by the fields, and why their work would be overseen by a professional with a whip. The children of the owners went to school in a building made of green logs, while the owned children carried water or worked in the fields. The stories were necessary because the bare facts were a nightmare.

Spring is when cotton is planted, and the spring of 1861 was a good one. Also that spring, fighting began at Fort Sumter.

The federal army was well equipped for war with Indians, but the rebels in South Carolina had artillery. Lincoln called for volunteers. Arkansas joined the Confederacy.

In June, the enslaved people on Isaac and Virginia Love's plantation weeded and hoed around the cotton plants. In July, Desha County organized a battalion. Isaac enlisted, then went back to the plantation. When the cotton was ready, the enslaved people dragged baskets or long sacks up and down the rows from daylight to dark.

Virginia's mother died. A judge assigned Isaac and his brother-in-law to oversee the division of her estate among her eight heirs. The estate included eleven slaves.

In Napoleon, someone set up a pair of cannon facing the Mississippi. They killed a passenger on a steamboat called the *Westmoreland.*

For cotton planters, it was a successful year. Three hundred thousand bales were stacked on landings along the Arkansas River, waiting to cross the ocean to be made into cloth for inexpensive shirts, pants, and dresses. Each bale was four hundred pounds and had required more than four hundred hours of human labor to urge it out of the soil and into a shippable package.

But the only way out was through New Orleans. In April 1862, the US Navy took that city. Facing the prospect of it falling into Union hands, the governor of Arkansas ordered all of the cotton burned. It took days. Newspapers reported that the sky was dark with smoke all along the Arkansas River.

In September, Lincoln promised to make slavery illegal wherever the Confederacy fell to Union control. In Napoleon, US troops established encampments, tearing the place up, burning wood they had pulled off of houses. The Confederates brought five thousand troops to Arkansas Post and set them up in a fort made of oak logs, dirt, and sheets of iron that were seven-eighths of an inch thick.

Lincoln's order, later called the Emancipation Proclamation, took effect on the first day of 1863. Nine days later, an ironclad Union gunboat steamed by the Loves' plantation, trailing black smoke as it went out of sight around the bend. Others followed, and they were soon heard firing on the fort. Thirty thousand US troops overwhelmed the Confederates there.

The war went on for another year and a half, and then it ended. At some point in 1865—the exact date was not written down—Isaac Love appeared before a federal officer in the bombed, ruined, and partly flooded city of Napoleon to sign an oath of loyalty to the Union. By his signature, the county clerk recorded the following description: "Isaac Love, born in Tennessee, age 47 years, 6 feet tall, auburn hair, light eyes, a farmer."

On Christmas Day 1865, four men traveled with Isaac Love to

Helena, to an office of the Bureau of Refugees, Freedmen, and Abandoned Lands. Lieutenant W. S. McCullough, a white officer serving with the 113th US Colored Infantry, witnessed a contract under which the four men, former slaves, not named, agreed to work on Love's plantation in Desha County, and Love agreed to pay them.

One year later, he took nine bales of cotton to Napoleon.

3. Settling

In his 2014 essay "The Case for Reparations," Ta-Nehisi Coates argues that "what is needed is an airing of family secrets, a settling with old ghosts."

The family secret I'm airing here was so well buried, my family didn't know it anymore. Then one day I was wasting time online and started googling my ancestors. I found a census document dated July 1860, headed "Schedule 2—Slave Inhabitants in Redfork Township in the County of Desha, State of Arkansas." On that form, Isaac Love is listed under "Names of Slave Owners."

It's not that I thought my family was innocent. It's more like my ancestors hadn't been real to me. Isaac Love was a character who stole a horse, a figure in a story to fall asleep to. The new facts changed the story.

Alongside his name, ten people are enumerated by age, sex, and color. Five male, five female; one mulatto, nine black. Their names are omitted. One boy was about the same age as Isaac's son.

What happened to that boy? I don't know how to find out.

Some facts are simply lost.

It is recorded that in 1885 the State of Arkansas offered ten dollars to anyone handing in the scalp of a panther.

Much would be written both by and about William Stanley, the Welsh boy who walked off his plantation job. After serving on both sides of the Civil War, he changed his name to Henry Morton Stanley and went to Africa, where he followed the Congo River to its source. As La Salle had done for Louis XIV—mapping a great river, claiming the land it drained, and setting up posts to extract that land's wealth—so Stanley did for King Leopold II of Belgium. The result was what Leopold called the Congo Free State, though in practice it was neither a state nor free.

The last American parakeet died in a zoo in Cincinnati in 1918.

No one has gotten a good look at an ivory-billed woodpecker since April 1944, when Don Eckelberry, an Audubon Society illustrator, spent two weeks in northeastern Louisiana sketching a female who had nested in an ash tree. She emerged from her hole every morning, pecked for grubs, gave her clarinet-like call, and came home alone every night.

In 1868, Isaac Love was pushing fifty and encumbered in a number of unwelcome ways. His older son had been badly wounded in a campaign in Missouri. In addition to the two younger children, Isaac and Virginia had an orphaned niece and nephew to care for, and Desha County was occupied by federal troops. They had options, though. They sold the farm and left.

Possibly they had guessed what was coming. Their land was inside a sharp bend. In time, the river shifted and cut it off; like the town of Napoleon, the Love plantation is gone now, washed away by flood.

Today, there is a levee to protect the cotton fields, but the 135 acres that the Loves used to own are on the river side of the levee, unprotected. The ground there is bumpy and wet. It is partly wooded, partly brush, and armadillos like it. Hunters set out corn for the deer. Poking around in the woods there in spring 2019, I found the jawbone of a pig on the ground. It's an impressive jawbone—eleven inches long, with a row of molars that could chew through a tree root and a pair of curved, three-inch tusks. Those tusks aren't for show. They are knife-edged. But it's not a rare find. Hogs have been loose in Arkansas for four hundred years. This one might have traced its family back to Hernando de Soto's herd, if there were an Ancestry.com for pigs.

Some facts aren't written down because people don't want them to be remembered. The mound containing corn husks, bones, and clay pots is still there, but the park service doesn't want people digging in it, so they don't advertise the location. The mound looks more or less like it did when Julia lived nearby. It's conspicuous. You wouldn't have to be an archaeologist to notice it and wonder. It's a sixty-foot fact in a field of grass.

In the case of Julia, across her whole life, care was taken not to record the facts I would need to piece her story together. When she gave birth to Mary Ann, a dash was entered in place of the father's name; when she gave birth to Louisanna, the father's surname was omitted. I know no way to trace these people. Every ten years, when the census enumerator came to her home, care was taken to count Julia in a way that would make her almost impossible to identify as an individual. Her name was usually omitted; she was sometimes called mulatto, sometimes black; her age was recorded with a striking imprecision. In the 1840 census, she was classified as a female slave aged at least twenty-four but no more than thirty-six years.

It's not that she wasn't kept track of. She was important. Her whole life, there were young people around her whom she raised. It's fair to say she cooked between forty and fifty thousand meals. That's a conservative guess. She must have been loved. Unkindness is everywhere, but kindness is, too, and love happens all the time. She mattered, and she was officially counted, but care was taken to hide certain connections. There is no way to know who her mother was or what happened to her daughters. It's as though her face has been blurred. She is there in the record, but the priests, enumerators, and county clerks have avoided any notation that would suggest the continuity of one human identity—a consciousness, a soul.

And yet, sometimes I catch a clear glimpse of her. A page from the 1870 census for Yell County, Arkansas, describes the new household of Isaac and Virginia Love. That is where they went, a hundred miles farther west along the Arkansas River, to higher ground. Their younger children were with them: the boy "at school," the girl "at home." Sharing their address was an older married couple, the Johnsons. Hesicah Johnson, born in Maryland, worked "around home," and Julia worked "in [the] kitchen."

There she is: Julia, "slave of Mr. Dumont," mother of Mary Ann, mother of Louisanna, wife of Hesicah, mulatto or black, born in Arkansas. It was the fifth of July 1870, and she told the census taker she was sixty-three.

JAMES MCAULEY

Memory's Cellar

FROM *Liberties*

YOU ENTER THE CAVE OF HORRORS in the basement of an Otto-manera house that is now a small yeshiva just outside the medieval walls of the Old City. On the one hand, there could be no better encapsulation of Jerusalem than this: disjointed histories piled one atop the other like dishes in the sink, all beneath the shade of Aleppo pines. On the other, there is something immediately decrepit about the place. It is wrenchingly nondescript; it looks like extra storage for folding chairs or even for cleaning supplies. Were it not for a Hebrew plaque on the limestone gate outside that reads *Martef HaShoah*, or the Holocaust Cellar, next to an arrow pointing in its direction, you would have no idea where you had arrived. Even now, no notice identifies this rough place as the first Holocaust memorial ever built.

The cellar was inaugurated in 1949 on Mount Zion. It is a monument to the destruction of the Jewish people, yes, but also a monument to the way the destruction was understood in its immediate aftermath by those who had survived, and in the newly established Jewish state. But despite its location, a stone's throw from King David's alleged tomb, the cellar is not, nor was it ever, an august institution that sought to stipulate a collective memory of catastrophe or to impose a narrative interpretation of any kind. No museology or mixed media went into the creation of this dark shrine. It is a site of raw memory, and also a kind of *Wunder-kammer* of catastrophe. There are many Holocaust memorials and museums in the world now, but there is no other place quite like this one. To enter it is to confront, without any philosophical or historiographical or aesthetic mediation, in the most startlingly direct way, the unvarnished blinding horror of a vanished moment, before that horror was sanitized into language and meaning. The place is truly terrifying.

The entire space is pitch dark, dank, and smells of mold from years of water dripping on ancient stone. This is a place where survivors brought whatever obscene relics they had salvaged from the camps and had somehow managed to carry to Palestine after the war: lampshades made from Torah scrolls, canisters of Zyklon B, the chemical used in the gas chambers, and bars of soap made from human body oil, all displayed in a candlelit cave in a prominent glass vitrine with a tattered green velvet lining. The soap bars turn out to be fake; there is no evidence that the Nazis ever made soap out of human flesh. But that is entirely beside the point: the soap represents one of the cruelest rumors that circulated in the camps, which these survivors believed to be true—and here, in this cellar, what you come to see is how *they* understood the catastrophe that *they* had endured, what *they* remembered of it and how *they* began to represent those memories with material objects. The mentality that tortured them and sustained them in equal measure is arguably the most important thing on display.

Toward the end of the cellar, to the extent that it has an exposition, is a small niche that resembles an oratory. Here you see ashes—called "martyrs' ashes"—from the concentration camps, brought to Israel in June 1949 in a series of glass jars, painted in blue and white stripes with yellow Stars of David, to mirror the uniform that so many Jews had worn up until their deaths. It is an indescribably desolating feeling to stand there in this putrid cellar, in front of those ashes, and to think of the unnamed bodies whose incinerated remains are blended in these peeling glass vials, to know only how those bodies had died and nothing of how they had lived. In any case, there is no attempt to explain or to tell those stories at Martef HaShoah, which is the source of its power. In the immediate aftermath of the war, these dark rooms were already a commentary on the futility, and even the perversity, of narrative.

These days, the memory of the catastrophe that we now call "the Holocaust" in English or "the *Shoah*" in Hebrew—as if there is a single word in any language that will capture it—has been spun over the years by governments and memorial institutions in Israel, the United States, Western Europe, and Eastern Europe into respective "lessons" that apparently teach us about this or that: about human rights, about collaboration with evil, about the necessity of Zionism, about the moral failings of bystanders. But these lessons, no matter how true or well-intentioned they may be, when they try to instruct, to caution, or even to inspire, tend to remove us from the actual details of the catastrophe, which is neither parable nor metaphor but quite simply a fact of extreme facticity—a catastrophe in the literal sense of the term—an epochal tragedy that defies facile explanation, a loss with many reasons and causes but above all a loss, devastating, final, incontrovertible. The most crushing horror of the catastrophe is that it happened at all—that facticity; and what, exactly, "it" was. In that sense, the world's first Holocaust memorial is also its most authentic. Here there is no narrative. Here there is only shock and stupefaction, frozen in cold stone.

We do not always get to choose the questions that we ask of the past, or the questions that the past asks of us. But we can ask why those questions are posed in the first place, why they are formulated in the way they are, and perhaps most importantly, what their place in our lives should be. I cannot remember a time when I was not aware of the Holocaust, when its shadow was not somehow a fundamental part of how I understood the world and—as perverse and as sad as this is—of how I understood my own Jewishness. I am Jewish, but I am not descended from survivors. And yet the catastrophe was something of a mediating filter to the entire identity for so many in my generation, the way it was taught to so many of us, the stories we heard as children, the ultimate reason we were told that we had to remain Jewish, as if Judaism was merely a form of resistance and not a thing of depth and beauty that had existed long before—and indeed, long after—those who tried to extinguish it. The first time I read Sartre's *Réflexions sur la question juive*, the postwar treatise in which he asserts with zero humility or shame that the anti-Semite "creates" the Jew, I was deeply unsettled, I think because I saw myself in his formulation, and I did not like what I saw. Was *this*, after all, what Jewish survival was meant to look like, an obsession with reading about the camps, and not, for instance, Yiddish poetry by Avraham Sutzkever and Peretz Markish?

As I got older, I began to question my own questions about the past, questions I had not chosen, but questions that were nevertheless suspect. Why should an event that essentially had nothing to

do with me, that certainly does not belong to me, come to occupy
so much space at the expense of so much else? Peter Novick and
others have shown that at least part of the answer is cultural: in the
1990s, when I grew up, the Holocaust became a public metaphor
for any number of things, not least because the murder of millions
of Jews in and of itself never seemed reason enough to rivet people's
attention. What seemed—and still seems—to concern most people
are the meanings that we have assigned to the catastrophe rather
than the brute horror of the catastrophe itself, the lessons, and
even the platitudes, that we teach our children about it. I have long
been struck by the reality of this elision—that even in our morbidly
identitarian moment, if one is to speak about this catastrophe, one
necessarily has to speak about something else. (A fine example is
Ken Burns's recent series on American indifference to Jewish refugees in the late 1930s and 1940s, a film that purports to be a documentary about the Holocaust but is mostly interested in parallels
between American immigration policy then and our present-day
troubles with immigration at the southern border.)

Maurice Halbwachs, the great French theorist of collective memory, said it best in the essay that introduced the concept. "In each
epoch," he wrote in 1925, "memory reconstructs an image of the
past that is in accord with the predominant thoughts of the society."
So it is today. We arrange for the past, especially the calamitous
past, to tell us what we wish to hear. Many of the Holocaust museums that now exist in virtually every large provincial American city
basically exhort their visitors to be nicer people. In Dallas, where
I grew up, the Holocaust and Human Rights Museum—again, it
is rarely enough for any of these museums to be only a Holocaust
museum—encourages visitors to be "upstanders" in their daily lives,
to step up when they see injustice happening. There is also a "Beyond
Tolerance Theater" that teaches viewers about unconscious bias on
the playground or in the workplace. In Los Angeles, the Museum
of Tolerance, a satellite of the Simon Wiesenthal Center, which recently opened another version of itself in Jerusalem, emphasizes
mutual respect in all its forms, and features a permanent exhibition entitled "Finding Our Families, Finding Ourselves," which
"showcases the diversity within the personal histories of several
noted Americans," including Maya Angelou, Kareem Abdul-Jabbar,
and Carlos Santana. The point is that we Americans are all different, and therefore we are all the same. This is one reason why the

Holocaust looms so large in contemporary life. It is so *usable*. Approaches such as these indulge, and even depend on, an individual and collective solipsism: the murder of millions of others in faraway lands is relevant only insofar as it is somehow related to me, to us.

That is why I had come back to Israel, a place where I have spent a great deal of time over the course of my life, to see this little cave: this is a relic of the time before collective memory crystallized, before the catastrophe became a fount of moral instruction seemingly open to all. I was interested in the aftermath from the very beginning, long before the era of platitudes and parables—interested in how, exactly, survivors who emerged from an inexplicable and indescribable hell built a durable memory from the ground up, and also in the sacrifices that had to be made for the sake of that memory, the omissions, the elisions, and the emphases. I took as my starting point a comment by Susan Sontag. "Strictly speaking, there is no such thing as collective memory," she remarked in *Regarding the Pain of Others*. Instead, "what is called collective memory is not a remembering but a stipulating: that *this* is important, and *this* is the story about how it happened." I don't think she was entirely right, in the sense that collective memory is a very real force for many communities, even those who did not experience a cataclysmic event. The mechanisms of collective memory may be mysterious, but the evidence that it works is visible in all our inherited cultures. But Sontag was right to see memory as a construction, as something that was not handed down from on high but actively constructed from below—and sometimes at great personal cost to those who built it. And this is why I had come to Mount Zion: the Holocaust Cellar is above all a chapter in the history of memory in its earliest and most unfiltered stages. To visit here is to return to the source.

In the beginning—or rather at the end—there was widespread indifference and the constant threat of oblivion. What had happened in Europe between 1933 and 1945 was a catastrophe so immense that its extent could not yet be fathomed, a rupture so profound that it could not yet be named, because naming implies narrative and narrative implies meaning. And who, in the rubble, would have the temerity to pronounce confidently, with the intellectual composure required for the task, on the meaning of what had just happened? Who would dare speak of such a thing? Millions had been murdered everywhere in Europe, gassed in windowless rooms and in the backs of trucks, shot at point-blank in wooded ravines, hunted in forests until they lost the strength and finally the will to run. Rich and poor, significant and insignificant, cruel and kind—in certain areas, a whole world was systematically reduced to nothing. The great cities of Yiddishland, an entire civilization between the Danube and the Volga, lay in ruins; smaller towns and shtetls simply disappeared from the map. The great synagogues that had been fixtures of urban landscapes for centuries were desecrated and ransacked and gutted. Jewish homes, even the meager ones, were sequestered, and their contents, even the worthless ones, plundered and thrown into piles—mounds of candlesticks, heaps of inexpensive china. What was the lesson in those piles and piles of teacups in makeshift warehouses? No, this was not a parable. This was an actual calamity of unprecedented scope and brutality, a calamity that in some ways had no religious or historical antecedent even in the experience of a people to whom history had already been merciless.

But along with the utter disbelief, the incomprehension, and the silent awe before the extent of the destruction, there was also a sense among survivors of the encroaching threat of oblivion, the most painful fate of all—one had seen a hellscape, lived to tell the tale, but emerged into a world in which there was no surviving proof of it and no audience eager to believe it or imagine it, all the photographs notwithstanding. Oblivion is the intersection of ignorance and indifference, and oblivion was always a fundamental aim of the Nazi genocide of the Jews, not only the oblivion of the liquidation of the Jewish people, but also the oblivion of *how* they were liquidated—the details of their destruction, the means of their murder. The Jews were simply to disappear, along with any and all traces of their disappearance. Martef HaShoah emerged precisely at this moment, when oblivion was at the door.

In the immediate aftermath of the war, the indifference was instantly palpable. "There was never any mystery about what had happened to Europe's Jews," Tony Judt writes in a remarkable discussion of the subject near the end of *Postwar*. "That an estimated six million of them were put to death during the Second World War was widely accepted within a few months of the war's end." Accepted, but not wrestled with. Few were really interested in the plight of the Jews. In the bloodlands of Eastern Europe, anti-Semitism remained, and

Jews who returned home after their liberation from the camps were sometimes met with further pogroms, most notoriously in Kielce, Poland, in July 1946. In the West, there was less outright violence but just as much elision. The French newspaper *Le Monde*, for instance, would write, even passionately, of *survivants des camps* and even of *déportés*, but it would never speak of Jews specifically. What began to matter to growing numbers of survivors was to preserve evidence and testimony, without which all would not only still be lost but also forgotten, which would be akin to losing it all again. As the philosopher Jean-François Lyotard observed, decades later, in *Le Différend*, a treatise that responded to a rising tide of denialism about Auschwitz, the after-effect of precisely this phenomenon:

> It is the nature of a victim not to be able to prove that one has been done a wrong. . . . The perfect crime does not consist in killing the victim or the witnesses . . . but rather in obtaining the silence of the witnesses, the deafness of the judges, and the inconsistency (insanity) of the testimony. You neutralize the addressor, the addresses, and the sense of the testimony; then everything is as if there were no referent (no damages).

This was why, even as the destruction was still underway, the fight against oblivion had already begun, the struggle to save the documentary evidence. The astonishing story of the Jewish historian Emanuel Ringelblum and the *Oyneg Shabbos* project in the Warsaw Ghetto is now well-known: Trapped in the ghetto, he and his group of fellow imprisoned historians risked their lives to preserve every trace they could find that revealed something, anything, about their own destruction. They collected quite a lot—diaries, posters, decrees, and about twenty-five thousand documents that detailed the extermination camps at Treblinka and Chelmno and the ghettos elsewhere in Poland. "It must be recorded with not a single fact omitted," read one of their circulars. "And when the time comes—and it surely will—let the world read and know what the murderers have done." The historical documentation assembled by these historians in extremis was then buried underground in three large milk cans, only two of which have been found. Ringelblum was murdered with his family in March 1944. Only one member of *Oyneg Shabbos* survived—the writer Rachel Auerbach, who later became the head of the testimonies department at Yad Vashem, an institution whose existence was still unimaginable at the end of the war.

Oyneg Shabbos was far from the only such enterprise. The documentary impulse was a form of resistance, and it appeared in Jewish circles across wartime Europe. The writers Vasily Grossman and Ilya Ehrenburg, Soviet soldiers at the time, were in the battalion that liberated Treblinka. Grossman was haunted by the gas chambers that he discovered there, which he struggled to grasp: "What are the pictures now passing before people's glassy dying eyes? Pictures of childhood? Of the happy days of peace? Of the last terrible journey?" But he concluded: "No, what happened in that chamber cannot be imagined." When the two returned home, they set about compiling *The Black Book of Soviet Jewry*, a sprawling five-hundred-page collection of memories from Jewish survivors, interviews with non-Jewish eyewitnesses, and dispatches by the authors themselves—a massive undertaking that was published in Yiddish, not Russian. Soviet censors initially ordered that the contents of the book be changed: they wanted to shift the focus away from Jewish suffering, and they wanted certain passages to be rewritten so as to downplay atrocities committed by Ukrainian civilians against Ukrainian Jews. By 1948, the censors took it one step further: they scrapped the book entirely, destroying even the typefaces used to print it. The attack on *The Black Book* was an opening salvo in Stalin's war against "rootless cosmopolitans," a favorite communist term for Jews, and one of the earliest state-sanctioned attempts after the war to condemn the catastrophe to oblivion.

Much the same was true in Western Europe, far from the slaughterhouses of the east. In occupied France, as early as 1943, Isaac Schneersohn, a rabbi-turned-industrialist from the family of the Lubavitcher rebbes, called a meeting of local Jewish leaders in the small apartment he was renting in Grenoble, then under Italian control. His aim was to document the atrocities that they saw unfolding everywhere around them. "These days, when we evoke the horrible figure of six million victims," Schneersohn later recalled, "the few Jews we ourselves witnessed being deported seem a little less weighty in comparison, even a drop in the ocean. But at the time, when we thought about what they went through, pushed up against cold walls, left in waiting rooms or in train stations, when we contemplated the sheer number of the elderly, of women, of the sick, we were seized with anguish and submerged in sadness." Far from the Warsaw Ghetto, he nevertheless responded in exactly the same way as Emanuel Ringelblum: what mattered was fighting oblivion until the very end. "No one among us believed he would emerge alive from that oppressive atmosphere where it was literally impossible to breathe. . . . And so I had only one desire: to record all these Nazi crimes so that those who survived could transmit the facts to future generations and record, for history, the memory of the atrocities perpetrated by the Nazis on the Jewish people." Schneersohn did survive, and his makeshift archive became the Centre de Documentation Juive Contemporaine (CDJC), the foundation for Paris's Mémorial de la Shoah, the first memorial of its kind in Western Europe, dedicated in 1953.

Almost immediately, the question became what to do with all this documentary evidence, hundreds of thousands of linear feet of archival material, diary entries, and typeset testimonies that sought to preserve traces of the inexplicable. In time, each of the names that began to emerge for the calamity was inadequate, because, again, names imply narrative, and each narrative somehow reduced the event into a particular frame that diminished either its horror or its totality, and sometimes both. In Yiddish, some survivors almost immediately began calling the Nazi attempt to liquidate the entire Jewish people a *khurbn*, a term that means "destruction" and originally referred to the destruction of the Second Temple by the Romans in approximately 70 CE, the watershed event in early Jewish memory. But the Nazi genocide of the Jews was hardly the same: this time what was destroyed was far more than sacred space—not the "cultic center" of a particular religion but an entire people, many of whom had nothing to do with the religion of their ancestors. By the late 1930s, journalists in Palestine were already using the biblical term *shoah*—Hebrew for "catastrophe"—to describe the great darkness that had fallen over the Jews of Europe. "That day is a day of wrath," we read in Zephaniah 1:15, "a day of trouble and distress, a day of *shoah* and desolation, a day of clouds and thick darkness." (The word *shoah* appears in a number of places in the Hebrew Bible, always to denote devastation.) For many at the time, that sense of biblical catastrophe, of primal destruction, encapsulated the Nazi assault. After the Nazis invaded Poland in September

1939, for instance, *Davar*, a great Hebrew daily now defunct, noted that "a terrible *shoah* befell the millions of Jews of Poland, a *shoah* whose scope and sights far exceed anything experienced in recent years." But *shoah* means catastrophe merely in the general sense of disaster, as in natural disaster, as if what happened came from nowhere and had nothing to do with human will.

And then, of course, there was "holocaust," soon to be the most prevalent of all the names and by far the worst of the lot. The word came from the ancient Greek translation of the Hebrew Bible, the roots *holos* and *kostos*, which together meant "totally burnt," completely consumed by the fire, as in an animal offered for ritual sacrifice. "Holocaust" already had a premonitory valence in English: Nathaniel Hawthorne had used the term in 1844 in "Earth's Holocaust," a short story that uncannily anticipated the Nazi book burning at Berlin's Bebelplatz in May 1933. It describes a great conflagration of the books of the world: "Thick, heavy folios, containing the labors of lexicographers, commentators, and encylopedists, were flung in, and, falling among the embers with a leaden thump, smoldered away to ashes like rotten wood." In 1933, *Newsweek* had used the term to describe the actual Bebelplatz book burning, and in 1943 the *New York Times* did the same to describe the plight of Jewish refugees in Palestine who had "surviv[ed] the Nazi holocaust."

But it was Elie Wiesel who was most insistent that "holocaust" be used to describe the catastrophe that he had witnessed. In the 1980s, he explained his reasoning in an appearance at a Chicago synagogue. The term, he said, enshrined the Jewish religious significance of the catastrophe, because it called to mind the *Akedah*, or the binding of Isaac, one of the most harrowing passages in the Bible, when God demands of Abraham that he sacrifice his son. "I call Isaac the first survivor of the Holocaust because he survived the first tragedy," Wiesel said. "Isaac was going to be a burnt offering, a *korban olah* [a type of sacrifice in the Temple that had to be entirely consumed by the fire on the altar], which is really the Holocaust. The word 'holocaust' has a religious connotation. Isaac was meant to be given to God as a sacrifice." But this is precisely the problem with the term. It paints a picture of Jews being led to their deaths like Isaac by Abraham, like lambs to the slaughter, devoid of agency or will, and it also casts the entire event as something ordained by God to purify the world. It confidently presumes a theology. It perversely sacralizes mass murder. And unlike in the story of Isaac's crucible, no angel appeared in the sky to prevent the murder.

Although the Holocaust Cellar appeared amid the emergence of these endless debates, it differed from other early attempts to come to terms with the catastrophe in two ways: it sought to show and not to tell—the articulateness of the place is not discursive but physical; and it was established in the nascent Jewish state, a representation of a world-historical event in a new place whose existence represented another world-historical event. Even now, the cellar is an interplay between destruction and redemption.

The principal architect of Martef HaShoah was Shmuel Zangwill Kahana, the Director General of the new state's Ministry of Religious Affairs, who served in that office for two decades. Kahana was born in Warsaw in 1905 into a family of distinguished rabbis, and he himself received rabbinical ordination from Rabbi Moses Soloveitchik (the son of the renowned Rabbi Haim Soloveitchik and the father of the renowned Rabbi Joseph B. Soloveitchik), as well as a doctorate in Middle Eastern studies from the University of Lieges in Belgium. With his wife and his parents he escaped Poland in 1940 and settled in Palestine. Kahana was a religious Zionist, in his ideology and his party affiliation, for whom the Holocaust—or the *Shoah*, or the *khurbn*, or whatever the catastrophe was to be called—belonged squarely within the long sequence of disasters in Jewish history, from the destruction of the Second Temple in 70 CE to the massacres by the Crusaders in the eleventh and twelfth centuries to the atrocities by the Ukrainians in the seventeenth century to the pogroms in Russia from the 1890s to the 1900s, a teleology of tragedy to which the establishment of the State of Israel was the ultimate rejoinder.

Kahana believed that commemoration should be something of a religious rite, that it should adhere to Jewish religious tradition and its inherited approaches to mourning. This is why the choice of location for the cellar was paramount. "The cellar projects onto Mount Zion," Kahana wrote shortly after the opening. "And Mount Zion in return projects onto the Holocaust cellar." (The road that winds up to the top of Mount Zion is named for him.) A verse in Obadiah declares that "upon Mount Zion shall be deliverance and there shall be holiness." But the choice of Mount Zion had also another significance: it projected onto Mount Moriah, where according to the biblical account Isaac was bound, farther to the east, where the gold-domed mosque now stood, still behind the ceasefire lines and beyond Israeli jurisdiction. That was not just co-incidence: for Kahana, as for Wiesel, Isaac was the first survivor. The religious dimension of the cellar is still unavoidable, though it does not interfere with the experience of the place. Nothing could.

As has been hotly debated for decades now, the Jewish community in Palestine, and later the State of Israel, had an impossible relationship with the catastrophe in Europe, when it was unfolding and especially when it was over. In the words of the Israeli journalist Tom Segev, the response during the war was "less than compassionate" and, in the uncertain aftermath "a great silence surrounded the destruction of the Jews." It was only in 1961, with the public trial of Adolf Eichmann, as Segev and others have insisted, that there began "a process of identification with the tragedy of the victims and survivors, a process that continues to this day." But other historians, most notably Anita Shapira, have convincingly complicated this view of Israeli diffidence or indifference, noting that, among other things, Ben Gurion's push for reparations from the German government in the early 1950s, as well as the ferocious pushback against that campaign, led by a young Menachem Begin, showed that Israel's establishment in those early years was not so much "silent" regarding the Holocaust as terrified of its explosiveness. Before the Eichmann trial, after all, there was the Kasztner trial, a major moment in the public consciousness of the new state, when, in 1953, a hotelier named Malkiel Gruenwald, who lost fifty-two relatives in Auschwitz, accused the Hungarian-born journalist and civil servant Rudolf Kasztner of collaborating with the Nazis, and Adolf Eichmann in particular. The government took Kasztner's side, suing Gruenwald for libel. But the courts acquitted Gruenwald and ruled that Kasztner had "sold his soul to the devil." When the government attempted to appeal the case, it collapsed under public outrage. Kasztner was assassinated by a group of veterans walking into his Tel Aviv apartment in March 1957. (His granddaughter is now the head of the Labor Party in Israel.) This was not silence; it was trauma.

But if there was not silence, there certainly was stigma. One of the reasons that the bars of soap on display in the cellar are so moving, inauthentic as they may be, is that in Hebrew survivors were often and cruelly called *sabonim*, which means "soapsters."

Among the Jews of Palestine, there was often an undisguised contempt for the fact that their European brethren had not defended themselves and had, at least in the eyes of some, allowed a terrible fate to fall on them. How could they have let the Germans turn them into soap? In 1944, *Davar* asked that question in a headline: "Why are the Jews of Hungary not defending themselves?" The Zionist ethos rebelled against the apparent lack of resistance. Likewise, Yitzhak Gruenbaum, a Polish Zionist leader who later became Israel's first Interior Minister, had nothing but disdain for the Jews of Poland who "had not found in their souls the courage" to defend themselves. In his mind, they had preferred "the life of a dog over an honorable death." These condescending Zionists exaggerated, of course: there certainly was Jewish armed resistance in the Nazi inferno. But there was not, nor could there have been, enough.

So many new citizens of the newly minted state had come from Europe and were stranded, as it were, in trauma and stupefaction. No one has written about this better than David Grossman, whose novel, *See Under: LOVE*, published in 1989, follows a young Israeli boy, Momik, the child of two survivors, who tries to exorcise what he calls the Nazi "beast" from his family's life. There is a moving passage early in the novel when Momik tries to get rid of the tattoo on his grandfather's arm. His grandfather is always muttering, locked in a trance, and Momik is convinced that the tattoo is the problem. "The numbers drove him crazy because they weren't written in ink and they couldn't be washed off with water or spit. Momik tried everything to wash grandfather's arm, but the number stayed fixed." Indeed, the numbers could never be washed away.

"The moment it happened it was known here," Yehuda Bauer, the great Israeli historian of the Holocaust, one of the first to study the subject seriously in any language, told me about the catastrophe. It was a late summer afternoon in Jerusalem, and Bauer, now ninety-seven, kindly received me in the small apartment that he keeps in an assisted living facility above an anonymous shopping center next to the Shaare Zedek hospital, not far from Yad Vashem. I brought a box of cookies from the bakery downstairs, and instantly regretted it: Bauer struggles to walk, and insisted on rummaging in his kitchenette for the right plate to serve the cookies. He and his family had left their native Prague on the night the Germans invaded Czechoslovakia, and his father brought the family to Palestine, where he has remained ever since. "We knew about the ghettos," he said. "What was clear was that if the Germans conquered Palestine we wouldn't survive." When he was a PhD student, Bauer told me, there were not yet any scholarly studies of the Holocaust, but he had been influenced by Abba Kovner, the Polish-Jewish writer and partisan leader who had led Nakam, a postwar paramilitary organization devoted to vengeance—to murdering six million Germans in exchange for the six million murdered Jews. Kovner fainted after giving testimony at the Eichmann trial, one of the most memorable moments in that ongoing drama, recorded on live television for all the world to see. "He persuaded me very early that the Holocaust was the most important event in the Jewish twentieth century, and maybe in all of Jewish history," Bauer said. "When I told him I didn't know the languages at the time, that I was scared, he said, 'that's fine—you should be scared.'"

It was clear from the very beginning that some edifice would have to be erected in Israel in commemoration of the catastrophe in Europe, but the government could not decide what form, exactly, that commemoration should take. The question became urgent in June 1949, when the Israeli government received a glass coffin containing thirty-one jars of "martyrs' ashes" from Austria. (Simon Wiesenthal led the group of survivors who brought them to Jerusalem, and their installation in the cellar is regarded as the first public ceremony of Holocaust commemoration in Israel.) But it was the Ministry of Religious Affairs, under Kahana's stewardship, that took charge of this occasion, not any other part of the government. He devised a major public spectacle: a coffin containing the jars lay in state in Tel Aviv, where thousands of people visited it, and it was later transported to Jerusalem by military convoy, wrapped in an Israeli flag. Kahana prepared for the arrival of the martyr's ashes in Jerusalem by soliciting many pieces of Judaica that local survivors had brought from Europe—Torah crowns, incense boxes, menorahs. His aim was clear: the cellar, quickly cleared from a basement in an old Ottoman building, was a response to the Destruction of the Temple, however small. The newspaper *Hatsofeh* put it this way: Kahana's cellar was "a counterpoint to the removal of the articles from the Holy Temple in

Jerusalem to Rome." The cellar was nothing less than a retort to the Arch of Titus. The symbolism was complete.

Before the Israeli government decreed, in April 1951, that Yom Ha'Shoah, or Holocaust Remembrance Day, would fall on the twenty-seventh day of Nissan, which was the date in the Hebrew calendar when the Warsaw Ghetto uprising was crushed in 1943, Kahana had his own ideas. In 1949, in keeping with his agenda, and his view of the Jewish past, Martef HaShoah was officially inaugurated on Tisha B'Av, the ninth day of the month of Av, a religious day of fasting that commemorates the day on which the Babylonians destroyed the First Temple, the Romans destroyed the Second Temple, and many other calamities befell the Jews across the centuries. In this way the Holocaust was fitted into the tragic pattern of Jewish history as enunciated by the great nineteenth-century Jewish historians— Heinrich Graetz, Leopold Zunz, even Simon Dubnow, murdered in Riga in 1941. But no interpretation, not even the lachrymose one, can master what one sees in those dark rooms: what they evoke is beyond a mere chapter in a saga of suffering. I actually thought of Dubnow when I wandered through the cave. "*Yidn, shraybt un far-shraybt,*" a number of survivors recall him saying before his murder— Jews, write and record. This is precisely what Martef HaShoah seeks to do, however humbly, however violently.

In the years that followed the establishment of the state, there were frequent attempts to establish the cellar as a site of political inspiration, as the historian Doron Bar has ably documented. Kahana arranged for Tisha B'Av to be commemorated in the cellar every year, with the ashes of murdered European Jews brought to the nearby synagogue at David's tomb. In 1950, the year after the cellar was dedicated, the ceremonies of Israel's Independence Day began on Mount Zion, and with one of the objects in the cellar— the blowing of a shofar that had been brought from Europe. Kahana was hopeful that all of these events would entrench his vision of what the catastrophe would mean in the eyes of the wider Israeli public. "The commemoration in the Holocaust Cellar," he said, "will undoubtedly penetrate wider public circles and bind them to the memory of the Holocaust, as specific dates become accepted. For the time being, we are laying the foundations and making attempts to establish special events. We will see the effects of those actions as time goes by." Those ambitions alienated some, including

Bauer. "I was never religious," he told me in Jerusalem, when I asked him what he thought about the cellar. "I was never interested in that sort of thing."

But this was really as far as "narrative" ever got on Mount Zion, at least in relation to Holocaust memory. Regardless of Kahana's intentions, the space that he cleared for his terrible chamber never quite became a museum that sought to depict the catastrophe in religious terms. This was because it became a space for survivors to come and grieve on their own terms, in a time when there was virtually nowhere else for them to go. In the north the kibbutz Lohamei Hagetaot, the Ghetto Fighters' kibbutz, had not yet opened its famed galleries, known as the Ghetto Fighters' House, and neither had Yad Mordechai in the south opened its museum. For a few short years, Martef HaShoah was essentially all there was, and it touched a nerve far beyond what Kahana imagined. People came from everywhere, carrying what they had—memories of lost loved ones, treasures from forgotten towns, objects that somehow testified to the destruction that they had survived. They did not come to Mount Zion to "tell a story" as much as they came to ensure that what they remembered did not vanish along with everything else they had known. During Hanukkah, a number of survivors would assemble in the cellar and light candles in lamps that had been brought from Europe.

In 1953, the fourth year of its existence, a local association of Hungarian survivors decided to establish an archive of sorts in the cellar—a *beit gnazim*, as they called it—that would record the names of the murdered along with any other relevant documents they had. Around the same time, small communities of survivors began to put up plaques with the names of their towns in Europe that the catastrophe had either devastated or eradicated altogether. By 1952, hundreds of these plaques were placed on the walls of the courtyard outside the cellar as well as inside, all over its dark walls. This was why one unnamed survivor told the religious Zionist newspaper *Hatsofeh* in December of that year that the site should be Israel's "traditional monument for the commemoration of the Holocaust," because there were publicly displayed names of "all the lost communities." In fact there was no room, in this small spot, for the names of all the communities, but the place-names that are given are deeply affecting. Each one represents countless graves that were never dug. They even look like gravestones.

At the same time, on the other side of the city, there was another Holocaust memorial project devoted to memorials and names, to be called Yad Vashem for precisely that reason. Its name derived from Isaiah 56:5: "And to them will I give in my house and within my walls a memorial and a name (*yad vashem*) that shall not be cut off." In August 1953, the Knesset passed the Yad Vashem Law, establishing the Holocaust Martyrs' and Heroes' Remembrance Authority, which was to be Israel's official national memorial to the Holocaust. Debates had raged since even before 1948 about what the place of Holocaust memory should be in the landscape of the new state, but Ben-Gurion had hesitated until memorials began to crop up all over Europe in the early 1950s. He had been present at the dedication of Isaac Schneersohn's Mémorial du Martyr Juif Inconnu in the Marais district of Paris in the summer of 1953, and had returned to Jerusalem adamant that the Jewish State, and nowhere else, be the official home of Holocaust memory. And so the purpose of the newfound memorial project, according to the law passed in the Knesset, "is to gather *in the homeland* material regarding all members of the Jewish people who laid down their lives, who fought and rebelled against the Nazi enemy and its collaborators, and to perpetuate their memory."

Martef HaShoah was a humble cellar outside the Old City, on the eastern side of Jerusalem, which derived its gravitas from its proximity to some of the holiest sites in Judaism and Jewish memory. Yad Vashem, which would not open to the public until 1973, very much derived its legitimacy from its position in the west of the city, the "new" city, on the slopes of Mount Herzl, the hallowed ground of secular Zionism. As it grew in size and stature in the decades after its opening, the newer memorial museum and archive became the place where Israel tells the story of the Holocaust—a sophisticated museological exposition of the European events, in various media, that ends with stunning views of Eretz Yisrael, the rightful home of the Jewish people. Point made. The site is now a massive complex with state-of-the-art technology, in a structure that the architect Moshe Safdie boldly cut through a mountain. This is where Israeli prime ministers bring endless delegations of foreign leaders to understand something about the Jewish, and the Israeli, past. The Zionist lessons of Yad Vashem are plain. IDF soldiers are routinely brought through the museum as part of their training. Rest assured they do not visit the cellar on Mount Zion, or even know that it exists.

They can be forgiven, as the site is open by appointment only, and even that is irregular. When I visited most recently, I had to beg for access. It was a stroke of luck that I was allowed in.

How far we have come from the cave on Mount Zion, from its rawness, from its urgency. Today much of Holocaust memory—or much of public Holocaust memory, I should say—is high-minded kitsch. In museums and memorials across the globe, it often seeks to sanitize and moralize in equal measure, to spin the nightmare of Auschwitz into some kind of sermon about the future. Forget, but only for a moment, that the cautionary power of Auschwitz has demonstrably failed: the memory of the past has not stopped genocides, even in Europe, nor has it impeded anti-Semitism, which, perhaps especially in the United States, is more than alive and well, and at a time when Holocaust education has never been more mainstream. Beyond all that, Holocaust memory has now become a pixilated performance, and sometimes even a genre of entertainment. This, it would seem, is the future of cautionary memory.

For many memorial institutions, the reigning anxiety is the impending disappearance of the last generation of survivors, women and men have been living custodians of memory for decades and who have helped the event come alive for generations of schoolchildren and others by means of memoirs, documentaries, and interviews. There is a manifest belief among the leaders of many of these institutions that survivors should simply not be allowed to die like everyone else, that somehow they owe us more of their time and more of their trauma beyond the grave. Hence the bizarre "Dimensions in Testimony" project, an initiative of Steven Spielberg's Shoah Foundation at the University of Southern California in Los Angeles, which has created literal holograms of twenty-five survivors, a technology now available at twelve different Holocaust museums worldwide, from Skokie, Illinois, to Sydney, Australia. In the words of the project's promotional materials: "Now and far into the future, museum-goers, students and others can have conversational interactions with these eyewitnesses to history to learn from those who were there."

Holograms! Spielberg was accused of kitsch, and worse, for *Schindler's List*, a film that actually dared to depict victims *inside* a gas chamber. "Dimensions in Testimony" is not nearly as impudent and outrageous as that, but it is cut from the same cloth. I have now seen a number of these spectacles of artificial intelligence in museums in different cities, and it is the "artificial" part of the "intelligence" here that bothers me most. After all, so much of the fight for Holocaust memory was, and remains, a fight for the truth, proving against the violence of denialism that the catastrophe really did happen, that it was not, in fact, a distortion or a hoax. And yet here we are, relying on literal distortion, on a technological hoax, to tell the story.

"Dimensions in Testimony" goes something like this. You sit down in an auditorium of some kind, the lights dim, and all of a sudden a hologram appears, a pixilated reconstruction of a smiling survivor, who is magically alive again, and gives a brief summary of his or her experience, and then takes questions. You can ask the survivor almost anything you want—their favorite color, their favorite food. In fact, that is the point: to make sure people know that these holograms are real people, which they are not. The docent running the show at one museum I visited told the audience that we should make sure to ask the survivor to tell us a joke. Someone even did, and people even laughed. I rubbed my eyes in disbelief. What stupendous disrespect! But this is where Holocaust memory, and collective memory, is headed: insults to decency and insults to intelligence in equal measure. Before you know it, sorrow will be fun.

Martef HaShoah is more or less entirely forgotten in our era of Holocaust holograms. But the cave of horrors bears revisiting, if only to confront anew the stupefaction, the muteness, the shock, the colossal humbling, that it offers. As we progress further and further from the catastrophe itself, that original sense of the smashing of the mind against it is too often forgotten. We think that we can believe that the catastrophe happened—obviously it happened, didn't it?—and we are no longer even all that afraid of it, because we have allowed it to make sense in some strange way, with all the arrogance of theory and hindsight. We are so familiar with it, when we think about it at all. But on Mount Zion familiarity is out of the question. There we are reminded that there is no narrative, no intellectual or religious or emotional framework, that can adequately capture the hopelessness and abjection preserved in these basement rooms, no lesson they can be said to teach. The ashes are the ashes; the soap is the soap.

RICHARD PRINS

Because:
An Etiology

FROM *Potomac Review*

BECAUSE SHE SAYS she's a simple lady. Because I don't believe her. Because she called herself convoluted just a minute ago. Because I'm trying to charm her. Because I say the path to simplicity is convoluted. Because it's five bucks for a beer and a shot. Because we have forty between us. Because we're riding the Q train home. Because my bed frame collapses beneath us. Because we're already doomed. Because breathing suddenly feels so much better. Because she forgets about the pill. Because her best friend kicks her out. Because she moves in with me and my wine-stained mattress. Because she sleeps with her ex before moving in. Because now she's ready to love me, too. Because they vacuum her cervix. Because we visit her mother in Zambia. Because she hasn't seen her mother in ten years. Because she was twelve when her father summoned her. Because education. Because the fuck kind of education was she getting in Texas. Because his wife was not her mother. Because his wife told the neighbors she was adopted. Because she wrote home every day for a year. Because she vomits on the plane. Because she keeps vomiting when we get there. Because her mother thinks she's pregnant. Because I think we've been safe this time. Because she thinks she's a stranger to her mother. Because she grew dreadlocks and is six feet tall. Because she never learned to speak Lozi. Because she never learned to cook nshima. Because she learned how to be Zambian but now she forgot. Because she needs a new passport. Because you're not allowed to have dread-

locks in your passport photo. Because you have to pay a bribe if
you have dreadlocks in your passport photo. Because her mother
still ceremonially attacks her with a hairbrush even after paying
the bribe. Because I'm not there for her. Because her brother
takes me out drinking. Because he keeps me out drinking until the
following afternoon. Because she can't wait to fly home. Because
she no longer knows what home is. Because she's a stranger to
herself now, too. Because she wants to break up with me. Because
she doesn't mean it. Because she takes it all back. Because she's
either broke or broken. Because she's still living with me even
though we broke up for real this time. Because the apartment
looks like every dresser drawer and closet just held a projectile
vomiting contest. Because our house is disgusted by the way we
squandered love. Because I find her a room in a friend's apartment. Because four hundred a month is a miracle in this city. Because she was supposed to move out yesterday. Because she hasn't
started packing. Because our mattress is sheeted with wrinkled dol-
lar bills. Because it's where she threw all her tips. Because she can't
stop sleeping with strangers. Because she hasn't slept in three days.
Because she says make love to me. Because I miss her like flame
misses water. Because no hold me first. Because she can't trust me.
Because somebody's been putting voodoo on her. Because she
isn't making sense. Because my heart reminds me she's like a
poem so she doesn't have to make sense. Because she heard a gun-
shot. Because that means the bartender's dead. Because or maybe
her mother or sister. Because somebody's gotta be dead. Because
she keeps killing people with her thoughts. Because she's Medusa.
Because it's New Year's Eve and she's in love with the bartender. Because it's her shift at the restaurant and also her wedding day.
Because the restaurant is actually a secret cult. Because she's
disturbing the customers. Because her boss calls her sister to take
her home. Because she tells her sister she murdered me. Because
her sister believes she really did stab me and leave me gasping my
last breaths in a pool of blood. Because her eyes are dancing
flames. Because her sister is the Antichrist. Because her niece is
also Satan. Because she needs me to take her to church dammit.
Because the apocalypse is happening right now. Because her hair
is Satan. Because she stabs at the back of her head with a razor
blade. Because one of the Satans is chasing her. Because she's running shoeless out the door. Because she tosses her phone in a trash

can. Because it won't stop ringing. Because her sister calls 911. Because it's never safe for a crazy black woman to be running loose in the streets. Because her sister says that not me. Because the cops show up before the ambulance. Because she asks if she's going to jail. Because the cop shrugs did you do anything to go to jail for. Because he's got a gun not an MSW. Because she steps into the ambulance with her arms spread balancing one foot in front of the other as if walking across a tension wire. Because she signs the consent form *The Devil* and that means she's officially The Devil. Because she knows people are being tortured behind the curtains. Because the nurse asks if she's been here before. Because what about drug use. Because were you smoking every day. Because was it once or was it twice. Because keep going it was more. Because do you have a diagnosis. Because her mother has high blood pressure. Because she's been drinking too much coffee so maybe it's just high blood pressure. Because the doctor interviews me in another room. Because recent mania. Because previous depression. Because prolonged breakup. Because in my opinion coming to America was the experience in her life which could most clinically be described as traumatic. Because couldn't moving from Zambia to Texas at the age of twelve make anyone psychotic. Because the doctor doesn't laugh at my joke. Because who said it was a joke. Because she asks me to marry her. Because she's been issued a pale blue gown. Because my eyes are bleeding grief. Because this isn't poetic. Because this isn't romantic. Because deep in my gut I wish I could marry her. Because she darts into the corner like I'm going to bite her. Because *Fuck you're the one who's there in the madness who else am I gonna call Ghostbusters?* Because it's Judgment Day. Because provisional diagnosis. Because at least (2) of the following. Because each present for a significant portion of time during a one-month period. Because delusions. Because hallucinations. Because disorganized speech. Because grossly disorganized or catatonic behavior. Because negative symptoms. Because an episode of the disorder lasts at least one month but less than six months. Because when the diagnosis must be made without waiting for recovery it must be regarded as provisional. Because the hospital discharges her. Because her clothes are still scattered across the living room floor. Because I didn't pick them up. Because she packs them all up. Because months pass and she still has a set of my keys. Because she's naked in my bed and cradling one of my dashikis when I get home. Because I get home drunk and lonely. Because I don't have to be drunk or lonely to crave her touch. Because I wish I could do it all over again. Because she snatches the condom off my penis. Because she says she's still on the pill. Because I want to believe her. Because I believe her. Because she's lying. Because she's pregnant. Because she says don't say I tricked you. Because I don't say but you did trick me. Because God and her mother don't want her to get another abortion. Because this wasn't an accident. Because this was flailing for control. Because nothing says control like a squalling malleable creature of your very own. Because she's too terrified to leave her apartment. Because she still thinks the world is ending. Because she flies home to her mother in Zambia. Because I fly there the week before she's due. Because of God's grace I'm not drunk when you are born. Because you are a miracle. Because you squeeze my index finger in your tiny wrinkled paw. Because joy is shooting up my limbs. Because it melts into regret the second it strikes my heart. Because I know how soon I will be leaving. Because I rock you to sleep singing Suzanne. Because Jesus knew for certain only drowning men would see him. Because I hate the sound of my quavery nasal voice. Because I keep singing anyway until my limbs are tingling. Because any appendage may tingle long after it is severed. Because these lopped-off arms of mine will keep bearing your weight after the rest of me flies home. Because at home I need anesthetic. Because I go drowning at a friend's pad. Because a line for each nostril. Because whiskey when we hit the dive. Because we crush his Dexedrine pills into an iridescent orange powder on the counter. Because the bartender doesn't even flinch. Because maybe he thinks we're snorting Pixy Stix. Because we dip into the club next door. Because I dip my finger in a little Ziploc. Because translucent crystals cling to my fingerprint. Because they dissolve on my tongue. Because Soul Brothers Six wails a rare B-side. Because it must be a love song to Jesus. Because I feel so fucking cleansed in that shower of strobing lights. Because maybe I'm not alone after all. Because I hear my sneakers squeaking on the beer-slick floor. Because we crash at Ari's house. Because our nightcap is a couple tabs of acid. Because sunrise catches me dancing in my underwear sucking on a Dragon Stout and trying to convince Ari the noisy air conditioner is actually his mother. Because if you think that's crazy guess what happens next. Because Donald Trump is elected president. Because a lawful permanent

resident (LPR) normally may travel outside the United States and
return. Because however there are some limitations. Because a
Permanent Resident Card (PRC). Because acceptable as a travel
document only if the person has been absent for less than one
year. Because if an LPR expects to be absent for more than one
year the LPR should also apply for a reentry permit. Because to
obtain a reentry permit file Form I-131. Because the LPR must
actually be in the United States when he or she applies for a reentry
permit. Because your mother has been absent for two years. Because your mother has never even heard of a reentry permit. Because that means you're getting on a plane. Because you're a baby
you fly in her lap. Because the customs officer says welcome home.
Because according to his discretion. Because the president isn't
yet ranting about shithole countries. Because he isn't president yet
the inauguration is next week. Because I find you a sublet with
bedbugs. Because the next sublet falls through. Because you move
in with my parents. Because you move to your auntie's pad in
Bushwick. Because your mother doesn't believe in therapists. Because she doesn't believe in taking pills. Because you say take care
of me. Because you say Mama cries all day. Because Mama can't get
out of bed in the morning. Because she stops taking you to day
care. Because she turns off the lights and tells me to come get her.
Because she looks like a train ran over her soul. Because she looks
at me like I'm a menacing stranger. Because I'm not sure I recognize her either. Because I get her in a cab to the hospital. Because
she won't talk or put on the gown. Because now I'm full-time
daddy. Because being your daddy is my first full-time job in ages.
Because I'm not a serious person. Because I'm terrified. Because I
think my world is ending. Because I'm becoming a more coherent
person. Because therapy. Because antidepressants. Because so
much for all those last-call nights. Because you're sleeping on my
couch. Because so many drunk and transient friends slept there
before you. Because I'm waiting for your mother to lurch down
the hall. Because glazed eyes and a papery green gown. Because
she hasn't spoken all week. Because another patient stomps at me.
Because he's a real person. Because look at the walls the ceiling
the lights. Because they're real. Because I can touch them. Because he is real, too. Because the nurse tells him to stop bothering
me. Because his pulsing eyes scare me. Because my own eyes itch
for my screen. Because distraction is downstairs in a locker. Be-

cause I'm even more scared of my newsfeed. Because the thumbnail won't go away. Because the little boy's eyes spit tears. Because he grips the links of his cage. Because he sought asylum. Because here I am inside an asylum. Because I have to scroll past never clicking. Because my government is abusing children. Because my government is putting them in cages. Because my government is doing it on purpose. Because the boy's face is pried open with grief. Because it looks too much like yours. Because you howl Mama. Because your jawbone will fly out of your mouth and slay me. Because your breath skips. Because a looping blurt of noise. Because a broken record repeats itself. Because cords of your snot smear my shoulder. Because you claw the buttons on my chest. Because you were nursing and then Mama vanished. Because I have no milk in my nipples. Because you're not in a cage you're safe. Because whose mind is really sick. Because what is a border if not a hallucination. Because your mother has a new diagnosis. Because an uninterrupted duration of illness during which there is a major mood episode in addition to criterion A. Because criterion A is as follows. Because two or more of the following presentations. Because at least one of these must be from the first three below. Because delusions. Because hallucinations. Because disorganized speech. Because hallucinations and delusions for two or more weeks in the absence of a major mood episode during the entire lifetime duration of the illness. Because symptoms that meet the criteria for a major mood episode are present for the majority of the total duration of the active as well as residual portions of the illness. Because don't cry baby we'll see Mama soon. Because your mother has supervised visits. Because she's taking the meds. Because she's starting to feel more balanced. Because I'm a flailing funambulist on the tension wire of fatherhood. Because I let you sleep some nights at your mother's apartment. Because she lands a barista job. Because she decides she doesn't need the meds. Because various factors have been linked with nonadherence in patients with a similar diagnosis. Because side effects. Because akinesia. Because akathisia. Because relapse of positive symptoms. Because poor therapeutic alliance. Because poor insight. Because younger age. Because low socioeconomic status. Because substance abuse. Because she's stoned at drop-off. Because she smokes all day when she smokes. Because you tell me Mama leaves you alone in the apartment crying. Because you're only three years old for

Christ's sake. Because your mother says she would never do that. Because I want to believe her. Because I can't believe her. Because I let you sleep there again. Because it's the night before your fourth birthday. Because your mother won't let you sleep. Because she wants to blow candles at midnight. Because she forgot the cake. Because she dashes you out to the bodega at midnight. Because your mother FaceTimes me after midnight. Because I know something's wrong. Because you are crying for Daddy. Because your mother is personally insulted. Because it's almost 12:35 and you were born at 12:35 so don't you realize how this makes her feel. Because *Come get her she's being a brat.* Because she's ranting and pacing when I get there. Because she's waving a flambeau of incense sticks. Because it stinks of weed or evil spirits. Because I see no safety in the blaze of her eyes. Because I pick you up *Baby it's time to go home.* Because you scream for Mama. Because I'm used to you screaming for Mama. Because this twinge in my heart as I think up anything to distract you. Because your mother shouts *Look now you're the one traumatizing her!* Because you stop wailing when we get home. Because I already wrapped all your birthday presents. Because I put them in easy-to-find hiding places. Because the next day you wear your new mermaid swimsuit and all your friends come to your party at the Splash Pad. Because your mother has fun at the party, too. Because Mama's not psychotic just stoned off her ass and snorting wild laughter. Because you will cherish your fourth birthday party as incomparably joyous not as that time your mother cracked up. Because your mother will crack up again. Because there's no way of knowing when. Because it's just a few months later. Because I call when she doesn't pick you up. Because she keeps trying to leave her apartment. Because she just can't make herself leave her apartment. Because stop it. Because stop it. Because I can't see through the phone but I swear she's slapping herself in the face. Because it's another month in the hospital. Because this time I don't even visit. Because I'm still her first stop after discharge. Because she's coming to borrow a screw gun. Because unspecified damage done to her apartment before the mobile crisis unit took her away. Because you don't even ask about Mama this time. Because you only remember to cry when I mention the hospital. Because you have already learned to compartmentalize. Because otherwise you are rolling with it. Because your teacher says you are just as ebullient as ever. Because you still make more friends on a Tuesday at the playground than I've made in years. Because you are so fucking radiant. Because how can the best thing that ever happened to me also be the most traumatic? Because I've never done anything better than being your daddy. Because think of what I would have done otherwise. Because my idea of living my best life was giving myself hangovers. Because I didn't consent to your existence. Because I can't regret your existence. Because cherishing your existence does or does not admit your mother did me a favor by tricking me. Because most of my adult interactions are with your friends' parents. Because I don't want them to know your mother is a mentally disturbed woman who tricked me into impregnating her. Because that's so very private. Because it's ethically questionable that I'm even writing about it. Because someday you will feel disturbed that you were made by reckless deception. Because if we want beauty we have to be just as dumb and wild as God made us. Because sometimes I *do* want the world to know your mother is indeed a severely troubled woman who tricked me into impregnating her. Because that's my inconvenient truth. Because that's the alarm that wakes me up every morning to brush your teeth and play a game of Candy Land before walking you to school. Because if they don't know the unflattering truth about your mother they will assume some unflattering truths about me. Because call me vain but I don't want the whole world thinking I'm some kind of asshole. Because consider a man who intentionally impregnates an African woman then dumps her then leverages his socioeconomic privilege to gain custody of their daughter. Because he sounds execrable doesn't he? Because that's not who I am. Because that's just who I look like. Because a multitude of paradoxes contains me. Because my silence is a child ripping the limbs off a daddy longlegs. Because I remember how severed my arms felt twitching. Because you lived so far away from me. Because now my arms feel like they will fall out of their sockets carrying your weight wherever I go. Because I can't let you walk across this tension wire all by yourself. Because I once told your mother the path to simplicity is convoluted. Because simplicity must not be where this tension wire is taking us. Because I can't see what's on the other end. Because I can only read the map. Because they used to write *Here Be Dragons*. Because your mother is the dragon and she's out there somewhere shrouded in her own smoke. Because that's exoticizing. Because that's pathologizing.

Because that's stigmatizing. Because nevertheless. Because studies of identical twins indicate genetic predisposition. Because factors such as urbanicity, migration, cannabis, and childhood traumas. Because your mother came here when she was twelve. Because you came here when you were one. Because your mother was separated from her mother when she came here. Because you were separated from your mother when she was hospitalized. Because your mother resented her father for taking her away from her mother. Because your father is me and I am all I can do. Because your childhood is trauma. Because schism. Because etymology is etiology. Because history is a broken record. Because lies scratch it. Because it skips then repeats. Because it's catching its breath. Because experience has taught us that we have only one enduring weapon in our struggle against mental illness: the emotional discovery of the truth about the unique history of our childhood. Because that's the first sentence of *The Drama of the Gifted Child*. Because here is a whole lot of truth. Because do you really need all this truth. Because if I were actually talking to you how much of this would I say. Because for starters probably not the parts about having sex with your mother. Because nobody wants to know how they got here. Because you're here though and I'm responsible. Because you call it Daddy's house even though it's your home now, too. Because here is a home. Because take it please before the very concept of home is snatched away from you. Because look at you. Because you found a sparrow in our backyard. Because its body was pulsing with ants. Because one lifeless eye pinched shut. Because it's bedtime. Because I cradle you in my arms no matter how they tingle with desire to go out writhing on some hazy strobe-lit dance floor. Because you still whisper Daddy sing Suzanne. Because I probably sound like a drowning man not a father. Because that's what coming up for air sounds like. Because you look up at me and speak. Because remember the birdie who died in the backyard. Because you saw me tie it up in a bag. Because your eyes ignite with manic revelation. Because you've been performing since you were a baby. Because if it wakes up what will it say? Because of those times your mother was catatonic. Because you shake your fist like a campy little spirit medium. Because the only defibrillator you had was your personality. Because you channel that bird. Because shocking your mother awake was a matter of survival. Because the bird is grouchy and baffled to find itself trapped in stygian plastic. Because not every child is gifted such drama. Because I'm in a bag! Because it's not fair! Because I don't want to go to sleep! Because you are my child. Because a child knows death is the nap you don't want to take. Because death is when you pass out somewhere that's not your home and wake up in darkness slung over a shoulder. Because every impulse that rooted you to the ground snaps like a brittle wishbone. Because that's the strange world passing you to yet another place.

As Big as You Make It Out to Be

FROM *Ploughshares*

IN MAY 2009, a year after I graduated from college, I found my-self in a mangrove swamp thirty miles east of Haikou, the capital city of China's southernmost province, Hainan Island, standing atop a massive, concrete floodgate. With me were six reporters from a Cantonese television station, the CEO of one of China's largest telecommunications companies, and a novelist who had fled China twenty years earlier after the massacre at Tiananmen Square. It was a hot, overcast day, and the tropical sunlight beat down in a sourceless glare as the reporters—twenty-somethings in T-shirts and khaki shorts, mopping their brows and chugging bottled water—trained their cameras on the two middle-age men, who were talking with great animation about the past.

To either side, the thin line of the seawall ran straight to the horizon, bifurcating the flat, green landscape. In front of us, a brown river wound through a wilderness of mangroves, and on its still surface several empty sampans drifted, clustered around a mooring post. Behind us, legions of ragged palm trees nodded their heads almost imperceptibly in the faint breeze, and rect-angular fishponds gleamed in the sun. Thirty-three years earlier, the businessman, Tony Fok, and the novelist, Su Wei, had helped create this landscape, quite literally, with their bare hands.

"If you stood here and looked out," Su Wei said, sweeping a hand toward the palm trees, "you'd see tents and thatch huts as far as the eye could see. At night, there were thousands of camp-fires glittering in the dark." During the years 1975 and '76, thirty thousand teenagers camped here in what was one of the largest

campaigns of the sent-down youth movement, the period immediately following the Cultural Revolution, when urban teenagers
were relocated to the countryside to "learn from the peasants."
It was a time when political winds blew through every corner of a
person's life, and the project, in its grandiosity and ambition, was
typical of its era, a time when it was believed possible to overcome
all material limitations by pure force of will. The goal was lofty: to
build a mile-long seawall to convert 1,500 acres of marshland to
rice paddies that would feed Chairman Mao's socialist utopia. The
means were primitive: heaving buckets of mud, day in, day out,
without the benefit of machines or pack animals, reshaping the
landscape by sheer human brawn.

"We were covered in mud from head to toe," Su Wei explained,
gesticulating in front of the big black cameras. "Every day, we had
to wade back and forth from there"—he pointed to the nearest
fishpond, a distance of about fifty feet—"to here, knee-deep in
mud. Just carrying one bucket of mud that distance took half an
hour." It was here, working on the seawall, that Su Wei and Tony
Fok met. Su Wei was a budding writer, Fok an aspiring composer,
and the two collaborated to write a triumphalist anthem they
called "Patrolling the Seawall." Su Wei would go on to join a circle
of writers who would pen some of the foundational works of Chinese literature after the Cultural Revolution; they would march
with the student protestors on Tiananmen Square, and afterward,
many would flee the country. Tony Fok would set aside music to
study wireless technology and later found a company that would
build the cell phone towers of much of south China. But the formative moments of their youths were spent here in Hainan, in
white undershirts and straw hats, under a punishing sun, trooping
through the wilderness to the drumbeats of crashing tree trunks—
summer camp on a Wagnerian scale.

Su and Fok, who reconnected later in life to collaborate on
a cantata commemorating the sent-down youth movement, had
flown back to Hainan to revisit the seminal sites of their adolescence. The film crew was along for the ride, capturing their reminiscences to produce a documentary about the making of the
cantata. In the film, which later aired on a major provincial TV
channel, Su Wei appears to be speaking to the camera. But in fact,
he is speaking to me. From time to time, the microphones pick up
my "uh-huhs," and occasionally the camera, following his gestures,

pans past a bearded American youngster in baggy pants, looking conspicuously out of place on these rutted dirt paths lined with rubber trees.

"This is one of the places we cleared to plant rubber trees," Su Wei says to the offscreen me. "This whole place used to be dense jungle. The hillside was swarming with people." The music swells to a climax, and the film cuts to a black-and-white montage of serious-looking kids wielding shovels and swinging axes.

Twenty million people—an entire generation—had their youths rerouted by a man with wild dreams who wrote a little red book. This, at least, was one thing I had in common with them. And this was what had brought me to Hainan Island. My book, however, was a red paperback novel called *The Invisible Valley*, which lay nestled in my satchel as I trooped through the rubber orchards with Su Wei, past brick-and-tile barracks, down overgrown stone steps toward the well where the "re-eds" used to wash. It's often said that a book can change the course of one's life—but for me, this was literally true. This is the story that I, at age thirty-three, now have to tell.

I was not the sort of person whose life you'd expect to be changed by a Chinese novel. I have no Chinese ancestry. Nor did I have any friends or family with ties to China. My relationship with China began in the dusty offices of the Yale Chinese department, where I took Mandarin during college, and it might well have ended there too had I not met Su Wei, who took a job as a lecturer at Yale not long after fleeing China and who, one afternoon during my junior year, made me an unusual proposal.

I had enrolled in Su Wei's upper-level Chinese course because a quirk of the curriculum left me no other choice. I had studied Chinese for a few years, more or less on a lark, and though my skills were still middling, I'd placed out of the classes intended for lower-level learners. Su Wei's class was the only option available. The idea was to improve students' language skills by reading literature, though in practice most students were of Chinese ancestry and took the class for an easy grade. The selections of Chinese fiction we read, which I had to painstakingly decode with a dictionary, were written by the now-famous writers of the 1980s, China's post–Cultural Revolution literary renaissance, most of them household names in China but completely unknown in the United States.

Up to that point, the Chinese classes I'd taken were mostly about forming sentences. "Which do you think is more important, family or career?" the teacher would ask us, calling on students one by one. "Use the *gen xiangbi* sentence pattern." The language was a glass vessel to be filled with any meaning we chose to pour into it, and the teachers did their best to make themselves transparent, too, serving as invisible conduits between the student and his or her intended meaning, studiously avoiding telling us anything about their own personal lives. There was too much vocabulary to be learned. Class time was too precious for such tangents.

Su Wei's class was different, though. On the first day of class, not long after plunking down his books at the head of the seminar table, he taught us what he promised was the worst insult in the Chinese language ("Repeat after me," he said with a twinkle in his eye and a backward glance out the door. "Fuck your family for eight generations back!") and plied us with gossip about the first writer in our spiral-bound course reader. "Back in the eighties, Teacher Su knew all these people," he said, referring to himself, as he often did, in the third person. "We were the first generation of writers to write 'serious literature' after the Cultural Revolution. And you know, back then, Teacher Su's apartment was very famous among intellectuals in Beijing."

It was a studio—hence, no roommates, a rare thing in those days—allowing Su Wei to convert it into a space to host literary gatherings. "Over there"—he gestured at one end of the classroom—"was a ring of sofas. Against the wall was an upright piano a musician friend gave me. I slept over there"—the other end of the classroom—"in a little nook by the door." Here he hosted meetings of his *sha long*, his literary salon, a term he used as unironically as Rousseau and Voltaire might have. He and his friends, some of them the writers whose works we were reading, would gather to listen to music, critique each other's novels, and discuss art and politics. China was opening up and seemed on the brink of great change. "We were all very 'idealism,' very 'romantics,'" Su Wei said, punctuating his speech, as he often did, with slightly ungrammatical English. "Let me tell you a story about the first time I met Shi Tiesheng, the next writer in our textbook . . ."

So he went on, week after week, beaming at us and waving his arms as if conducting an orchestra. The vocabulary words, the sentence-correction exercises—these things were an afterthought.

The real subject of the class was Su Wei himself. He would regale us for half a class period with the story of how he'd bicycled through the streets of Beijing to collect signatures for a petition from the city's most prominent intellectuals, a toothbrush in his backpack in case the secret police following behind him apprehended him and took him to jail. He would tell how, on the eve of the massacre, when he was camped out in Tiananmen Square, he would slip back once a day to his apartment, risking capture, in order to feed his cat, Aïda, who'd just borne a litter of kittens. Sometimes, in a nod to the needs of the non-native speakers in the classroom, he annotated himself by scribbling words at odd angles on the board. But often he just addressed us as he would another Chinese person, sentences spilling forth in torrents, so it required all my powers of concentration to follow him.

Now the Chinese language was not just a blank substratum. It was an alternate universe, a dusky continent teeming with storylines that revealed itself against the college's bright, tree-lined streets, along which I walked to and from Su Wei's class. Here, for once, was proof that real life could have the same epic sweep as stories in books.

I used to visit my Chinese teachers' office hours for explanations of difficult vocabulary, and I kept up this habit with Su Wei, though it felt weird to prevail upon a famous exiled writer to explain the difference between "either" and "neither." "Clutter" was the obvious word to describe Su Wei's office, but it didn't quite do the place justice. More or less every square inch of space was occupied, either by books, papers, tea tins, mugs, brushes, calligraphy scrolls, ink paintings, Greek busts, or myriad tchotchkes including inkstones, pieces of gnarled wood, figurines, and hand-drawn cards given to him by his students. Three large tables dominated the room, piled high with books and oddments, one of them heaped so deep with literary magazines that their undulating pages, visible from one side, looked like a cross section of sedimentary rock. The fat leaves of a tropical plant glowed in the occasional dusty sunbeams that penetrated the perennially closed blinds. Above the door hung two enormous characters: *Cheng Zhai*—"The Studio of Lucidity." It was through this door that I began passing every Tuesday afternoon.

Su Wei seemed happy to help me stammer through sample

sentences and explain the subtle differences between words. His explanations often spun off into whimsical tangents about ancient Chinese poetry or long-winded reminiscences about his own literary exploits, and soon the vocabulary list would be forgotten altogether. He took such genuine pleasure in art and literature and the Chinese language, jumping up again and again to scrawl characters on the chalkboard, that we developed a tacit understanding that if we alighted on an interesting side topic—the ancient nudist Taoist eccentrics known as the Seven Sages of the Bamboo Grove, for instance, or our shared passion for classical music, or an esoteric word with a story behind it—there was no need to address the questions I'd actually brought.

"I think you and I are quite similar, Wen Houting," he said, addressing me using the Chinese name I went by in class. "I can tell that you're the kind of person who—here's a phrase you'll like," he said, scribbling sideways in my notebook, "doesn't 'eat amid the cooking smoke of humanity,' *bu chi renjian yanhuo*. When I was young, I was just the same. But to write well you have to *ru shi*—you know, to enter society, to get mixed up in things. . . ."

He didn't know it, but I was fascinated with Su Wei in part because I wanted to write, too. I hadn't yet admitted this to myself, though. Wanting to be a writer felt corny somehow. And I knew that no one wanted to read about the small, soft problems of another boy from the Boston suburbs. For this reason, listening to Su Wei's stories gave me a strangely wistful feeling. I hadn't been born into a time when there were so few writers that simply being one made you part of literary history. I didn't have a despotic government to stare down—not that anyone, rationally, would want one—or live in a society in which artists were seen as powerful and dangerous. I loved listening to his tales, but it felt like pressing my face against a shop window, gazing at something I couldn't let myself desire, something that wasn't given to me to have. I didn't have a life—not the way Su Wei did.

Then, the following fall, during one of our office-hour bull sessions, Su Wei asked me, seemingly out of the blue: "Do you want to translate my novel?"

Actually, what he said was, "Do you want to translate my *Mi Gu*?" The name of the book means "enchanted valley" or "valley by which one is enchanted, or in which one gets lost." Su Wei had written a number of books, but I could tell by the way he constantly compared what we read in class to "my *Mi Gu*," the way he bragged about it and relished reliving its details, that this was the one he felt really mattered. That summer, while taking language classes in Beijing, I'd come across a stack of copies on display in a bookstore, hefty red paperbacks with a stylized cloud pattern on the cover and a blurb on the back calling it a "work of genius." I'd picked up a copy and tried to read it, but the language was too hard, and I didn't get far.

"Think about it," Su Wei said, rising to refill his mug of green tea, then returning to the enormous, shapeless armchair in which he took his regular afternoon nap. I sat on one of the half dozen straight-backed chairs along the wall—I later noticed these came in handy for accommodating the occasional delegations of visiting Chinese dignitaries he hosted—my notebook of now-irrelevant vocabulary questions balanced on my knee. "It would be a big project," he said. "Maybe too big." He paused, gazing downward into his tea as if searching for something within himself. For a moment, he seemed smaller, less sure, more vulnerable than his normally buoyant self. "I don't usually seek out my students to translate my work. But I'm pretty sure you're the one to do it. I wouldn't recommend it to anyone else."

At this point, I should note that it's fairly unusual for an author, particularly a well-known one, to entrust an untried student with the translation of their most important work. Usually a publisher, already interested in an author's work, will approach a translator; or, if an author is particularly keen to be read abroad, he or she will seek out a translator through professional connections. But I didn't know this at the time, and it didn't occur to me that it might be an odd thing to do.

All I knew was that an unbelievable opportunity had descended upon me—the very thing I'd wanted without knowing I could want it. Could I really translate Su Wei's book? Was I really the one? The improbability of it was heady enough to convince me it could be true. I rushed back to my dorm room, clutching the copy of the novel Su Wei had just given me, feeling like a great, rare bird had dived out of the sky and alighted on my wrist. Yes, I would be Su Wei's translator. The mixture of fear and desire I felt at that moment is something I've experienced at only a few, rare moments in

life. It was the thrill of contemplating the imminent rearrangement
of one's soul.

At the beginning of *The Invisible Valley*, a twenty-year-old boy is working on a rubber plantation in the hills of Hainan Island, around the
year 1970. Lu Beiping is a city kid—he grew up in Guangzhou, Su
Wei's hometown—but the fickle winds of the times have blown him
to a rural backwater where his job is to dig holes in the ground.
This is where we meet him, a middle-class, educated youngster
thrust into highly unusual circumstances, yet unaware that they are
unusual; to him, his daily routine planting rubber trees on the farm
has become tediously, mind-numbingly ordinary. Then, one day,
on the way back to camp, he notices something odd: a scrap of red
paper lying at the edge of a rubber grove, covered in unrecogniz-
able glyphs.

He picks it up, and unbeknownst to him, by pure chance, he
has marked himself out for a still more unusual fate. According
to local custom, he must now marry the spirit of a dead girl in an
arrangement known as a "ghost marriage." The spirit in question
belongs to the daughter of the most powerful man in the camp,
Foreman Kau. The foreman, knowing that these superstitions are
not exactly compatible with the Marxist atheism he is supposed to
espouse, gives his newlywed "son-in-law" a questionable blessing:
Lu Beiping will now spend his days minding the work unit's herd
of cattle up on the mountain, alone in the jungle, where people
will be less likely to gossip about him. It is there, by chance, that
Lu Beiping meets a band of woodcutters with some even stranger
beliefs than the foreman's, and slowly, he finds himself drawn into
their world.

Holding this book in my hands in my dorm room at Yale, I
didn't know any of this; in fact, I had only the faintest idea what
the book contained. Flipping through the first chapters, I could
tell the landscape was important. There were eerie, red cloud
formations called "snakeclouds" and a creek with five bends like
fingers winding across the landscape, giving the place a primor-
dial feel. I knew, because Su Wei had told us in class, that the
novel was set on a fictional mountain in a real county in Hainan,
that it had a lot of sex in it, and a lot of *tuhua*—local dialect—as
well as an enormous, mythical snake and some deep philosophical

ideas. It sounded both like and unlike the kind of book I could imagine myself writing, if I'd had anything near the kind of life experiences that Su Wei had. And here it was now, very solid and real, its red cover cool to the touch: a message out of another world, a thick brick of strange glyphs that would take me, if I allowed them, Elsewhere.

This invitation came at an opportune time, for it answered a question that had been vexing me: Whatever was I to do after college? Most of my classmates were already laying the groundwork to capitalize on their Ivy League educations in all the traditional ways: getting jobs at investment banks and consulting firms, applying for prestigious fellowships, applying to grad school, landing journalism internships. I, though, hadn't a clue what to do. For what single reality was I to exchange the manifold possibilities of my Promise, that gleaming passport that had gotten me into Yale? With this book, at least I could put off that decision. I figured I could get a part-time job—I envisioned some sort of stereotypical light manual labor, like working in a coffee shop—and spend a year translating the novel while I figured out "the next step." At the very least, I'd have a good excuse to keep listening to Su Wei tell stories, and who knows? Maybe a novel by an exiled Chinese writer, who'd never before been translated into English, could make a splash.

Later that semester, I received an email from Su Wei with another interesting invitation. Did I want to take a trip with him into New York City, he asked, to hear a poetry reading by Bei Dao, China's most famous contemporary poet? Bei Dao, who rose to fame during the heady years before Tiananmen, was sort of the Bob Dylan of his generation: student protestors chanted lines from his poetry while marching on the square in '89. Needless to say, I said yes—this was just the kind of experience I was hoping for.

"Buckle up," Su Wei told me as I climbed into his dusty red sedan in front of the Chinese department. "My wife told me to be extra careful taking a student with me on the road." He'd packed us dinner to go, mostly consisting of the individually packaged Chinese snacks that he kept in vast quantities in his office, plus some strange, tiny hamburgers he'd microwaved in their plastic wrapping just before we left.

Su Wei launched into his story immediately as we pulled away from the curb. In the days leading up to June 4, tensions were mounting. The students had begun hunger striking, and the government had declared martial law. In an attempt to end the standoff, twelve public intellectuals, including Su Wei, arranged to meet with representatives of the government to negotiate the students' withdrawal from the square. Bei Dao was among them. This was Su Wei's first encounter with the poet, marching together with him through the sea of protestors, across the square, toward the Great Hall of the People. "The crowd was *teeming* with secret police," he said, gesturing dramatically as he steered us past the New Haven Green. I remember this sentence clearly—it was the first time I heard the word "teeming" in Chinese.

As anyone familiar with that chapter of history knows, their attempt was unsuccessful. The students stayed, and in the early dawn hours of June 4, the People's Liberation Army marched into the square and opened fire on the protestors. Su Wei, who got out in the nick of time, managed to get on a train to Guangzhou with the aid of a stranger's ID card, found by pure chance on the street. While he was laying low with a distant relative, an official announcement declared that all student leaders and members of the Federation of Independent Intellectuals—this included Su Wei—must surrender themselves to the authorities. Any who resisted would be shot. By luck, a midnight phone call alerted Su Wei to a way out of the country, and the next day, he was hidden in the hold of a smuggler's speedboat, churning down the Pearl River toward Hong Kong.

Of course I would translate Su Wei's book. "This sounds like the kind of opportunity that doesn't come along more than once in your life," my father admitted, taking me out to dinner at a nice restaurant near campus. This was 2007, a year before the financial crisis, and it seemed conceivable back then that after spending a year on this project, full-time employment would simply descend on me, as easy as that.

I have only the vaguest memories of that poetry reading. There were two brothers with scraggly long beards who made a splatter painting on an enormous calligraphy scroll while Bei Dao read his poetry aloud; then there was a screening of a long, pretentious art movie, which Su Wei and I lost patience with and walked out of. What I remember most clearly, though, was leaving for it: driving off in that little red car into what was certain to be an adventure. We were so absorbed in conversation that Su Wei accidentally drove up the exit ramp to the highway—and for a brief, hair-raising moment we watched the rain of oncoming cars hurtling toward us before Su Wei pulled a frantic U-turn and managed to get us going in the right direction.

That same autumn, during one of my office hour visits, Su Wei gave me an unusual assignment. "If you want to translate my book," he said, "I'm giving you a piece of homework. You need to fall in love."

By this point, I wasn't unused to being surprised by the things that came out of Su Wei's mouth. Operating in a foreign language, I had no benchmark for what was normal, and the things that happened in Chinese seemed to occupy a parallel universe where the usual laws of physics sometimes didn't apply. One of his favorite topics was contemplating shining visions of my future, ones in which I would become, say, a famous writer, or an esteemed professor, or the greatest Chinese-English translator of my generation. *Ei! Ni bie shuo!* ("And it just could be that . . . !") he'd say whenever some grand new possibility swung into view. Sometimes he'd direct his attention to a potential fault in my character, as if I were the protagonist of a novel he was envisioning, and he'd tell me what I needed to learn to counteract this tendency so it wouldn't trip me up on my road to greatness. Never before had I had a teacher who saw it as within his purview to scry into my future or judge the shape of my soul. I wasn't sure to what degree this was a cultural difference or just a reflection of Su Wei's own eccentricities and his particular liking for me. But all the same, his assignment made me feel a bit dizzy as I descended the steps of the Chinese department afterwards. This was foreign territory.

In the book, Lu Beiping also quickly finds himself wading into unfamiliar waters. One day, while searching for a bull that's wandered off into the jungle, he stumbles into a clearing, where he sees what, to him, seems like a vision out of another world. Sitting on a moss-covered log, a foraging basket on her knees, is an outlandish-looking woman, clad in a flowered dress and old-fashioned dangly earrings, smoking a hand-rolled cigarette. (In those days, the prevailing female fashion was green military fatigues and an emphatic absence of makeup or jewelry.) The woman, Jade, leads him up into a hidden valley on the mountainside, where he meets a collection of rough-cut men, all of them outcasts from mainstream society, who call themselves "the driftfolk" and make a meager living hewing timber and selling it on the black market. This is Jade's family. With these men she has a fluid, polyamorous marriage, and the resulting litter of semi-feral children of uncertain parentage they raise together in a pair of crowded shacks by the creek's edge.

Needless to say, this would be utterly heretical in the society Lu Beiping comes from, rife with dogmas and taboos, where even holding hands with a member of the opposite sex is an invitation for raised eyebrows and possibly much worse. Either in spite of or because of their differences, the mountain woman and the bespectacled city boy develop feelings for each other. When Lu Beiping and she "make good," as she calls it, Lu Beiping finds himself a permanent guest in this odd little community, where men walk around naked and the children know full well what their parents do at night, and he must rapidly adjust himself to a very different definition of normal.

It was true; I'd never been in love. Would that really make a difference in how well I could translate this book? "Love is one of the most central, universal human experiences," Su Wei said to me. "Every writer should have it—you should, too." It wasn't a stretch to see how romantic experience was relevant to this novel, but I sensed that Su Wei was perhaps more concerned for my growth as a human being. Though I aced all my Chinese tests, he would later tell me that he'd noticed how I rarely came to or left class together with other students. I was *du lai du wang*: solitary, someone who "comes and goes all alone."

Right around this time, I went to one of the end-of-semester parties that Su Wei liked to throw for his students and colleagues, and at which I would later become a frequent guest. Su Wei's house was a white clapboard affair on the most ordinary-looking of suburban streets, with a plaster angel on the lawn and a trampoline out back. But stepping inside it was like entering another world. Heavy wood furniture and fat, green couches reposed among paintings and calligraphy and teapots and inkstones, surrounded by enormous tropical plants spilling vines and leaves every which way. The rooms were permanently imbued with the odors of cooking oil and dog hair and long years of living. Su Wei's wife, Mengjun, also taught Chinese at a nearby college, and my first impression of her was as a vortex of activity in the kitchen, whipping up a dozen dishes and turning down my offers to help, while Su Wei held court in the living room, giving guests tours of his myriad artifacts or regaling them with his stories. Photographs of Mengjun as a strikingly beautiful young woman hung on the walls. They were one of the first adult couples—other than my parents—whose marriage I remember having a distinct impression of. Unlike my parents, who never disagreed in front of the children, Su Wei and Mengjun would spar publicly over the smallest things, barking orders at each other from separate rooms like sailors on a ship. Their teenage daughter, Emily, seemed to inhabit a world of her own, clambering up the stairs and disappearing into the lavender cave that was her bedroom while her father and his friends recited classical poems and banged on the piano as the night drew on.

What would it be like, I wondered, growing up in a house like this? Even in my own culture, I had very little knowledge of how other families arranged their lives.

Lu Beiping wonders the same thing, waking up in the driftfolk's shack and gazing through the patched mosquito net at Jade's bamboo pipe, her stone cookstove, the children's laundry hung out to dry, these accoutrements of another person's existence. How much of this, he wonders, will be—can be—compatible with the "me" I know? And how much must I change my shape to fit it?

Later that year I would, much earlier than I expected to, complete Su Wei's homework assignment. I met a girl and fell in love with her; a year later, we were sharing an apartment in Brooklyn. It was there that I began working on the English version of *The Invisible Valley*.

Needless to say, Su Wei was eager to take credit for my new relationship and showered his blessings on us when I took my new girlfriend up to the "Studio of Lucidity" to meet the eccentric Chinese novelist I'd told her so many stories about. I cannot say that his assignment was directly responsible for my finding a partner, and I took care not to give the impression that it was. But the human psyche is a complex place, a soup with many ingredients at work. If there was one key ingredient, it's that by that point, I'd become a bit more open to letting the current of my own life mingle with, and be altered by, the lives of others.

In a creative writing class I took in college, my teacher told me that my characters needed "backstory": some hint of where they came from, their families or careers, what experiences shaped them and made them act the way they did. Lu Beiping has almost none of this. We know his father was a percussionist in a Western-style symphony orchestra, and that's about it. It's as if he's a blank canvas being painted into being by the story as it unfolds. If he has one distinct, unchanging character trait, it's a kind of compulsive curiosity and openness to new experience that bears him deeper and deeper into the tale. Whenever chance offers up some mystery or opportunity, whether in the form of a scrap of red paper or the advances of a wild mountain woman, his answer is always *yes, yes,* and *yes* again.

In New York, one thing led to another. My girlfriend, also a writer, was employed as a magazine editor, and I was spending the mornings translating *The Invisible Valley* and the afternoons doing whatever I could to make money. Having only one marketable skill, the ability to read Chinese (at about an eighth-grade level) and write English, I hung out my plaque as a Chinese-English translator, translating press releases for the Taiwanese cultural attaché's office, subtitles for a documentary film, newspaper articles from overseas Chinese newspapers, whatever would pay the bills. This was temporary, I told myself; it was a means to an end. We were young in New York; we cooked beans and counted pennies; we sweated in subway stations on summer nights.

Practicality was not my muse. Nor was it Su Wei's. Perhaps that, more than anything, was the reason we got along.

Every month or so, I rode the rattling Metro-North train up to New Haven, where Su Wei would pick me up at the station, and we would drive out to his house in the suburbs. There, I would spend a weekend camped in his living room with an enormous sheaf of printouts, copies of the novel's Chinese manuscript, the margins of which gradually filled with a riot of notes and questions and impromptu illustrations that Su Wei scribbled in an attempt to render the world of the novel imaginable to me. Here are the rubber groves; here is where the river runs. Here is the spot where Lu Beiping meets Jade. This is what a *wopeng* looks like—a kind of A-frame hut in which many of the novel's characters lived— and these are the two different kinds of kerosene lanterns that the characters would use to light their way through the jungle at night. Pages spread out on the coffee table before us, we would *zou* (walk through) a chapter together, reliving scenes that Su Wei had imagined years ago. Though the novel wasn't autobiographical, these scenes seemed as real to him as if he'd lived them, as if Jade and Lu Beiping and the woodcutters had an ongoing existence independent of him that he could tune into at any time he wished.

Later, it would dawn on me just how intimate and flattering the experience of being translated could be, to feel the full force of another intellect beamed onto your work, to see that the fiction you've imagined matters enough to another writer that he or she has made it their job to *be* you. This, I'm sure, was one of the reasons why Su Wei was willing to spend so many weekends with me in this way. Bathing in the afterglow of his creation, we would *zou* through chapter after chapter, taking breaks to replenish our mugs of green tea, walk the dogs, or retire to our rooms for the Cantonese habit of a midafternoon siesta, which Su Wei still maintained even after having lived for twenty years in New England. It was work; it was play; and I was certain—as we trailed after his lumbering golden retriever, Liangliang, and his hyperactive white lapdog, Lilia, on our regular orbits through his suburban neighborhood, bantering in Mandarin as we walked—that no one else was doing anything quite like what we were doing.

Gradually, the world of *The Invisible Valley* took form in my mind. Its geography solidified, its characters acquired fixed personality traits and ways of speaking in English that I could reliably anticipate. At the same time, they gained English names that seemed as inevitable as their Chinese ones. And so, on the slopes of Mudkettle Mountain, along the bends of Mudclaw Creek, Lu Beiping became more and more entangled in the strange world of the driftfolk: brash, uninhibited Jade; stern, bald Kingfisher; jovial Stump; melancholy Autumn; and their children, Smudge, Tick, and Roach. Their world became his, and though Lu Beiping tells himself that this is a brief interlude in his life, that sooner or later things will go back to normal, we know he's lying to himself.

The driftfolk's unusual family structure, he soon discovers, is just the tip of the iceberg. Ruling over the ragtag band is Kingfisher, a forbidding man whose unconventional beliefs shape how the driftfolk live and account for their radically open sexual relations. Unlike the Communist cadres, who fear no divine retribution for decimating the forests, Kingfisher believes in the supernatural; he believes the tales of the god-serpent dwelling deep in the mountains, believes a human misstep can trigger a typhoon. And at the heart of his beliefs is a provocatively simple idea, that death is the only evil, love the supreme good, and that, therefore, any kind of affection between human beings, no matter its form, is permissible.

Is this a cult? Lu Beiping wonders as he gets to know Jade's folk better. Are these people crazy? Or are they the only clear-eyed ones? The deeper in he gets—the more of Jade's foraged greens he eats and the more of their home-brewed yam liquor he drinks—the harder it is to tell. And so his initiation into adulthood is, at the same time, his initiation into this strange, miniature society, which seems to be an upside-down mirror of his own.

"Kingfisher's philosophy," like so much else Su Wei talked about, had a fixed, eternal quality to it, as if he'd discovered it himself up there on Mudkettle Mountain and brought it back with him, just as he'd brought back so many other tall tales out of the roiling drama of recent Chinese history. And the story's significance, just like its trees, its valleys, and its characters, was something that, to him, felt solid and certain. Though he was under no illusions that he was anywhere near as famous as the writers on his syllabus, the ones who'd sat in his literary salon or marched with him on Tiananmen Square, he nevertheless had utter confidence in the value of his work, a Victorian poet's conviction that his writing would stand as a monument to posterity. "Nobody can go around this book," he would say, as if *The Invisible Valley* were a mountain sitting solidly in the path of future literary critics. It might not be famous, but it could still be Great, and in any event, there was no other book about the Cultural Revolution quite like it; of this he was sure. I knew no other Chinese novelists or literary critics, so I had to take his word for it.

"Things are as big as you make them out to be," he would tell me years later, advising me about how to make one's way in the world as an artist. In some ways, it was the mantra by which he lived every day of his life. I could tell that this touch of grandeur was the necessary glue that held together Su Wei's being; without it, he wouldn't be Su Wei—he would be someone else entirely.

And so, after our "work" was done, after we'd retired to his study to shoot the breeze amid the cheerful clutter of books and photographs, we'd turn in for the night, get up the next morning, and prepare to repeat the whole process. Refilling his Big Gulp–size glass mugs with the expensive green tea he received as gifts when being fêted on official occasions, we'd ready ourselves for another day on Mudkettle Mountain. Over breakfast, Mengjun

would confide in me her worries about her daughter—worries
that she thought perhaps I, having myself been an American teenager, might be able to speak to (high-school boyfriend, college
applications, dubious friends from the cheerleading squad)—
while Su Wei grunted from behind the pages of the *World Journal*
that everything would be okay. Mengjun had come to the US as a
young woman to marry a political exile she barely knew—they'd
courted mostly by international mail; she'd thought it romantic to
be marrying a novelist—yet the practicalities of raising a child in
a foreign country had hardened her pragmatic side in opposition
to her husband's quixotic nature. On the way out the door, she'd
press upon me fruit and snacks to make sure I wouldn't go hungry on the road, adding to the weight of the whimsical souvenirs
that Su Wei always bestowed on me. These included an imitation
jade bracelet he'd bought at a Zen Buddhist pilgrimage site on a
recent trip to China; heavy wooden paperweights carved with the
Three Character Classic, the primer from which Chinese children
once learned to read; a cheap sandalwood fan; a tin of vanilla-
flavored tea; books of poetry way too difficult for me to read; the
long, black zither he'd acquired in a transient burst of enthusiasm
for Chinese classical music and then promptly gave up on; and a
battered, brown coat he gave me when it was raining outside and
I had nothing to wear. It still hangs in my closet.

Arriving back in Brooklyn, I'd feel as if I'd emerged out of a
secret world, a parallel life that was even more difficult to translate
into English than the novel I spent my mornings poring over. I
found that I stopped even trying to explain to my girlfriend what
we did and talked about on these visits. To my friends, to my parents, *The Invisible Valley* was a steadily growing mystery, a strange
emptiness into which more and more of my time poured.

Then, about a year after we moved to New York, I got a call
from Su Wei with another surprising proposition.

"*Houzi*," he said—by now, he'd taken to calling me by this pun-
ning nickname, which sounded at once like "monkey" and the
name of a Confucian disciple—"I'm going back to Hainan Island.
Do you want to come along?"

The first thing Su Wei had to do when he arrived on Hainan
Island as a sent-down youth was to publicly denounce his family.
His father had been a secret agent for the Communists working

in the Kuomintang government during the Chinese Civil War, but when Chairman Mao incited the nation's adolescents to "Smash the Four Olds" and weed out reactionary elements, the stain of his involvement with the Kuomintang was enough to land him, his wife, and several of Su Wei's sisters in jail. "Our house was ransacked seven times," Su Wei told me, describing the chaos when the Cultural Revolution swept his native city of Guangzhou. "I had to stand by and watch while a soldier whipped my grandma with a bicycle chain. I was only fifteen years old, but as the oldest son present, I had the responsibility of looking after what was left of my family. I still remember walking along the banks of the Pearl River and thinking that I might as well just jump in and drown myself. At that point, the call came for students to go to the countryside for reeducation. I was too young to be required to go, but I signed up anyway. There was nothing left for me at home."

On the rubber plantation to which Su Wei was assigned, each newly arrived city kid had to stand in front of the assembled work unit and report their family's political background. When Su Wei spoke, the crowd was aghast: his was the worst of the worst, a *sha guan guan zidi*—the child of parents who had been "killed, imprisoned, or put under surveillance." Immediately, the older students singled him out for harassment, stealing his diary and writing out private passages on the public announcement board, or secretly putting water in his kerosene lantern so it would explode when he tried to light it in order to read at night.

"That time was a turning point for me," Su Wei told me as we walked alongside the dilapidated barracks in the mountain encampment where he and his peers had lived. "I used to be a spineless little kid. I was scared of the dark. I'd suck up to other kids when they bullied me. But in Hainan, at that moment in my life, something in me fundamentally changed." He resolved to toughen himself up. He forced himself to carry two hundred buckets of water from the well to the rubber groves every day, read biographies of Mao's early years to stoke his resolve to make something of himself. (To this day, he attributes his short stature to the weight of those buckets pressing on his shoulders—as well as to the effects of malnourishment.)

Though at first Su Wei was ostracized for his bookish tendencies, it wasn't long before the leader of the work unit took note of his budding literary talent. He was soon deployed as a propaganda writer, traveling between remote encampments to report on the achievements of the Agricultural Reclamation Corps, the military-style apparatus of state-run farms to which most sent-down youth from Guangzhou had been assigned. The Corps's main mission on Hainan was to end China's dependence on imported rubber by leveling the tropical rainforest that blanketed the hills and planting rubber trees in their place. The massive seawall where Su and Fok met, which would be the final stop on our journey, was another of the Corps's "campaigns," aimed at boosting rice production in order to achieve agricultural self-sufficiency, another of the nation's heroic ambitions.

Standing atop that solid, concrete floodgate with the camera crew, thirty years later, it was hard to imagine what it must have looked like as this structure was being built. A thirty-foot-tall rampart heaped up out of mud and stones, stretching as far as the eye could see in either direction; around it, the murky water of the mangroves and thousands of teenagers waist-deep in it, carrying buckets. Between the two segments of advancing seawall, tall wooden pilings were rammed into the water as a skeleton to support the earthen edifice as it grew. Once, Su Wei said, he led a group of visiting writers for a walk along the wall till it gave way to the wooden pilings. While the visitors hung back fearfully, and the workers on the other side watched in awe, he hopped along the top of the pilings, thirty feet above the waves, till he reached the far side. "By that point," Su Wei told me, "I wasn't afraid of anything."

How would I have fared if I'd had the same experiences that Su Wei did? This was the question echoing in the back of my mind whenever I listened to his stories. Having grown up in a time of peace and plenty, I had no stories of triumph over adversity with which to answer his. The only things that had ever pushed me close to despair were negligible by comparison: all-nighters in high school, fears of disappointing my teachers, anxiety over whether to drop the classical music studies in which I and my parents had heavily invested. "A writer needs to be sensitive," Su Wei told me right around the time he assigned me to fall in love, "but if you have one fault, it's that you're *too* sensitive." I wondered: Had I been in his position, would I have changed in the same ways he did? Would I have unlocked some inner reserve of strength I didn't know I had and emerged, phoenixlike, a different and more resilient me? No one in their right mind would want to have such experiences, but listening to him tell the tale, it was hard, in a perverse way, not to want to have *had* them.

Though Su Wei would later come full circle in his attitude toward that era's ideology, he was very much a product of a pre-ironic age. It was an era that produced romantic myths rather than dispelled them, and despite the deprivations that they suffered, one could tell, from the way Su Wei and Tony Fok reminisced as they reunited with weatherworn farmhands or posed for photos in front of the old mess hall, that they still had fond feelings for those days. In retrospect, they knew full well how awful the trials were that the Cultural Revolution put them through. Yet its dreams were still their first dreams, its heroes their first heroes. I once found Su Wei in his office at Yale watching a YouTube video of a Revolutionary Model Opera, the era's only officially sanctioned form of entertainment. The music was pure schmaltz, bombastic, yet at the same time, viscerally stirring. A black-and-white photo of him from that period shows a grinning, bespectacled pipsqueak in what looks like a military uniform, standing in a triumphant pose with one foot on the tread of a bulldozer.

One day in 1976, when Su Wei and Tony Fok were working on the seawall, a photojournalist from Beijing arrived to photograph the construction project for *China Pictorial*, a glossy, large-format magazine whose mission was to publicize the revolution to foreign audiences. The project's leaders were excited at the chance for some good publicity, and it fell to Su Wei to take the visitor around the site to document their titanic undertaking. Later, though, when the journalist looked at the pictures he'd taken of the construction site, his face darkened, and he seemed on the verge of tears. Su Wei asked him what was wrong.

"We thought it looked epic," Su Wei explained thirty years later as he and I walked along the completed seawall, after the documentary crew had finished filming us. "But from his perspective, he knew there was no way he could use those photos. We were an army of children, dressed in tattered clothing and covered in mud, a seething sea of bodies. He saw those photos through different eyes and saw what we didn't: we looked like Roman slaves."

Several years later, at one of Su Wei's parties, as he and his friends happily banged out songs from the now widely performed *Cantata for the Sent-down Youth* on the piano, a Chinese graduate student took me aside, scowling, and said in English, quietly, "That period of time was evil. There's no other word for it. I can't stand how they insist on telling stories that glorify it."

I saw his point. Su Wei didn't idealize those times, nor did he skirt difficult topics, but even when recounting his most harrowing experiences, he seemed to draw a kind of emotional sustenance from them, relishing every dramatic twist and turn of the tale. It was as if his life had been a movie he'd watched and starred in at the same time. Somehow, he managed to savor them as aesthetic experiences without reexperiencing the pain of those memories.

The wall ended up being a failure. The soil reclaimed from the thousands of acres of tropical mangroves ended up being too salty to plant rice, and in the end sustained only a meager crop of coconut palms and fish farms. It was, like so many of the era's undertakings, a grand, symbolic gesture, the real-world implications of which hadn't been well thought out: brilliant theater with little practical value. Mao was, let it not be forgotten, a poet as well as a political leader, and he governed with a poet's sensibilities.

At one point during our trip to Hainan, in a van bumping down a mountain road between two of the rubber plantations where Su and Fok had spent their teenage years, I found myself sitting next to a local worker who, it turned out, had also been relocated from the city as a teenager during the Cultural Revolution. However, his life had taken a different course from theirs. Like Su Wei, he came from a "bad family," politically speaking—the man's father had been an intellectual who worked in the Kuomintang government before the Communists took over. Unlike Su Wei's, though, his family background kept him from ever returning to the city and getting an education. He'd spent his whole life on the plantation, married a local woman, and become, essentially, a peasant. His teeth were black, and he spoke Mandarin with such a thick, rural accent that I had to lean close and ask him to repeat himself over and over again as he told his story. Seeing this, several members of the film crew sitting in the back of the van began to laugh. (I cannot remember what Su Wei was doing throughout all this— probably in the middle of telling a story.)

It was true, I was too sensitive. I began to wonder: In times like those, did the sensitive people simply go insane or commit suicide, leaving the hardy ones to tell the tale? Years later, a Chinese student of mine would write a story about a strange woman who lived in her neighborhood growing up. Impeccably dressed in a red felt hat and green coat, she would stand at the gate of the school, day after day, gazing in at the classroom building. It turned out that the woman had been driven to madness during the Cultural Revolution, when her husband, a teacher, had been humiliated and beaten to death by his students and colleagues.

And then there were those who didn't survive at all. After leaving the seawall, we visited a graveyard where several dozen sent-down youth were buried. We bowed to the graves—cameras rolling—then departed, leaving behind a bright emptiness of sunlight, tall grass, and the buzz of cicadas.

"I'm lucky," I later heard Su Wei tell a table of Chinese graduate students whose eyes had just widened at some unbelievable detail of a story he was telling. "I'm like an elephant. I have a thick skin."

At which point Mengjun shouted from the kitchen: "Anyone wonder what it's like, being married to an elephant?"

One of the men who cohabitates with Jade in her mountain hideout is a shy, melancholy fellow named Autumn. Unlike Stump and Kingfisher, rough-cut woodsmen who spit and swear and fight, Autumn comes from an educated family, but he had to break off his schooling and flee into the wilderness when the Cultural Revolution began. In Lu Beiping Autumn sees a fellow intellectual, and the two quickly become friends, bonding over poetry and working together to decipher an ancient stone inscription that Autumn finds on the mountainside.

Autumn's job in the band of woodcutters is to explore the jungle in search of promising timber to log and sell. This has given him an encyclopedic knowledge of tropical hardwoods and also fueled an erudite fascination with their uses and histories, particularly in the making of fine furniture for the scholar-gentry of the past. The pinnacle of classical hardwoods in Autumn's pantheon is *zitan*, a deep purple-black wood once used to make furniture for the imperial court; among the heirlooms Autumn's family lost in the revolution were three pieces of *zitan* furniture said to have been inherited from distant ancestors. For centuries, the tree that produced *zitan* wood was thought to be extinct. But Autumn is convinced that *zitan* still grows in the rainforests high up on Mudkettle Mountain, and he has become obsessed with finding it.

Zitan is conventionally translated into English as "purple sandalwood." I could tell immediately, though, that this phrase wouldn't do. It was obvious from the way Autumn basked in the very idea of *zitan* that, for him, its name was rich with symbolic resonance, evoking a millennia-old heritage, a lost world of elegance and refinement. "Sandalwood" sounded brittle and aromatic, like something used to line a drawer. I needed a name with a different feeling, something that conveyed a sense of majesty and age. In the end, I settled on "amaranthine rosewood."

Su Wei himself owned a piece of amaranthine rosewood. It was a gift from his sister who had made a fortune in textiles after China opened up its markets to the outside world. One morning over breakfast, he took it out and showed it to me. After reading Autumn's rhapsodies, it looked surprisingly quotidian: a medallion of rough, unfinished gray wood about the diameter of a softball, mounted on a polished ornamental base.

At Su Wei's parties, in addition to the graduate students who TA'ed his classes, and whom he often roped into giving musical performances, one was likely to encounter other intellectuals who, like him, had left China under unusual circumstances. There was a professor who'd run into political trouble for trying to translate *Doctor Zhivago* into Chinese and for publishing a feminist manifesto; he would sometimes, unaccountably, start speaking to me in Russian, and liked to make wisecracks when Su Wei got up to recite poetry. There was a kindly older gentleman with a leonine mane and scraggly gray beard who'd camped out on Tiananmen Square with Su Wei, who I later learned spent two years living undercover, disguised as a peasant woodcutter, before managing to escape to the US. These people left China trailing their own stories and their own versions of its history, stories that lived on in enclaves like these, in the living rooms of clapboard ranch houses, behind the windshields of Subarus on I-91 between Hartford and New Haven. It was in such company, at Su Wei's house in August 2008, that I watched the opening ceremony of the Beijing Olympics, saw gargantuan footprints of fireworks explode over the skyline and an army of synchronized dancers act as an enormous human printing press, spelling out a message of national rejuvenation. I don't know what complicated feelings went unspoken in that room that evening, but I have to imagine they must have included some mixture of sadness and pride.

What was it like, I wondered, to have lost one's country?

As the plot of *The Invisible Valley* deepens, Autumn's quest for amaranthine rosewood takes on a powerful symbolic dimension, and it becomes clear that this is where the story's emotional center lies. Deep in the jungle—just maybe—grows one last amaranthine rosewood tree; and there, too, high in the mountains, in a primeval rainforest untouched by man, lurks the Snakeweird, the god-serpent feared by Kingfisher but not by the cadres: a fabled creature that may or may not exist, depending on whose version of the tale you believe. Though, occasionally, far off in the distance, you'll hear its unmistakable cry, sounding eerily like the wail of an infant.

Back in Brooklyn, my own quest to translate *The Invisible Valley* went from a diversion to something more serious.

I completed a draft of the novel, but I could tell that what I'd put on the page didn't do justice to the life these characters now lived in my head, to the world I'd inherited from Su Wei by listening to his stories and going with him to Hainan. I started again. I borrowed money to go to grad school for creative writing, thinking this would give me the tools I needed to make the novel truly come alive in English. My girlfriend and I agreed that we'd wait to leave New York till I'd finished this project, at which point I'd get a "real job" and we'd plan the "next step" of our lives.

One year stretched into two, then three, then five. My younger sister graduated from college, bought a car, then a house. Rejection letters from publishers and grant applications piled up. And gradually, something else became clear to me. As a college student, I'd imagined translating *The Invisible Valley* as an easy leg up, a way to launch a career as a writer without the risk and heartbreak of writing my own book. Now, I saw that it wasn't that simple. *The Invisible Valley* wasn't going to help me. Instead, it needed my help. To bring it into the world, I needed to give it everything I had.

One evening, when I was back home in Boston, my mother burst into tears. "This time you've spent . . ." she said. "You could have used it to start a career!"

"You *have* to stop translating," one of my writing teachers said. "I just do not understand why you would put your time and your education at the service of *someone else's work*."

Still, every couple months or so, whenever a convenient weekend presented itself, I'd take the train up to New Haven. Su Wei would pick me up at the station, and we'd drive off together in that dusty red sedan, gabbing happily in Mandarin. "Whenever I see you," he said, "I find we have *liaobuwan de huati*—so much to talk about!"

Liaobuwan de huati. I would tell him about how I'd just proposed to my girlfriend, presenting her with a ring fashioned out of a twig and a maple bud. He would tell me about some recent string of coincidences—his stories often involved fateful coincidences, like a Dickens novel—say, an old friend from China, for years thought dead, rematerializing to make a surprising confession. I would tell him about our new parakeet, which would perch on my Chinese copy of *The Invisible Valley* and nibble the pages as I worked; he would tell me about an ancient bird-loving scholar who wrote with his pet bird nestled in his pen-hand. Inevitably, he'd tell me about his latest hobbies and ambitions, whether it was to get serious about calligraphy, or write first-rate song lyrics, or master the art of classical poetry. A year or two after I met him, he resolved to become "as good as anyone alive at writing classical Chinese verse," which I suppose is a bit like wanting to go down in history as the twenty-first century's greatest sonneteer. For years, he took this vow quite seriously, studying and imitating the complex tone patterns of the Tang and Song Dynasty, and in his bathroom, I'd often find books of thousand-year-old poetry stuffed into the magazine holder. Later, he'd write a poem in a Song Dynasty rhyme scheme for me and my fiancée and read it on the day of our wedding.

"Friends of mine say I seem like a person out of a former age," Su Wei once told me. "They say, 'When Bei Dao gets drunk at parties, he sings revolutionary songs; you sing folk songs and Peking opera.'"

It was true; his passions always tended toward the past. But at the same time that there was something eternally old about him, there was also something eternally youthful. Even as his hair began to gray, he saw life as containing infinite possibilities. The great classical landscape painter Huang Gongwang didn't start painting till his fifties, he told me. As a writer, he was still young, and his best days might lie ahead of him. He was preparing to write an epic picaresque novel; he was preparing to write his own autobiography; he was always preparing. *Wo hai zai zhang shenti*, he told me excitedly, flexing his arms—"I'm still growing!"

I was growing, too. Over six years and countless trips from New York to New Haven, I watched Emily, who I first saw riding a little pink bike, graduate from middle school, then graduate from high school, then go off to college. Over those six years, Su Wei went from a legendary figure before whose office door I'd hesitate nervously, to a man who I often heard out in the backyard cajoling his white lapdog in a singsong voice, "Lilia, time to poop!" Mengjun and I grew closer, and when I visited them, I began to feel that it was as much to see her as to see him. Over meals, Emily and I would speak to her parents in Mandarin and to each other in English; I realized that, because she'd never learned to read Chinese, one of the most meaningful things I could do as a translator was to translate her dad's stories for her. As the years passed, I came to see that it wasn't so much the world inside *The Invisible Valley* that needed to be preserved and transmitted, but the reality it reflected, the stories surrounding it.

Everything got smaller, the way a playhouse does as a child grows older and the world around it gets larger—and more interesting.

Yet I wondered: Was I any closer to becoming the person I wanted to be, back when I first set foot in the dusty interior of "The Studio of Lucidity," back when I first fondled *The Invisible Valley* longingly in that Beijing bookstore? Was I any closer to acquiring a story of my own to tell? Or had I merely borrowed one, become a shadow flickering at the edges of someone else's life? And was there any difference?

One day, I was sitting at Su Wei and Liu Mengjun's dinner table, chatting about where life might take me now that I was almost done translating *The Invisible Valley*. I was looking into teaching jobs, though part of me rebelled at the idea of indefinitely spinning on this life lived only in and through books. My wife and I were touring towns in the Northeast with an eye to settling down and having children. Or perhaps we might move to China—who could say? In any case, visions of unwritten novels needed to be put aside temporarily in the face of more pressing economic needs. (What I might write about, though, I hadn't any more clue than I did years back when I started this project.) At some point in the conversation, I made an offhand remark that began, "I might not become a famous novelist, but . . ."

I can't remember exactly how this sentence ended, but I do remember his response. Later that evening, in the privacy of his office, he said to me gravely, "As soon as I heard you say that, I thought, 'Houzi is done for.' If you don't think you can be, you never will be. Remember: things are as big as you make them out to be."

Nide xin you duome da, shiqing jiu zheme da. Or another way you could translate that, I suppose, is: "Things are exactly as big as your heart is."

The Invisible Valley, like most stories, is about a detour. By chance, Lu Beiping picks up a scrap of red paper, goes into the forest, and comes out different. None of this was part of the plan, just as Lu Beiping's going to Hainan in the first place wasn't part of the plan; just as Su Wei's going to Hainan, where he conceived this story, wasn't part of the plan; just as fleeing China for the US, where he passed the story on to me, wasn't part of the plan. Life did not take its expected trajectory; it took a detour, and that detour itself became life. Life is what happens instead.

I did end up moving to China, after all. Really—how could I not? I would go deeper into the story because the story was all I had. Later that year, an opportunity would fall into my lap to teach at the same university in southern China where Su Wei, by coincidence, had gone as an undergraduate. I took it, following another red scrap of paper farther into the jungle. Five years later, *The Invisible Valley* having finally been published, I would still be in China, teaching literature to college students, with no immediate plans to return. The world of the novel opened into the world of real life, into skyscrapers and bullet trains, into the roiling, changeful epic of a country renewing itself before my eyes like a snake eating its own body, like a book rewriting itself in real time—a book one could spend one's life translating.

I didn't know that then, though. I didn't know whether *The Invisible Valley* would amount to anything. It seemed like my six years spent with Su Wei on Mudkettle Mountain, like so many youthful adventures people like to tell stories about, might end up boiling down to Something I Once Did, a curious interlude before I moved on with my life.

I have a memory of a weekend I spent one summer at Su Wei's—or perhaps it was multiple weekends blended together; in retrospect, it's hard to say. We'd just pulled in, and I was greeted as usual with a hug from Mengjun and the slobbery licks of the golden retriever, Liangliang. We must have been talking about trees on the ride from the train station—perhaps I'd told him about the enormous oak tree that my fiancée and I liked to read under in Prospect Park—because he said, "I have to show you something!" and rushed me out to the back porch. He gestured up at three trees whose canopies spread high above us, shading the yard and melting into the teeming greenness of the New England summer. "These are my trees," he said. "An oak, a maple, and a pine. I think of them as my old friends. I've always felt like trees have spirits. Sitting out here, I like to give them names and imagine myself talking to them, having conversations with them."

Because another friend was visiting that weekend, I didn't sleep in the guest room as usual, but on the living room couch. In the middle of the night, I woke to the sound of Liangliang's claws clicking on the floorboards as he shuffled somnolently around the sofa where I lay. Moonlight silvered the room, casting bright rhomboids on the floor and ballooning the black silhouettes of the tropical plants nodding near the window. Next to me was the coffee table where we'd pored over *The Invisible Valley* for so many hours, where we'd unwrapped countless snacks and drunk so much tea and relived so much history—history that had begun to feel like mine, even though it wasn't.

A year later, Liangliang would die of old age. Su Wei and Mengjun would sell that house with the three trees in back, and Mengjun would be battling cancer. I would be a continent away. In that moment, though, I knew none of this. I felt happy, at ease, at peace. I felt at home in the world, treasuring this unlikely place I'd discovered, this rare inheritance I'd stumbled into, fixing the table, the moonlight, and the clicking of Liangliang's claws in my mind lest any of this be forgotten.

Love Is a Washing Line

FROM *Prairie Schooner*

Day 57.

You are (a) married and (b) in love.

And you are eating weird shit: fried hake on oats and rye bread. Melted cheese on top of steamed rice. Salads.

You are fucking eating salads.

Younger you is caning himself right now because you are (a) married, (b) in love, and (c) eating salads. These must be the end times. Armageddon in the morning is the only explanation for this out-of-character behavior.

As far as you know this is what people in love do when they are married: they eat gluten-free pizza with basil pesto and yesterday's pan-fried calamari like it is Jiro Ono's Michelin star–winning sushi; they laugh at each nearly missed rent payment and high-five each other when they just about make it; they attend family lunches and dinners, and plan clan holidays—the dysfunction of one family is multiplied by two, then dialed to one hundred. They change diets to suit each other.

Because marriage.

Because love.

Day 206.

As the bottom falls out of the economy and the middle-class safety nets of your tax brackets become porous, you learn to fix holes with holes. When one of you has the foolish dream to become a full-time writer, luxuries like ethical, 70 percent cacao dark chocolate vanish from the top shelf. They are not replaced. (She does not complain.)

When she is finally diagnosed with food intolerances of all kinds, she will denounce meat. The fridge will fill with odd tropical fruits and vegetables glowing with essential vitamins and minerals. (You will bitch about the blandness of omega-3 for days.) At first, you will join her on her new nutrition journey because it is romantic—being recognized as a supportive spouse comes with a strange kind of status. While most wives are opening fantasy football accounts to have something in common with their husbands, your taste buds which hitherto could not differentiate between varying shades of chlorophyll can now taste the difference between iceberg lettuce and Swiss chard. (Side note: it is all in the price.) The diet will become a duty; there is only so much mushrooms can do to replace meat. Then it will become an irritation: you live in a country of limited dietary options; carnivores thrive, vegetarians and vegans wilt and die in the heat.

At some point you will stop with the romantic culinary pretensions. Not to worry, though. You will still be (a) very married and (b) sufficiently in love, but you'll also be (c) doing the thing you vowed never to do: hitting terminal velocity, not falling more deeply in love, just falling at a constant speed.

Condition *c* is going to wreak havoc on everything. It will morph the morning greetings into grunts. Kisses will curdle. Passion will ferment. The atrophied attraction of the past becomes the archeological marker of a time gone by.

It has not even been a year.

Day 345.

To overcome the slump, the two of you have been going for silent walks in the evening. You also used to commute together in the mornings until you realized your schedules were not compatible. Plus you hate the music she plays on the radio. It is always too early to listen to TLC's *FanMail*. You still dance together and you both attend the same gym, though. You have also invested in board games you do not play.

You did all these things because you are determined (a) to be married and (b) to return back to the way things were before (c) life took control.

Then you did something strange: you both signed up for boxing classes.

Day 366.

It was an unconventional anniversary gift. Tradition states paper for the first year, cotton the second, and steel for the eleventh. But, no, the two of you got each other hand wraps, eight- and fourteen-ounce gloves, and focus mitts. A bag hangs under the tree in the backyard, the strange fruit of this young union.

When you showed up to the boxing club, a room full of sweat and testosterone, eager and curious, you did not realize it was the best thing the two of you had done since you got married.

Day 0.

That is what your boxing coach, a small, spry, sinewy man made of fluid movements and a critical eye, says: "It's always Day Zero if you're boxing. Everything has to feel new, even if it isn't. Otherwise you start slacking. No slackers at my gym."

The two of you "Yes, Coach!" like some new military recruits.

He laughs and says: "We'll see."

You are both orthodox—power in your right hand, vows on your left. He shows you how to stand: left foot forward, right foot anchored, with a bounce in your knees to facilitate quick, bobbing motions. He makes the two of you box shadows for a while to see how you move. Because you are both dancers your bodies respond instinctively to motion. But you are both raw, untrained. Nonetheless he says he has something to work with: "Okay, let's get you fit."

Day 0.

The progress is slow and demanding. Each day launches a fresh assault on your legs, lungs, and desire to stay committed to training.

The jab is never smooth or straight enough. Your boxing coach wants you to hit the mitts hard and recoil, ready to block or counter. He wants each punch to be precise, each combination to be concise, like a tight sentence which conveys only what it has to. A jab is a capital letter, it is always starting something; or it is a comma or semicolon, breaking a longer pattern of pain into parts. A double jab says *stay there*—"Yes, you don't want him coming after you. So you tell him to stay back! Let's go—jab, and jab, and double jab!" A cross is a conclusion. "You hit someone with that and that's the end of the story," the coach says. You have a lot to learn. The physics behind throwing, blocking, and taking a punch are almost magical. Just like there is more than biology involved in staying married. There is plenty the film training montages and running-through-the-airport-to-declare-undying-love scenes do not show.

Unquantifiable forces go into staying married: kindness, compassion, compromise, sacrifice. These are the ones you know of so far. They were exercised pretty easily in the early days. They seemed bottomless, gratuitous aspects of human nature, especially for those in love like ye anointed ones: after all, you were both married to each other, the loves of each other's lives. (This was before you realized the love of your life might be such only between five o'clock in the evening when she came home and seven o'clock in the morning when she went back to work—those early days of lockdown were nightmarish.) Everything, back then, was new: kindness was automatic; compassion was subliminal; compromise was easy because it did not cost much; and sacrifice was self-righteous.

Everything was new. And because it was new it did not slacken.

Day 0.

After a week of boxing classes you start speaking like a ringside veteran: *Sometimes you've got to roll with the punches. Everything's about not staying still—move your feet, use your legs to throw your punches. You stay still, you get hit. Move, move, move. Hit, but don't get hit.*

It is not long before everything becomes a pugilistic metaphor: *Don't let success go to your head, man, and most importantly: never let failure go to your heart.* This is what you will say to yourself and others when they sense a victory or when failure swoops down for them.

Why? It is what your coach told you when you were clobbered in the sparring session by the other beginner in the gym you do not like. *Keep your guard up*: what you will tell one of your female friends when she says a first date went pretty well. *Take it on the chin*: when your best friend does not get the promotion he was waiting on for the past eight months. *Keep it light, keep it moving. Stay loose, stay ready. Chances make champions.* You will not even be halfway to throwing a decent punch before you start summarizing everything with some prizefighting pun.

Another strange thing: everyone who throws a punch automatically becomes a boxer, but not everyone who walks down the aisle knows what it means to be married.

Day 380.

After a year of marriage, you will not know jack shit about anything. Not your wife and best friend whom you vowed to love, forsaking all others. (These words will not make sense after the first major bust-up.) Not your friends who are still wandering from pillows to panties, bedposts to breakups. (You were on the same wavelength when you were all single, but now that you are married their problems seem infantile—you will lose some because of your judgment.) You thought you knew your married friends. They seemed to have it all figured out. You said as much at the couples dinner you had two months ago. They are getting a divorce now. Some of your newly divorced friends will become strangers because, heck, what do they know? It is always doom and gloom with them, or touch and go whenever any discussion about love comes up.

Day 0.

There is refuge in boxing. It favors the quick, the alert, the smart defenders, the aggressive counterpunchers, and the knockout kings. While training, the snap movements of muscle memory and the split-second judgment calls will become your greatest asset even as the motions of marriage and the routines of consideration and consultation become your worst enemies. And even that realization has a contradiction: the ring has a routine, a carefully choreographed dance of boxer and trainer. But to you, everything involving marriage—a tango and tangle of lovers and quarrelers—is the chaos before creation.

When you get better, your boxing coach will say you have two rounds of skipping and seven of pad work—murder on your shoulders when he Maxim guns combinations, shouting at you to focus. "You stop focusing and you're fucked!" He says you have got to hit the pads harder, you acquiesce. When he tells you to close up and be compact, you mimic his defensive stance: "If you stay open like this"—he prods at your stomach—"you'll be closed out!" He taps your chin lightly to show you where the dark switch to your consciousness can be found. When he corrects your movement, tweaking your cross, adjusting the momentum of your left hook or right uppercut, you and your wife obey without question. "Yes, Coach! Yes, Coach! Yes, Coach!" You are both supplicants of the sweet science, willing to be taught, willing to learn, eager to please, pupils of pain, eager to deal out violence in the prescribed manner. This is the thrill of boxing: designated hit points, cordoned rings, protective cups and mouth guards, twelve rounds of boxing, judges, a referee to make sure everything is fair and clean—boxing has rules, clear ways to determine winners and losers.

> Marriage is a madman's alchemy. It is some shamanic bullshit.
> It works only if you believe in it.
> And sometimes, not even then.

Day 255.

When you have to serve up kindness to your wife, you will hesitate. There will always be time to be kind later, you think. It sounds strange right now, but marriage will expose weakness in your character. Kindness is like a boxer's fitness—it flags in a fight. Eventually, it slips, and that is when the bad form and wild swinging will come through. The dishes are never clean enough; she even stopped stacking the dishwasher because you told her she is useless at it. That was the word you used: *useless*. She makes too much noise when she is cleaning. The bed is never made to army standards. There are shoes everywhere. Demarcations of space will need to be arbitrated by the International Court of Justice, and even then you will still annex whatever you want, whenever you want—everything that is yours is Russia; everything that is hers is the Ukraine. In conversation, you will throw barbed jabs at her when she least expects it. And when she loses her balance, makes the slightest mistake, or stands still, shell-shocked by some small cruelty she did not think you were capable of, you will go after her looking for the sixth-round stopper.

It is in these heightened moments of drama and confrontation, when you have to resist the urge to leave her splayed out on her ass, that you will be found wanting.

What about that time?
What about that thing?
And you said this but did that!

A magnificent combination of past hurts, present grudges, and future judgments—you will even throw a sly, well-aimed *Well, fuck you then!* after the bell has gone.

Day 0.

For better or for worse—this is how the marital vows go. Once you start sparring, which will not be too long because you will be itching to throw some real hands, you will realize worse always comes first in the boxing ring.

Jab, jab—boom! —*cross!* Foolishly, you go after your opponent.
Jab, cross, left hook! You eat punches like it's communion.

The small ring of your anus feels like it's in Pluto's orbit—that is how far outside of your body you have been hit. Your coach is screaming at you to remember the fundamentals. *Defend. Move. Make the angles. Attack.* Too many variables, too much to think about, too many fists to focus on. Messages from your brain are not sent quickly enough to your feet.

Boom. Boom. Boom.

You try to back away, but there is nowhere to hide in the ring; it exposes you in ways your nuptials cannot.

Day 390.

There is always a corner in which to hide in a marriage. The distance can be blamed on work: that deadline, that assignment, that client, that colleague. You can explain away the absence of time like a Trump White House press officer: *There's no time to attend to this right now because there's, in fact, no such thing as time.* Every single one of your shortcomings is fake news; any consequence of your wrongdoing is an alternative fact. David Attenborough might have to do a nature documentary on you because humans have not been known to shelter in shells. Not the Philly shell that is the Mayweather hallmark; we are talking about the calcified shell of silence which gets harder to break with each passing day and moment.

In a boxing ring worse always comes first. In a marriage, knowing the difference between better and worse really depends on how honestly you respond to each situation, how courageously you fight the fear to hide behind excuses and hurts, how sincerely you follow through on action plans and promises.

Day 0.

The coach ties a string across the ring's diagonal: "Bob underneath. Quickly. Don't let the string touch you. Quicker. Faster. Focus."

The string is tight, a taut line that makes your legs burn with the effort of maintaining perfect form slips. But you are motivated. This is training. This is boxing. This is preparation for victory. This is how you win.

Your marriage has a line, too. It stretches from "I do" until *death do us part.*

Except it is not tight. It is more like a washing line, weighed down by laundry, buoyed down by time. It can carry a lot. Until it cannot.

Day 0.

Your boxing coach will show you how to tie hand wraps: "Twice around the wrist, four times around the palm." He will show you how to stand, how to find jaw-breaking power in your small toe. He will teach you how to dig deep and persevere through pain. And even in the small gym in the hood with nothing but your coach and your reflections for witnesses you will be a boxer from the first moment you take your stance: left for reach, right for power.

But at the altar in the presence of dearly beloveds, after the reception, dancing, and wedding cake, after the settling into new roles and responsibilities, even after a year of being married, you will not know how to be a husband.

Kindness in your right, vows in your left—southpaw, marriage is unorthodox.

Day o.

A day—any day.

You are (a) married and (b) fluctuating between love and whatever it is you feel two years into the journey.

The coach's words: *Everything has to feel new, even when it is not. You either focus or fold.*

The lessons so far: kindness, compassion, compromise, sacrifice, and patience. (God: patience!) And reserved silence, too. Sometimes you just have to take the hit without countering. These are the motions. These are the combinations. And every day you work on keeping the line tight.

Because if you do not, you start slacking.

ANNE MARIE TODKILL

Storm Damage

FROM *The Fiddlehead*

To dwellers in a wood, almost every species of tree has its voice
as well as its feature.
　—Thomas Hardy, *Under the Greenwood Tree*

Here shall he see
No enemy
But winter and rough weather.
　—William Shakespeare, *As You Like It*

LOOKING OUT FROM his brother's hospital room, my husband
noticed it was raining; it wasn't until later, leaving the city, that he
saw a row of buckled hydro towers and realized something big had
happened. Waiting with our daughter's family an hour and a half
away, I'd been trying to read the sky over cornfields, feeling de-
fenseless in a landscape as open as Dorothy's Kansas and wondering when we should head for the basement. As it happened, the
derecho tracked just north of us as it gouged a thousand-kilometer
line across southern Ontario and eastern Quebec. But we were
worried about our own house, a half day's drive northwest in cot-
tage country, where even under normal circumstances we keep a
saw in the car in case a tree falls across our road. I sent a text
to a neighbor, asking for news. She sent a phone pic of the only
obstruction on our track: a single, slender poplar. That's lucky, I
replied. We can handle that.

We heard the reports of damage, injury, and death. Our own
escape—house, woodshed, solar array unscathed—was so arbitrary
as to seem surreal, but we still congratulated ourselves for having
had a danger tree near the house cut down the summer before.

"If you're starting to think a tree needs to be taken down," the arborist had said, "it's time to take it down." But none of this held me back from erupting into tears when I saw what our neighbor hadn't mentioned: a glorious, eighty-foot American basswood, toppled over in the meadow below the house. Can you *love* a tree? If so, that was the one, the view-defining tree I admired every day, in every season, that I loved truly. Why, among so many acres of trees, was it singled out? Was it to atone for how lightly, as it seemed, the storm had roughed us up otherwise? For the fact that my brother-in-law was beating the odds of a terrible illness? For the uncountable things in my life that could have, but so far haven't, gone wrong? My husband was surprised at first: such a carry-on for a tree. I agreed, but kept crying regardless.

Before we moved here, I'd never noticed the specific comeliness, the gestalt, of *Tilia americana*. There are some fine specimens in our clearings: multi-stalked, hence rhythmic; stately and generous; pastoral in evocation. I took them as models of their kind until a friend pointed out that basswoods typically have a single trunk. This would mean that, whether by grazing animal, fire, or axe, those basswoods were pollarded early in their growth, and that the derecho's victim had already survived a brush with death. In fact, there'd been a second near miss: an infestation of the *Lymantria dispar dispar* moth, whose caterpillars defoliated nearly 1.8 million hectares of eastern Ontario forests in 2021. A single LDD caterpillar can eat, and excrete, a square meter of greenery before it pupates (it poopates, then pupates), and despite our efforts to bandage the lower trunks with burlap traps, we watched in horror as the mighty basswood was stripped to the last leaf. In our deciduous woods more generally, I felt a miserable anger as the canopy was reduced to thready lace. For the first time I questioned our move to the country: If this was the state of nature now, if it can spiral into ruin so uncontrollably, did I really want to watch at close range? Given the intensity of the infestation, the falling frass sounded like the patter of a fine, refreshing rain—an observation that put a cruel twist on my disgust. (Even the discovery that there is a word for caterpillar shit infuriated me.) We also learned that if a deciduous tree is defoliated early in the season it can remount its leaves and survive. But if this repeats for successive summers it will exhaust itself and die. I watched with faint hope for signs of LDD population collapse—caterpillars turned to ooze, hanging in an inverted V (in which case, nuclear polyhedrosis virus), or shriveled, hanging vertically (in which case, *Entomophaga maimaiga* fungus), that would signal the beginning of the end of a multi-year cycle. COVID-weary, I uttered curses that would bring upon the caterpillars their own incurable plague. Some weeks later, our bare basswood took a stab at immortality, performing a second, astonishing leafing-out. There were, indeed, signs of population collapse, but I think it was a prolonged dose of Arctic air that winter that, as well as freezing our water lines, made the spongy egg masses nonviable and reprieved our woods. And so it came to pass that the queen of the basswoods was alive and nearly in full leaf on May 21, 2022, when a low-pressure system west of Lake Erie set in motion the chaos that eventually caught her like a sail, dashing her without mercy to the ground.

Maybe it's the times, or maybe it's my age, but I've fallen into a habit of anticipating loss, waning, and even erasure, in every lovely, natural thing I have the good luck to gawp at in the day-to-day. I take the measure of our woods and imagine the whole shebang obliterated by wildfire. I sit beside wetlands, watching for ducks and herons, pondering the inexorable advance of *Phragmites australis*, an out-of-place, habitat-choking reed. I try to discipline these thoughts, to redirect them toward the necessity and productiveness of change, such as the resurgence in our sandy clearings of the native white pine hurled down a century and a half ago by settlers. I think of the carbon storage that, by mindful neglect, we might achieve here. But it's also true that I had never admired the basswood tree without speculating about which of us would outlast the other. Truly, not once.

Now I know.

Or maybe I don't. A few roots are still anchored where the tree was tipped out of the mound of sandy earth and cleared fieldstone where it grew. Perhaps the derecho brought about another pollarding, and nothing more. I doubt it, but it might be too soon to tell. The only thing I know right now is that a groundhog likes to survey its kingdom from the top of the root ball, and also, when alarmed, to take cover in a new burrow underneath.

So much for the tree. As for the forest, it took us a long time to inspect every corner of our rough ground for damage. Some spots are accessible only in winter, when traveling on snowshoes makes it possible to weave through a confusing, fractal system of wetlands without losing your mind. A drone would have come in handy. It was soon obvious, though, that the path to our kayak-launching spot would have to be remade. This area has always been prone to wind damage, but this time the wind-snaps and blowdowns were more dramatic than we'd ever seen. Ditto for other places where we often see balsam and spruce splintered like exploded firecrackers after a high wind, of which there are plenty in summer. Our woods are tired looking, rather threadbare, a little rickety, and the pruning carried out by any strong wind is part of the normal order here. But this was wind of a different order, wind that moved like a hurricane, but without rotation, a juggernaut that dropped explosives: downbursts, microbursts, EF1 and EF2 tornadoes.

In our township, the hardest blows were dealt at The Ridge, a dome of good land that has been farmed since the 1860s. Wooded areas were reduced to an agonal twist of broken and scrambled trees, trampled under the boots of a crazed colossus. Once-glorious hardwood rows edging broad fields were left in tatters. A friend, sheltering in her farmhouse when the wind tore through, and not knowing where her beloved dog was hiding, was certain the roof would come off. This fear, although unrealized, was entirely rational. (The dog survived.) Up the road, a cattle farmer had received no warning; the storm bore down when he was out with a bucket of fence staples, doing repairs; he ran into the wind so he could see, and thus dodge, falling trees. He made it home without injury to a collapsed barn and a ruined store of hay. A tiny redbrick church used for prayer on Sundays and euchre on Thursdays remained intact, dwarfed within a stand of tall white pine that had always struck me as fate-tempting; sure enough, some of the crowns snapped—falling on tombstones, though, not the church roof, which must have given the faithful something fresh to ponder. Even a year later, an acquaintance near The Ridge was still limbing and bucking fallen trees. "I lost a thousand," he told me, adding with particular regret, "a lot of big pine."

Neither of us voiced the obvious: they won't be restored in our day. Another friend, surveying the damage in his fifty-acre lot, fell and broke his ankle. It took him six hours to crawl through the tangle back to the off-grid cabin where his wife waited; she hadn't realized until the third hour of his absence that something was wrong. The question of where to begin looking for him was unanswerable: a crushed forest is a hellish infinity.

A local logging company made omelets with broken eggs, harvesting almost nothing but wind-tips and snapped trees until the following spring. Preparing to log in the concession below ours, they smoothed out the road allowance that runs along our south edge. One Sunday afternoon in winter, when there was no truck traffic, we took advantage of the easier walking to have a look. A neighbor working at his hunt camp told us that another neighbor's hundred acres were gone. "How do you mean, *gone?*" we said. "*Gone,*" he repeated. "Just *gone.*"

We thought we might as well check our east, rarely traveled property line to see how things looked there and whether any of the survey tape that marked it needed replacing—a task worth attention every few years. Some of those flags, it turns out, will never be seen again—a sizable section of conifers got clobbered, and even with a heavy snowpack to lift us above much of the debris, it was impossible to get through. A jumble of balsam had evidently made good shelter for hares and good hunting for marten. But I doubt anything bigger than a fox would bother to traverse that mess. Near the same area, a trail we'd made with considerable effort the summer before to a sun-warmed backrest of rock beside a pond was well and truly buried. The wind had taken a wrecking ball to paradise.

Two months after the derecho, on July 25, a supercell tornado traveled more than fifty-five kilometers through some townships south of us, crushing barns and houses and doing bizarre things to trees. Whereas drone footage of the derecho damage shows downed trees lying like iron filings in an identical direction, the tornado produced an unmethodical and ghoulish mangling. Among fallen hardwoods, white pines were left standing, shorn of branches, as if a harvester machine had malfunctioned, given up, and stuck the mutilated trunks back in the ground. I've heard a meteorologist make a respectable argument that derechos are not necessarily more frequent in our region than they used to be. Or at least, given current practices of surveillance, we can't make meaningful comparisons with the past. Land surveyors in the mid-1800s noted evidence of old hurricanes in these parts. I know a woman whose family farm was obliterated—and a childhood friend killed—in a tornado that touched down in our township in

1947. And yet, standing open-mouthed before the derecho wreck-age, and then the centrifuged properties an hour south, it's hard not to think of these disasters as connected to one another and to the shame of the rapidly unfolding climate-change clusterfuck for which we are to blame.

One day soon we're going to get tarps ready to hang at a mo-ment's notice inside the windows of our unshuttered, uncur-tained, and basement-less house. We want to be ready for the next whackadoodle storm warning, to protect ourselves from side-bursts of shattered glass.

Every time we cut a new path through our bush we make distances seem shorter and the terrain more intelligible. It's a domestication, but also a way of confining the damage caused by footfalls. One winter day we used Google Earth to plan bearings and distances for a new trail to get us from the logging road to the beaver pond, which is difficult to approach from the south. And then we set out to flag it, zigzagging up toward the edge of the pond, where the storm damage turned out to be much worse than we'd guessed, and then swinging west to loop round an awkward spur of wetland. From there the ground rises to an open hardwood ridge, from which we can descend to our track, the lower clearings, the solar towers, and, on a smaller rise, our house. Standing on that ridge, we realized that we were in line with the fallen basswood, facing into what would have been the blast of wind, and saw how narrowly the solar towers had been spared. Around us, rather than an im-passible snarl of debris, was an open wood punctuated by massive wind-throws—mainly maples and ash, pointing east, the spreading, shallow disks of their root balls heaved from the ground along with an impressive quantity of rock, their bare crowns a mirrored intricacy many feet distant.

As obviously dendritic as these fallen forms were, they also struck me, as none of the storm damage had before, as humanoid. Perhaps there was a particular gravitas in the effect—the trees lying at some distance from one another, like casualties on a battlefield where the slain were not mown down en masse but picked off, one by one, each victim retaining the dignity of individuation. Here, one could see the trees for the forest. Again, I pondered: By what caprice was this or that tree taken, but not those others? Some of the ash hadn't been tipped so much as folded in half, the leathery bark buckled in a half loop away from an already rotten core. Those trees, it was now clear, were already on the hit list of the emerald ash borer before the derecho finished them off. But the toppled trees, bodies of wood, on that open ridge got me thinking about the terror of being singled out in a general catastrophe: how it must feel to anticipate death in a time of crisis as a hit-or-miss matter of dire chance.

In summer 1944, from "Somewhere in France," a young lieutenant in the Canadian Scottish Regiment wrote to his mother in British Columbia, asking for shaving supplies, socks, and light novels. He answered to his middle name, Kenneth. When I met him, a few years before I married his elder son, he was in his eighties and his memory of the war was reduced to a single anecdote about his fear of getting water in his boots during the landing at Juno Beach. But, at the age of twenty-two, he reported that "fighting morale is at top pitch" and described how one might be in a slit trench in the rain "with the mud oozing in" and still feel "relatively safe" provided the "Moaning Minnies" were "a couple of hundred yards away." This, on a day when "three of us captured 12 Jerries including an Officer. I made quite a haul. A set of binoculars, a Luger pistol and a copy of Hardy's *Under the Greenwood Tree* in English, so in the next spell of shelling I will have something to read." In another letter, he interrupts himself: "Hold it for a moment, here comes 'Moaning Minnie'—I'm still okay, they weren't even close." Was this a way of invoking his mother's presence at what might well have been his hour of death? A later sequence of letters, written from hospital, refers cryptically to events in a grain field in Normandy. "There was no cover, just open wheat fields, with the grain cut and the occasional hedge." There, his "platoon was quite a bit reduced," his "mortar man dropped with a bullet through the head," and he himself was taken out of action by "a good clean bullet wound" through the thigh. There was sangfroid in the doing—"I told [the reserve corporal] to go ahead and fight the war"—and bravado in the telling. "My nervous system," he avowed, "is good." He is candid, though, about the damage caused by the liberators themselves: "Nearly all the towns and villages we pass through are knocked almost flat by our shells & bombs and

there are many casualties among the civilians." And later: "And
then they smile and welcome us and shrug their shoulders saying
'*C'est la guerre.*'"

It is axiomatic in battle stories that a sense of agency, and the
conviction of one's purpose, can edge terror out of the way, making room for brave acts. We call this valor. And it is this quality
in the Ukrainian resistance—and counteroffensive—that speaks
compellingly to people of my postwar generation (a problematic
label, given that military conflict has never ceased), raised on
Allied narratives of the Second World War and for whom the injustice of Putin's invasion, no less than Hitler's serial occupations, is
incontrovertible. Perhaps this helps to explain why, standing in that
graveyard of trees, my thoughts turned to Ukraine without pausing
over any other conflict zone. I thought of mortars dropping with
cynical premeditation on apartment blocks, theaters, hospitals, and
schools; of women in childbirth; of the waste of peaceful cities; and
the objective of this terror, which is to demonstrate that, without
submission, there can be no safe place. The experience of terror,
because existential, has temporal and spatial dimensions: this is
happening to *me, now, here.* One way or another, we are pinned by
fate to some place on earth. I know this is apples and oranges, a
category mistake—but, thinking about the deliberated catastro-
phes of war, I looked at our broken woods and thought: This is
nothing. Stop complaining. Your grief is misplaced.

I keep wondering how Thomas Hardy's second novel came into
the possession of a German soldier. It seems likely he made it
home; perhaps some descendant knows the story of his capture
and eventual repatriation; of the possessions he and his comrades
forfeited in the episode; and whether he was a habitual reader of
English novels. What eventually happened to the book, and the
binoculars, is unknown; as for the Luger, a bigger prize, my father-
in-law believed it to be stolen by an orderly when he was in military
hospital. Had the German taken the book from an Allied soldier,
dead or alive? Was he trying to improve his English (in case of capture, or opportunities for espionage?), or to understand a people
that the Führer professed to admire? Had he asked that English
novels be sent to him, just as young Kenneth, bored in convales-
cence, asked his mother to send him novels in French rather than
English? Was this soldier well educated? What was his cast of mind?

Did he, like Kenneth and his mother, read Tolstoy, and would he have agreed with them that the horse-race scene in *Anna Karenina* was especially fine? Had Hardy's novel been recommended as inoffensive to the Nazi aesthetic of close-to-nature living and ethnic purity? I'd like to know how much of it he had a chance to read; whether he struggled with Hardy's archaisms and his rendition of "Wessex" dialect; whether he recognized the nostalgia as patronizing, or that it was nostalgic at all; whether it made him homesick to read about a village where social bonds ran deep, and on Christmas Eve a rustic band of musicians traveled through the parish until every family had heard at least one traditional tune. Also, did he agree that young men must beware the irresolute hearts of young women? How real was any of this to him? Did he read it as his Canadian captor planned to, to take his mind off the sound of shelling? I'd like to know how much he minded the book being confiscated.

I'd like to know if he was a total bastard. I'd like to know how much he longed for peace.

My father-in-law wrote: "If you know of anyone coming of age for the Army advise them to join the Air Force, or the Navy, where you don't see the results of your guns, the suffering, the sorrow and the devastation—where you don't come face to face with the enemy and personally have to account for him."

He also added: "But then, for myself, I would rather be here than in any plane, ship or tank, or behind any artillery piece. The mud and blood, dirt & grime and the excitement gets in your blood I guess."

In the woods my mood used to waver between relief and unease. Relief, because urban environments are not my jam. Unease, by virtue of a sense of trespass. Whose woods these are I supposedly know: On paper, they belong to my husband and me. That ownership is provisional, an amateur custodianship practiced within traditional Anishinaabe territory. Moreover, land ownership cannot be construed as absolute. It is a form of tenancy, a holding. I would argue that to think less of owning and more of holding—not as in holding back, but holding dear—has something to recommend it in a respectful relationship to land. But, as for my "unease," no doubt this has a cultural lineage, descended from the bias by which Suzanna Moodie viewed the "green prison" of the bush as a shadow looming over her aspirational clearing. In settler consciousness, the forest is a place of bounty and danger, refuge and menace, fabular but also actual wolves (which, I'm happy to say, live here still). It contains anything one's ambition or apprehension might hold. It is unsupervised—that is, unless you've set up cams to detect wildlife or intruders, it lacks surveillance in the manner of city intersections and subway platforms. For me, the absence of an obvious societal frame offers a delicious invisibility, an extraordinary privacy. By the same token, it engenders a self-consciousness that disrupts the very solitude I crave. Where exactly *am* I? Is it okay that I'm here? Am I hurting anything? For someone who, as a child, believed herself to be under the surveillance of a benevolent, judgmental, and masculine God, this must surely be a dilution, a displacement, of the question, "Does God see me in this place?" But the animate presences here leave no room— not for me—for a churchy sort of deity. And so, the question of visibility settles into two pragmatic matters: First, what creatures are aware of me just now, even if I'm not aware of them? Second, suppose I break my ankle: How would anyone find me?

Anxiety in the forest used to hang around me like a compromising odor. I've learned to ignore it, or else gear up. I enter the woods in the armor of the citizen scientist, rationalizing the near-wild by means of phone apps, binoculars, a camera. In this way I cast the forest as a fragile character in need of my understanding and diligent surveillance. The forest is a mental construct, precipitated out of a cluster of values—environmentalism, climate-change anxiety, a zeal for species protection—together with a socially phobic disposition. But even this is a proprietary sort of performance. Besides, it's a geeky and peculiar way to live.

But those acres within "our" woods that were flattened by the derecho—well, those are no longer intelligible to me. They are bewildered, disordered. They cannot be traversed or inventoried. They are defamiliarized in the way that all sites of catastrophe— bomb craters, apartment blocks fractured by earthquakes—are recognizable but made strange. Punched down like rising dough, the woods have been reduced to a thing that is neither forest nor clearing. If we brought in the logging company, the shattered trees would become "matériel" in a sense akin to Don McKay's parsing of the term, in his essay "Baler Twine," as "a denial of death altogether, as in the case of things made permanent and denied access to decomposition, their return to elements." Without human harvesting to complete the storm's reduction of living trees to lumber, we might imagine a reversion to Aristotles's *hyle*, unformed matter—a term that, as Robert Pogue Harrison points out in his cultural history, *Forests*, was the Greek word for forest before its appropriation by Athenian philosophy. (Moreover, as Harrison also notes, the Latin *materia* refers to "the usable wood of a tree" and has the same root as *mater*, mother. How organically these cognates are nested. And there we go again.) But, thinking of mere matter, it helps to consider that the "gone" sections of our woods, reduced to a shapeless condition (unless, for instance, we clamber around with hand lenses, examining mosses), are also full of potency. Besides, as much as we might want to ascribe to "acts of nature" the human attribute of violence, we might just as well call them innocent, not to mention creative. Here's McKay, in "Contemplating the K-T (Mass Extinction #5)":

> [. . .] At any rate,
> we must be grateful to the blessèd asteroid,
> slayer of dinosaurs, facilitator
> of our green and pleasant, if now pretty
> iffy, biosphere.

Let us be consoled by the vegetation under the leveled trees; the soil, plants, fungi, lichen; the habitat for snails, insects, and hence for birds; the living space for rodents, hence snakes and mustelids; and, without resorting to classification, the whole bubbling soup of genetic material. What comes next will be a highly localized remounting of the self-willed wild. So then, what is so distressing about "gone" woods? Perhaps that they are untraversable, inaccessible, and, in that sense, no longer for us homebody humans a *place*. There is barely any *there*, there.

I am by no means out of these woods yet.

Let's say, for the sake of argument, that the derecho's connection with climate change, and hence with human action, is tenuous. This is not to counsel denial, but to keep our eye on degrees of culpability. Behind the storms of summer 2022, there was no conscious Gilgamesh felling a cedar forest to make for himself a name. Or at least, there was no *proximate* Gilgamesh, no single

megalomaniac available to collar for the crime. When it comes to
climate change, culpability is so diffuse as to seem unassignable to
specific events. But that's not quite it. For many of us, the guilt of
everyday actions, purchases, and habits is almost paralyzing, while
government and industry answer to venal interests, carrying on
their myopic business. But let's stick for now to the contemplation
of deliberate environmental atrocities arising from war. McKay,
following Harrison, laments "the darkest element in our use of
the land—the urge to *lay waste,* to render the material world as
matériel, to make of our capacity for destruction an enduring sign
and so achieve fame" ("Otherwise than Place"). This is the impulse
of the tyrant, the psychopath, the totalitarian, the murderer. Harrison describes the historically repeating "gesture of Gilgamesh," in
which assaults on nature go beyond the human need for resources
or domestication and arise from a kind of rage against limitation.
Writing in 1991, he might as well have been summing up Vladimir
Putin's delusional motives in present-day Ukraine: "There is a kind
of childish furor that needs to create victims without in order to
exorcise the pathos of victimage within." Thus, the abused sons of
Russia are told that their "special military operation" will rout out
an incipient Nazism and resurrect the glories of the past. Moreover,
they are instructed that Ukraine does not exist. By this logic it matters nothing if people, towns, cities, habitats, are smashed down in
a senseless bewildering.

   As I write, Bakhmut, city of wine and salt, is now a city of ash:
pulverized, hollowed, drained of meaning as a habitable place.
There is not much *there* left there. The combatants still regard this
scorched earth as territory, but how do we construe its ground—or
the ground of any devastated city—as *land?* What natural thing
remains? At what cost can the debris be disposed of, the soil
decontaminated, the apartment blocks rebuilt?

   We are territorial but, *primum,* we are terrestrial. We are not
meant for the moon, or Mars. We are not meant to be giants, like
Gilgamesh. We are not meant to be immortal. The facet of war's
violence now called "ecocide" could also be described as a denial
of our rootedness on earth, or, more plainly, as the absence of
humility, whose flip side is gratitude. Actions of war abuse land
as if it were nothing. As if it were collateral damage, merely. As if
the earth will shrug it off, in a *c'est la guerre* kind of way, forgiving

the crackpot fantasy that a new social and political order can arise from ashes, rubble, wreckage, and radioactive dust *as if organically.* History's despots are but merry bakers, punching down the world's social and environmental assets like so much dough.

It should be said that, before Putin's invasion, Ukraine was no environmental angel. One source maintains that the war "rages over one of the most heavily industrialized and polluted territories in the world." If anything, this amplifies the likelihood of environmental catastrophe, especially in the Donbas, where shelling unleashes poisons into groundwater, air, and soil. This is to say nothing of the burning of forests, ruin of arable land, loss of species, and damage to wetlands and other fragile eco-zones. Scientists and others are keeping a tally—including a price tag for reparations—of environmental degradation resulting from Russian aggression, and citizen science has taken a dark turn with an official hotline for the reporting of ecological crimes. "What's interesting about this war," one commentator notes, "is it's probably going to be the best-documented conflict in terms of environmental damage that we've ever seen." If true, that would be something to be grateful for. But isn't that observation—what makes this war *interesting*—just a bit meta, as if there is nothing peculiar about thinking about an unfathomable tragedy in terms of an identifiable brand, on trend with the greening of the zeitgeist?

Volodymyr Zelenskyy has said, "There can be no effective climate policy without peace on earth." Indeed. Would it be fatuous, or featherheaded, to propose a corollary? That there can be no war so long as there is scrupulous regard for the earth? The notion of the "rights of nature" is fairly new in law and governance, and points to a radical revision of our sense of human dominion. Until such personification of nature is rooted in our global consciousness as more than symbolic, more than metaphorical, more than sentimental, it seems unlikely that any future Gilgamesh will acquire the humility needed for restraint.

Such thoughts follow me into the bush like a weasel on the hunt, ferreting out despair, rage, and cynicism, and feasting on it lustily in the very place where I seek refuge from such feelings. In the woods I have enjoyed respite from social complication, emotional short circuits, and a human sense of time. But not now so much. I live in the embarrassment of having been, so far, in my preferred place on earth, spared. And I fear that above the forest's sweet Dionysian shade is the white-hot glare of a vengeful sky.

Before the snow was gone, I went up the ridge to where the toppled ash and maple lie, armed with my camera and lenses, hoping to record their melancholic, monumental forms; the gigantic, yet shallow, root balls; the rock laid bare or hoisted up amid roots— flat sedimentary flakes and round granite boulders, the interleaved substrates of this region. But no focal distance did the trick for me that day—not a wide angle, or a short telephoto, and not a 50 mm, which is often described as a good approximation of the human field of view. I could find no frame that rendered, emotionally, the way a fallen tree stood out for me as a signifier. In a long view, the tree lost mass, figure flattening into ground; closer up, a sense of scale was lost; keeping the near end sharp, the far end blurred, lost the distance between root and crown. In every attempt, what I saw as calamitous looked like a tangle much like any other woodland tangle. There lies the failure of my amateur craft, which leads me to seek the Instagram-ready icon rather than submitting to a totality that cannot be grasped.

One day, soon after the storm, I lay down on the widest trunk of the windfelled basswood. I'm not sure why its solidity against my back seemed surprising. Or why I felt that it held the warmth of muscle and bone, that it was a living, relatable body, merely asleep.

ED PAVLIĆ

Anita Baker Introduced Us and Patrice Rushen Did the Rest

FROM *Oxford American*

12:45 a.m. September 2, 1986.

It's dark now and the balcony makes it seem like we're sitting up in the middle of the night sky high above the glow from Dayton Street in Madison. Ric talks and I think, "Well he's not small because he don't eat that's for damn sure." An empty carton of mozzarella sticks sits open on a large pizza box, also empty, which covers most of the patio-type table we made from two milk crates emptied of my records. Remembering Liz's lesson from last summer about drinking vodka with grapefruit juice has helped me defend myself against repeating unavoidable evenings like that one that got out of hand at La Maison du Caviar in Paris. I've mixed the grapefruit *between* as much ice and as little liquor as possible, so this tastes like cold juice with some distant heat lost in it. I don't see the point of drinking at all but, up here, tonight, and diluted as much as possible, okay I don't mind it. And Ric's not all theatrical and pushy about it like Claude Haddad and his Lebanese-exile crew yelling at me, "Yalla, Eddie, Yalla!"

"They don't scratch, ever, and you can set them to repeat like an auto-reverse tape deck. Just think: pure music, no skipping and popping." Ric's convinced CDs are the future and that we'll need a CD player in here asap. Back down the hall in the living room

Anita Baker's singing about *See about me . . . Come on see about me.*
Her scatting fades out and Ric rises up out of his chair, saying, "See
this, I'm talking about no getting up to flip the record." I can see
it. But then what happens to the records? We gotta buy it all again?
I'd heard "Sweet Love" and "You Bring Me Joy" on the radio, but I
hadn't heard *Rapture* before leaving for Boston for work last spring
and then on to France for the summer. I take a moment to feel
the dark breeze curl over the low balcony wall and notice how
three radio towers slow-strobe in the distance. Ric steps back onto
the balcony followed by a woman singing *turning back the hands
of time . . .* "Mystery," first song, side two on *Rapture.* I'm not sure
if it's the trip back from Greece to Paris to Chicago to Madison
and then today and the run-in with the sheriff and the mess with
Terrance, or if it's something else that feels like it's coming out
from behind the air in every direction at once, but I haven't ever
heard anything like *this* album on *this* balcony before. Did she just
sing *Only images survive?* Ric sees this in my face: "I'm telling you,
E, you stay over there too long and get culturally deprived. Might
as well be *sub*-urban." He says that last part like it's a synonym for
subhuman then, "Hell, Madison's bad enough! But at least I can
get home in a hour." I think, home? To Chicago? In an *hour?*

I want to tell him about the no-gravity-suspended feeling among
the murmurs of Parisians in the streets of Beaubourg, the relief
from the way everything in the United States feels like it's trying to
tear itself (or at least me) apart. But it's not the time. I'm watching
him talk and mostly listening to the album and balancing what
Anita Baker's doing with these songs against the grim imitations
of togetherness I remember from those Paris discos. I haven't
even noticed the invisible things weaving Ric and me into each
other right here yet; it's too close. Instead, I'm feeling that moment when the Commodores' "Lady" appeared out of Euro-drone
in the disco and the warmth of people dawned behind my eyes
like it was cut through by the vanishing groove in the cold spray
from the brick saw. That warmth and those people weren't in that
disco, that was all in me. That image, though, the diamond blade,
the vanishing groove, comes and goes from my body like it's made
itself a home in me. Like maybe it *is* only images that survive?

Twelve hours ago I was sitting on a picnic table at the Union with
no place to live. I hadn't planned on coming back to school at all,

at least not now. My plan—which okay wasn't a *plan*—had been to stay in Paris, where I'd lived half the summer riding along with the modeling industry run amok, my girlfriend T and her roommates and the agency owner Claude and a buzzing cloud of his generously pushy friends whose need for "company" seemed as endless as their cashflow. I had the little money I'd made earlier this summer running a brick saw for a small construction crew in the tank room of a Budweiser brewery in New Hampshire. Don't ask. I'm not sure about how it all comes together either.

Twelve hours ago I hadn't really even met Riccardo Williams, who, somewhere between noon today and midnight tonight became my best friend, and, who, a little less than a year from now, and according to a scale of lived time there's no measure for, will die of a sickle cell crisis and vanish from—but leave a permanent hole blasted out of—my life as fast as he'd appeared into it. Before today I'd mainly known Ric through Terrance, who I'd run into just before leaving town last spring; Terrance talking about they might be looking for a roommate for next fall and would I be down? I'd said I'd think about it and then forgot about it. Until the moment my plane touched down at O'Hare yesterday at 5:05 p.m. and I realized I'd returned to school and I had nowhere to live.

So, then, a few minutes before noon today: I rang the buzzer to this apartment, #902, unannounced; woke up Ric, who had rolled into town himself about an hour before me and gone back to sleep; asked Ric if he was cool with another roommate; drove across town to clear it with Terrance at his shady-ass job "selling art" for a boss who's about as legit as the bootleg Patrick Nagel prints he had Terrance hawking by phone; went back, moved in our stuff, and got to cleaning the place after Terrance and whoever else had hurricane'd in it all summer, which went along okay but for a hole smashed in the hallway wall and a football-shaped spot burned into the carpet—Ric: "I can't believe them fools was 'basin' in here"—in the living room; talked for the first time with Ric over Parthenon Gyros and George Howard's *A Nice Place to Be*, a conversation that began to distantly sparkle over Howard's version of Sade's "The Sweetest Taboo" just when the sheriff showed up with an eviction notice talking about how no rent (which, each month, Ric had sent to Terrance) had been paid all summer and so we, or someone, owed $1,575 before Friday or we best get to packing up or deputies would do it for us starting end of this week at eight a.m.; agreed to Ric's claim that if I "invested" $1,000 of my savings from the brick saw in the brewery into paying the back rent and solving the shit with the sheriff it would pay off and pay off quick; then paused the cleaning work to pack up all Terrance's shit in Hefty bags—everything except his Raleigh Technium road bike that Ric said he'd deal with after he figured out exactly how pissed he was and how pissed he wasn't—and deliver the load to shady bossman's ranch-style house where Terrance—talking about "man I know, my bad on the rent man, my bad"—had already been staying; then finished finishing the cleaning, leaving the oven— Jesus, the *oven*—for later and Ric saying how he thought this was a day that could end with a six-pack of La Cerveza Mas Fina between new roommates but that was now going to have to be an evening with a bag of ice and a bottle of Stolichnaya and whatever I want in between—and me: "in between?" and Ric: "between the vodka and the ice!" and me keeping quiet about the fact that I drank alcohol reluctantly and only when it absolutely couldn't be avoided, like with Claude and his gold-Cartier'd, red-Ferrari'd, silk-unbuttoned confrères and Ric looking me directly in my eyes and saying without saying this was absolutely one of those unavoidable nights I was keeping quiet about.

All that earlier today and yet still spiraling through the cooling evening air around us.

Rapture and us on this balcony casts the sun, the saw, *and* the vanished groove. All of it. One after another these songs start in some small, safe, and secure place, places that feel cozy or blurry or both, it's *home,* a home in people, home between people. But sleepy. Then, in a few minutes, and without ever *leaving* home, which, when she sings it, like *a picture in a frame, it remains the same,* these songs sear and soar and search. Wide awake: See *about me, come see about* me-e; it's a desperate plea and an open taunt. Basic as Ms. Baker barefoot on the album cover. All these songs say "Come closer, I *dare* you." But, closer to what? We take turns getting up, flipping the record over, and playing it again. This is how we meet. Each other, yes, but also something far, far beyond ourselves: a need, a burning, to make a formal acquaintance with flaming mysteries we'll never understand. Come closer to that. Flames we have to keep and connect and not let burn the whole shit down. Saying far more than it'll ever say, a song about how something or someone been so long sings *I need you to come closer, I can't hide.* And when she sings "hide" the word opens up, wide, and there they are: *all* the people. We talk on and on. Each song searches itself, searches us both, and, without us noticing, pushes us closer. This started right here above Dayton Street on September 1, 1986. And meantime all this—the meeting up inside the meeting up—happens far, far away from here and, probably, a long, long time ago. As if from far away and long ago, the soaring and searching inside these songs release a meeting up from inside our meeting up. There's a rhythm up in this, too, and another rhythm up inside that. I feel my weight shift in my chair as the balcony, or the building, or the whole hemisphere begins to rock back and forth.

Over Anita Baker singing about without who she can't do and don't ask her to, Ric describes his family. He's the only child and lives in a townhouse on South Michigan Ave. with his mom and dad. There are family businesses, vaguely described, an office on South Vincennes Ave., city contracts, a trucking company, the Tree House, a hotel in Negril, Jamaica, where he says we *need* to go. A grandmama he calls Ms. Lou is married to a South Side alderman, Beavers, which, as Ric puts it, "covers a whole lot. *And* with Harold Washington in office? A *whole* lot." He looks at me and asks, or really he just states:

"*You* know what I mean."

"Yeah I get it."

I have no idea what he means. From comings and goings of friends and family when I was a kid, from following Chicago Public League basketball over the years, and from coming to know all the Black students in the AOP during my first year at UW, I'd learned about a range of Chicago high schools: Taft, Westinghouse, CVS, Kenwood, Lindblom, Mendel, Whitney Young, Simeon, and MLK along with South Shore High School, where my mother graduated. But Ric says he went to a school on the Near North Side, at North Ave. and Clarke St., near Lincoln Park: "Latin. The Latin School of Chicago?" I say I never heard of it. He laughs and says that's because it's a small private school, "probably the best in the city." Then he leans back and smiles, "See you don't know nothing about that, I tried to tell you the way we got it covers a *lot*." *Are you happy now with your life?* blows onto the balcony from *Rapture* and I remember, just a few hours ago, how Ric, sounding a lot like he just did, had handled that sheriff like a charmer handles a snake.

As he talks to me Ric spins a thin ring, a gold snake with ruby eyes that wraps almost three times around his right pinkie finger. The light on the balcony gathers around the ring and loops back and forth between the eyes of the snake and the matching shimmer from a gold Mercedes-Benz medallion that hangs from a thin chain high in the middle of his chest. Ric weaves through sentences the same as he'd driven through traffic earlier today. I follow along remembering those few times last year how space seemed to clear out in conversations among us when he spoke. He says last year he flew home (*flew* home? So that's the "home in a hour" thing) about twice a month but he plans to cut that back to maybe once a month this year. Ultimately, he doesn't see graduating from UW, more likely he'll transfer to a Chicago school, probably Northwestern, maybe junior year. I say I go to UW because in-state tuition is like $350 a term. Ric says his high school cost *waaay* more than his out-of-state tuition at UW. He mostly came up here for a little independence that was also close to home and, then holding up his cloudy glass of vodka and grapefruit juice on ice, "because the drinking age up here is eighteen. My Ps play me pretty close. And I love 'em but damn."

We talk and talk more about France and last year at school and T and Valerie and Feeda and the Ferraris and about, before that, how I finished high school trapped in a little all-white town in Wisconsin, "that shit was like a blizzard that never stopped." Ric says, "My brother I *know* they musta loved them some you." Ric's got at least one serious-sounding girlfriend in Chicago, Lisa, a connection as he describes it that feels familiar to me from mine in France. Then he says "but if I go home and don't want to *be* home I can always stay with Deborah, one of my pops's women." I let that one go by. None of the details we're saying really matter that much. Whatever's really happening is far away and also riding inside these words like whatever imminence has been hiding behind the air for about the last ten hours since the sheriff interrupted our conversation over gyros and George Howard. Anita Baker's *Rapture* blooms searing searches out of simple, sleepy scenes and sentences and, by ten p.m., after a box of mozzarella sticks, a large pizza, and a few splashes of heat into glasses of grapefruit juice, we both feel this thing—bottomless and nameless—start to pour over us or out of us or into us as if the air itself is doing that thing where you turn your T-shirt inside out without taking it off. A song says *been so long missing you baby*. But what's there for two twenty-year-olds who, anyway, just met to *say* about that? A few minutes later, and after who knows how many times we'd flipped the record over, Anita Baker rips apart some silly sentence about how no one in the world loves her and she's *breaking inside* and the words burn around us in the air, flare after flare softens the sharp edges of the late-summer night as it cools into tomorrow.

Ric stands up, stretches, and says, "Come on let's finish fixing this place and get it into shape suitable for guests who ain't baseheads."

"Who," I ask, "do you have in mind?"

"We'll see about that this week." He goes inside and walks over to the wall between the door to the hallway and the row of closets Terrance's bike leans against. On that wall hangs a poster of a white Porsche 911, the one with the whale tail spoiler. It's unframed but fixed to a plastic foam mat. "Hold this," Ric says to me, taking down the poster. He holds up his chin with his hand, thinker style, and then, "I know what goes here." Removing a gold thumbtack from the wall, he turns around and digs a folder out of a bookbag sitting on the foot of his bed. He opens the folder and takes out a six-inch slip of paper. Maybe a half-inch wide, it looks like a headline or a piece of ad copy he's cut out of a magazine. He turns back around and pierces the gold tack through the slip of paper and then sticks it back in at the center of the wall where it used to hang the poster of the Porsche. Ric steps back making a fake camera frame by touching index fingers and thumbs extended. He nods approvingly, "That'll work." I turn to my right so I can see what he did on the wall around the poster I'm holding. A headline:

THIS MAN GETS A NEW CAR EVERY DAY

Now I hand him the poster, "Okay my turn." Leaving the bedroom I enter my room via the hallway door and take out a red folder where I keep clippings like that. Mine are mostly photos of the best moves I cut from *Sports Illustrated*. Moves like the one where Dr. J dunks on Bird and the whole Celtics squad. But I know exactly the one I'm looking for. Coming back in I tell Ric to turn around and, just below the headline, I tack the photo to the wall with one of the gold thumbtacks lying on top of his dresser: This photo's not large, about 5 × 7, so it fits underneath the headline, which now reads like the photo's caption.

"Now okay turn around."

"Oh man, MJ, yes! Look at the wrist. Fingers extended—He's gonna take the *whole* city. He'll take the league, too, if they can get him a team. Brad Sellers ain't it. You should have heard Bonnie DeShong all summer throwing it at MJ on WGCI inviting him over to her house so she could play piano for him in the dark."

"For real? I thought she did traffic."

"*Exactly!* She keeps taunting him with traffic updates and the hours of night when the travel times are best."

Next we take the Porsche poster into the hallway across from the bathroom where the wall's busted in. Ric pushes in another gold thumbtack and hangs the poster over the hole in the wall.

"That'll just about do that. What do you think?"

"Works for me."

"Imma get me one of these." He gestures to the car on the poster.

I laugh. "Yeah right, me, too."

But Ric doesn't laugh. He points his thin finger at me, cocks his head to the side and says, "Man, you know what?" I'm not sure which "what" he means so I shake my head. Ric turns toward the living room, takes one step and then turns back to me. Side two of *Rapture* is coming to an end, again. Anita Baker's howl-searching something about *the way* you-u . . . *the way you* live . . . *the way you live your* life. Ric says, "*All* spring Terrance asking if he could come to Chi for the summer and work for the family, you know, 'drive a *truck*.'" I don't know why he makes the finger quotes around "drive a truck." Then, "Man, can you imagine Terrance pulls some shit like he did with the rent on *my* pops?! Nooo buddy." Shaking his head, he turns around to walk toward the living room and I assume he's going to flip the record over again. But after two steps Anita Baker's *take it easy, you better, better take it easy* ricochets down the hall and, as if on cue, Ric turns around and steps toward the bedroom. I hear him whisper "damned straight" as he walks past me and through the door and turns left into the room. I'm not sure if he was talking to me or to himself, talking back to the record, to Terrance and the finger-quote "truck," or to the Porsche he's saying he's getting. But I'm wrong. It's none of that. Turns out it's about how pissed he is or isn't. Turns out it's "is."

A few seconds later Ric passes across the open doorway holding Terrance's Raleigh Technium road bike over his head. Holding up the bike he disappears past the doorway to the right and I run the few steps to the door. I hear myself think, "*oh*-shit." I look to the right and see Ric, all in one motion, turn to the side, step one foot through the sliding doors, and heave the bike to his left and over the railing. Ninth floor. The whole-ass Raleigh Technium road bike over the edge. When he turns back around Ric's wipe-clapping his hands together and making that frowning-certain face you make when you've just finished a solid and sensible task. A job well done. When I hear the soft smash of metal down below I'm still hesitating over a shocked cloud of what-ifs: what if the bike doesn't clear the sixth-floor balcony below; what if someone's walking on the sidewalk at the wrong time; what if the fucking cops the fucking cops the fucking cops? Untouched by these what-ifs, Ric looks up to me:

"Like she said we better take it easy."

2:45 a.m. September 2, 1986.

My plan is to use this thin futon as a bed for the year. Almost as much a padded rug as a futon, it fits perfectly in the corner of this small room between the outside wall and the path of the door that swings in from the hallway. In the morning I can roll it back up and slide the folding door open to the living room. That'll expand the space. Plus this corner stays dark despite the yellow light that, even with the blinds closed, spills through the window at night. Classes start tomorrow, well, *today*, and I still need to register, but I'll start thinking about that when it's really tomorrow. I can't get to sleep with the last twelve hours whirling in my arms and legs and that smug-ass sheriff in my face at the door when I close my eyes and Ric talking to him over my shoulder like he's laying down winning cards in a poker game we'd just found out we were playing.

The flight of Terrance's Raleigh Technium road bike from Capitol Centre's apartment #902 ends our first night on the balcony. After the bike leaves the building, even with Ric's don't-give-a-fuckism, we

agree it would be wise to move inside. The spur-of-the-moment ceremony of the bike's exit also changes the air, or maybe it makes us
notice all the changed air all around us all between us. Ric makes
himself another glass of Stoli and grapefruit on ice. Inside the living
room now everything feels like it's leaning toward everything else. Yellow light from the street hazes across the ceiling. Ric sits down leaning
forward with his legs wide apart and talking about when he gets married he's going to sing "Ribbon in the Sky" at the wedding. He has no
plans, understand, but, he says, he's gonna sing it when she's coming
down the aisle. He's been practicing. A closeness gathers around us.
He says living beyond fifty is pointless; fifty years should be plenty. I
notice a little yellow haze from the ceiling gathers and mixes in his
bright, dark eyes. I don't know about all that "should be plenty" stuff
but fifty's so far off it's strange to even mention it. I say I'm not trying
to sing at my wedding but it's got to have music. He leans back at the
kitchen table rotating his glass, looks up at me and asks what song I'd
play to dance to, like for that first dance? I'm surprised to be talking
about this at all, really, but I look away from him toward the window
and, under the air conditioner, on the floor, Patrice Rushen still
stares out from the cover of *Pizzazz*. So I say maybe "When I Found
You," which floats and then has that great breakdown at the end. Ric
doesn't remember that song but wants to hear that breakdown part.

So I take off *Rapture* and pick up *Pizzazz*. But when I turn it over
"When I Found You" isn't on there. Then I remember it's on her
earlier album *Patrice*. You know, *Pizzazz-Patrice*, it's close. I'm saying
how after "Forget Me Nots" in high school I'd bought as many of
her previous records as I could find. And *Now*, too, with "Feels
So Real," which is up there with Niecy's "Do What You Feel" and
"I'm So Proud." Come to think of it "I'm So Proud" might be a
contender for the wedding-dance thing itself but, no, not quite.
My fingers walk through the records and find *Patrice*. There it is:
"When I Found You," second song, after "Music of the Earth," on
side one. I put the record on, drop the needle, and catch the last
breaths and congas of "Music of the Earth." Then static in the
pause before "When I Found You" comes on and, by the time the
horns introduce the theme, soft, and I sit back down on the futon
in front of the poster of the blown-away Maxell tape dude on the
living room wall, the rest of all what's been hiding behind the air
is on its way out front. It's like every inch of air in the room is invisibly tsunami-ing into every other inch of air in the room. Also

it's as if the room has somehow rotated 90 degrees inside itself like north is now east, east is now south, and south has moved around to nine o'clock. And where the songs on *Rapture* start up close and then sear and search and tear out the walls while leaving them in place, "When I Found You" starts all up under your ear, whispering, and then draws all distance into this first closeness that really sounds like touch, I mean if you listen—or touch—close enough: a centripetal closeness; a gathered togetherness. The kind of closeness where the closer you get the further out—and back that togetherness extends. That's when things like balconies and buildings and hemispheres start to rock back and forth.

Ric sits at the table, sips his grapefruit juice, and acts unimpressed. But he's nodding his head up and down to the slow beat and shaking it side to side with the lyrics, *and now I can say for me it's a brighter day,* when he turns his head my way his eyes are closed, brows up, which somehow opens his face wide. It's like that; it sneaks up on you. Every time. If you've heard this song you know that the lyrics are featherlight, riding on an easy rhythm, a soft rolling sea. Then the strings follow the saxophone solo and lift the song, lighter than before. It's pure sweetness. But then toward the last minute, when Patrice Rushen repeats the chorus, held up by the strings, she pins the "me" in "for *me*" up an octave and then bends the line about "a brighter day" down into a minor key. The water darkens. This signals the beat to come back, doubled up at the start of like every fourth measure, and a little harder, more urgent, and the breakdown I was talking about begins. Now most people I know, and *all* the dudes I know, would have been talking about something by now and so the load of brick brought down by these subtle shifts in voice, by the beat inside the beat, and by the heat inside the dark, would get talked over. But Ric hasn't said shit since the needle dropped. In the wedding fantasy, as it appears to me in this moment, this, when the water darkens, when the waves rise up, is where the families join in dancing—which should have signaled something about just *what* families are gonna be joining which dancing. But my mind's too far behind all this to see any of that. So we can leave that for later.

In the living room of apartment #902 right now, with the song turned up and the air turned inside out and the walls drawn in around us and Patrice Rushen repeating Baby *when I found . . .* and twisting the *You-*u like she's wringing out her next breath from the word itself, the word inside the word, Ric Williams rises up from his chair holding his glass in his right hand, left hand snapping and flipping twice with the double-first beat in those measures. "Oh, snap, yes, *yes* . . ." he says under his breath and slow-drags a two-step in a circle around the living room, dipping his shoulder forward like he's headed out from the beach moving through the darkened waves. The song fades and the urge begins to hear it again, to feel it go over the edge, again, into the breakdown. Again. As I watch Ric dance his little dance and chop out that double-beat with his left hand, stepping out with his right foot when the high hat closes, and while the backup chorus and Patrice Rushen trade repetitions of *Baby when I found you*, I know I've arrived somewhere I've never been. For all we know it's a place *that's* never been; maybe whenever something like this happens it happens for the only time. And again. Every time. And maybe one day this song *will* be about a wedding, a wedding inside some unrealized revolutionary rocking back and forth, but here and now it's about a meeting, a friendship, an intimacy even closer than skin on skin. And it's about the turned-inside-out, tsunami'd-ass-air in this *living* room—living room, I think suddenly—with some basehead's burnt-blind eye in the carpet, in this ninth-floor apartment that's but recently been vacated of a Raleigh road bike off its balcony.

CHRISTIENNE L. HINZ

A Rewilding

FROM *Terrain*

I THINK I MIGHT BE A WEED.

A weed is any plant that dares show its face in an unexpected place without the gardener's express permission. A weed takes up space that belongs to the tea roses, sucks up water and nutrients meant for perpetually hungry heirloom tomatoes. Weeds are ugly: too tall, too thick, sloppy, disorganized, utterly devoid of charm. We are fecund hussies, as well: setting seed so copiously that if we manage to get a foothold in your yard, this time next year, all our kinfolk are sure to move in next door, play loud music at odd hours, barbecue in the driveway, ruin the neighborhood ambiance, and drive down property values.

Twenty-plus years ago, I fetched up, a newly minted PhD in southern Illinois suburbia, not because 1,300 square feet of a 1970s suburban ranch house was my dream home, but because the 120' × 90' lot was fenced for my dog. The roof didn't leak, its concrete slab wasn't cracked, and the monthly mortgage payment was less than my student loan payment. I bought it, and told myself, "Self, just thank God for small favors."

The neighborhood, at the time, consisted mostly of working-class retirees. It looked (and still looks) the way baby formula looks. And tastes. It's white. Very white. But its whiteness has never been my primary objection. My objection has always been its grinding architectural and landscaping homogeneity. The homes are neat-as-pins ranches tucked on professionally fertilized and manicured lawns. The landscaping consists of cookie-cutter foundation shrubs, featuring obligatorily sterile flowering specimen trees, or perhaps a fast-growing shade tree dying of the power company's arboreal butchery. The trees and shrubs, all of them, are trademarked versions of about two dozen species that many homeowners and most gardeners know by name.

The one saving grace, I believed, about moving to Similac suburbia was the opportunity to plant a vegetable garden, some raspberries, and dwarf plum trees. I remember my grandmother's plum trees. She was a stern, deeply unhappy woman who certainly loved hard but did not always do so kindly. Rather, she communicated love in the products of her own manual labor. And she was a gardener's gardener. As a toddler I would ride on her hip through the garden, skin tingling from the heat of the sun. She would reach up, pluck a plum from one of her trees and hold it to my mouth. I would just gum, gnaw, and suck. Plum juices burst from behind that blue-black skin to pour hot liquid summer down my throat. That's what her love tasted like. I wanted to give that love to my child. To myself.

Now, the human imposition of monoculture on nature, in this case the tyranny of the suburban lawn, is a profound trauma to an ecosystem. A suburban landscape usually begins as farmland or recovering farmland whose soil structure has been deeply damaged by commercial agricultural practice. Years of being crushed beneath the weight of heavy farm equipment compacts the soil, disrupting its ability to hold water. Soil nutrients, and sometimes even organic matter, have been exhausted, and the mycorrhizal fungi symbiotes that transfer water and nutrients to plant roots have been disrupted by annual tilling. Insect and weed pests, evolved to be indifferent to chemical controls, abound.

When residential developers purchase such land, the first thing they do is strip it bare-assed naked by bulldozing the topsoil away (which they sell to landscaping companies who make you, the homeowner, buy it back in bags). The exposed clay is further compacted to hardpan beneath the treads of the bulldozers. The streets are laid, the houses are built, and the entire neighborhood is landscaped with a few dozen alien and even invasive commercially available cultivars that can tolerate such blighted conditions.

Then insult of insults, landscaping companies lay sod directly on top of clay scraped bare of its original fertility. Now the homeowner has to pay good money to continually water grass planted on clay that can no longer sequester water. Now the homeowner has to pay good money, annually, to fertilize the lawn with nitrogen (which runs off in the rainwater that can't be sequestered by the hardpan clay). Now the homeowner has to pay good money to poison the very plants evolved to repair disturbed ecosystems: dandelions, plantain, violets, clover, lamb's quarters, purslane, and sorrel.

The impact of that trauma was everywhere visible in my suburban neighborhood, and in my backyard. Rather than a few representatives of a diverse range of flora and fauna, my property crawled with millions of individuals of only a few species. Without topsoil beneath the lawn, there was nary an earthworm to be found, no matter where I looked, but there were phalanxes of Japanese beetle grubs curled between the clay and the sod, contentedly chewing roots, fattening themselves for metamorphosis, and a summer of drunkenly skeletonizing the leaves of the neighborhood's costly ornamental shrubs. Mole tunnels snaked beneath the lawn from grub patch to grub patch.

As for birds, there were the usual bird-feeder bullies: cardinals, sparrows, and ground feeders big enough to hold their own against predators: robins, mourning doves, grackles, and Brewer's blackbirds. Scrawny rabbits gnawed hostas to the ground in search of water or nutrients. Slugs as long and fat as Cuban cigars hitched rides on your pant legs, and made slime trails up and down the siding and window screens. Chains of ants marched in disciplined lines from beneath the house's foundation through the electrical outlets and into my house to raid bags of pet food and spilled sugar in the kitchen cupboards.

"You can't grow vegetables around here," my elderly neighbor sagely opined, watching as I sweated to tote wheelbarrow after wheelbarrow of topsoil and compost into the backyard with which to build tumuli beds. "There's nothing here but pure clay."

Now, I was raised by a long line of hardheaded Black women who worked close beneath the supervision of the white aristocracy and its terrible critical Gaze. The White Gaze is a bulldozer that crushes the Black soul flat. It compresses our strength to hardpan. The bulldozing White Gaze scrapes clean away the fertility native to us, packages it, and sells it on the open market where we pay to buy it back. Weeds endowed by their Creator with the capacity to help us heal are rounded up in the industrial school-to-prison pipeline.

As a child, I was taught by my elders that the key to surviving the

weight of the White Gaze is to become absolute masters of the Cult
of Respectability. To master the Cult of Respectability is to adopt the
standards, practices, manners and mannerisms of the aristocracy. We
were only allowed to speak "the King's English." My grandmother
taught us the uses and correct placement of the silver at a formal
table. I learned to clean a house so well, guests could eat off the
floor, and the women in my family didn't think anything of trash-
talking another woman's house where you couldn't.

The Cult of Respectability was both a tyranny and a Holy Grail.
It took a lot of living between being a little Black girl at Grandma's
knee to a grown-assed natural Black woman to unpack how the
Cult of Respectability is built on a chassis of racism and self-hatred,
and to understand—even more importantly—*that it does not work.* It
doesn't save anyone. It only makes us docile. The Cult of Respectability is the bit between our teeth, the spur in our flanks. It makes
of us the instrument of our own domestication.

I am a traumatized person. I have never NOT lived in fear. I
have never NOT lived in existential danger. I have never NOT been
crushed to hardpan beneath the weight of the White Gaze. I have
never NOT needed a resting place, where I could hide, and secretly
blow upon the flickering flame of wildness that should have been
mine but for the obliterating weight of history.

So here I am—this weed—fetched up in southern Illinois
suburbia where the Cult of Respectability has been imposed upon
the landscape, where the ecosystem's inborn wildness and fecundity have been crushed to hardpan and scraped away. I needed
my home to be a shelter, but there was no shelter in suburbia for
me and my son, no way to press a fresh plum, hot from the sun,
against his lips. He would not be able to taste the summer as I had
tasted it from the safety of my grandmother's hip. Where would
he catch praying mantises, purple his face with mulberries, pull
spicy radishes straight from the ground, poke garter snakes, and
learn the names of butterflies? How could he discover his own
inborn wildness?

He couldn't. He wouldn't, and neither would I, unless I found
a way to break suburbia's coercive White Gaze, and the Cult of
Respectability inherent to it. To restore the ecosystem which lived
in me, to recover some of my own inborn wildness, I had to restore
the ecosystem in which I lived. I had to help it recover some of its
own inborn wildness.

And so, I decided to make myself a splinter in the eye of the White Gaze.

I first defied the suburban Cult of Respectability by refusing to rake up my leaves in the autumn. "Those leaves will kill your grass, you know," my neighbor opined, wringing her hands in consternation. I stole her pile of leaves, too, which her husband had raked into the street for the city to take away.

The next spring, nitrogen-fixing "weeds" popped up wherever the grass had died under the damp mats of moldering leaves. I left the weeds to do what weeds do. Native bees began to visit the clover and violets that filled in the bare patches. Dandelion and plantain punched through the hardpan beneath the lawn, adding porosity to the clay. The increased plant diversity in the lawn gave rabbits something to eat besides grass, so they began to let my vegetable garden and the hostas be. But no lie: I sweated through the censorious gazes of old folks walking their Chihuahuas. And every week I was throwing away doorknob advertisements from lawn care companies.

I next defied the Cult of Respectability by taking three whole years to establish a clay-busting native shortgrass prairie on the sunny side of my front lawn. This involved smothering the grass with unsightly cardboard, newspapers, and tarps. Boxes full of bare-root plants arrived by mail, bags of mulch and bales of straw stacked up in front of the garage. The driveway became cluttered with misplaced shovels, forgotten buckets of garden tools, and unspooled garden hoses.

VILLAGE CITATION 1: "Noxious weeds are not allowed within the village. Remove all weeds within 5 days or you will be billed for weed removal."

VILLAGE CITATION 2: "flowers taller than 12 inches are not allowed within village limits. Mow areas to regulation height within 5 days or you will be billed for mowing."

I shadowboxed myself around village complaints for two years; and I kept hold of my sanctity with neighbors who regularly led their dogs to pee on the prairie seedlings struggling to grow by the curb.

But by the third year, the prairie finally matured and exploded into blossom, lighting up the street like a wildfire. Three varieties of purple and yellow echinacea, red and yellow Ratibida, and lemon-yellow helianthus, goldenrod, and purple New England aster, rare

native grasses whose seeds songbirds go to war for: side oats grama
with its teeny red flowers, little bluestem, and wild sea oats. Purple
and white prairie clover; varieties of milkweed, green, pink, and
orange, for the monarch butterflies; spiky blazing stars; and larger
species like rattlesnake master and even cup plant, which tops ten
feet.

By coloring outside of the landscaping lines, I seduced the return
of earthworms. House finches, goldfinches, dragonflies, skippers,
and orb spiders soon followed. Insects whose names I'll never know
began chewing through the prairie's detritus, making compost.

Prairies require fire to thrive. The first time I burned my front
yard prairie, the neighbors stepped out of their houses to stare,
slack-jawed. But . . . one morning, I found a card in my mailbox,
addressed to "Our Neighbor":

> "I've watched you working in your front yard, and I wanted
> you to know that I make a point of driving by your house every
> morning on the way to work to see what's blooming. Thank
> you for adding such joy to the neighborhood."

That was the end of the village's noxious weed citations.

I really wanted birds to choose to nest in my yard rather than
just "drop by for a visit." Wherever birds nest, they are particularly brilliant at pest control, something vital to the organic
gardener. To seduce a wider variety of birds, I determined to
establish a miniature woodland area around the raggedy sweet-
gum tree behind the garage. I reimagined this lonely old thing as
the forest "canopy," and planted native understory trees—downy
serviceberry, hawthorn, and redbud to give it some company. I
filled in the shrub layer with natives that thrive in partial to deep
shade—bottlebrush buckeye, witch hazel, black haw viburnum,
Carolina spicebush, hearts-a-bustin', chokecherries, and the like.
These provided year-round food sources for birds. Slowly over
the years I added native perennials for the herbaceous layer, and
ephemerals for the ground layer. Jacob's ladder, Solomon's seal,
black cohosh, goatsbeard, wild ginger, mayapple, fire pinks, Virginia bluebells, and spring beauties.

I took away the Cult of Respectability's power to disallow red-eared
sliders right-of-way through my property to wherever it is turtles
go in the late summer. The Cult of Respectability didn't get to de-

home the house wrens and flickers that arrived to keep the ants out of my house. The Cult of Respectability no longer decided who can and who can't raise their babies in my yard. Black-capped chickadees, titmouses, juncos, blue jays, and barred owls, ruby-throated hummingbirds, blue skinks, brown snakes, toads, thumbnail-size green frogs, and butterflies beyond number found sanctuary on less than 1,000 square feet of suburban lot.

I haven't had problems with cigar-size slugs since.

African American trauma might be unique, but trauma is not unique to African Americans. Despite America's cultural myth of individualism, all of us are crushed, in some manner—let's say oppressed—by toxic social norms. Too fat, too thin, too young, too old, too brown, too queer, too foreign, too poor, too disabled, too smart, too ignorant, too religious, too heathen, too liberal, too conservative. We are a traumatized people living in a traumatized ecosystem. Our history and culture have profoundly alienated us from nature, from our own natures, from each other's natures.

My neighborhood has changed over the years: fewer retirees and more working families with children. My neighbors have three little girls like stairsteps, something like six, eight, and ten years old. One evening, their parents brought them out to their backyard to see the fireflies twinkling in mine. Their mother whispered to me that her kids only knew about fireflies from seeing them depicted in storybooks. "Hell," she said ruefully, "I've never seen so many fireflies in one place at the same time."

It made my heart hurt, really hurt, to think we have raised a generation of children so profoundly disconnected from a natural world in need of mending. I captured some fireflies in a mason jar so the kids could see what they look like up close. Their awed gazes and murmurs of appreciation were payment in full for the time, money, physical and psychic labor I've spent seducing a backyard ecosystem's revival.

I say be a weed. Find your inborn wildness. Don't let anyone rob you of your fecundity. Set copious seed. Your offspring and their friends, and their offspring and their friends, are welcome in my yard. We'll play loud music and party in the driveway until the sun goes down. And we'll watch the fireflies come out.

Contributors' Notes

Notable Essays and Literary Nonfiction of 2023

Contributors' Notes

KATHLEEN ALCOTT is the author of three novels and one short story collection. Her short fiction and essays have appeared in *Harper's Magazine*, *The Best American Short Stories*, the *New York Times Magazine*, *The Guardian*, *Elle*, *Tin House*, and *The Baffler*. She has been nominated for the Joyce Carol Oates Prize and the *Sunday Times* Short Story Award, and in 2023 received an O. Henry Prize. A fellow of MacDowell, Alcott has taught at Columbia University and Bennington College.

BROCK CLARKE's books include the novels *Who Are You, Calvin Bledsoe?*, *The Happiest People in the World*, and *An Arsonist's Guide to Writers' Homes in New England*; the short story collection *The Price of the Haircut*; and, most recently, the essay collection *I, Grape; or The Case for Fiction*. His tenth book—the short story collection *Special Election*—will be published in 2025. He lives in Portland, Maine, and is the A. LeRoy Greason Professor of English and Creative Writing at Bowdoin College.

MICHAEL W. CLUNE is the author of two critically acclaimed memoirs: *White Out* was named a "Best Book of 2013" by *The New Yorker*, NPR, *The Millions*, and elsewhere; *Gamelife* appeared in 2015. *White Out* was reissued in 2023. His writing has appeared in *Harper's Magazine*, *The Atlantic*, *Granta*, and *Tin House*, among other places. He received his BA at Oberlin and his MA and PhD at Johns Hopkins University. He was a 2019 Guggenheim Fellow, and he is a professor of English at Case Western University. His first novel, *Pan*, is forthcoming.

TEJU COLE is a novelist, essayist, and photographer. His books include *Open City, Known and Strange Things, Tremor,* and *Pharmakon.*

JONATHAN GLEASON is a writer, university instructor, and medical interpreter, currently living in Chicago. He is a graduate of the University of Iowa's Nonfiction Writing Program and a recipient of a 2023 grant from the Elizabeth George Foundation. His writing has appeared in *The Sun* magazine, Literary Hub, *New England Review, The Kenyon Review, Michigan Quarterly Review,* and others. His collection of essays about illness and medicine was shortlisted for the Graywolf Press Nonfiction Prize and a finalist for the Miami Book Fair Emerging Writer Fellowship.

CHRISTIENNE L. HINZ is a PhD in modern Japanese history and has published articles on entrepreneurship among nineteenth- to twentieth-century Japanese women. She is a Pushcart Prize–nominated memoirist, an essayist, a poet, and a Master Gardener specializing in organic gardening, orcharding, and sub/urban ecosystem restoration. A beekeeper, a ceramicist, and a textile artist, Christienne enjoys life with her partner of twenty-five years, and her two children.

YIYUN LI is the author of eleven books, including *Wednesday's Child, The Book of Goose,* and *Where Reasons End.* Her work has been translated into more than twenty languages. Li's honors and awards include a MacArthur Foundation Fellowship, a Guggenheim Foundation Fellowship, a Windham Campbell Prize, the *Sunday Times* EFG Short Story Award, the PEN/Faulkner Award, the PEN/Jean Stein Award, the PEN/Malamud Award, the PEN/Hemingway Award, and others. She is a member of both the American Academy of Arts and Sciences and the American Academy of Arts and Letters, and was named a 2023 International Writer from the Royal Society of Literature. Her work has appeared in *The New Yorker, The Atlantic, Harper's Magazine,* and other places. She is a professor at Princeton University, where she directs the creative writing program.

NICOLE GRAEV LIPSON is the author of the forthcoming memoir-in-essays *Mothers and Other Fictional Characters* (February 2025). Her essays and criticism have appeared in *Virginia Quarterly Review, The Sun, The Gettysburg Review, River Teeth, Fourth Genre, The Millions,* the *Washington Post,* and the *Boston Globe,* among other publications. She is the recipient of a Pushcart Prize, and her work has been nominated for a National Magazine Award. Lipson received her MFA from Emerson College and lives outside of Boston with her family.

AMY MARGOLIS is the longtime director of the Iowa Summer Writing Festival at the University of Iowa. Her fiction appears in *The Iowa Review*. "1978" is part of a memoir-in-shards about her life as a dancer in the late 1970s and early '80s, at the onset of the AIDS crisis.

JAMES MCAULEY is a writer in New York. He is the author of *The House of Fragile Things: Jewish Collectors and the Fall of France*, which won the National Jewish Book Award in 2022. He holds a PhD in modern history from Oxford, where he was a Marshall Scholar, and is a former Paris correspondent for the *Washington Post*. His writing has appeared in the *New York Review of Books*, the *New York Times*, *The Economist*, and other outlets.

RÉMY NGAMIJE is a Rwandan-born Namibian author, editor, publisher, photographer, literary educator, and entrepreneur. His debut novel, *The Eternal Audience of One*, was first published in South Africa by Blackbird Books. In 2022, it was honored with a special mention at the inaugural Grand Prix Panafricain De Littérature and won the inaugural African Literary Award from the Museum of the African Diaspora. He won the Africa Regional Prize of the 2021 Commonwealth Short Story Prize and was short-listed for the AKO Caine Prize for African Writing in 2021 and 2020. He was long-listed and short-listed for the 2020 and 2021 Afritondo Short Story Prizes respectively. In 2019, he was short-listed for Best Original Fiction by Stack Magazines. Rémy is the founder and chairperson of Doek, an independent arts organization in Namibia supporting the literary arts, and the editor in chief of *Doek! Literary Magazine*, Namibia's first and only literary magazine. He is also the founder and director of several literary initiatives such as the Bank Windhoek Doek Literary Awards, the Doek Literary Festival, and the Doek Anthology. He has served as a judge of the Kalemba, Kendeka, Commonwealth, and Plaza short story prizes. His fiction, nonfiction, and poetry have appeared in *The Johannesburg Review of Books*, *American Chordata*, Lolwe, Lit Hub, *Granta*, *One Story*, *Prairie Schooner*, and many other places. More of his writing can be read on his website: remythequill.com.

ED PAVLIĆ is author of thirteen books written across and between genres. His most recent works include: *Call It in the Air* (2022), *Outward: Adrienne Rich's Expanding Solitudes* (2021), *Let It Be Broke* (2020), and *Another Kind of Madness* (2019). An editor with the Arts in Society Project at *Boston Review*, he is Distinguished Research Professor of English, African American Studies, and Creative Writing at the University of Georgia.

RICHARD PRINS is a lifelong New Yorker. His poetry has appeared in publications such as *Gulf Coast*, *jubilat*, and *Ploughshares*, and his essays have previously been listed as notable in *The Best American Essays* and *The Best American Travel Writing*. His translations of Swahili literature have been awarded a 2023 PEN/Heim Translation Fund Grant and a 2024 National Endowment for the Arts Translation Fellowship.

COURTNEY MILLER SANTO is the author of two novels published by Harper-Collins: *The Roots of the Olive Tree* and *Three Story House*. Her essays, poems, and stories have appeared in *The Los Angeles Review, Swing, The Missouri Review, New Letters,* and *Third Coast.* She teaches in the MFA program at the University of Memphis, where she also serves as the editor in chief of *The Pinch.* Find her on Instagram @courtneysanto or online at courtneysanto.com.

JENNIFER SENIOR is a staff writer at *The Atlantic* and winner of the 2022 Pulitzer for Feature Writing. Prior to joining *The Atlantic,* she spent five years at the *New York Times*—first as one of its daily book critics, then as columnist for the Opinion page. Before that, she spent eighteen years as a staff writer for *New York Magazine.* Her first book, *All Joy and No Fun: The Paradox of Modern Parenthood,* spent eight weeks on the *New York Times* best-seller list, was named one of Slate's Top 10 Books of 2014, and has been translated into twelve languages. In addition to the Pulitzer, Senior has won a variety of journalism prizes, including a National Magazine Award, a GLAAD award, two Front Page Awards from the Newswomen's Club of New York, and the Erikson Prize in Mental Health Media. Her work has been anthologized four times in *The Best American Political Writing,* and her profile of the psychologist Philip Brickman was selected for *The Best American Science Writing of 2021.* She lives in New York with her husband and son.

JENNIFER SINOR is the author of several books of literary nonfiction. Her most recent book, *The Yogic Writer: Uniting Breath, Body, and Page,* joins the practice of writing and the practice of yoga. Her essay collections include *Sky Songs: Meditations on Loving a Broken World* and *Letters Like the Day: On Reading Georgia O'Keeffe.* She teaches creative writing at Utah State University, where she is a professor of English.

SALLIE TISDALE is the author of many essays. Her most recent book is *The Lie About the Truck: Survivor, Reality TV, and the Endless Gaze.*

ANNE MARIE TODKILL lives off-grid in North Hasting, Ontario, within the treaty lands of the Michi Saagiig Anishinaabeg. Her essays, short fiction, and poems have appeared in various Canadian literary magazines and anthologies, including *The Fiddlehead, The Malahat Review, The New Quarterly, The Best Canadian Poetry in English* series, and the *Best Canadian Stories* series. Her first collection of poetry, *Orion Sweeping*, was published in 2022. "Storm Damage" is part of a collection-in-progress.

JERALD WALKER's latest book, *Magically Black and Other Essays*, which includes "It's Hard Out Here for a Memoirist," was published in September 2024. He is also the author of two memoirs and the essay collection *How to Make a Slave*, a finalist for the 2020 National Book Award and winner of the 2020 Massachusetts Book Award. His work has appeared in publications such as *Harvard Review*, *Creative Nonfiction*, *The Iowa Review*, the *New York Times*, the *Washington Post*, and *Mother Jones*, and it has been widely anthologized, including this sixth time in *The Best American Essays*. A recipient of a Pushcart Prize, the PEN/New England Award for Nonfiction, and fellowships from the Guggenheim Foundation, the National Endowment for the Arts, and the Michener Foundation, Walker is a professor of creative writing at Emerson College.

JENISHA WATTS is a senior editor at *The Atlantic*. Before joining *The Atlantic* in 2020, she was a culture editor for ESPN's *The Undefeated* and a features and commentary editor for *espnW*, and she edited articles for *ESPN The Magazine*. She's also held editorial roles at *Time* Books, *Essence*, and *People*. She lives in Maryland with her husband and son.

JAMES WHORTON JR. is a former Mississippian now living in Rochester, New York. He is author of the novels *Approximately Heaven*, *Frankland*, and *Angela Sloan*. His short stories and essays have appeared in *Oxford American*, *The Gettysburg Review*, *The Iowa Review*, *The Southern Review*, *Mississippi Review*, *Chicago Quarterly Review*, and *The Sewanee Review*. He teaches at SUNY Brockport.

AUSTIN WOERNER is a Chinese-English literary translator whose work has appeared in *Ploughshares*, *Poetry*, the *New York Times Magazine*, and elsewhere. He is the translator of a novel, *The Invisible Valley*, by Su Wei, and two volumes of Ouyang Jianghe's poetry, and the editor of *Chutzpah!: New Voices from China*. He has taught creative writing and translation in China for many years, first at Sun Yat-sen University in Guangzhou and then at Duke Kunshan University in Suzhou, and he is currently a teaching fellow in translation studies at the University of Leeds.

Notable Essays and Literary Nonfiction of 2023

SELECTED BY KIM DANA KUPPERMAN

ABOUT

MARINER BOOKS

MARINER BOOKS traces its beginnings to 1832 when William Ticknor cofounded the Old Corner Bookstore in Boston, from which he would run the legendary firm Ticknor and Fields, publisher of Ralph Waldo Emerson, Harriet Beecher Stowe, Nathaniel Hawthorne, and Henry David Thoreau. Following Ticknor's death, Henry Oscar Houghton acquired Ticknor and Fields and, in 1880, formed Houghton Mifflin, which later merged with venerable Harcourt Publishing to form Houghton Mifflin Harcourt. HarperCollins purchased HMH's trade publishing business in 2021 and reestablished their storied lists and editorial team under the name Mariner Books.

Uniting the legacies of Houghton Mifflin, Harcourt Brace, and Ticknor and Fields, Mariner Books continues one of the great traditions in American bookselling. Our imprints have introduced an incomparable roster of enduring classics, including Hawthorne's *The Scarlet Letter*, Thoreau's *Walden*, Willa Cather's *O Pioneers!*, Virginia Woolf's *To the Lighthouse*, W.E.B. Du Bois's *Black Reconstruction*, J.R.R. Tolkien's *The Lord of the Rings*, Carson McCullers's *The Heart Is a Lonely Hunter*, Ann Petry's *The Narrows*, George Orwell's *Animal Farm* and *Nineteen Eighty-Four*, Rachel Carson's *Silent Spring*, Margaret Walker's *Jubilee*, Italo Calvino's *Invisible Cities*, Alice Walker's *The Color Purple*, Margaret Atwood's *The Handmaid's Tale*, Tim O'Brien's *The Things They Carried*, Philip Roth's *The Plot Against America*, Jhumpa Lahiri's *Interpreter of Maladies*, and many others. Today Mariner Books remains proudly committed to the craft of fine publishing established nearly two centuries ago at the Old Corner Bookstore.

EXPLORE THE REST OF THE SERIES!